Collins

WATERWAYS GUIDE 3

Birmingham & the Heart of England

CONTENTS

Mapping sourced from Ordnance Survey®

Published by Nicholson
An imprint of HarperCollins Publishers
Westerhill Road, Bishopbriggs, Glasgow G64 2QT
www.harpercollins.co.uk

Waterways guides published by Nicholson since 1969
This edition first published by Nicholson and Ordnance Survey 1997
New edition published by Nicholson 2000, 2003, 2006, 2009, 2012, 2014, 2018

Wildlife text from *Collins Complete Guide to British Wildlife* and *Collins Wild Guide*.

This product uses map data licensed from Ordnance Survey © Crown copyright and database rights (2017) Ordnance Survey (100018598)

Researched and written by Jonathan Mosse.

The publishers gratefully acknowledge the assistance given by Canal & River Trust and their staff in the preparation of this guide. Grateful thanks are also due to the Environment Agency, members of the Inland Waterways Association, the Friends of the Cromford Canal, and CAMRA representatives and branch members.

Photographs reproduced by kind permission of: Jonathan Mosse p14, 47–61, 51, 62–77, 63, 66, 73, 75, 77, 79, 134–135, 164, 172; Alamy 15–27, 28–37, 38, 39–45, 46, 78–85, 86, 87–115, 117–137, 138, 139–147, 148, 149–157, 159–163, 165–171, 173–189; Paul Huggins (paulhugginsphotography.com) 150, 170 (banded demoiselle) 171 (moorhen, mute swan); 171 Frank Lane Picture Agency/Ted Benton (marsh fritillary); Shutterstock 52 (Bildagentur Zoonar GmbH), 155 Dave McAleavy, 170 Christian Musat (speckled wood), Steve McWilliam (large skipper), Robert Hardholt (holly blue), Jens Stolt (orange tip) 171 Andrey Novikov (devil's bit scabious); HarperCollins Publishers (great crested grebe).

A catalogue record for this book is available from the British Library

Printed in China by RR Donnelley APS Co Ltd

ISBN 978-0-00-825799-6

10 9 8 7 6 5

MIX
Paper from
responsible sources
FSC™ C007454

This book is produced from independently certified FSC™ paper to ensure responsible forest management.

For more information visit: www.harpercollins.co.uk/green

INTRODUCTION

Wending their quiet way through town and country, the inland navigations of Britain offer boaters, walkers and cyclists a unique insight into a fascinating, but once almost lost, world. When built this was the province of the boatmen and their families, who lived a mainly itinerant lifestyle: often colourful, to our eyes picturesque but, for them, remarkably harsh. Transporting the nation's goods during the late 1700s and early 1800s, negotiating locks, traversing aqueducts and passing through long narrow tunnels, canals were the arteries of trade during the initial part of the industrial revolution.

Then the railways came: the waterways were eclipsed in a remarkably short time by a faster and more flexible transport system, and a steady decline began. In a desperate fight for survival canal tolls were cut, crews toiled for longer hours and worked the boats with their whole family living aboard. Canal companies merged, totally uneconomic waterways were abandoned, some were modernised but it was all to no avail. Large scale commercial carrying on inland waterways had reached the finale of its short life.

At the end of World War II a few enthusiasts roamed this hidden world and harboured a vision of what it could become: a living transport museum which stretched the length and breadth of the country; a place where people could spend their leisure time and, on just a few of the wider waterways, a still modestly viable transport system.

The restoration struggle began and, from modest beginnings, Britain's inland waterways are now seen as an irreplaceable part of the fabric of the nation. Long-abandoned waterways, once seen as an eyesore and a danger, are recognised for the valuable contribution they make to our quality of life, and restoration schemes are integrating them back into the network. Let us hope that the country's network of inland waterways continues to be cherished and well-used, maintained and developed as we move through the 21st century.

If you would like to comment on any aspect of the guides, please write to Nicholson Waterways Guides, Collins, Westerhill Road, Bishopbriggs, Glasgow G64 2QT or email nicholson@harpercollins.co.uk.

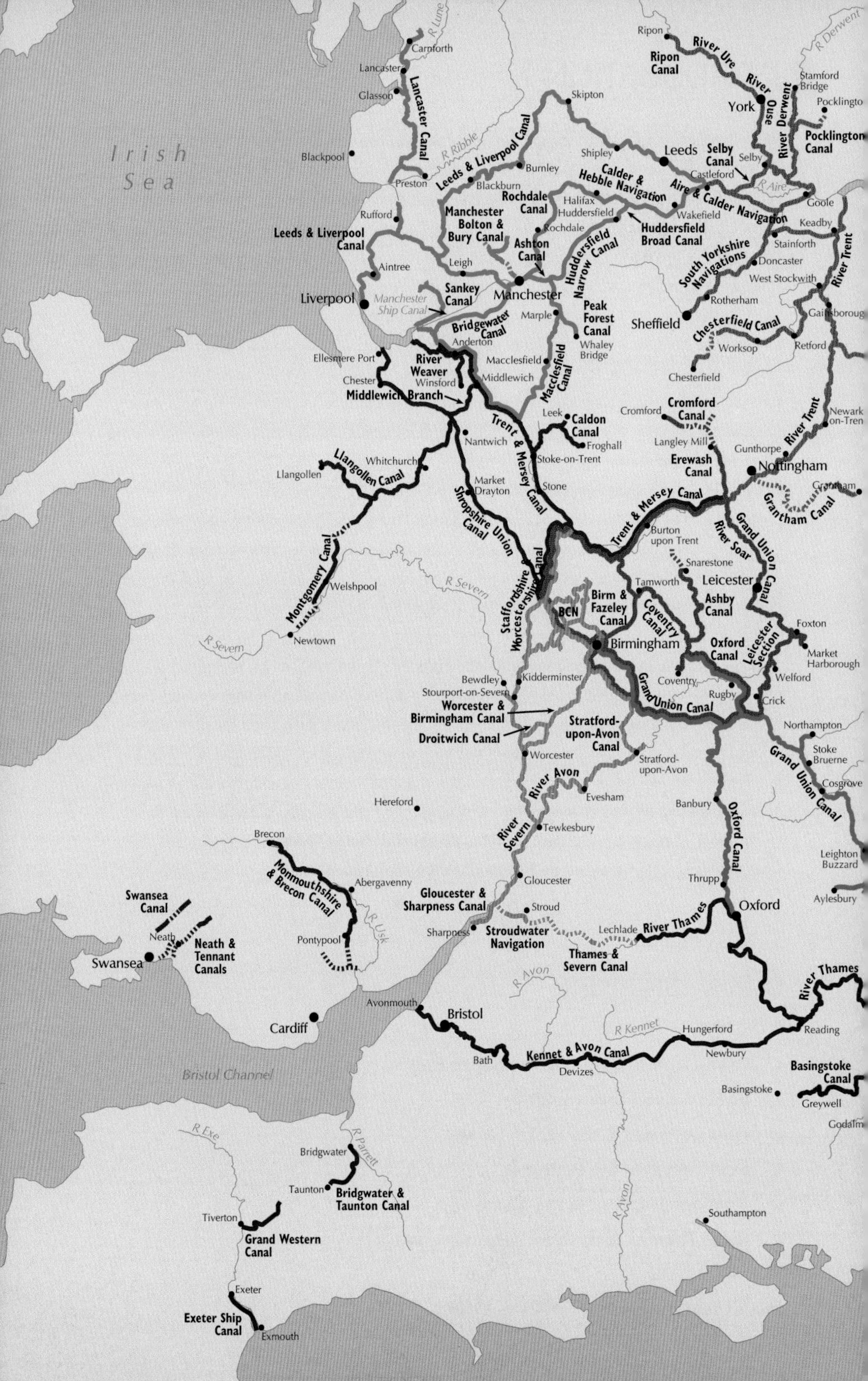
Irish Sea
Bristol Channel
Lancaster Canal
Ripon Canal
River Ure
River Ouse
River Derwent
Pocklington Canal
Selby Canal
Leeds & Liverpool Canal
Calder & Hebble Navigation
Aire & Calder Navigation
Rochdale Canal
Manchester Bolton & Bury Canal
Huddersfield Broad Canal
Huddersfield Narrow Canal
Ashton Canal
South Yorkshire Navigations
River Trent
Sankey Canal
Manchester Ship Canal
Bridgewater Canal
Peak Forest Canal
Chesterfield Canal
River Weaver
Macclesfield Canal
Middlewich Branch
Trent & Mersey Canal
Caldon Canal
Cromford Canal
Erewash Canal
Llangollen Canal
Shropshire Union Canal
Grantham Canal
Montgomery Canal
River Soar
Grand Union Canal
Staffordshire & Worcestershire Canal
Birm & Fazeley Canal
BCN
Coventry Canal
Ashby Canal
Oxford Canal
Leicester Section
Worcester & Birmingham Canal
Droitwich Canal
Stratford-upon-Avon Canal
River Avon
River Severn
Monmouthshire & Brecon Canal
Gloucester & Sharpness Canal
Stroudwater Navigation
Thames & Severn Canal
River Thames
Swansea Canal
Neath & Tennant Canals
Kennet & Avon Canal
Basingstoke Canal
Bridgwater & Taunton Canal
Grand Western Canal
Exeter Ship Canal
R Lune
R Ribble
R Aire
R Severn
R Usk
R Avon
R Kennet
R Exe
R Parrett
Carnforth
Lancaster
Glasson
Blackpool
Preston
Rufford
Aintree
Liverpool
Ellesmere Port
Chester
Ripon
York
Stamford Bridge
Pocklington
Skipton
Shipley
Leeds
Selby
Castleford
Goole
Burnley
Blackburn
Halifax
Huddersfield
Wakefield
Rochdale
Keadby
Stainforth
Doncaster
West Stockwith
Leigh
Manchester
Rotherham
Sheffield
Gainsborough
Marple
Whaley Bridge
Worksop
Retford
Anderton
Macclesfield
Winsford
Middlewich
Chesterfield
Leek
Froghall
Cromford
Newark-on-Trent
Nantwich
Langley Mill
Gunthorpe
Nottingham
Whitchurch
Llangollen
Stoke-on-Trent
Market Drayton
Stone
Grantham
Burton upon Trent
Snarestone
Welshpool
Tamworth
Leicester
Newtown
Birmingham
Foxton
Market Harborough
Bewdley
Kidderminster
Stourport-on-Severn
Coventry
Welford
Rugby
Crick
Northampton
Stoke Bruerne
Worcester
Stratford-upon-Avon
Cosgrove
Hereford
Evesham
Banbury
Tewkesbury
Brecon
Leighton Buzzard
Abergavenny
Gloucester
Thrupp
Aylesbury
Stroud
Oxford
Neath
Sharpness
Lechlade
Pontypool
Swansea
Avonmouth
Bristol
Cardiff
Hungerford
Reading
Bath
Newbury
Devizes
Basingstoke
Greywell
Godalming
Bridgwater
Taunton
Tiverton
Southampton
Exeter
Exmouth

The Waterways of Britain

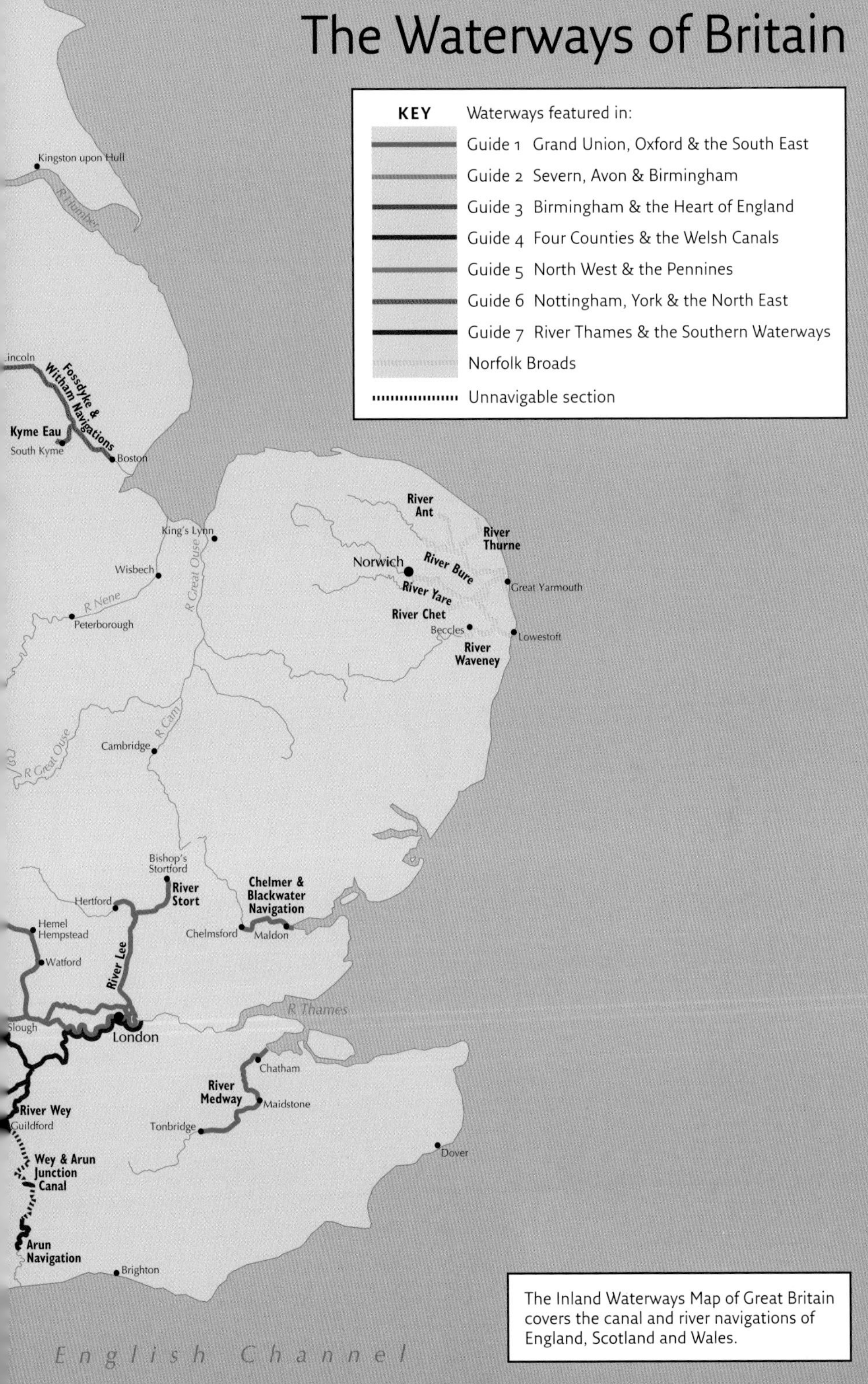

The Inland Waterways Map of Great Britain covers the canal and river navigations of England, Scotland and Wales.

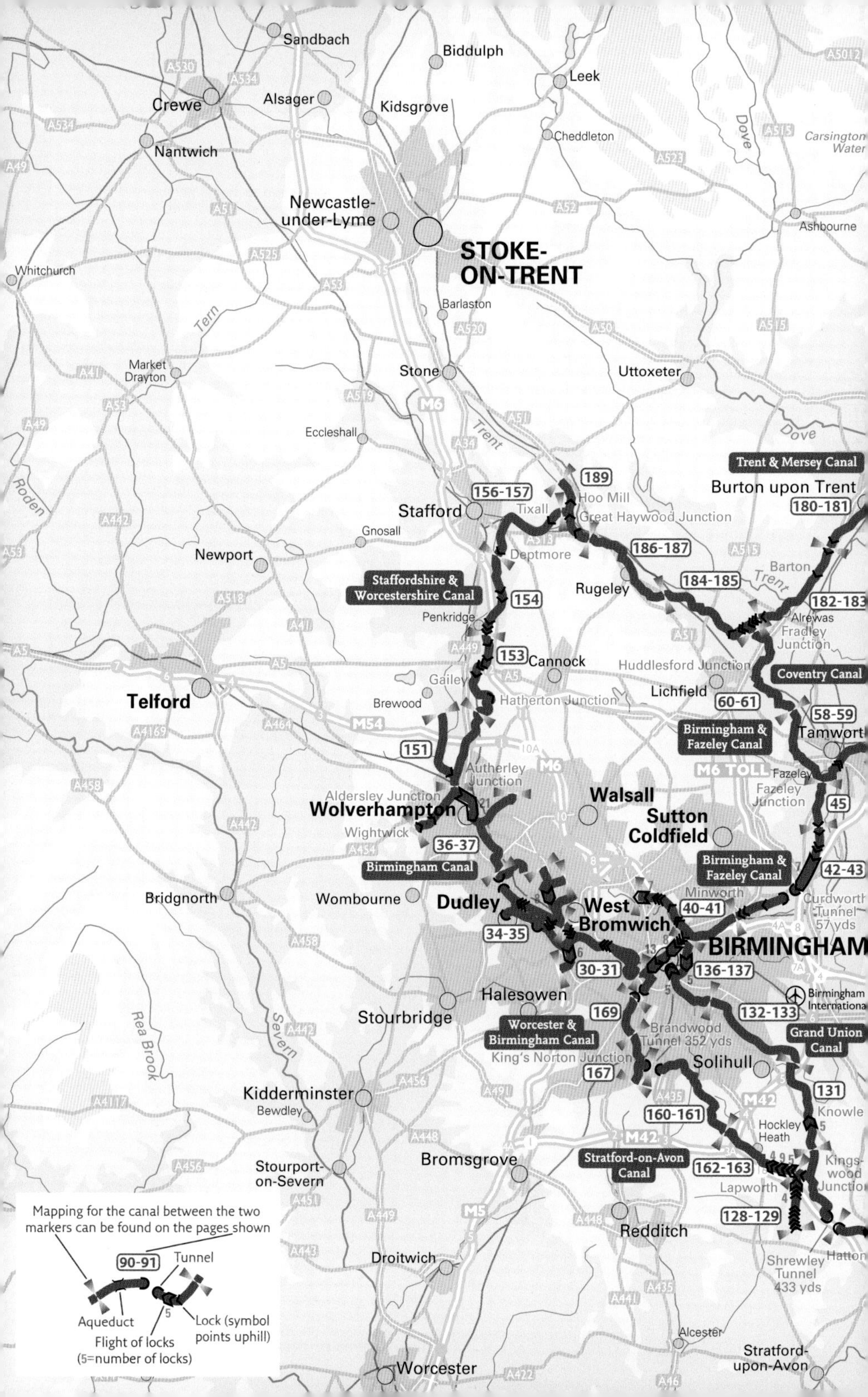

Sandbach
Biddulph
Leek
Crewe
Alsager
Kidsgrove
Cheddleton
Nantwich
Dove
Carsington Water
Newcastle-under-Lyme
STOKE-ON-TRENT
Ashbourne
Whitchurch
Barlaston
Tern
Market Drayton
Stone
Uttoxeter
M6
Eccleshall
Trent
Dove
Trent & Mersey Canal
Roden
189
Hoo Mill
156-157
Burton upon Trent
Stafford
Tixall
180-181
Great Haywood Junction
Gnosall
Deptmore
186-187
Newport
Barton
Staffordshire & Worcestershire Canal
154
Rugeley
184-185
Trent
182-183
Penkridge
Alrewas
Fradley Junction
153
Cannock
Huddlesford Junction
Coventry Canal
Gailey
Lichfield
Telford
Hatherton Junction
60-61
58-59
Brewood
M54
Birmingham & Fazeley Canal
Tamworth
151
10A
Autherley Junction
M6
M6 TOLL
Fazeley
Fazeley Junction
Aldersley Junction
Walsall
Wolverhampton
Sutton Coldfield
45
Wightwick
36-37
Birmingham & Fazeley Canal
42-43
Birmingham Canal
Minworth
Curdworth Tunnel 57 yds
Bridgnorth
Wombourne
Dudley
West Bromwich
40-41
34-35
BIRMINGHAM
30-31
136-137
Birmingham International
Halesowen
132-133
Rea Brook
169
Stourbridge
Worcester & Birmingham Canal
Brandwood Tunnel 352 yds
Grand Union Canal
Severn
King's Norton Junction
Solihull
167
Kidderminster
131
Bewdley
160-161
Knowle
Hockley Heath
M42
Stratford-on-Avon Canal
Bromsgrove
Kingswood Junction
Stourport-on-Severn
162-163
Lapworth
128-129
M5
Redditch
Hatton
Droitwich
Shrewley Tunnel 433 yds
Alcester
Stratford-upon-Avon
Worcester
Mapping for the canal between the two markers can be found on the pages shown
90-91
Tunnel
Aqueduct
Flight of locks (5=number of locks)
Lock (symbol points uphill)

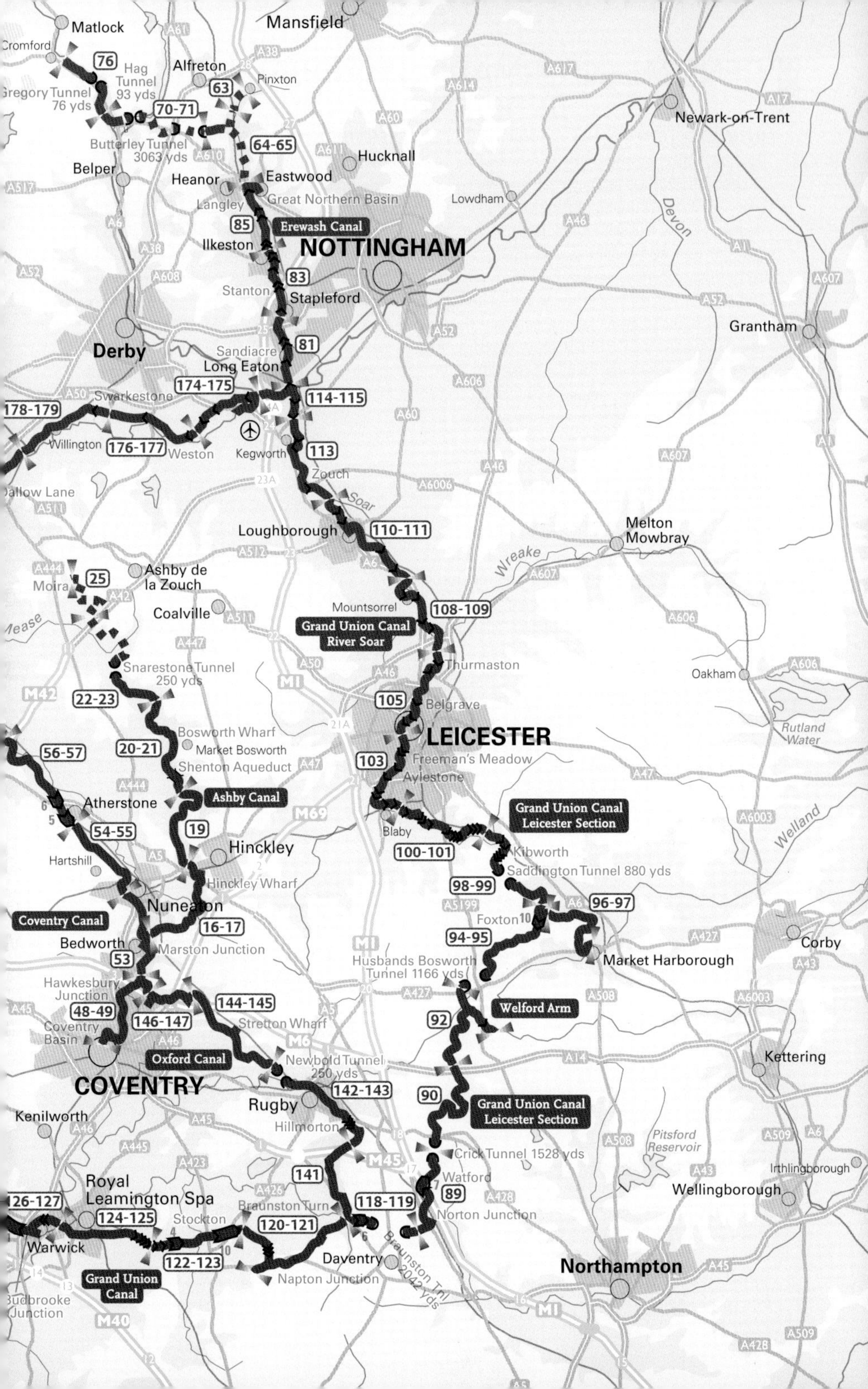

Matlock
Mansfield
Cromford
Hag Tunnel 93 yds
Gregory Tunnel 76 yds
Alfreton
Pinxton
Butterley Tunnel 3063 yds
Newark-on-Trent
Hucknall
Belper
Heanor
Eastwood
Langley
Great Northern Basin
Lowdham
Erewash Canal
Ilkeston
NOTTINGHAM
Stanton
Stapleford
Grantham
Derby
Sandiacre
Long Eaton
Swarkestone
Willington
Weston
Kegworth
Zouch
Soar
Loughborough
Melton Mowbray
Wreake
Ashby de la Zouch
Moira
Coalville
Mountsorrel
Grand Union Canal River Soar
Mease
Snarestone Tunnel 250 yds
Thurmaston
Oakham
Belgrave
LEICESTER
Rutland Water
Bosworth Wharf
Market Bosworth
Shenton Aqueduct
Freeman's Meadow
Aylestone
Atherstone
Ashby Canal
Grand Union Canal Leicester Section
Blaby
Welland
Kibworth
Hartshill
Hinckley
Saddington Tunnel 880 yds
Hinckley Wharf
Nuneaton
Foxton
Coventry Canal
Bedworth
Marston Junction
Corby
Husbands Bosworth Tunnel 1166 yds
Market Harborough
Hawkesbury Junction
Welford Arm
Coventry Basin
Stretton Wharf
Oxford Canal
Newbold Tunnel 250 yds
Kettering
COVENTRY
Rugby
Grand Union Canal Leicester Section
Kenilworth
Hillmorton
Pitsford Reservoir
Crick Tunnel 1528 yds
Watford
Irthlingborough
Royal Leamington Spa
Wellingborough
Braunston Turn
Norton Junction
Stockton
Warwick
Daventry
Braunston Tnl 2042 yds
Northampton
Grand Union Canal
Napton Junction
Budbrooke Junction
76
63
70-71
64-65
85
83
81
174-175
114-115
178-179
176-177
113
110-111
25
108-109
22-23
105
20-21
56-57
103
19
54-55
100-101
98-99
16-17
96-97
94-95
53
48-49
146-147
144-145
92
142-143
90
141
89
126-127
124-125
118-119
120-121
122-123

GENERAL INFORMATION FOR WATERWAYS USERS

INTRODUCTION

Boaters, walkers, fishermen, cyclists and gongoozlers (on-lookers) all share in the enjoyment of our quite amazing waterway heritage. Canal & River Trust (CRT) and the Environment Agency, along with other navigation authorities, are empowered to develop, maintain and control this resource. It is to this end that a series of guides, codes, and regulations have come into existence over the years, evolving to match a burgeoning - and occasionally conflicting - demand. Set out in this section are key points as they relate to everyone wishing to enjoy the waterways.

The *Boater's Handbook* is available from all navigation authorities. It contains a complete range of safety information, boat-handling know-how, warning symbols and illustrations, and can be downloaded from www.canalrivertrust.org.uk/boating/navigating-the-waterways/boaters-handbook. It is complemented by this excellent video relating specifically to safe lock operation: www.youtube.com/watch?v=3UIW7VotJpM.

CONSIDERATE BOATING

Considerate Boating gives advice and guidance to all waterway users on how to enjoy the inland waterways safely and can be downloaded from www.canalrivertrust.org.uk/boating/navigating-the-waterways/considerate-boating. It is also well worth visiting www.considerateboater.com. These publications are also available from the Customer Services Team which is staffed *Mon-Fri, 08.00-18.00*. The helpful staff will answer general enquiries and provide information about boat licensing, mooring, boating holidays and general activities on the waterways. They can be contacted on 0303 040 4040; customer.services@canalrivertrust.org.uk; Canal & River Trust, Head Office, First Floor North, Station House, 500 Elder Gate, Milton Keynes MK9 1BB. Visit www.canalrivertrust.org.uk for up to date information on almost every aspect of the inland waterways from news and events to moorings.

Emergency Helpline Available from Canal & River Trust outside normal office hours on weekdays and throughout weekends. If lives or property are at risk or there is danger of serious environmental contamination then contact 0800 47 999 47 immediately for emergency help.

ENVIRONMENT AGENCY

The Environment Agency (EA) manages around 600 miles of the country's rivers, including the Thames and the River Medway. For general enquiries or to obtain a copy of the *Boater's Handbook*, contact EA Customer Services on 03708 506 506; enquiries@environment-agency.gov.uk. To find out about their work nationally (or to download a copy of the *Handbook)* and for lots of other useful information, visit www.gov.uk/government/organisations/environment-agency.
The website www.visitthames.co.uk provides lots on information on boating, walking, fishing and events on the river.

Incident Hotline The EA maintain an Incident Hotline. To report damage or danger to the natural environment, damage to structures or water escaping, telephone 0800 80 70 60.

LICENSING - BOATS

The majority of the navigations covered in this book are controlled by CRT and the EA and are managed on a day-to-day basis by local Waterway Offices (you will find details of these in the introductions to each waterway). All craft using the inland waterways must be licensed and charges are based on the dimensions of the craft. In a few cases, these include reciprocal agreements with other waterway authorities (as indicated in the text). CRT and the EA offer an optional Gold Licence which covers unlimited navigation on the waterways of both authorities. Permits for permanent mooring on CRT waterways are issued by CRT.

Contact Canal & River Trust Boat Licensing Team on 0303 040 4040; www.canalrivertrust.org.uk/boating/licensing; Canal & River Trust Licensing Team, PO Box 162, Leeds LS9 1AX.

For the Thames and River Medway contact the EA. River Thames: 0118 953 5650; www.gov.uk/government/organisations/environment-agency; Environment Agency, PO Box 214, Reading RG1 8HQ. River Medway: 01732 223222 or visit the website.

BOAT SAFETY SCHEME

CRT and the EA operate the Boat Safety Scheme - boat construction standards and regular tests required by all licence holders on CRT and EA waterways. A Boat Safety Certificate (for new boats, a Declaration of Conformity), is necessary to obtain a craft licence. CRT also requires proof of insurance for Third Party Liability for a minimum of £2,000,000 for powered boats. The scheme is gradually being adopted by other waterway authorities. Contact details are: 0333 202 1000; www.boatsafetyscheme.org; Boat Safety Scheme, First Floor North, Station House, 500 Elder Gate, Milton Keynes MK9 1BB. The website offers useful advice on preventing fires and avoiding carbon monoxide poisoning.

TRAINING

The Royal Yachting Association (RYA) runs one and two day courses leading to the Inland Waters Helmsman's Certificate, specifically designed for novices and experienced boaters wishing to cruise the inland waterways. For details of RYA schools, telephone 023 8060 4100 or visit www.rya.org.uk. The practical course notes are available to buy. Contact your local boat clubs, too. The National Community Boats Association (NCBA) run courses on boat-handling and safety on the water. Telephone 0845 0510649 or visit www.national-cba.co.uk.

LICENSING - CYCLISTS

You no longer require a permit to cycle on those waterways under the control of Canal & River Trust. However, you are asked to abide by the ten point Greenway Code for Towpaths available at www.canalrivertrust.org.uk/see-and-do/cycling which also provides a wide range of advice on cycling beside the waterways. Cycling along the Thames towpath is generally accepted, although landowners have the right to request that you do not cycle. Some sections of the riverside path, however, are designated and clearly marked as official cycle ways. No permits are required but cyclists must follow London's Towpath Code on Conduct at all times.

TOWPATHS

Few, if any, artificial cuts or canals in this country are without an intact towpath accessible to the walker at least and the Thames is the only river in the country with a designated National Trail along its path from source to sea (for more information visit www.nationaltrail.co.uk). However, on some other river navigations, towpaths have on occasion fallen into disuse or, sometimes, been lost to erosion. The indication of a towpath in this guide does not necessarily imply a public right of way or mean that a right to cycle along it exists. Horse riding and motorcycling are forbidden on all towpaths.

INDIVIDUAL WATERWAY GUIDES

No national guide can cover the minutiae of detail concerning every waterway, and some CRT Waterway Managers produce guides to specific navigations under their charge. Copies of individual guides (where available) can be obtained from the relevant CRT Waterway Office or downloaded from www.waterscape.com/things-to-do/boating/guides. Please note that times - such as operating times of bridges and locks - do change year by year and from winter to summer. For free copies of a range of helpful leaflets for all users of the River Thames - visit www.visitthames.co.uk/about-the-river/publications.

STOPPAGES

CRT and the EA both publish winter stoppage programmes which are sent out to all licence holders, boatyards and hire companies. Inevitably, emergencies occur necessitating the unexpected closure of a waterway, perhaps during the peak season. You can check for stoppages on individual waterways between specific dates on www.canalrivertrust.org.uk/notices/winter, lockside noticeboards or by telephoning 0303 040 4040; for stoppages and river conditions on the Thames, visit www.gov.uk/river-thames-conditions-closures-restrictions-and-lock-closures or telephone 0845 988 1188.

NAVIGATION AUTHORITIES AND WATERWAYS SOCIETIES

Most inland navigations are managed by CRT or the EA, but there are several other navigation authorities. For details of these, contact the Association of Inland Navigation Authorities on 0844 335 1650 or visit www.aina.org.uk. The boater, conditioned perhaps by the uniformity of our national road network, should be sensitive to the need to observe different codes and operating practices.

The Canal & River Trust is a charity set up to care for England and Wales' legacy of 200-year-old waterways, holding them in trust for the nation forever, and is linked with an ombudsman. CRT has a comprehensive complaints procedure and a free explanatory leaflet is available from Customer Services. Problems and complaints should be addressed to the local Waterway Manager in the first instance. For more information, visit their website.

The EA is the national body, sponsored by the Department for Environment, Food and Rural Affairs, to manage the quality of air, land and water in England and Wales. For more information, visit its website.

The Inland Waterways Association (IWA) campaigns for the use, maintenance and restoration of Britain's inland waterways, through branches all over the country. For more information, contact them on 01494 783453; iwa@waterways.org.uk; www.waterways.org.uk; The Inland Waterways Association, Island House, Moor Road, Chesham HP5 1WA. Their website has a huge amount of information of interest to boaters, including comprehensive details of the many and varied waterways societies.

STARTING OUT

Extensive information and advice on booking a boating holiday is available from the Inland Waterways Association, www.visitthames.co.uk and www.canalrivertrust.org.uk/boating/boat-trips-and-holidays. Please book a waterway holiday from a licensed operator – this way you can be sure that you have proper insurance cover, service and support during your holiday. It is illegal for private boat owners to hire out their craft. If you are hiring a holiday craft for the first time, the boatyard will brief you thoroughly. Take notes, follow their instructions and do ask if there is anything you do not understand. CRT have produced a 40 min DVD which is essential viewing for newcomers to canal or river boating. Available to view free at www.canalrivertrust.org.uk/boatersdvd or obtainable (charge) from the CRT Customer Service Centre 0303 040 4040; www.canalrivertrust.org.uk/shop.

PLACES TO VISIT ALONG THE WAY

This guide contains a wealth of information, not just about the canals and rivers and navigating on them, but also on the visitor attractions and places to eat and drink close to the waterways. Opening and closing times, and other details often change; establishments close and new ones open. If you are making special plans to eat in a particular pub, or visit a certain museum it is always advisable to check in advance.

MORE INFORMATION

An internet search will reveal many websites on the inland waterways. Those listed below are just a small sample:

National Community Boats Association is a national charity and training provider, supporting community boat projects and encouraging more people to access the inland waterways. Telephone 0845 0510649; www.national-cba.co.uk.

National Association of Boat Owners is dedicated to promoting the interests of private boaters on Britain's canals and rivers. Visit www.nabo.org.uk.

www.canalplan.org.uk is an online journey-planner and gazetteer for the inland waterways.

www.canals.com is a valuable source of information for cruising the canals, with loads of links to canal and waterways related websites.

www.ukcanals.net lists services and useful information for all waterways users.

GENERAL CRUISING NOTES

Most canals and rivers are saucer shaped, being deepest at the middle. Few canals have more than 3-4ft of water and many have much less. Keep to the centre of the channel except on bends, where the deepest water is on the outside of the bend. When you meet another boat, keep to the right, slow down and aim to miss the approaching craft by a couple of yards. If you meet a loaded commercial boat keep right out of the way and be prepared to follow his instructions. Do not assume that you should pass on the right. If you meet a boat being towed from the bank, pass it on the outside. When overtaking, keep the other boat on your right side.

Some CRT and EA facilities are operated by pre-paid cards, obtainable from CRT and EA regional and local waterways offices, lock keepers and boatyards. Weekend visitors should purchase cards in advance. A handcuff/anti-vandal key is commonly used on locks where vandalism is a problem. A watermate/sanitary key opens sanitary stations, waterpoints and some bridges and locks. Both keys and pre-paid cards can be obtained via CRT Customer Service Centre.

Safety

Boating is a safe pastime. However, it makes sense to take simple safety precautions, particularly if you have children aboard.

- Never drink and drive a boat – it may travel slowly, but it weighs many tons.
- Be careful with naked flames and never leave the boat with the hob or oven lit. Familiarise yourself and your crew with the location and operation of the fire extinguishers.

- Never block ventilation grills. Boats are enclosed spaces and levels of carbon monoxide can build up from faulty appliances or just from using the cooker.
- Be careful along the bank and around locks. Slipping from the bank might only give you a cold-water soaking, but falling from the side of, or into a lock is more dangerous. Beware of slippery or rough ground.
- Remember that fingers and toes are precious! If a major collision is imminent, never try to fend off with your hands or feet; and always keep hands and arms inside the boat.
- Weil's disease is a particularly dangerous infection present in water which can attack the central nervous system and major organs. It is caused by bacteria entering the bloodstream through cuts and broken skin, and the eyes, nose and mouth. The flu-like symptoms occur two-four weeks after exposure. Always wash your hands thoroughly after contact with the water. Visit www.leptospirosis.org for details.

Speed

There is a general speed limit of 4 mph on most CRT canals and 5 mph on the Thames. There is no need to go any faster - the faster you go, the bigger a wave the boat creates: if your wash is breaking against the bank, causing large waves or throwing moored boats around, slow down. Slow down also when passing engineering works and anglers; when there is a lot of floating rubbish on the water (try to drift over obvious obstructions in neutral); when approaching blind corners, narrow bridges and junctions.

Mooring

Generally you may moor where you wish on CRT property, as long as you are *not causing an obstruction*. Do not moor in a winding hole or junction, the approaches to a lock or tunnel, or at a water point or sanitary station. On the Thames, generally you have a right to anchor for 24 hours in one place provided no obstruction is caused, however you will need explicit permission from the land owner to moor. There are official mooring sites along the length of the river; those provided by the EA are free, the others you will need to pay for. Your boat should carry metal mooring stakes, and these should be driven firmly into the ground with a mallet if there are no mooring rings. Do not stretch mooring lines across the towpath and take account of anyone who may walk past. Always consider the security of your boat when there is no one aboard. On tideways and commercial waterways it is advisable to moor only at recognised sites, and allow for any rise or fall of the tide.

Bridges

On narrow canals slow down well in advance and aim to miss one side (usually the towpath side) by about 9 inches. *Keep everyone inboard when passing under bridges and ensure there is nothing on the roof of the boat that will hit the bridge.* If a boat is coming the other way, the craft nearest to the bridge has priority. Take special care with moveable structures - the crew member operating the bridge should be strong and heavy enough to hold it steady as the boat passes through.

Going aground

You can sometimes go aground if the water level on a canal has dropped or you are on a particularly shallow stretch. If it does happen, try reversing *gently*, or pushing off with the boat hook. Another method is to get your crew to rock the boat from side to side using the boat hook, or move all crew to the end opposite to that which is aground. Or, have all crew leave the boat, except the helmsman, and it will often float off quite easily.

Tunnels

Again, ensure that everyone is inboard. Make sure the tunnel is clear before you enter, and use your headlight. Follow any instructions given on notice boards by the entrance.

Fuel

Diesel can be purchased from most boatyards and some CRT depots. To comply with HMRC regulations you must declare an appropriate split between propulsion and heating so that the correct level of VAT can be applied. However, few boatyards stock petrol. Where a garage is listed under a town or village's facilities petrol (and DERV) are available.

Water

It is advisable to top up daily.

Pump out

Self-operated pump out facilities are available at a number of locations on the waterways network. These facilities are provided by CRT and can be operated via a 25-unit prepayment card. Details of how to buy a pump out card either online, by phone or in person are available from www.canalrivertrust.org.uk. The cards provide for one pump out or 25 units of electricity. Cards can be obtained from CRT Waterway Offices, some Marinas and boatyards, shops and cafés.

Boatyards
Hire fleets are usually turned around at a weekend, making this a bad time to call in for services.

VHF Radio
The IWA recommends that all pleasure craft navigating the larger waterways used by freight carrying vessels, or any tidal navigation, should carry marine-band VHF radio and have a qualified radio operator on board. In some cases the navigation authority requires craft to carry radio and maintain a listening watch. Two examples of this are for boats on the tidal River Ouse wishing to enter Goole Docks and the Aire & Calder Navigation, and for boats on the tidal Thames, over 45ft, navigating between Teddington Lock and Limehouse Basin.
VHF radio users must have a current operator's certificate. The training is not expensive and will present no problem to the average inland waterways boater. Contact the RYA (see Training) for details.

PLANNING A CRUISE

Don't try to go too far too fast. Go slowly, don't be too ambitious, and enjoy the experience. Mileages indicated on the maps are for guidance only. A *rough* calculation of time taken to cover the ground is the lock-miles system:

Add the number of *miles* to the number of *locks* on your proposed journey, and divide the resulting figure by three. This will give you an approximate guide to the number of *hours* your travel will take.

TIDAL WATERWAYS

The typical steel narrow boat found on the inland waterways is totally unsuitable for cruising on tidal estuaries. However, the adventurous will inevitably wish to add additional 'ring cruises' to the more predictable circuits of inland Britain. Passage is possible in most estuaries if careful consideration is given to the key factors of weather conditions, tides, crew experience, the condition of the boat and its equipment and, perhaps of overriding importance, the need to take expert advice. In many cases it will be prudent to employ the skilled services of a local pilot. Within the text, where inland navigations connect with a tidal waterway, details are given of sources of advice and pilotage. It is also essential to inform your insurance company of your intention to navigate on tidal waterways as they may very well have special requirements or wish to levy an additional premium. This guide is to the inland waterways of Britain and therefore recognizes that tideways - and especially estuaries - require a different approach and many additional skills. We do not hesitate to draw the boater's attention to the appropriate source material.

LOCKS AND THEIR USE

A lock is a simple and ingenious device for transporting your craft from one water level to another. When both sets of gates are closed it may be filled or emptied using gates, or ground paddles, at the top or bottom of the lock. These are operated with a windlass. On the Thames, the locks are manned all year round, with longer hours from April to October. You may operate the locks yourself at any time.

If a lock is empty, or 'set' for you, the crew open the gates and you drive the boat in. If the lock is full of water, the crew should check first to see if any boat is waiting or coming in the other direction. If a boat is in sight, you must let them through first: do not empty or 'turn' the lock against them. This is not only discourteous, and against the rules, but wastes precious water.

In the diagrams the *plan* shows how the gates point uphill, the water pressure forcing them together. Water is flooding into the lock through the underground culverts that are operated by the ground paddles: when the lock is 'full', the top gates (on the left of the drawing) can be opened. One may imagine a boat entering, the crew closing the gates and paddles after it.

In the *elevation*, the bottom paddles have been raised (opened) so that the lock empties. A boat will, of course, float down with the water. When the lock is 'empty' the bottom gates can be opened and the descending boat can leave.

Remember that when going *up* a lock, a boat should be tied up to prevent it being thrown about by the the rush of incoming water; but when going *down* a lock, a boat should never be tied up or it will be left high and dry.

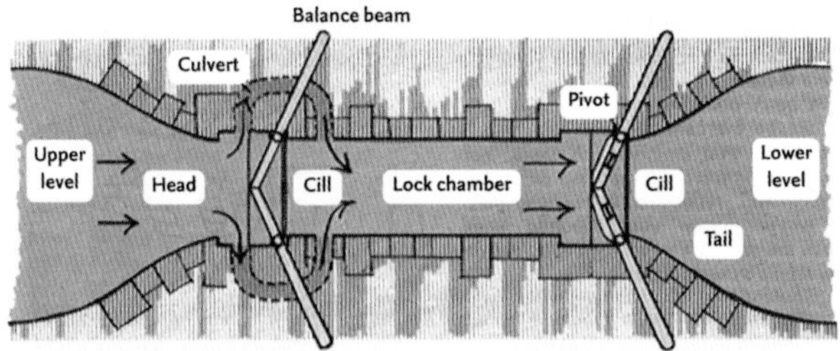

Ground paddles open. Water fills the chamber through the culverts.

Gate paddles closed, retaining water in the lock chamber.

A plan of a lock filling.

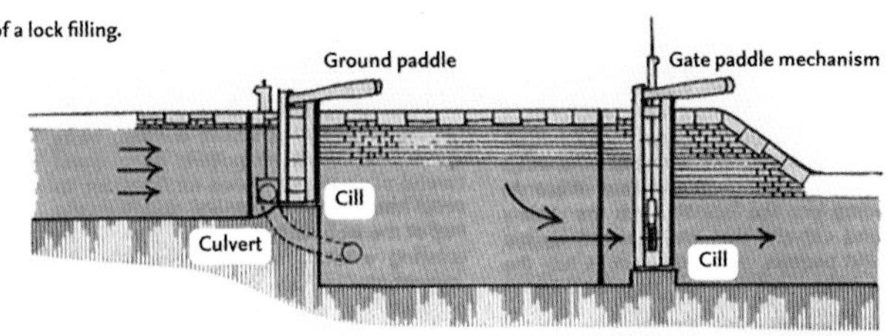

Ground paddles closed preventing water from the upper level filling the chamber.

Gate paddles open. Water flows from the chamber to the lower level.

An elevation of a lock emptying.

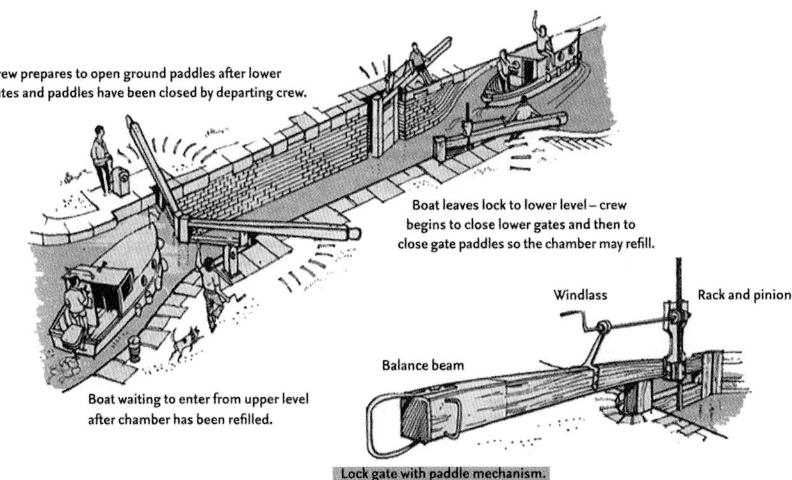

Lock gate with paddle mechanism.

- Make safety your prime concern. *Keep a close eye on young children.*
- Always take your time, and do not leap about.
- Never open the paddles at one end without ensuring those at the other end are closed.
- Keep to the landward side of the balance beam when opening and closing gates. Whilst it may be necessary to put your back behind the balance beam to gain a better purchase when starting to close a gate, always move to the correct position as soon as possible.
- Never leave your windlass slotted onto the paddle spindle – it will be dangerous should anything slip.
- Keep your boat away from the top and bottom gates to prevent it getting caught on the gate or the lock cill.
- Never drop the paddles – always wind them down.
- Be wary of fierce *top gate* paddles, especially in wide locks. Operate them slowly, and close them if there is *any* adverse effect.
- Always follow the navigation authority's instructions, where given on notices or by their staff.

Boats moored at Wharf Bridge, Stoke Golding, on the Ashby Canal

ASHBY CANAL

MAXIMUM DIMENSIONS

Length: 72'
Beam: 7'
Headroom: 6' 6"
Draught: 3' 6"

MILEAGE

MARSTON JUNCTION (Coventry Canal) to:
Burton Hastings: 3 miles
Hinckley Wharf: 6 miles
Stoke Golding Wharf: 8¾ miles
Dadlington: 10 miles
Shenton Aqueduct: 13 miles
Market Bosworth Wharf: 15 miles
Congerstone: 17¼ miles
Shackerstone: 18¼ miles
Snarestone Tunnel: 21 miles
HEAD OF NAVIGATION: 22 miles

No locks

MANAGER

0303 040 4040
enquiries.westmidlands@canalrivertrust.org.uk

Looking at this canal on a map it appears to be very much out on a limb. In fact the Ashby Canal was originally intended to be a through route from the River Trent at Burton to the Coventry Canal near Bedworth, but this plan was repeatedly shelved. In 1792, however, an Ashby Canal Company was formed and a Bill promoted, mostly by the owners of Leicestershire limeworks and the new coalfields near Ashby de la Zouch, who decided that an outlet southwards was required from their various works. The problem that soon arose was that, while the proposed canal could be built level for 30 miles (following the 300ft contour) from the junction with the Coventry Canal at Marston Jabbett, near Bedworth, to Moira, the section north of Moira would require expensive and complicated works, including locks, reservoirs, pumping engines and possibly a tunnel. Part of this cost was, in fact, avoided by building an extensive system of tramroads to and around the various coalmines and limeworks. However, while the canal was still being built (by a succession of engineers - Jessop, Outram, Whitworth senior and junior, and Thomas Newbold), the new coalmines near Ashby Wolds were found to be less productive than had been hoped. This, combined with the fact that the canal was never extended north to the Trent, was instrumental in preventing the Ashby Canal from making a profit for 20 years. However, a new coal mine sunk at Moira in 1804 eventually produced coal of such excellent quality that it became widely demanded in London and southern England. The canal flourished at last.

In 1845 the Midland Railway bought up the Ashby Canal - with the approval of all concerned except the Coventry and Oxford canal companies, who stood to lose a lot in tolls if the coal traffic from Moira switched to rail carriage. These two companies managed to hamstring the Midland Railway so effectively over its management of the canal that, instead of switching to carriage by rail, the coal traffic from Moira continued along the canal at a substantial level through to the turn of the century. It is therefore hard to see what real benefit the railway company gained from buying the canal.

Subsidence from the coal mines near Measham (now stabilised with the completion of mining in the area) has caused great damage in this century to the canal that served them. This subsidence has brought about the abandonment of over 8 miles of the canal, so that the waterway now terminates just north of Snarestone, outside the coalfield. The last load to be carried along the canal was coal to Croxley (Herts), from Gopsall Wharf in 1970. Ambitious plans are in hand to re-open the waterway through to Moira, making use of the abandoned railway line in Measham. Already a new 1¼ mile section, complete with a lock in water, has been constructed beside Moira Furnace.

Burton Hastings

At Marston Junction the Ashby Canal branches east off the Coventry Canal. Under the bridge there is a box containing guides to the waterway produced by the Ashby Canal Association. As soon as it leaves Marston, the canal changes completely and dramatically. The industry and housing estates that had accompanied the Coventry Canal through the Nuneaton–Bedworth conurbation suddenly vanish to be replaced by green fields, farms and trees. In this way the character of the Ashby Canal is established at once: also the first of the typical stone-arched bridges occurs which, together with the shallow and relatively clear water, suggests a rurality far from the industrial Midlands. Only the power lines that criss-cross this stretch are a memory of the other world to the west. A long wooded cutting leads the canal towards Burton Hastings, a typical farming village. Then the canal turns north, setting a course for Hinckley passing, to the east of bridge 13, Stretton Baskerville, a 'lost' village and scheduled ancient monument. The A5 (Watling Street) and the A47 cross near Hinckley. There is no navigation on the Hinckley Wharf Arm, which is used as a boat club mooring. However there are good *moorings* west of bridge 16 and to the north and south of the marina complex beyond bridge 17 (but ask at the marina first). Keeping west of the town, the canal continues through the fine rolling farmland that typifies the Ashby Canal.

Boatyards

Ⓑ **Trinity Marinas** Wharf Farm, Coventry Road, Hinckley LE10 0NF (01455 896820; www.trinitymarinas.co.uk). D E Pump out, gas, overnight and long-term mooring, wet dock, DIY facilities, chandlery, brokerage, books, maps and gifts, telephone, toilets, showers, solid fuel, laundrette, restaurant and hotel. Boat licensing at marina office.

WALKING AND CYCLING

The condition of the towpath has been greatly improved and erosion in the bridgeholes has been made good. This is a very rural waterway, so few sections of the towpath have an all-weather surface, making progress for walker and cyclist difficult in some areas during the winter months. Hinkley and Bosworth Borough Council publish four guides which detail walks that include sections of the canal. These are available from local Tourist Information Centres.

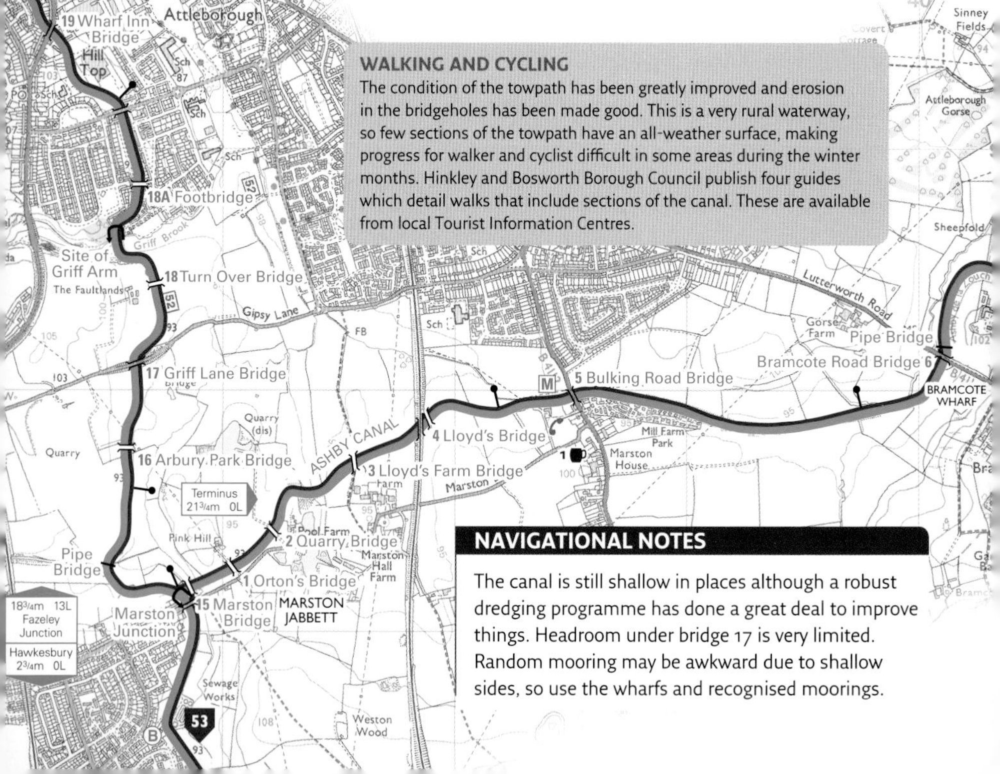

NAVIGATIONAL NOTES

The canal is still shallow in places although a robust dredging programme has done a great deal to improve things. Headroom under bridge 17 is very limited. Random mooring may be awkward due to shallow sides, so use the wharfs and recognised moorings.

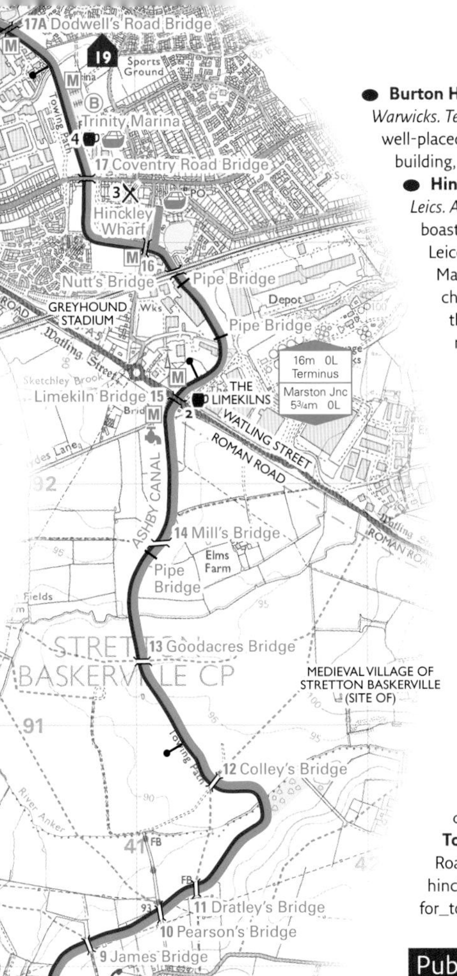

● **Burton Hastings**
Warwicks. Tel. A quiet village set on a hill in open farmland. The well-placed church dedicated to St Botolph is a Grade II listed building, parts of its construction dating back to the 14th C.

● **Hinckley**
Leics. All services. A hosiery manufacturing town that can boast having installed the first stocking machine in Leicestershire, in 1640. Buildings of interest include St Mary's church with the 'bleeding' tombstone in the churchyard; the Great Meeting Chapel (1722) and the museum. Only the bailey and part of the moat remain of the Norman castle. There is a coffee bar and second hand bookstall in the church *open Mon-Sat 10.00-16.00.* The shop on Coventry Road is *open Mon-Sat 05.30-21.00 & Sun 06.00-17.00;*

Concordia Theatre Stockwell Head, Hinckley LE10 1RE (01455 615005; www.concordiatheatre.co.uk). Small local theatre with performances *all year round.*

Hinckley and District Museum Framework Knitters Cottages, Lower Bond Street, Hinckley LE10 1QU (01455 251218; www.beehive.thisisleicestershire.co.uk). Established in a row of restored 17th-C thatched cottages once used for framework knitting, the museum houses displays on the town and area from prehistoric to medieval times. Also depicted are the hosiery and boot and shoe making industries together with annually changing exhibitions reflecting different aspects of local history. *Open Easter Mon-Oct, Sat and B Hol Mon 10.00-16.00, Sun 14.00-17.00 Jun-Sep Mon 11.00-15.00.* Tearoom and cottage garden. Small admission charge.

Tourist Information Centre The Library, Lancaster Road, Hinckley LE10 0AT (01455 255805; www.hinckley-bosworth.gov.uk/info/200096/information_for_tourists).

Pubs and Restaurants

1 The Corner House Hotel 454 Nuneaton Road, Bulkington, Bedworth CV12 9SB (02476 386159; www.cornerhousepubnuneaton.co.uk). South of bridge 5 on B4112. Large friendly pub orientated around family eating. Real ales. Food available *all day, every day.* Children welcome. Patio. *Open 11.00-23.00.*

2 The Lime Kilns Inn Watling Street, Hinckley LE10 3ED (01455 631158; limekilnsinn.co.uk). Canalside at bridge 15. Old coaching house and family pub serving real ale and bar food *L and E, daily (not Sun E)* Children's menu. Canalside seating, garden and children's play area. Traditional pub games, real fires and Wi-Fi. Mooring. *Open Mon-Fri L and E & Sat-Sun 12.00-23.00 (Sun 22.30).*

3 Simla 314 Coventry Road, Hinckley LE10 0NQ (01455 633955; www.simlarestauranthinckley.co.uk). Friendly, welcoming Indian restaurant keen to uphold the maxim that 'a guest does us honour by visiting for a second time.' Takeaway service with free delivery within a three-mile radius. *Open daily 17.30-23.30 (Fri-Sat 00.00).*

4 The Marina Trinity Marinas, Wharf Farm, Coventry Road, Hinckley LE10 0NB (01455 636493; www.brewersfayre.co.uk/pub-restaurant/Leicestershire/Marina-Hinckley.html). In the marina complex together with a Premier Inn Hotel, offering full breakfast *06.30-10.30.* Also *daily* buffet, a la carte menu and *Sun* carvery. Family-friendly and outside seating. Wi-Fi. B&B. *Open 12.00-23.00.*

Stoke Golding

The canal now runs fairly directly to Stoke Golding where there is one of the finest churches in Leicestershire. Just to the west of Wharf Bridge 25 there is an excellent *farm shop* (01455 212199) selling both *home-produced meat and vegetables*. An even wider range of *fresh farm produce*, together with *milk, bread, coal, logs and gas*, is available beside Bridge 23 (01455 212445/07971 851680). There are no locks, but the typical Ashby accommodation bridges occur regularly. The Ashby Canal is remote and rural, an ironic contrast to its raison d'être, the Ashby coalfields. After Stoke Golding the contours cause the canal to meander carelessly, passing Dadlington, heading in a northerly direction towards Sutton Cheney Wharf (*showers and toilets*) and the Bosworth Battlefield Centre nearby.

Pubs and Restaurants

1 The Oddfellows Arms 25 Main Street, Higham on the Hill, Nuneaton CV13 6AE (01455 212097). Good, all round village pub with attentive staff and welcoming family atmosphere. Home-cooked food available *Tue-Fri L and E (not Tue E) Sat 12.00-20.30 & Sun 12.00-15.30*. Child- and dog-friendly, garden. Traditional pub games and real fires. Quiz *Tue*. *Open Mon-Thu L and E (not Mon L) & Fri-Sun 12.00-00.00 (Sun 23.00).*

2 The White Swan High Street, Stoke Golding, CV13 6HE (01455 212313; whiteswanstokegolding.co.uk). Real ale and real cider dispensed in a homely village local with friendly staff. Food available *Tue-Sat L and E (not Tue E) & Sun 12.00-16.00*. Dog- and child-friendly, garden. Real fires and Wi-Fi. *Open Tue-Sat L and E (not Tue E) & Sun 12.00-00.00.*

3 The Mango Tree 3 High Street, Stoke Golding CV13 6HE (01455 213861; www.threehorseshoesstokegolding.co.uk). Award-winning Indian restaurant and takeaway behind the **Three Horseshoes pub** *open daily 17.30-23.00*. Real ale and real fire. The pub itself (01455 212263) is a typical three-roomed local serving real ale. Dog- and family-friendly, garden. Traditional pub games, sports TV and Wi-Fi. *Open Mon-Sat E and Sun 12.00-23.00.*

4 The George & Dragon Station Road, Stoke Golding CV136EZ (01455 213268; www.churchendbrewery.co.uk/pubs). The first Church End Brewery pub. Real ale. Traditional pub lunches, homemade from fresh, local ingredients, served *Tue-Sat L*. The pub also sells freshly baked bread, local cheeses and pork pies to eat in or takeaway. Real cider. Dog- and family-friendly (children *until 19.00*). Garden. Traditional pub games, real fires and Wi-Fi. *Open Tue-Thu L and E & Fri-Sat 12.00-23.00 (Sun 22.30).*

5 The Dog & Hedgehog 2 The Green, Dadlington CV13 6JB (01455 213151; www.dadlington.com/village/dogandhedgehog.php). Historic and charming village pub serving *Mon-Sat L and E (not Sun E)*. Real ales and good pub food made from fresh, local and seasonal produce *Mon-Sat L and E & all day Sun*. Real ales and a real fire in *winter*. Children and dogs welcome. Gardens. Booking recommended. *Open all day, every day (but closes 20.00 Sun).*

6 Café Wharfside Sutton Cheney Wharf, Wharf Lane, Sutton Cheney CV13 0AL (01455 213838). Friendly café serving tasty homemade dishes, tea, coffee, snacks and ices from breakfast through to tea. Muddy boots and well-behaved dogs on leads are welcome. *Open Tue-Fri 10.00-16.00 & Sat-Sun 09.30-16.30.*

7 The Hercules Revived Main Street, Sutton Cheney CV13 0AG (01455 699336/07795 973258; www.herculesrevived.co.uk). This recently refurbished, 17th-C country Inn has a relaxed bar and simple dining area on the ground floor with a large open fire, and a series of elegantly decorated, cosy restaurant rooms on the first floor. Home-cooked food, made from locally sourced ingredients wherever possible, is available *L and E (not Sun E)* and children are welcome. Outside seating. Wi-Fi. *Open Mon-Sat L and E & Sun 12.00-16.00.*

WALKING AND CYCLING

In Shenton Cutting, waymarked from Railway Bridge 34A, there is a wildlife walk and a bird-watching hide.

Boatyards

Ⓑ**Ashby Boat Company** The Canal Wharf, Stoke Golding, Nuneaton CV13 6EY (01455 212671; www.ashbyboats.com). **D** Pump out, narrowboat hire, gas, day-hire craft, chandlery, boat and engine repairs, welding, painting, solid fuel, crane, DIY facilities, Wi-Fi, toilets. *Emergency call out.*

Ⓑ**Ashby Canal Centre** Willow Park Marina, Stoke Golding, Nuneaton CV13 6EU (01455 212636; www.ashbycanalcentre.co.uk). **E** Short and long-term moorings, slipway, covered wet dock, boat brokerage, boat painting, welding, engine sales, DIY facilities, boat and engine repairs, boat surveys, BSS inspections, toilets.

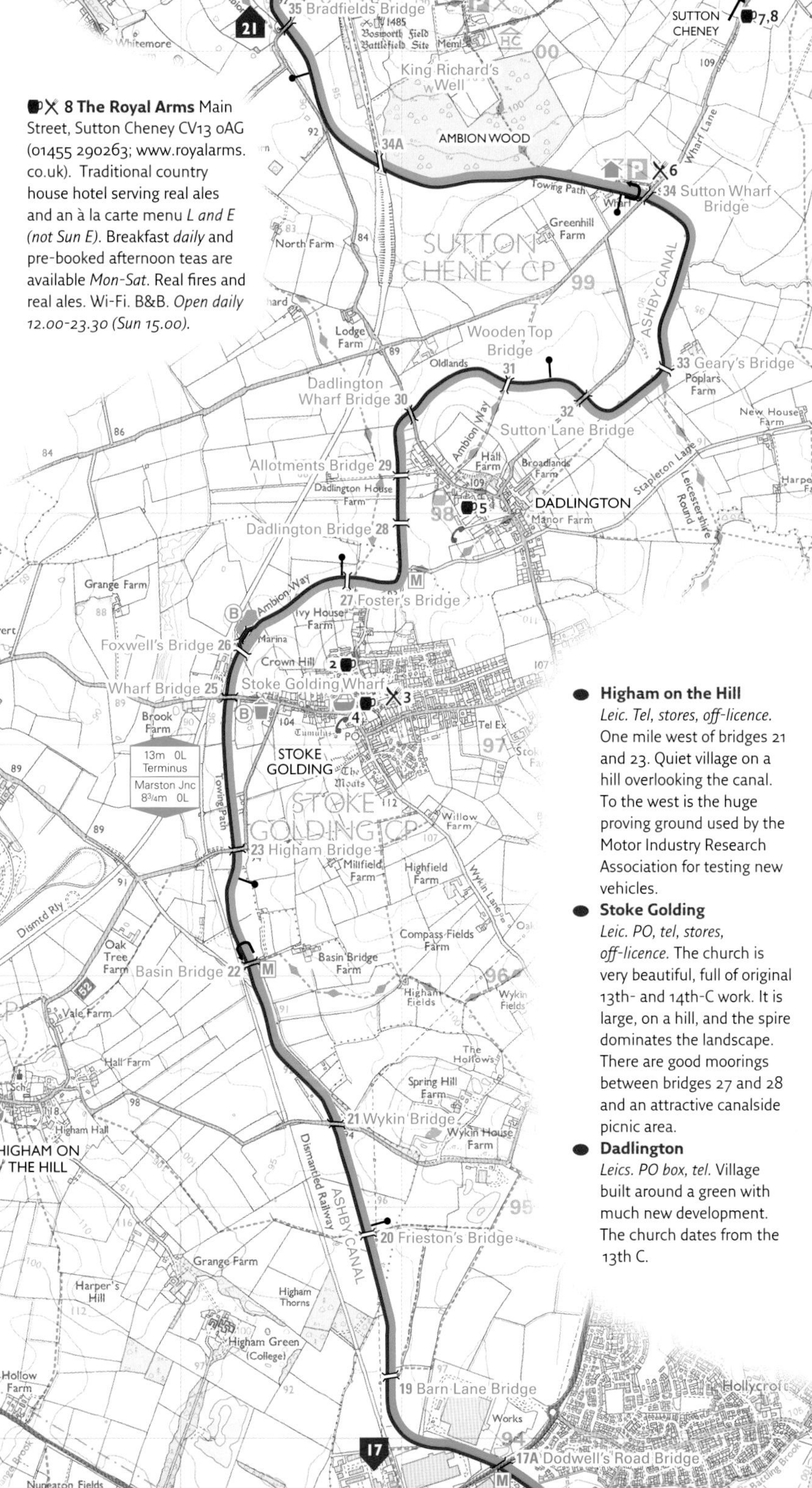

8 The Royal Arms Main Street, Sutton Cheney CV13 0AG (01455 290263; www.royalarms.co.uk). Traditional country house hotel serving real ales and an à la carte menu *L and E (not Sun E)*. Breakfast *daily* and pre-booked afternoon teas are available *Mon-Sat*. Real fires and real ales. Wi-Fi. B&B. *Open daily 12.00-23.30 (Sun 15.00).*

- **Higham on the Hill**
Leic. Tel, stores, off-licence. One mile west of bridges 21 and 23. Quiet village on a hill overlooking the canal. To the west is the huge proving ground used by the Motor Industry Research Association for testing new vehicles.
- **Stoke Golding**
Leic. PO, tel, stores, off-licence. The church is very beautiful, full of original 13th- and 14th-C work. It is large, on a hill, and the spire dominates the landscape. There are good moorings between bridges 27 and 28 and an attractive canalside picnic area.
- **Dadlington**
Leics. PO box, tel. Village built around a green with much new development. The church dates from the 13th C.

Market Bosworth

Just before Shenton Aqueduct there are good *moorings* for the Battlefield Centre. Shenton Park is passed on an embankment, and then the aqueduct carries the canal over the road to Shenton village. It continues towards Congerstone, with Market Bosworth and Carlton away to the east. There are good *moorings* between bridges 49 and 50, and north of bridge 51. Beyond Congerstone the navigation crosses the River Sence.

Shenton
Leics. Tel. Estate village clustered around the Hall, a house of 1629 much rebuilt in the 19th C.
Battle of Bosworth Field 22 August 1485 Ambion Hill, Sutton Cheney. The battlefield where Richard III, last of the Plantagenets, was killed by Henry Tudor who thus became Henry VII. 3/4 mile walk from Shenton Embankment to the **Bosworth Battlefield Heritage Centre** Sutton Cheney CV13 0AD (01455 290429; www.bosworthbattlefield.org.uk). Award-winning interpretation of the battle. Restaurant, shop. Toilets. Visitor Centre *open 10.00-17.00 (16.00 Nov-Mar). Closed over Xmas and throughout Jan.* Charge. Footpaths *open all year in daylight hours.* Disabled access to Visitor Centre and Battlefield Trails.
Whitemoors Antique and Craft Centre Main Street, Shenton, Market Bosworth CV13 6BZ (01455 212250/07709 394841; whitemoors.co.uk). Gardens, craft and antique centre. Tearooms. *Open daily 11.00-17.00 (16.00 Mon-Fri in winter). Closed over Xmas and New Year.*

Market Bosworth
Leics. Tel, stores, chemist, bank, butcher, takeaways, fish & chips, greengrocer, bakery. Almost a mile east of its wharf. Small market town remaining much as it was in the 18th C. Shop *open Mon-Sat 08.00-20.00 and Sun 09.00-18.00.*

Battlefield Line Shackerstone Station, Shackerstone CV13 6NW (01827 880754; www.battlefieldline.co.uk). Preserved railway line. A ride can be linked in with a visit to the Bosworth Battlefield Visitor Centre. *See* page 23 for further details.
Bosworth Water Trust Far Coton Lane, Wellsborough Road, near Nuneaton CV13 6PD (01455 291876; www.bosworthwatertrust. co.uk). Just to the west of Bosworth Wharf Bridge 42. Large leisure park with a 20-acre lake for water pursuits. Wetsuits and craft for hire. Changing rooms, toilets, showers and snack bar *open during main season.* Site *open all year, daily 10.00-dusk.* Charge.

Congerstone
Leics. Tel. Scattered village.

Pubs and Restaurants

1 The Black Horse Inn 17 Market Place, Market Bosworth CV13 0LF (01455 290278; www.theblackhorserestaurant.co.uk). Old-world country pub dispensing real ales. Snacks and meals available *L and E, (Sun 12.00-16.00)* in both bar and restaurant. Champagne breakfasts *Sat & Sun 10.00-12.45.* Children welcome. Outdoor patio and gazebo. *Open L and E (not Sun E).*

2 Victorian Tea Parlour 7 Market Place, Market Bosworth CV13 0LF (01455 290190). Off the courtyard. Step back in time and enjoy a trip down memory lane together with teas, coffees, snacks and light lunches. Children welcome. Pretty garden. *Open daily 11.00-17.00.*

3 The Dixie Arms (incorporating La Bella Piazza) 7 Main Street, Market Bosworth CV13 0JW (01455 290218; www.dixiearmshotel.co.uk). 400-year-old hostelry in the town centre. Bar meals are served *L* and the piazza is *open Mon-Sat E.* Real ales. Garden, traditional pub games, newspapers, real fires and sports TV. B&B. *Open 12.00-23.00 (Sun 22.30).*

4 Ye Olde Red Lion Hotel 1 Park Street, Market Bosworth CV13 0LL (01455 291713; www.redlionmarketbosworth.com). Another 400-year-old hotel and public house in the town centre serving real ales. Home-made snacks and meals available *Mon-Fri L and E & Sat and Sun all day.* Children and dogs welcome. Patio. Newspapers, real fires, sports TV and Wi-Fi. B&B. *Open 11.00-23.00 (Sun 22.30).*

5 The Gate Hangs Well Barton Road, Carlton CV13 0DB (01455 290806; www.gatehangswell.net). Welcoming, small country pub with warm, cosy interior. Real ales. Children and dogs welcome *(dogs in conservatory area only).* Garden, traditional pub games, newspapers, real fires, sports TV and Wi-Fi. *Open Mon-Thu E, Fri L and E & Sat-Sun 12.00-23.30.*

6 The Horse & Jockey Bosworth Road, Congerstone CV13 6LY (01877 881220; www.horsejockey.co.uk). Attractive country pub/restauarant serving real ales and food *L and E (not Mon L and Sun E).* Dog- and family-friendly, garden. Real fires and *regular* live music. *Open L and E (not Mon L and Sun E).*

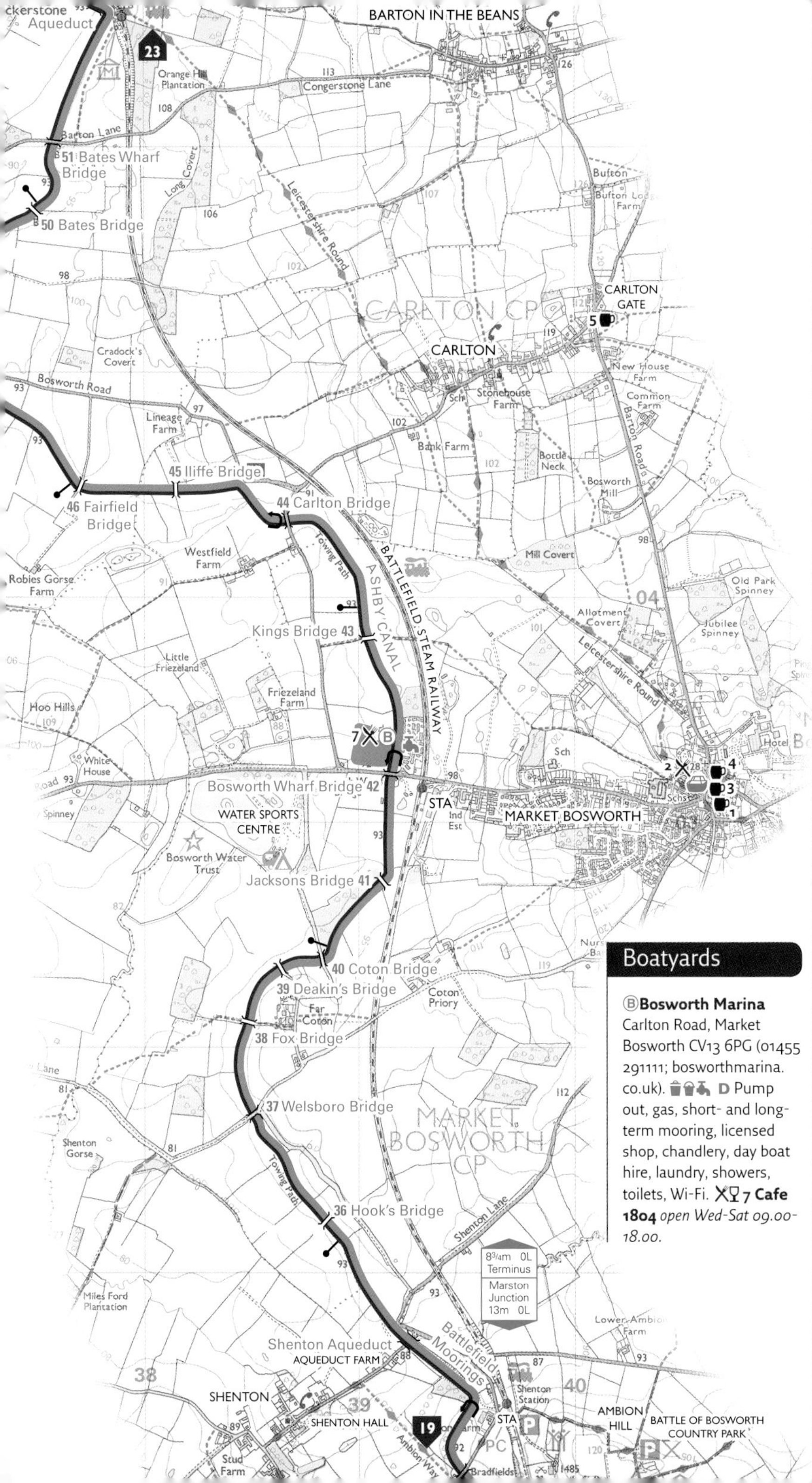

Boatyards

Ⓑ**Bosworth Marina** Carlton Road, Market Bosworth CV13 6PG (01455 291111; bosworthmarina.co.uk). D Pump out, gas, short- and long-term mooring, licensed shop, chandlery, day boat hire, laundry, showers, toilets, Wi-Fi. **7 Cafe 1804** *open Wed-Sat 09.00-18.00.*

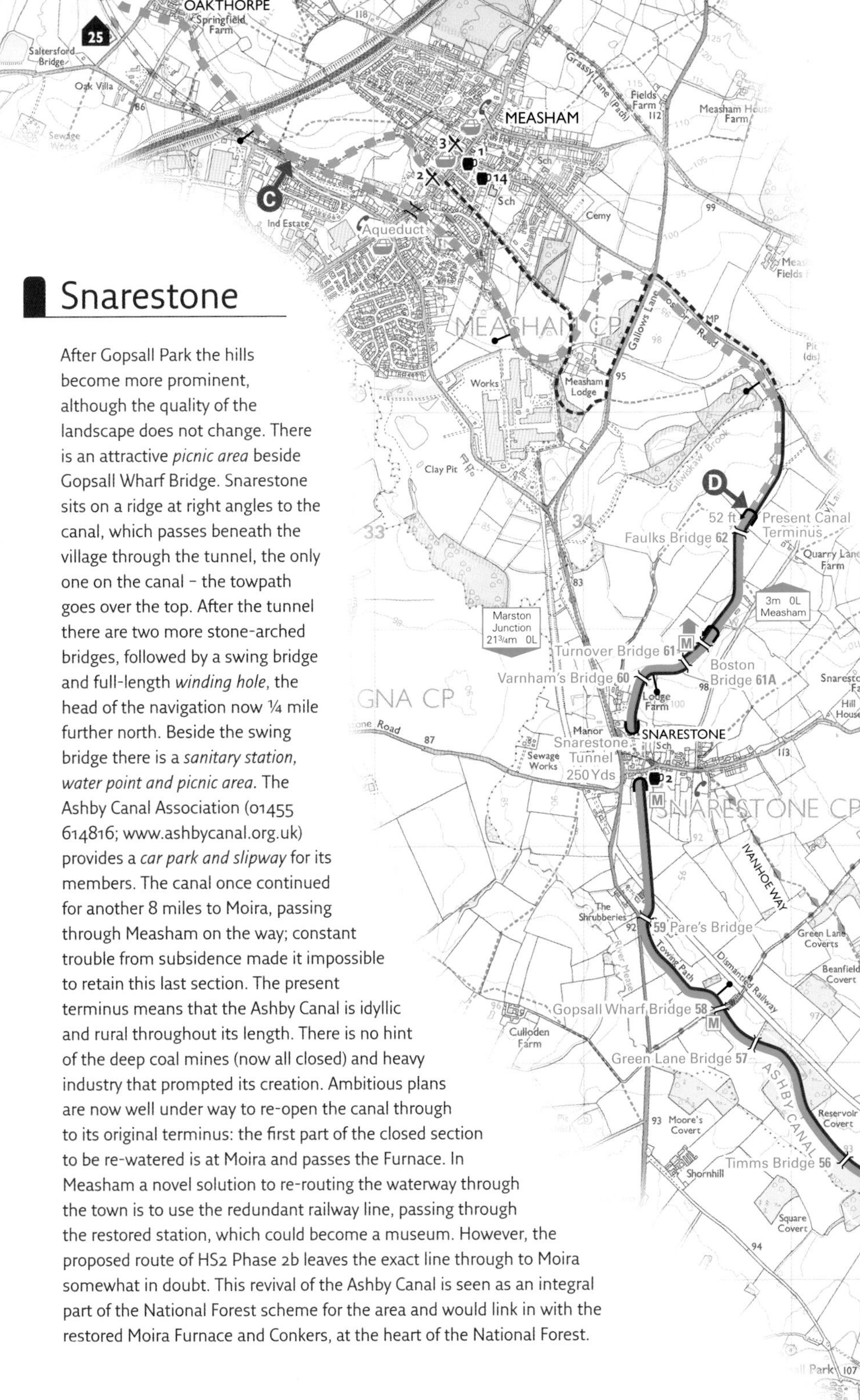

Snarestone

After Gopsall Park the hills become more prominent, although the quality of the landscape does not change. There is an attractive *picnic area* beside Gopsall Wharf Bridge. Snarestone sits on a ridge at right angles to the canal, which passes beneath the village through the tunnel, the only one on the canal – the towpath goes over the top. After the tunnel there are two more stone-arched bridges, followed by a swing bridge and full-length *winding hole*, the head of the navigation now ¼ mile further north. Beside the swing bridge there is a *sanitary station, water point and picnic area*. The Ashby Canal Association (01455 614816; www.ashbycanal.org.uk) provides a *car park and slipway* for its members. The canal once continued for another 8 miles to Moira, passing through Measham on the way; constant trouble from subsidence made it impossible to retain this last section. The present terminus means that the Ashby Canal is idyllic and rural throughout its length. There is no hint of the deep coal mines (now all closed) and heavy industry that prompted its creation. Ambitious plans are now well under way to re-open the canal through to its original terminus: the first part of the closed section to be re-watered is at Moira and passes the Furnace. In Measham a novel solution to re-routing the waterway through the town is to use the redundant railway line, passing through the restored station, which could become a museum. However, the proposed route of HS2 Phase 2b leaves the exact line through to Moira somewhat in doubt. This revival of the Ashby Canal is seen as an integral part of the National Forest scheme for the area and would link in with the restored Moira Furnace and Conkers, at the heart of the National Forest.

Shackerstone

Leics. Undeveloped and unchanged, Shackerstone is a farming village that reflects the pre-industrial feeling of the whole of the Ashby Canal. West of the village the canal flanks Gopsall Park; the house where Handel is reputed to have composed the *Messiah* was pulled down in 1951, and the park has since lost its original dignity and quality.

Battlefield Line Shackerstone Station, Shackerstone CV13 6NW (01827 880754; www.battlefieldline.co.uk). Although the railway line that follows the Ashby Canal is now closed, the former Shackerstone Junction station (near canal bridge 52) has come to life again as a small railway museum *(open 11.00-17.00* on train running days) and a depot for preserved steam locomotives which run 9-mile round trips to Shenton, via Market Bosworth, *Mar-Dec* – visit the website for the full timetable. The railway runs a mix of steam and diesel traction according to availability. Victorian tearooms and on-train catering with bar. Souvenir shop. Charge. Can be linked in with a visit to the Bosworth Battlefield Centre.

Snarestone

Leics. Tel. An 18th-C farming village built over the top of the canal, which passes underneath through the crooked tunnel (250yds).

Twycross Zoo East Midland Zoological Society, Burton Road, Atherstone CV9 3PX (0844 474 1777; twycrosszoo.org). World Primate Centre set in more than 80 acres, with around 500 animals of almost 150 species, including many endangered animals and native species in the Zoo's Nature Reserve. You can walk with ring-tailed lemurs in their walk-through enclosure, see a troupe of emperor tamarins leap above your head in their treetop exhibit and watch Humboldt penguins take their daily walk. Keepers present *regular* talks and feeds where you can learn more about the animals such as chimpanzees, Asian elephants and South African coatis. Indoor soft play area, outdoor play area, together with 'wet and wild' water play area. Restaurant and café. *Open 10.00-18.00 in summer with reduced hours during winter months – see website for details.* Charge.

Tourist Information Centre 5 North Street, Ashby de la Zouch LE65 1HU (01530 411767; www.nwleics.gov.uk/pages/tourist_information). *Open Mon, Tue, Thu & Fri 10.00-17.00 and Sat 10.00-13.00.*

Pubs and Restaurants (bottom half of map)

1 Rising Sun Church Road, Shackerstone CV13 6NN (01827 880215; risingsunpub.com). A range of real ales and real cider served in a wood-panelled bar in this old village pub. Food available *Wed-Sat L and E & Sun 12.00-21.00.* Dog- and family-friendly, garden. Traditional pub games, sports TV and Wi-Fi. *Open Mon-Thu L and E (not Mon L) and Fri-Sun 11.30-23.00.*

2 The Globe Inn Main Street, Snarestone DE12 7DB (01530 272020; www.theglobeinnsnarestone.co.uk). A good selection of real ales served in a relaxed and friendly atmosphere. Boaters are welcomed and reasonably priced meals and snacks are available in both the bar and restaurant *L and E (not Sun E).* Child- and dog friendly, garden and play area. Real fires and Wi-Fi. *Open 12.00-00.00.*

NAVIGATIONAL NOTES

Headroom in Snarestone Tunnel decreases towards the northern portal. It is not safe for two boats to pass in the tunnel.

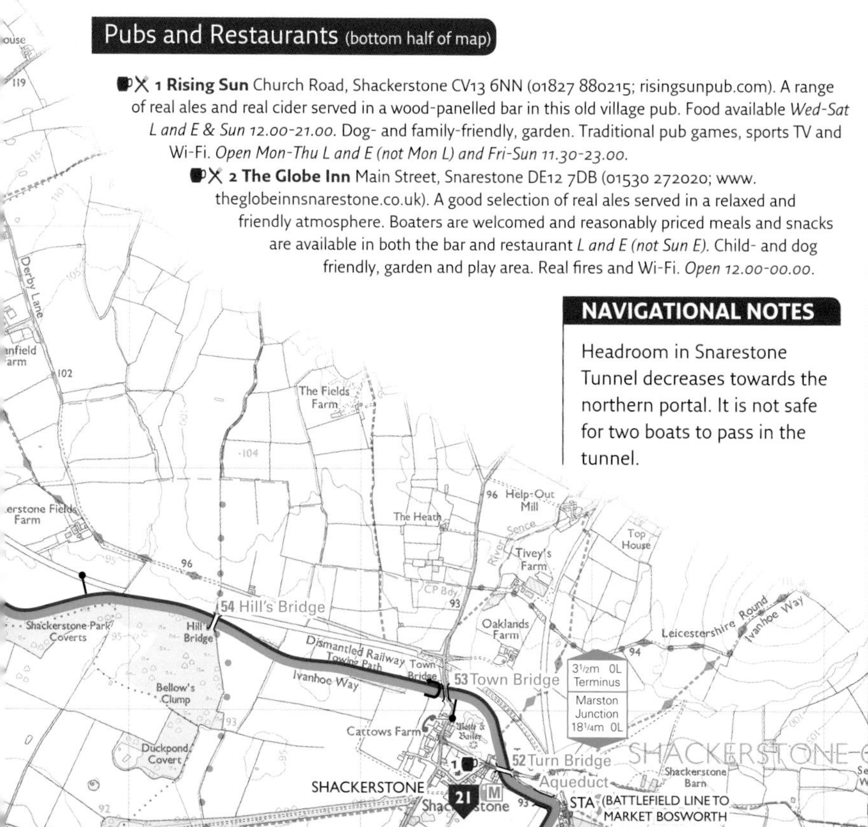

Moira

The 8-mile section of canal, beyond the present terminus at Snarestone, is under consideration for re-opening in three distinct sections; the most northerly, at Moira, being already completed. From the terminus, the first length (C–D on the map) is already the subject of a Transport and Works Act Order and substantially follows the line of the original navigation. However, it deviates outside Measham to make use of the alignment of the disused railway, making an aqueduct crossing over the High Street a likely outcome. This length then terminates before reaching the A42 which, together with the proposed route of HS2 Phase 2b, pose the major obstacles in the way of the second section (B–C). Once under these two potential obstructions, the waterway can largely follow its old, meandering course through to Donisthorpe where it will meet the third and already re-watered section (A–B) leading past Moira Furnace and into the basin beside Conkers. The countryside between Snarestone and Moira is a mixture of rolling Leicestershire arable land and the residues of extensive coal mining and clay extraction which are now the focus for imaginative landscaping, re-development and afforestation, as part of the National Forest.

- **Measham**
  Leics. PO, tel, stores, takeaway, chemist, library, off-licence, butcher, hardware, fish & chips, garage. Thriving industrial centre even before the arrival of the canal, with coal pits at Oakthorpe and clay deposits that led to the development of a pottery and sanitary ware industry. Famed for its pottery, much prized amongst boating families. The shop is *open daily 06.00-23.00.*
  Measham Museum Measham Station, Off Mannings Terrace, High Street, Measham DE12 7HU (01530 271724; www.meashammuseum.btck.co.uk). Follow the line of the old canal, from the present terminus at Snarestone, into Measham. Opposite St Lawrence's church. A uniquely personal history of a small community spanning 100 years as seen through the documents, artefacts and illustrations preserved by a former village doctor and his father. *Open Tue & Sat 10.00-12.00 & Tue and Thu 14.00-16.00.* Small charge for adults.
  Measham Community Office 56 High Street, Measham DE12 7HZ (01530 273956). This is the base of Leicestershire County Council's Ashby Canal restoration project and of the Ashby Canal Trust (www.ashbycanaltrust.co.uk). There is a small exhibition on the canal and a leaflet is available on the current state of the canal restoration.
- **Oakthorpe**
  Leics. Tel, fish & chips, off-licence. One-time mining village beside the Ashby Woulds Heritage Trail (*see* Walking & Cycling).
- **Donisthorpe**
  Leics. Tel, PO box, stores. 19th-C Perpendicular style church, constructed of grey sandstone, dedicated to St John the Evangelist. Another ex-mining village, now at the start of the isolated length of the newly re-watered canal and close to the Saltersford Valley Picnic Area.
- **Moira**
  Leics. PO, stores, off-licence. Source of the majority of the coal exported along the canal to Oxford, London and the Home Counties. The name derives from the Moira Estates in Ireland, owned by Baron Rawdon who developed the colliery, foundry and furnace in the area. Saline springs in the area also produced health-giving water but potential visitors were put off 'taking the waters' by the proximity of the coal mines and it was transported to Ashby-de-la-Zouch for final consumption.
  Ashby Woulds Heritage Trail Moira (0116 305 5000; www.leics.gov.uk/ashbywoulds.htm). A 3-mile local history and heritage trail for walkers and cyclists connecting Conkers to Measham and laid out along the old trackbed of the Ashby and Nuneaton Joint Railway Line. Access points link attractions and numerous country sites.
  Conkers Rawdon Road, Moira DE12 6GA (01283 216633; www.visitconkers.com). Ambitious project bringing the visitor close to nature in all its myriad forms. This hands-on experience, at the heart of the National Forest, offers a host of indoor and outdoor activities for all the family. *Open Apr-Oct 10.00-18.00 & Nov-Mar 10.00-17.00 (Jan 16.30).* Charge.
  Just Bikes Cycle Hire 7/8 The Green, Ashby-de-la-Zouch (01530 415021; www.justbikesashby.com). *Open Mon-Sat 09.00-17.00.*
  National Forest Cycle Centre: Hicks Lodge, Willesley Woodside, Moira LE65 2UP (01530 274533; www.forestry.gov.uk/hickslodge). Café, bike hire and repair shop, showers and a wood-burning stove for chilly days. Also a selection of cycle trails for both novice and experienced riders. *Open daily 09.00-17.00 (Thu 20.00).*
  Moira Furnace Furnace Lane, Moira DE12 6AT (01283 224667; www.visitnationalforest.co.uk/view/?id=Moira-Furnace). The furnace, completed in 1806, is a focus for a variety of hands-on exhibitions and outdoor attractions including a 150-year-old deciduous woodland plantation, lime kilns and a wildflower meadow, adventure playground, tea rooms and craft centre. The furnace itself had a short working life and so remains in superb condition today, providing an excellent means of accessing the industrial archaeology of this important area. Horse

riding and cycling trails; regular special events and children's fun days; guided heritage walks. Furnace *open Apr-Sep, school hols, Tue-Sun 11.00-16.00 & term time Sat-Sun 11.00-16.00*. Charge. **Traveline** (0871 200 22 33; www. traveline.info). Comprehensive bus information.

- **Ashby de la Zouch**
  Leics. All services (except station). Ashby is mentioned in the Doomsday Book as a settlement of approximately 100 people largely situated round the present site of St Helen's church. In 1160 a Norman nobleman, Alain de Parrhoet la Zouch, became lord of the manor by marriage so bestowing the somewhat striking addition to the town's name. During the 15th C, Ashby Manor was gifted to Lord Hastings by Edward IV and the town became the main seat of the Hastings family. The noble lord converted the manor house into a castle and extensively rebuilt St Helen's church. The Grammar School was founded in 1567 against a backdrop of growth and general prosperity as skilled craftsmen – swordsmiths, gold beaters, pewter workers, clockmakers and silversmiths – set up in 'courts' in the area of Market Street. Inevitably it was a Royalist garrison that occupied the castle during the Civil War under the command of Henry Hastings, later Lord Loughborough. It fell to the Parliamentarians in 1646 after a year-long siege and was all but destroyed. With the publication of Sir Walter Scott's classic romance in 1820, the castle regained something of its former prominence, this time as a romantic backcloth to Ivanhoe's victorious tournament and Robin Hood's arrow-splitting exploits. Two years later Ashby took on the mantle of Spa Town with the construction of the Ivanhoe Baths and the Royal (then Hastings) Hotel. Ironically enough, its fortunes were founded upon imported water, brought by canal from nearby Moira and discovered in the course of coal extraction. It was felt that mining was a somewhat less than salubrious companion to taking the waters! This was a relatively short-lived prosperity and following a steady decline, the Baths were closed in 1884. Today Ashby is both a centre for light industry and sought after as a residential area.

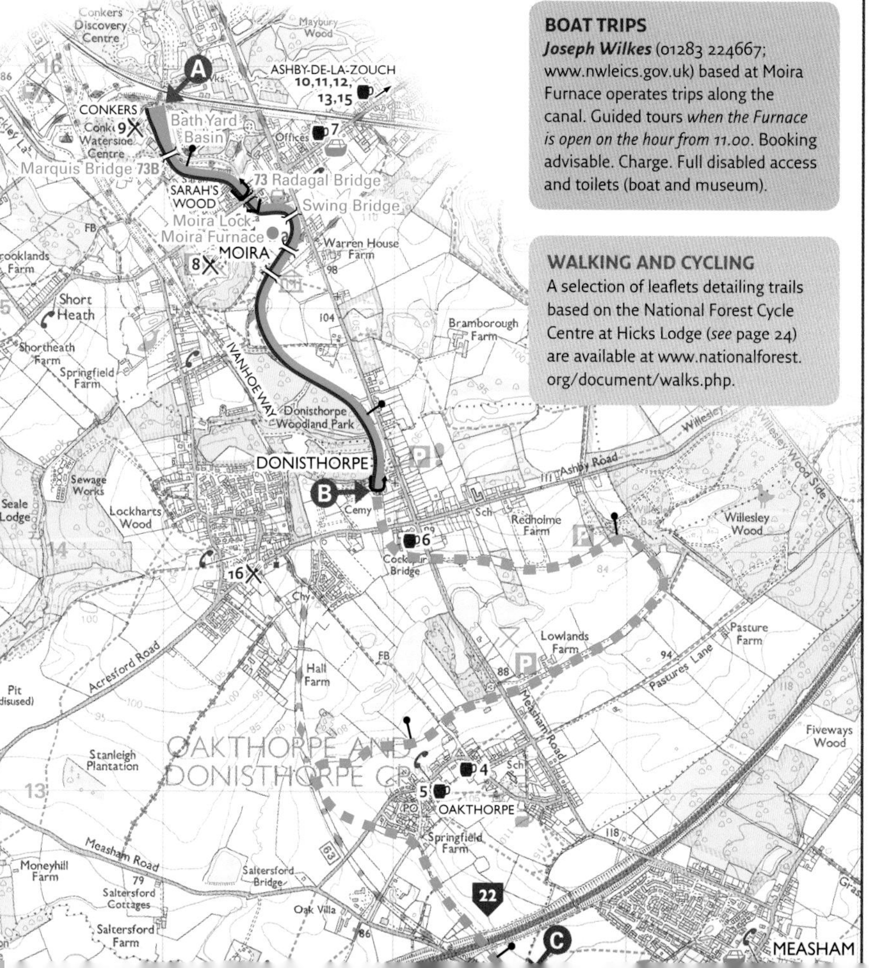

BOAT TRIPS
Joseph Wilkes (01283 224667; www.nwleics.gov.uk) based at Moira Furnace operates trips along the canal. Guided tours *when the Furnace is open on the hour from 11.00*. Booking advisable. Charge. Full disabled access and toilets (boat and museum).

WALKING AND CYCLING
A selection of leaflets detailing trails based on the National Forest Cycle Centre at Hicks Lodge (*see* page 24) are available at www.nationalforest.org/document/walks.php.

Ashby de la Zouch Museum 5 North Street, Ashby de la Zouch LE65 1HU (01530 560090; www.ashbymuseum.org.uk). A permanent display of the history of Ashby and its environs, archives of its rich heritage and a model of the castle as it was during the year-long siege of the Civil War. *Open Mon-Fri 11.00-13.00 & Sat 10.00-15.00. Closed over Xmas and New Year for two weeks.* Disabled access and toilets. Small charge.

Ashby Castle South Street, Ashby de la Zouch LE65 1BR (01530 413343; www.english-heritage.org.uk). While some early remains date back to its 12th-C manor house origins, the most striking feature is the 75' Hastings Tower standing gaunt amongst the ruins. As the castle was designed to resist siege, this tower was connected by underground passage to the kitchens, which can still be explored today. *Opening times vary considerably, according to the time of year*, so telephone for details. Charge.

St Helen's Church 66 Market Street, Ashby de la Zouch LE65 1AN (01530 413336; www.sthelensashby.co.uk. In Perpendicular style, this church was built by Lord Hastings in 15th C on the site of an earlier Norman building. Enlarged and restored in 1880, it contains much of interest including a rare finger pillory (said to be used in the punishment of those misbehaving in church), glass from Ashby Castle chapel and a series of windows portraying the life of Christ.

Tourist Information Centre 5 North Street, Ashby de la Zouch LE65 1HU (01530 411767; www.nwleics.gov.uk/pages/tourist_information). *Open Mon, Tue, Thu & Fri 10.00-17.00 and Sat 10.00-13.00.*

● **Staunton Harold**

Leics. Tel. A hamlet of isolated farms, cottages and the Hall, two miles north of Ashby. There are early Saxon references to the manor of Staunton Harold which passed to the Normans following the Conquest of 1066. Later in the hands of the Ferrers family and subsequently held by the Shirleys. The Palladian style hall is now a Sue Ryder Home and is private.

Ferrers Centre for Arts and Crafts Staunton Harold, Ashby de la Zouch LE65 1RU (01332 864863; www.ferrerscentre.co.uk). Stable block now home to a thriving and diverse selection of craftsmen and women. Tea room (01332 864617) and gift shop situated in the courtyard together with the Ferrers Gallery (01332 863337) who hold regular exhibitions and artist-led workshops. *Open Tue-Sun 11.00-16.00.* Ground floor disabled access. Free (although parking charge at weekends). Many studios (and the tea room) are *closed Mon except B Hols.*

Holy Trinity Church Staunton Harold, Ashby de la Zouch LE65 1RW (01332 863822; www.nationaltrust.org.uk/staunton-harold-church). One of the few churches to have been built during the Commonwealth Period, in 1653. It contains a splendid painted ceiling, fine panelling and still has the original hangings, cushions and pews. *Opening times vary considerably, according to the time of year*, so telephone for details. Donation. Coffee shop at the Hall.

Calke Abbey Ticknall, Derby DE73 7LE (01332 863822; www.nationaltrust.org.uk/calke-abbey). An extraordinairy establishment: on the face of it another Baroque mansion from the early 18th C surrounded by extensive park and woodlands. It is in fact a time capsule depicting a grand country house in decline, the clock having stopped with the death of Sir Vauncey Harpur-Crewe in 1924. Since then little has altered either inside, or outside within the 750 acres of park, the stable block or Gothic-style church. Shop and information room. Restaurant. Disabled access including buggy driven by volunteers for access around the grounds. *Opening times vary considerably, according to the time of year*, so telephone for details. Charge

WALKING AND CYCLING

Although there is still a long way to go before the Ashby Canal is fully complete between Marston Junction and Moira, this is nevertheless a paradise for the walker and cyclist wishing to enjoy the countryside free from the motor car. Starting at the present canal terminus north of Snarestone, a portion of the old waterway route can be walked into Measham. Where a stream makes the path impassable, go down onto Bosworth Road to the right, turn left and proceed to the crossroads and then turn left again. Rejoin the canal on your right near Measham Lodge and follow it into the village. To reach Moira by foot (or bicycle) join the Ashby Woulds Heritage Trail (*see* details in text) in Measham. *A Family Cycling Guide* (free) is published by North West Leicestershire District Council (www.nwleics.gov.uk) and details a variety of local routes, together with publications that cover cycling further afield in north west Leicestershire. For the most part these are off-road cycleways or include substantial traffic-free sections. Another excellent leaflet from North West Leicestershire DC, this time for the walker, is *Exploring the Ashby Woulds – A Guided Walk and Things To Do.* Free.

Pubs and Restaurants (pages 22 and 25)

✕ 1 **Gilly's Pantry** 53A High Street, Measham DE12 7HR (01530 270066). Serves breakfasts and lunches. Children welcome.

✕🍷 2 **The Link Cantonese Restaurant** 22 High Street, Measham DE12 7HR (01530 272766). Highly regarded Chinese restaurant serving generous portions. Excellent, attentive, friendly service. Families welcome. Take away service. Buffet *Tue & Sun.*

✕ 3 **Bunnies Tearoom & Patisserie** 32 High Street, Measham DE12 7HZ (01530 274442). Wide range of filled baguettes and Paninis. Jacket potatoes, cakes and *all day* breakfasts. Teas and coffees.

🍺✕ 4 **The Hollybush Inn** Main Street, Oakthorpe, Swadlincote DE12 7RB (01530 270943). Large rambling establishment - the oldest building in the village. This pub serves real ale and a wide and appetising range of English and continental food *Tue-Sat E & Sun L.* Children and dogs (in bar) welcome. Garden and children's play area. Sports TV. *Open Mon-Fri 16.00-23.00 & Sat-Sun 12.00-23.00.*

🍺✕ 5 **Shoulder Of Mutton** 6 Chapel Street, Oakthorpe DE12 7QT (01530 229225). Welcoming village hostelry serving real ales and homemade food *L and E Tue-Sun (not Sun E).* Children welcome. Outside seating. Traditional pub games. *Open 12.00-23.00.*

🍺 6 **The Mason's Arms** 1 Church Street, Donisthorpe, Swadlincote DE12 7PX (01530 515515). An attractive exterior and a friendly welcome inside. This hostelry dispenses real ales and home-made traditional pub food *daily 12.00-21.00.* Family-friendly, garden. Sports TV and Wi-Fi. *Open Mon-Sun 12.00-23.00 (Fri-Sat 00.00).*

🍺 7 **The Railway Inn** 31 Ashby Road, Moira, Swadlincote DE12 6DJ (01283 217453). Small, welcoming local dispensing real ale *Mon-Fri L and E & Sat-Sun 11.00-23.00 (Sun 12.00).* Dogs welcome, patio seating. Real fires, sports TV and Wi-Fi.

✕ 8 **The Hub Café** Furnace Lane, Moira, Swadlincote DE12 6AT (01283 226666; www.hub-cafe.co.uk/moria.php). Serving a variety of home-made lunches, teas and snacks in a relaxed and friendly atmosphere. Children welcome. *Open daily 10.00-15.00.*

✕ 9 **Conkers** Millennium Avenue, Rawdon Road, Moira, Swadlincote DE12 6GA (01283 216633; www.visitconkers.com). Traditional English fayre and snacks available in each of two fully licensed, lakeside restaurants, *The Olive Tree* and *The Waterside.* Children welcome. *Open daily 10.00-17.00.*

🍺 10 **The Plough Inn** The Green, Ashby de la Zouch LE65 1JU (01530 412817). Serves an excellent and ever-changing range of real ales. Traditional pub games. Open fires in *winter.* Outside seating and disabled access. *Open Mon-Sun 11.30-23.00 (Sun 11.00).*

✕🍷 11 **La Zouch** 2 Kilwardby Street, Ashby de la Zouch LE65 2FQ (01530 412536; www.lazouch.co.uk/restaurant.html). A family-run restaurant serving an English/French style table d'hôte and à la carte menu *E,* together with morning coffee, snacks and light meals *L, Sun afternoon* tea and traditional *Sun* roasts. Children welcome. *Open Tue-Wed 09.00-18.00, Thu-Fri 09.00-21.00, Sat 09.00-19.00 & Sun 11.00-16.00.* Also *morning* coffee and *afternoon* teas. Shop selling fine wines and spirits.

✕ 12 **Tudor Court Tearooms** 51A Market Street, Ashby de la Zouch LE65 1AG (01530 417610; www.ashbyonline.co.uk/main.php?Tudor+Court+Tea+Rooms&businessID=160). Snacks, lunches and cream teas in a charming tearoom or outside under parasols in verdant surroundings. All food is home made. Children welcome. *Open Mon-Sat 08.30-16.30 & alternate Sun 12.00-15.00.*

🍺✕ 13 **Smisby Arms** Nelson Square, Smisby, Nr Ashby de la Zouch LE65 2UA (01530 412677). Set in a peaceful hamlet 2 miles north of Ashby. Traditional village local serving real ales and an appetising range of food *Mon-Sat L and E & Sun 12.00-20.30.* Young children not encouraged. Real fires and patio seating. *Open Mon-Sat L and E & Sun 12.00-22.00.*

Also try: 🍺 14 **The White Hart** 13 Bosworth Road, Measham DE12 7LG (01530 270459); 🍺 15 **The White Hart** Market Street, Ashby-de-la-Zouch LE65 1AP (01530 414531; www.whitehartpubashbydelazouch.co.uk) and 🍺✕ 16 **The Halfway House** 65 Church Street, Donisthorpe, Swadlincote DE12 7PX (01530 588783; www.halfwayhousedonisthorpe.com).

BIRMINGHAM CANAL NAVIGATIONS (BCN) - MAIN LINE

MAXIMUM DIMENSIONS

Length: 70'
Beam: 7' 0"
Headroom: 6' 6"

MANAGER

0303 040 4040
enquiries.westmidlands@canalrivertrust.org.uk

MILEAGES

Birmingham Canal new main line

BIRMINGHAM Gas Street to:
SMETHWICK JUNCTION (old main line): 2⅞ miles

BROMFORD JUNCTION: 4⅞ miles

PUDDING GREEN JUNCTION
(Wednesbury Old Canal): 5⅝ miles

TIPTON FACTORY JUNCTION
(old main line): 8¾ miles

DEEPFIELDS JUNCTION
(Wednesbury Oak loop): 10 miles
(Bradley Workshops: 2¼ miles)

HORSELEY FIELDS JUNCTION
(Wyrley & Essington Canal): 13 miles
Wolverhampton Top Lock: 13½ miles

ALDERSLEY JUNCTION
(Staffordshire & Worcestershire Canal): 15⅛ miles

Locks: 24

Birmingham Canal old main line

SMETHWICK JUNCTION to:
SPON LANE JUNCTION: 1½ miles

OLDBURY JUNCTION
(Titford Canal, 6 locks): 2½ miles

BRADESHALL JUNCTION
(Gower Branch, 3 locks): 3½ miles
Aqueduct over Netherton Tunnel Branch: 4⅜ miles
TIPTON JUNCTION (Dudley Canal): 5½ miles
FACTORY JUNCTION (new main line): 6 miles

Locks: 9

Netherton Tunnel Branch

WINDMILL END JUNCTION to:
DUDLEY PORT JUNCTION: 2⅞ miles

No Locks

Wednesbury Old Canal

PUDDING GREEN JUNCTION to:
RYDER'S GREEN JUNCTION: ⅝ mile

No locks

Walsall Canal

RYDER'S GREEN JUNCTION to:
Ryder's Green Bottom Lock: ¼ mile
DOEBANK JUNCTION: 1⅜ miles
WALSALL JUNCTION: 6⅞ miles

Locks: 8

Walsall Branch Canal

WALSALL JUNCTION to:
BIRCHILLS JUNCTION (Wyrley & Essington Canal): ⅞ mile

Locks: 8

Wyrley & Essington Canal

HORSELEY FIELDS JUNCTION to:
SNEYD JUNCTION: 6¼ miles
BIRCHILLS JUNCTION (Walsall Branch Canal): 8 miles
PELSALL JUNCTION (Cannock Extension): 12⅞ miles
Norton Canes Docks: 1½ miles
CATSHILL JUNCTION: 15⅜ miles
OGLEY JUNCTION (Anglesey Branch): 16⅜ miles
Anglesey Basin and Chasewater: 1½ miles

No locks

Daw End Branch

CATSHILL JUNCTION to:
LONGWOOD JUNCTION (Rushall Top Lock): 5¼ miles

No locks

Rushall Canal

LONGWOOD JUNCTION to:
RUSHALL JUNCTION: 2¾ miles

Locks: 9

Tame Valley Canal

DOEBANK JUNCTION to:
RUSHALL JUNCTION: 3½ miles
Perry Barr Top Lock: 5½ miles
SALFORD JUNCTION: 8½ miles

Locks: 13

The Birmingham Canal Company was authorised in 1768 to build a canal from Aldersley on the Staffordshire & Worcestershire Canal to Birmingham. With James Brindley as engineer the work proceeded quickly. The first section, from Birmingham to the Wednesbury collieries, was opened in November 1769, and the whole 22½-mile route was completed in 1772. It was a winding, contour canal, with 12 locks taking it over Smethwick, and another 20 (later 21) taking it down through Wolverhampton to Aldersley Junction. As the route of the canal was through an area of mineral wealth and developing industry, its success was immediate. Pressure of traffic caused the summit level at Smethwick to be lowered in the 1790s (thus cutting out six locks - three on either side of the summit), and during the same period branches began to reach out towards Walsall via the Ryder's Green Locks, and towards Fazeley. Out of this very profitable and ambitious first main line there grew the Birmingham Canal Navigations, more commonly abbreviated to BCN.

As traffic continued to increase so did the wealth of the BCN. The pressures of trade made the main line at Smethwick very congested and brought grave problems of water supply. Steam pumping engines were installed in several places to recirculate the water, and the company appointed Thomas Telford to shorten Brindley's old main line. Between 1825 and 1838 he engineered a new main line between Deepfields and Birmingham, using massive cuttings and embankments to maintain a continuous level. These improvements not only increased the amount of available waterway (the old line remaining in use), but also shortened the route from Birmingham to Wolverhampton by 7 miles.

Railway control of the BCN meant an expansion of the use of the system, and a large number of interchange basins were built to promote outside trade by means of rail traffic. This was of course quite contrary to the usual effect of railway competition upon canals. Trade continued to grow in relation to industrial development and by the end of the 19th C it was topping 8½ million tons per annum. A large proportion of this trade was local, being dependent upon the needs and output of Black Country industry. After the turn of the century this reliance on local trade started the gradual decline of the system as deposits of raw materials became exhausted. Factories bought from further afield and developed along the railways and roads away from the canals. Yet as late as 1950 there were over a million tons of trade and the system continued in operation until the end of the coal trade in 1967 (although there was some further traffic for the Birmingham Salvage Department), a pattern quite different from canals as a whole. Nowadays there is no recognisable commercial traffic - a dramatic contrast to the roaring traffic on the newer Birmingham motorways.

As trade declined, so parts of the system fell out of use and were abandoned. In its heyday in 1865, the BCN comprised over 160 miles of canal. Today just over 100 miles remain, and much has been done in recent years to tidy these up. This is now having a noticeable effect. Where once there were the old and run-down relics of industry, there is now much new housing, and stylish industrial estates. Of course some of the older vestiges of industry can still be found, and we hope that their most charming manifestations are kept for future generations to see and enjoy. But overall (and noting the exceptions and inevitable run-down areas) it is a fascinating environment. Just do not treat it like the remoter parts of Cheshire and Shropshire - it will always be subjected to the stresses of inner-city life, and you must always exercise caution. But it remains an area of retreat for the harassed city dweller and a new area of exploration for the canal traveller.

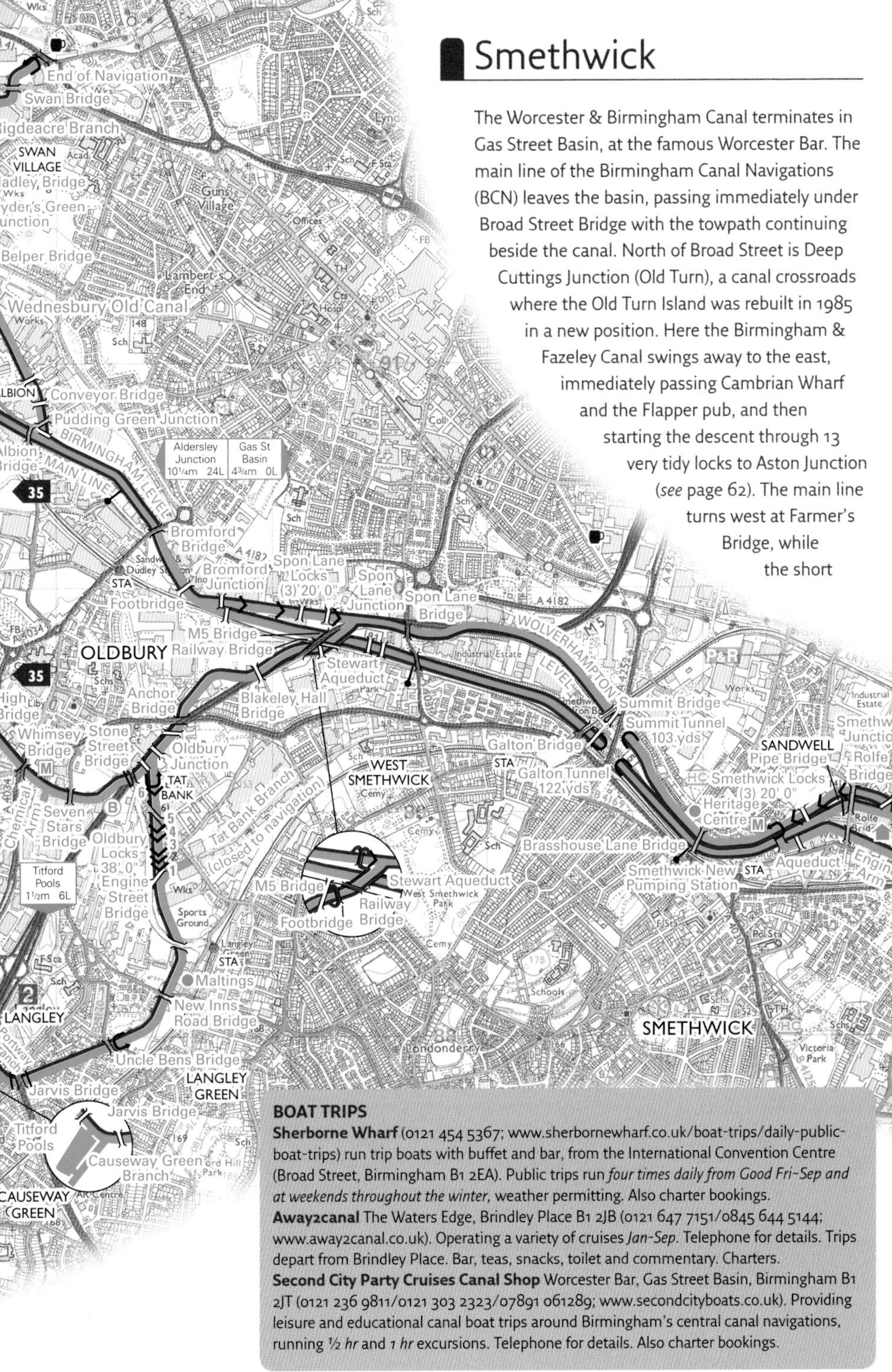

Smethwick

The Worcester & Birmingham Canal terminates in Gas Street Basin, at the famous Worcester Bar. The main line of the Birmingham Canal Navigations (BCN) leaves the basin, passing immediately under Broad Street Bridge with the towpath continuing beside the canal. North of Broad Street is Deep Cuttings Junction (Old Turn), a canal crossroads where the Old Turn Island was rebuilt in 1985 in a new position. Here the Birmingham & Fazeley Canal swings away to the east, immediately passing Cambrian Wharf and the Flapper pub, and then starting the descent through 13 very tidy locks to Aston Junction (*see* page 62). The main line turns west at Farmer's Bridge, while the short

BOAT TRIPS

Sherborne Wharf (0121 454 5367; www.sherbornewharf.co.uk/boat-trips/daily-public-boat-trips) run trip boats with buffet and bar, from the International Convention Centre (Broad Street, Birmingham B1 2EA). Public trips run *four times daily from Good Fri-Sep and at weekends throughout the winter*, weather permitting. Also charter bookings.
Away2canal The Waters Edge, Brindley Place B1 2JB (0121 647 7151/0845 644 5144; www.away2canal.co.uk). Operating a variety of cruises *Jan-Sep*. Telephone for details. Trips depart from Brindley Place. Bar, teas, snacks, toilet and commentary. Charters.
Second City Party Cruises Canal Shop Worcester Bar, Gas Street Basin, Birmingham B1 2JT (0121 236 9811/0121 303 2323/07891 061289; www.secondcityboats.co.uk). Providing leisure and educational canal boat trips around Birmingham's central canal navigations, running *½ hr* and *1 hr* excursions. Telephone for details. Also charter bookings.

Oozell's Street loop goes to the south, quickly disappearing behind new apartments. This loop, which now houses a boatyard and moorings, and the others further along, are surviving parts of Brindley's original contour canal, now known as the Birmingham Canal Old Main Line. The delays caused by this prompted the Birmingham Canal Company to commission Telford to build a straighter line, the Birmingham Canal New Main Line. This was constructed between 1823 and 1838, and when completed reduced Brindley's old $22\frac{1}{2}$-mile canal to 15 miles. The Oozell's Street loop reappears from the south, and then, after two bridges, the Icknield Port loop leaves to the south. This loop acts as a feeder from Rotton Park Reservoir and rejoins after $\frac{1}{4}$ mile at another canal crossroads – the Winson Green or Soho loop, which leaves the main line opposite the Icknield Port loop. This last loop is the longest of the three, running in a gentle arc for over a mile before rejoining the main line again. It was the only loop to have a towpath throughout its length until the recently completed towpath on the Oozell's Street loop. At its eastern end is Hockley Port, formerly railway-owned but now used for residential moorings. There are houseboats, a community hall, dry docks and workshops. The main line continues towards Smethwick Junction. Here there is a choice of routes: Brindley's old main line swings to the right, while Telford's new main line continues straight ahead – the old line is the more interesting of the two. The two routes run side by side, but the old line climbs to a higher level via the three Smethwick Locks. Here there were two flights of locks side by side. Beyond the junction, Telford's new line enters a steep-sided cutting. This 40ft-deep cutting enabled Telford to avoid the changes in level of the old line and thus speed the flow of traffic. The two routes continue their parallel courses, the one overlooking the other, until the lower line passes under the Telford Aqueduct. This elegant single span cast iron structure carries the Engine Arm, a short feeder canal that leaves the old line, crosses the new line and then turns back to the south for a short distance. There is a *laundry* in the *facilities block* here. The arm is named after the first Boulton & Watt steam pumping engine to be bought by the Birmingham Canal Company. This continued to feed the old summit level for 120 years. It was then moved to Ocker Hill for preservation and demonstrations, until the 1950s, when it was finally retired. The sides of the cutting are richly covered with wild flowers and blackberry bushes, and the seclusion of the whole area has turned it into an unofficial nature reserve. The old pumping station at Brasshouse Lane has been restored after years of disuse as part of the new Galton Valley Canal Park development. A Tangyes Engine has been installed to replace the original. The New Main Line continues through natural wilderness to Galton Tunnel. Telford's Galton Bridge crosses the cutting in one magnificent 150ft cast iron span. This bridge is preserved as an ancient monument. The old and the new Birmingham canal lines continue their parallel course, and soon the pleasant semi-rural isolation of the cutting ends, to be replaced by a complex meeting of three types of transport system. The M5 motorway swings in from the east, carried high above the canal on slender concrete pillars; the railway stays close beside Telford's new line; and the canals enter a series of junctions that seem to anticipate modern motorway practice. The new line leaves the cutting and continues in a straight line through industrial surroundings. It passes under Stewart Aqueduct and then reaches Bromford Junction. Here a canal sliproad links the old and the new lines via the three Spon Lane Locks, joining the new at an angle from the east. Note the unusual split bridge at Spon Lane top lock, which was rebuilt in 1986. The old line swings south west following the 473ft contour parallel to the M5, crossing the new line on Stewart Aqueduct. Thus canal crosses canal on a flyover. Spon Lane Locks, the linking sliproad, survive unchanged from Brindley's day and are among the oldest in the country. The old and the new lines now follow separate courses. The old line continues below the motorway to Oldbury Locks Junction. Here the short Titford Canal climbs away to the south via the six Oldbury Locks; this canal serves as a feeder from Titford Pools to Rotton Park Reservoir. After the junction the old line swings round to the north west and continues on a parallel course to the new line once again. After Bromford Junction the new line continues its straight course towards Wolverhampton. At Pudding Green Junction the main line goes straight on; the Wednesbury Old Canal forks right to join the Walsall Canal, which in turn joins the Tame Valley Canal at Doebank Junction.

WALKING AND CYCLING

Much of Birmingham's 100-mile network of canals offers excellent opportunities for walkers and cyclists, and provides the chance to explore a side of the city well away from the obvious tourist attractions and close to the area's industrial roots. From a more formal approach, Birmingham is a crossroads for the National Cycle Network with Route 5 approaching from Kings Norton via Worcester & Birmingham Canal. Route 81 follows the Birmingham Level Main Line from the city to Wolverhampton, to eventually head into Mid Wales. Several excellent routes lead out from the city centre along traffic-free or contraflow cycle lanes. Further details are available from www.sustrans.org.uk/ncn/map/themed-routes-0/urban-adventures/top-cycle-routes-and-around-birmingham and by visiting http://bhamcyclerevolution.org.uk. On the Mainline the south side tow path is no longer usable between Rolfe Bridge and Bromford Junction.

NAVIGATIONAL NOTES

Since the Titford Canal is the highest level on the BCN, it is advisable to telephone the Canal & River Trust Waterway Office (0303 040 4040; enquiries.westmidlands@canalrivertrust.org.uk) to check that there is adequate water before you visit the canal. You will need a standard T-shaped water conservation key (aka 'handcuff key') for Oldbury Locks in order to access this canal.

Boatyards

Ⓑ **Sherborne Wharf** Sherborne Street, Birmingham B16 8DE (0121 455 6163/0121 454 5367; www.sherbornewharf.co.uk). On the Oozell's Street Loop. **D E** Pump out, gas, day-hire boats, overnight mooring, long-term mooring, wet docks, dry dock, winter storage, chandlery, boat repairs, engine repairs, welding, fabrication, crane, books, maps and gifts, DIY facilities, electrical hook-up, solid fuel, toilets, showers, laundrette, Wi-Fi, large supermarket nearby. *Emergency call out. Open 7 days.*

The Titford Canal

Built in 1837 as part of the original Birmingham Canal scheme, acting as a feeder to Spon Lane, the Titford Canal served Causeway Green. This must have been a very busy canal in its heyday, with many branches, wharves and tramways connecting it to the surrounding mines and engineering works. Today it survives in shortened form and has the distinction of being the highest navigable part of the BCN, with a summit level above Oldbury Locks of 511ft. The locks are sometimes referred to as the Crow – a branch which left the canal above the third lock and served the alkali and phosphorus works of a local industrialist and benefactor Jim Crow. The last surviving recirculatory pumphouse can be seen by the top lock. The building has been completely restored and is now the home of the Birmingham Canal Navigation Society (01902 788441; www.bcnsociety.com). The waterway terminates at the wide expanse of water of Titford Pools.

Tourist Information Centre *see* page 66.

Pubs and Restaurants (pages 30-31)

In a large city such as Birmingham there are many fine pubs and restaurants. As a result of the development of the area adjoining the canal, between Gas Street Basin and Cambrian Wharf, there are now approaching two dozen eating and drinking establishments. This choice is further expanded by walking south along Broad Street, from Broad Street Bridge, at Gas Street Basin. However beyond the canalside the enterprising boater (walker and cyclist) might like to seek out some of the City's more diverse hostelries:

1 The Flapper Cambrian Wharf, Kingston Row, Birmingham B1 2NU (0121 236 2421; www.theflapper.co.uk). Student-type pub majoring on bottled beers, cocktails and music. Canalside terrace seating. *Open Mon-Thu & Sun 16.00-23.00 and Fri-Sat 12.00-01.00.*

2 The Brasshouse 44 Broad St, Birmingham B1 2HP (0121 633 3383; www.brasshouse birmingham.co.uk). Busy, modern pub serving *all day* breakfasts and good value bar meals, together with real ales. *Fri and Sat* night discos. Children allowed *until 18.00* if eating. Wi-Fi. *Open daily from 08.00 'til late.*

3 The Prince of Wales 84 Cambridge St, Birmingham B1 2NP (0121 643 9460). Popular hostelry situated behind the NIA and ICC serving real ales and inexpensive food *Tue-Sat 12.00-20.00.* Dogs welcome and live music *Sun 16.00-19.00. Open daily from 11.00 (Sun 12.00) 'til late.*

4 The Old Contemptibles 176 Edmund St, Birmingham B3 2HB (0121 200 3310; www.nicholsonspubs.co.uk/theoldcontemptiblesedmundstreetbirmingham). Close to Snow Hill Station. This comfortable, wood-panelled pub serves a good selection of real ales (nation-wide micro-breweries being well represented) and excellent food *Mon-Fri 11.00-22.00, Sat 12.00-22.00 & Sun 12.00-18.00.* Pump clips carry tasting notes and you can sip before you buy. Also real cider. *Open Mon-Sat 11.00 'til late (Sat 12.00) & Sun 12.00-18.00.*

5 The Figure of Eight 236-239 Broad St, Birmingham B1 2HG (0121 633 0917; www.jdwetherspoon.co.uk/home/pubs/the-figure-of-eight). Sensibly priced real ale in a pub handy for Gas Street Basin. Disabled access and outside seating. Wi-Fi. *Open all day from 07.00* serving breakfast and food *all day.*

6 The Wellington 37 Bennett's Hill, Birmingham B2 5SN (0121 200 3115; www.thewellingtonrealale.co.uk). Busy, CAMRA award-winning pub, with up to 17 hand pumps and a choice of real ciders. No food but customers are welcome to consume their own on the crockery provided. Also foreign bottled beers. Traditional pub games, garden, newspapers, sports TV and Wi-Fi. *Open 10.00-00.00.*

7 The Post Office Vaults 84 New St, Birmingham B2 4BA (0121 643 7354; www.postofficevaults.co.uk). Close to New Street Station. Wide range of real ales, ciders and perries available *daily 11.00-23.00 (Fri-Sat 00.00).* Also well over 300 foreign bottled beers to choose from. Free bar billiards, dog-friendly, newspapers and Wi-Fi.

8 The Old Joint Stock 4 Temple Row, Birmingham B2 5NY (0121 200 1892; www.oldjointstock.co.uk). Real ales and tasty food is served *Mon- Sat 08.00-11.00 and 12.00-22.00 & Sun 10.00-16.00* in an elaborately decorated, Grade II listed, Victorian building. Once a joint stock bank, there is now a theatre upstairs. Outside seating, children welcome, traditional pub games, newspapers and Wi-Fi. Live jazz *Sun. Open Mon-Sat 08.00-23.00 & Sun 09.00-18.00.*

9 The Old Royal, 53 Church St, Birmingham B3 2DP (0121 200 3841; www.theoldroyal birmingham.co.uk). Serving real ales and traditional pub food (including breakfast) *all day* from behind an elegant city centre façade. Sports TV and Wi-Fi. *Open daily 10.00-23.00 (Sat-Sun 12.00).*

10 The Shakespeare 21 Lower Temple St, Birmingham B2 4JD (0121 616 2196; www.nicholsonspubs.co.uk/theshakespeare lowertemplestreetbirmingham). Beside New Street Station. Attractively refurbished Victorian pub serving real ales and cider, together with quality pub food *daily from 10.00-22.00. Open Mon-Sat 10.00-23.00 (Fri-Sat 00.00) & Sun 10.00-22.30.*

Dudley

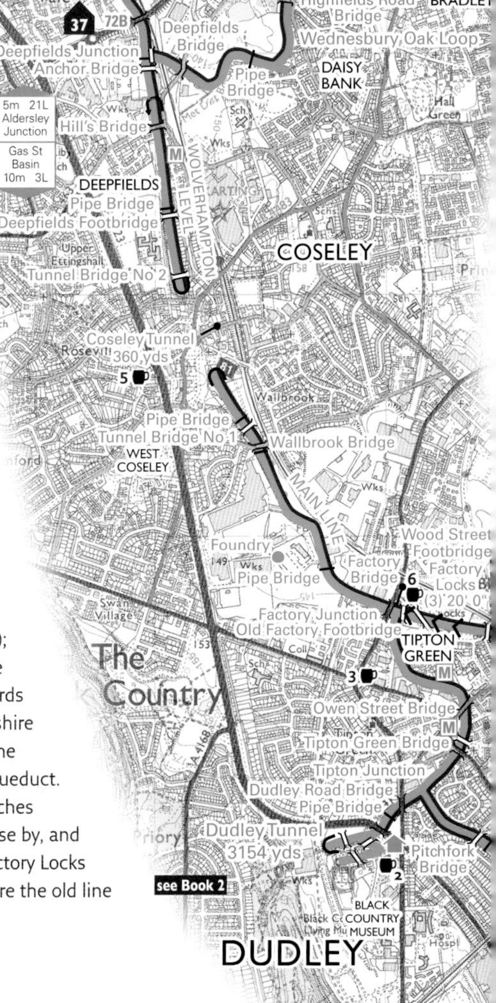

At Bradeshall Junction the Gower Branch links the two lines, descending to the lower level of the new line through three locks. To the south west of Tipton Junction is the branch leading to the Black Country Museum and the Dudley Tunnel. This branch connects with the Dudley Canal, the Stourbridge Canal, and thus with the Staffordshire & Worcestershire Canal. The old line turns north at the junction, rejoining the new line at Factory Junction. At Albion Junction the Gower Branch turns south to join the old line at Bradeshall. At Dudley Port Junction the Netherton Tunnel Branch joins the main line. The Netherton Tunnel Branch goes through the tunnel to Windmill End Junction (note the west side towpath through the tunnel is closed); from here boats can either turn south down the old Dudley Canal to Hawne Basin, or west towards the Stourbridge Canal, and thus to the Staffordshire & Worcestershire Canal. North of Dudley Port the new line crosses a main road on the Ryland Aqueduct. Continuing its elevated course the new line reaches Tipton, where there are *moorings* with *shops* close by, and a small basin. The new line climbs the three Factory Locks and immediately reaches Factory Junction, where the old line comes in from the south.

Pubs and Restaurants

1 The Old Court House 57 Lower Church Lane, Tipton DY4 7PE (0121 520 2865). North east of Dudley Port Station. Food available *L and E, daily* in a pub that used to be the holding cells for the police station across the road. Children and dogs welcome. Outside seating, traditional pub games, newspapers, sports TV and Wi-Fi. *Open Mon-Thu E & Fri-Sun 12.00-01.30 (Sun 23.30).*

2 The Bottle & Glass Inn Black Country Living Museum, Tipton Road, Dudley DY1 4SQ (0121 557 9643; www.bclm.co.uk/locations/bottle-and-glass-inn/28.htm#.WZBUXK2ZMUE). Real ale in a wonderful old pub, moved to the site. Snacks available *all day. Open daily 10.00-17.00.* More substantial refreshment available in the nearby **Gongoozler Restaurant** (0121 520 3200) and 1930s fish & chip shop.

3 Mad O'Rourke's Pie Factory 50 Hurst Lane, Tipton DY4 9AB (0121 557 1402; www.madorourkes.com). Quirky, popular eatery renowned for its world-famous, Desperate Dan cow pies, serving real ales, real cider and food *daily 12.00-21.30 (Sun 21.00). Sun L* carvery. Garden, family-friendly, real fires and Wi-Fi. Live music *Fri & Sat.* B&B. *Open Mon-Sat 11.00-23.00 & Sun 12.00-22.30.*

4 The Tamebridge 45 Tame Road, Tipton DY4 7JA (0121 557 2496). Friendly, welcoming family pub serving a changing range of real ales. Garden, dog- and family-friendly. *Monthly* live music. Real fires, sports TV and Wi-Fi. *Open 12.00-23.00.*

5 The New Inn 35 Ward Street, Coseley WV14 9LQ (01902 670669). Friendly pub dispensing real ale and bar snacks. Family-friendy. Traditional pub games, real fires and Wi-Fi. *Open Mon-Fri E (Fri 15.00) & Sat-Sun 12.00-00.00 (Sun 22.30).*

Also try: **6 The Barge & Barrel** Factory Road, Tipton DY4 9AJ (0121 520 6962; thebargeandbarreltipton.weebly.com).

Boatyards

Ⓑ**Caggy's Boatyard**
Watery Lane, Tipton DY4 8EZ (0121 520 5362/07710 343773). D
Pump out, overnight mooring, boat repairs, engine sales and repairs, welding, fabrication, boatbuilding, boat fitting out, dry dock, wet dock, DIY facilities, chandlery, toilets, books, maps, gifts, toilets, showers, solid fuel. *Emergency call out.*

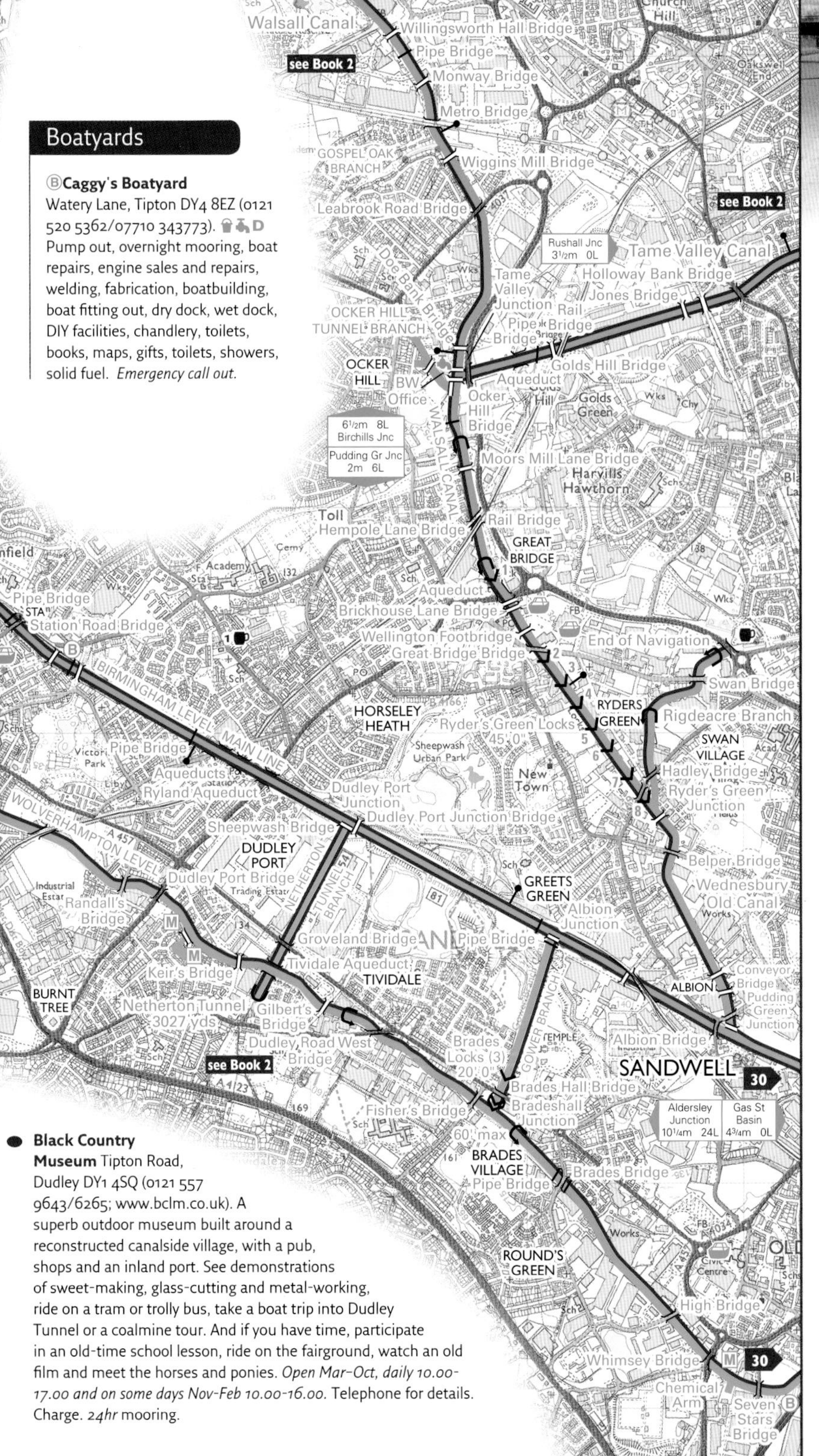

● **Black Country Museum** Tipton Road, Dudley DY1 4SQ (0121 557 9643/6265; www.bclm.co.uk). A superb outdoor museum built around a reconstructed canalside village, with a pub, shops and an inland port. See demonstrations of sweet-making, glass-cutting and metal-working, ride on a tram or trolly bus, take a boat trip into Dudley Tunnel or a coalmine tour. And if you have time, participate in an old-time school lesson, ride on the fairground, watch an old film and meet the horses and ponies. *Open Mar–Oct, daily 10.00-17.00 and on some days Nov-Feb 10.00-16.00.* Telephone for details. Charge. *24hr* mooring.

Wolverhampton

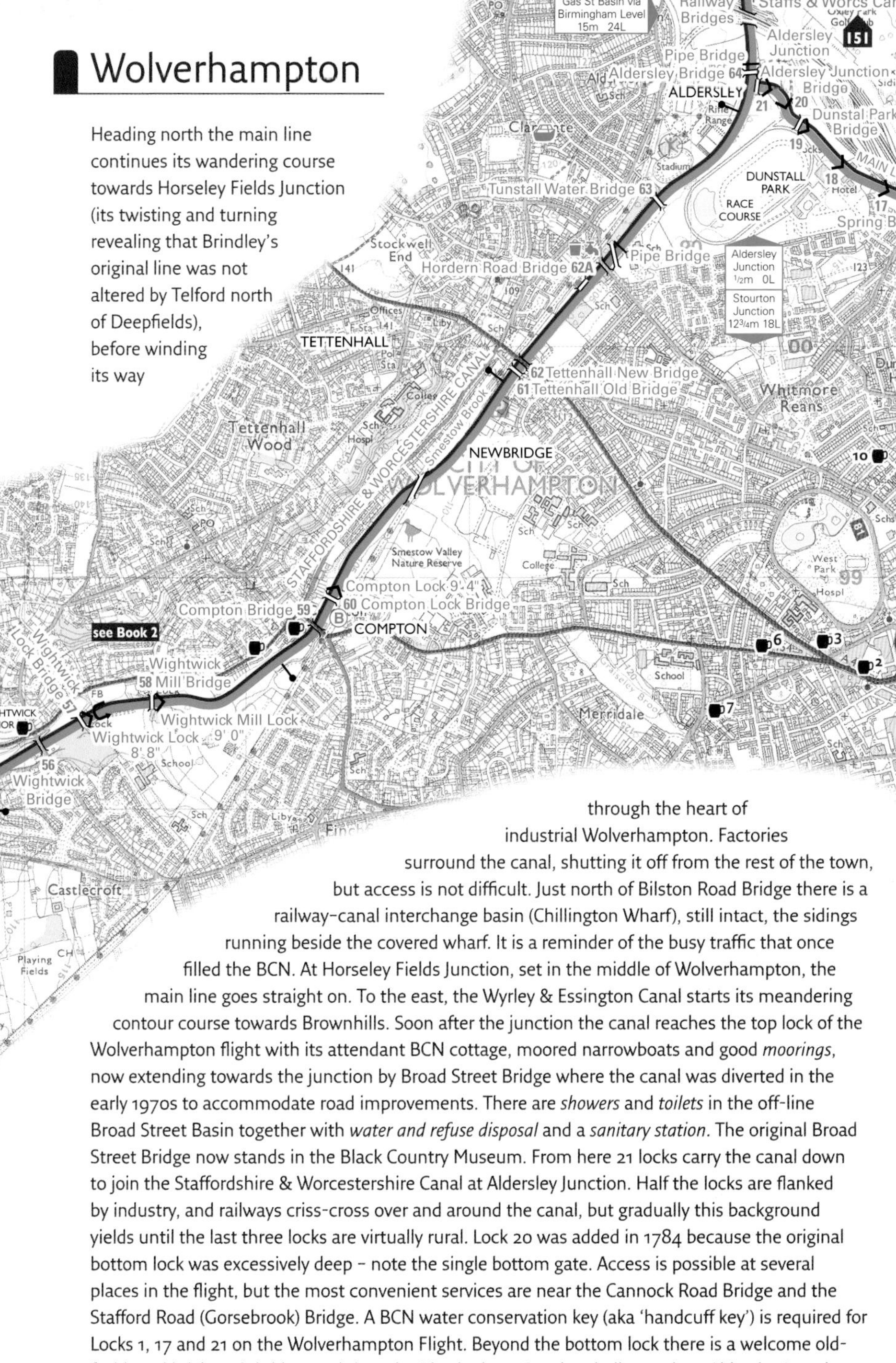

Heading north the main line continues its wandering course towards Horseley Fields Junction (its twisting and turning revealing that Brindley's original line was not altered by Telford north of Deepfields), before winding its way through the heart of industrial Wolverhampton. Factories surround the canal, shutting it off from the rest of the town, but access is not difficult. Just north of Bilston Road Bridge there is a railway-canal interchange basin (Chillington Wharf), still intact, the sidings running beside the covered wharf. It is a reminder of the busy traffic that once filled the BCN. At Horseley Fields Junction, set in the middle of Wolverhampton, the main line goes straight on. To the east, the Wyrley & Essington Canal starts its meandering contour course towards Brownhills. Soon after the junction the canal reaches the top lock of the Wolverhampton flight with its attendant BCN cottage, moored narrowboats and good *moorings*, now extending towards the junction by Broad Street Bridge where the canal was diverted in the early 1970s to accommodate road improvements. There are *showers* and *toilets* in the off-line Broad Street Basin together with *water and refuse disposal* and a *sanitary station*. The original Broad Street Bridge now stands in the Black Country Museum. From here 21 locks carry the canal down to join the Staffordshire & Worcestershire Canal at Aldersley Junction. Half the locks are flanked by industry, and railways criss-cross over and around the canal, but gradually this background yields until the last three locks are virtually rural. Lock 20 was added in 1784 because the original bottom lock was excessively deep – note the single bottom gate. Access is possible at several places in the flight, but the most convenient services are near the Cannock Road Bridge and the Stafford Road (Gorsebrook) Bridge. A BCN water conservation key (aka 'handcuff key') is required for Locks 1, 17 and 21 on the Wolverhampton Flight. Beyond the bottom lock there is a welcome old-fashioned brick-arch bridge, and then the Birmingham Canal main line ends at Aldersley Junction, inconspicuous when approached from the Staffordshire & Worcestershire Canal (*see* page 123).

NAVIGATIONAL NOTES

1. A standard T-shaped water conservation (aka 'handcuff key') is needed to operate Tipton Factory Locks.
2. Bradeshall Bridge, on the Gower Branch (page 43) has an air draught of 6' 6".

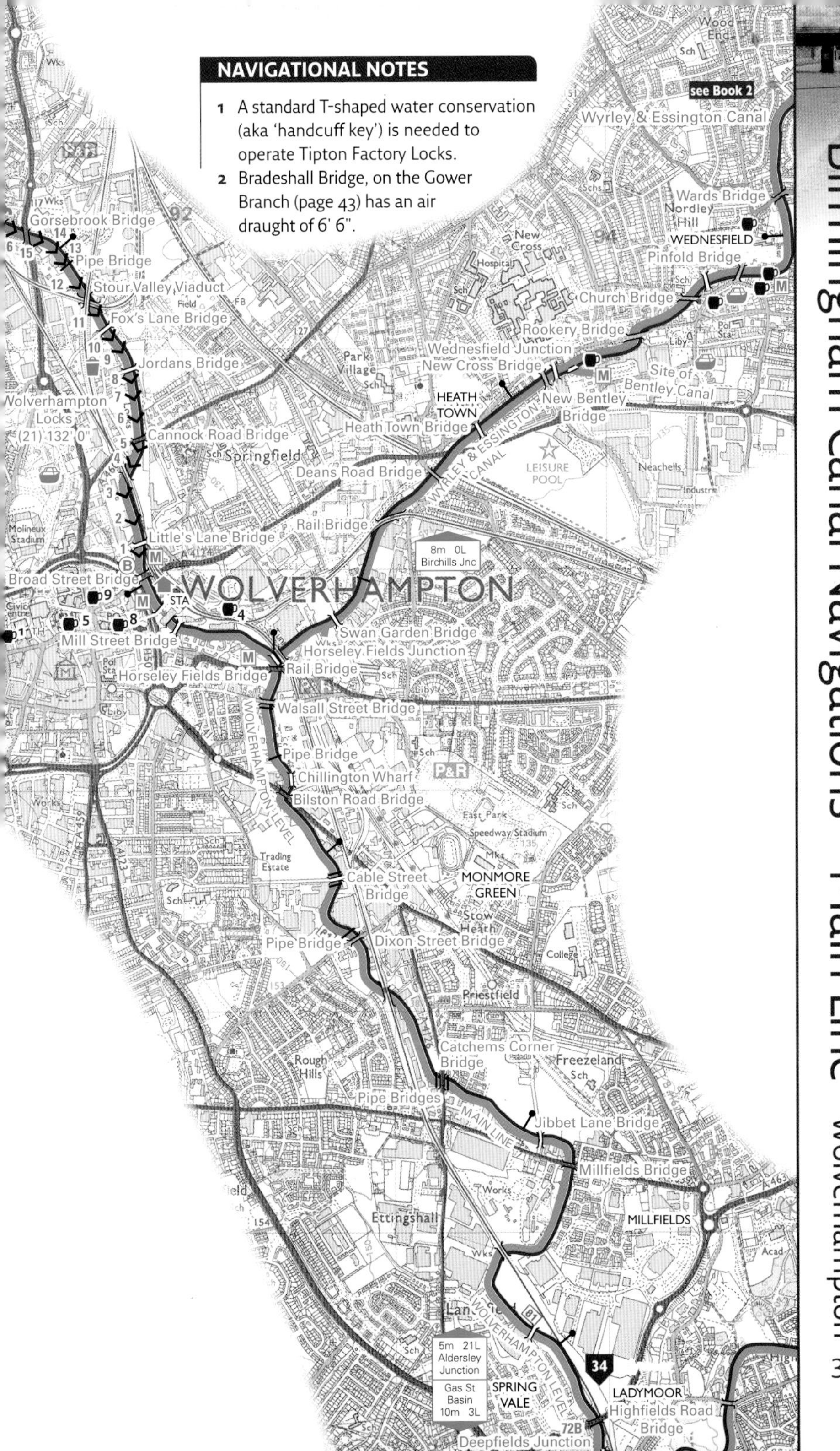

Pubs and Restaurants (pages 36-37)

In a town such as Wolverhampton there are many pubs to choose from. Below are a selection for the enterprising to seek out:

1 The Lych Gate Tavern 44 Queen Square, Wolverhampton WV1 1TX (01902 399516; lychgatetavern.co.uk). With its 16th-C timber-framed interior and an early 18th-C Georgian façade, this pub is one of the city's oldest buildings, now dispensing an ever-changing range of real ales and real cider. Home-made cobs available or bring your own food. Terrace, newspapers, real fires and Wi-Fi. *Open 11.00-23.00 (Fri-Sat 00.00).*

2 The Clarendon 38 Chapel Ash, Wolverhampton WV3 0TN (01902 420587; www.clarendonhotelpub.co.uk). Banks brewery tap serving real ale and food *daily 12.00-21.00 (Sun 19.00). Thu & Fri* live music. Dog- and family-friendly, outside seating. *Sun* quiz, sports TV and Wi-Fi. *Open Mon-Sat 11.30-23.00 (Fri-Sat 23.30) & Sun 12.00-22.30.*

3 The Combermere Arms 90 Chapel Ash, Wolverhampton WV3 0TY (01902 421880). Real ale served in a terraced house look-alike: both cosy and intimate. Renown for the tree growing in the gents lavatory! Open fires, a family room and outdoor drinking area. Sports TV and newspapers. Food available *Tue-Fri L. Open Mon-Thu L and E & Fri-Sun 12.00-00.00 (Sun 22.30).*

4 The Great Western Sun Street, Wolverhampton WV10 0DJ (01902 351090; www.holdensgreatwesternwolverhampton.co.uk). Real ale, railway memorabilia and good local cooking *L (not Sun).* Dog- and family-friendly, outside seating. Real fires, sports TV and Wi-Fi. *Open 11.00-23.00.*

5 The Posada 48 Lichfield Street, Wolverhampton WV1 1DG (07967 185830). Grade II listed building with its striking tiled frontage. A good range of real ales. Outdoor drinking area. Family-friendly, sports TV and Wi-Fi. *Open Mon-Sat 12.00-23.00 (Fri-Sat 00.10) & Sun 12.00-22.30.*

6 The Royal Oak 70 Compton Rd, Wolverhampton WV3 9PH (01902 422845; royaloakwolverhampton.co.uk). Traditional, single-room, community pub serving real ales and fresh cobs. Live music *Fri & Sat.* Outside seating, family- and dog-friendly. Newspapers, sports TV and Wi-Fi. *Open Mon-Sat 11.00-23.00 (Fri-Sat 00.00) & Sun 12.00-23.00.*

7 The Chindit Inn 113 Merridale Rd, Wolverhampton WV3 9SE (07986 773487; www.thechindit.co.uk). Originally built as an off-licence, this 1950's hostelry serves a good range of real ales. Outdoor drinking area, children welcome *until 19.00.* Live music *Fri & Tue.* Traditional pub games, sports TV and Wi-Fi. *Open Mon-Fri L and E, Sat 12.00-00.00 & Sun 14.00-23.00.*

8 The Moon Under Water 53-55 Lichfield Street, Wolverhampton WV1 1EQ (01902 422447; www.jdwetherspoon.co.uk/home/pubs/the-moon-under-water-wolverhampton). Situated in the ground floor of the former Co-op building this busy city centre pub serves real ales and food *all day* including breakfast. Children welcome. *Open all day from 07.00.* Wi-Fi.

9 The Hogs Head 186 Stafford St, Wolverhampton WV1 1NA (01902 717955; www.craft-pubs.co.uk/hogsheadwolverhampton). CAMRA award-winning pub serving a range of real ales (including beers from local micro-breweries) and real cider. Food is available *daily 10.00-22.00.* Outdoor drinking area. Quiz *Wed.* Children welcome *until 21.00* if eating. Pool, sports TV and Wi-Fi. *Open daily 10.00-00.00 (Fri 01.00 & Sun 00.20).*

10 The Stile Inn 3 Harrow St, Wolverhampton WV1 4PB (01902 425336). Friendly Victorian, street-corner hostelry serving real ales and food (including Polish dishes) *daily 12.00-20.30 (Fri-Sat 21.30).* Child- and dog-friendly, outside drinking area. Traditional pub games, newspapers, sports TV and Wi-Fi. *Open daily 11.30-23.00 (Fri 00.00 & Sat 01.00).*

Boatyards

Ⓑ**Oxley Marina** The Wharf, Oxley Moor Road, Wolverhampton WV10 6TZ (01902 789522; www.oxleymarina.co.uk). **D** Pump out, gas, overnight and day boat hire, over night and long-term mooring, slipway, solid fuel, winter storage, lifting facility, DIY facilities, boat sales and repairs, engine sales and repairs, welding and fabrication, toilets, car parking, *emergency call out.* Licensed bar *evenings and at weekends.* Snacks.

Supposedly haunted, the Coseley tunnel

BIRMINGHAM & FAZELEY CANAL

MAXIMUM DIMENSIONS

Length: 70'
Beam: 7'
Headroom: 6' 6"

MILEAGE

FARMER'S BRIDGE JUNCTION
(Birmingham Canal) to:
ASTON JUNCTION (Digbeth Branch): 1½ miles
SALFORD JUNCTION
(Tame Valley Canal): 3¼ miles
Minworth Top Lock: 6¼ miles
Curdworth Tunnel: 8½ miles
Bodymoor Heath Bridge: 11½ miles
FAZELEY JUNCTION (Coventry Canal): 15 miles
Hopwas: 17¾ miles
Whittington Brook: 20½ miles

Locks: 38

MANAGER

0303 040 4040
enquiries.westmidlands@canalrivertrust.org.uk

The Birmingham & Fazeley Canal was authorised in 1784, after a great deal of opposition from the well-established Birmingham Canal Company (who very soon merged with it), as a link between Birmingham and the south east. Until then, London-bound goods from Birmingham had to go right round by the River Severn. Naturally, the canal was useless until the Coventry Canal had at least reached Fazeley, but the new Birmingham & Fazeley Company ensured – even before its enabling Act was passed – that the other canals important to its success were completed. Thus at Coleshill in 1782 the Oxford Canal Company agreed to finish its line to Oxford and the Thames; the Coventry Canal Company agreed to extend its line from Atherstone to Fazeley; the new Birmingham & Fazeley Company agreed to build its proposed line and continue it along the defaulting Coventry route from Fazeley to Whittington Brook; and the Trent & Mersey Company pledged to finish the Coventry's line from Whittington Brook to Fradley Junction on the Trent & Mersey Canal.

This rare example of cooperation among canal companies paid off when, in 1790, the great joint programme was finished and traffic immediately began to flow along the system.

The Birmingham & Fazeley Company employed John Smeaton to build their canal: he completed it in 1789. The flights of narrow locks at Farmer's Bridge and Aston became very congested, especially after the Warwick canals had joined up with the Birmingham & Fazeley Canal at Digbeth; two new canals were built to bypass this permanent obstacle, one on each side. The Tame Valley Canal and the Birmingham & Warwick Junction Canal were opened in 1844, and traffic flowed more smoothly. After this the Birmingham & Fazeley Canal became more attractive to carriers and it continued to be an important link route. It still provides this link, but is now worthy of exploration in its own right.

The Tame Valley Wetlands Landscape Partnership Scheme (01675 470917; www.tamevalleywetlands.co.uk) aims to restore a 37 sq mile area of the landscape between Tamworth and Birmingham, in North Warwickshire and southeast Staffordshire. An area rich in natural and built heritage, this scheme would result in significant enhancement to the River Tame, its floodplain and the wider landscape, with improvements to access and the provision of training and volunteering opportunities for local people. The canal is an important part of this £2.4m project, which has recently been awarded £1.7 million from the Heritage Lottery Fund.

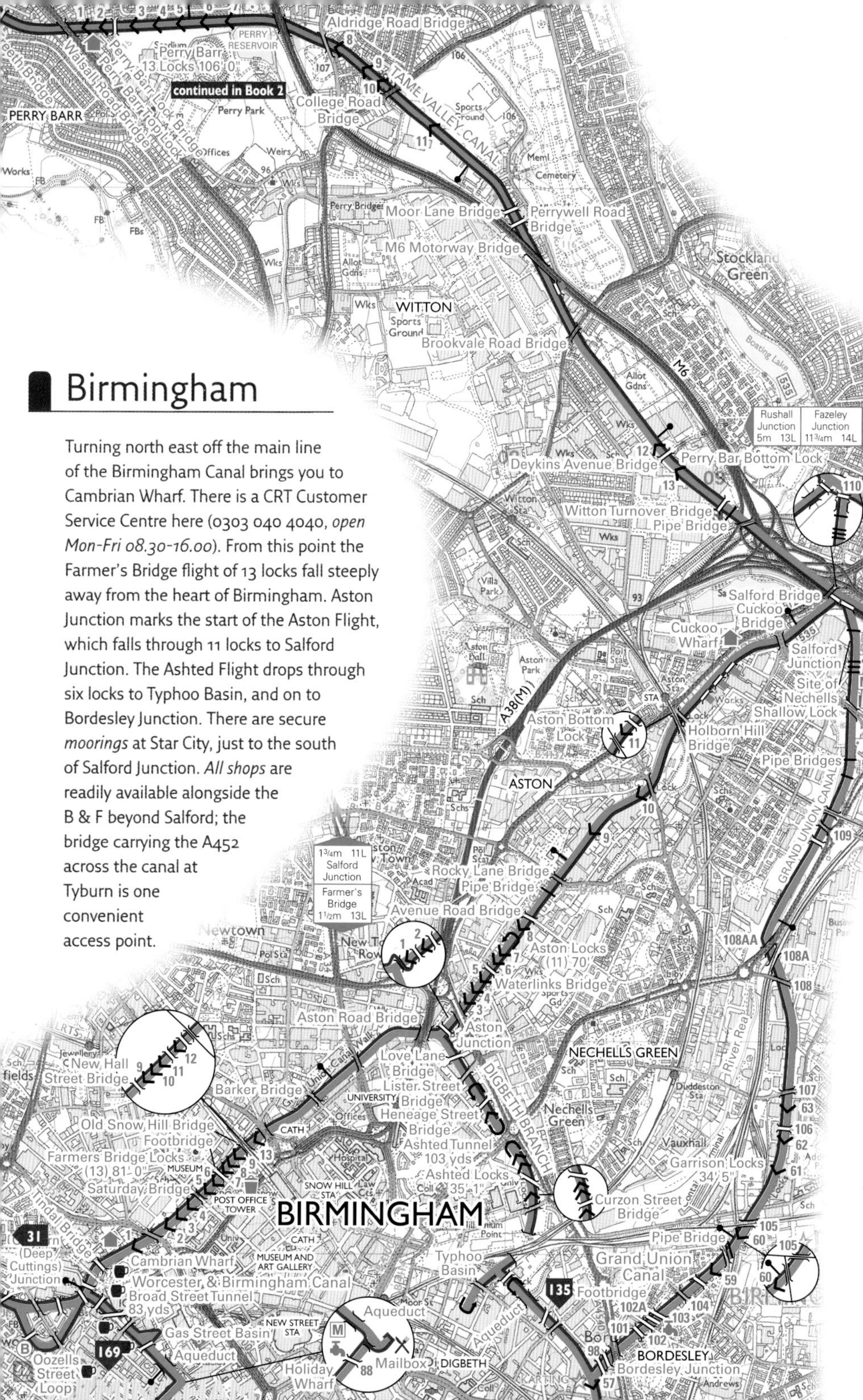

Birmingham

Turning north east off the main line of the Birmingham Canal brings you to Cambrian Wharf. There is a CRT Customer Service Centre here (0303 040 4040, *open Mon-Fri 08.30-16.00*). From this point the Farmer's Bridge flight of 13 locks fall steeply away from the heart of Birmingham. Aston Junction marks the start of the Aston Flight, which falls through 11 locks to Salford Junction. The Ashted Flight drops through six locks to Typhoo Basin, and on to Bordesley Junction. There are secure *moorings* at Star City, just to the south of Salford Junction. *All shops* are readily available alongside the B & F beyond Salford; the bridge carrying the A452 across the canal at Tyburn is one convenient access point.

Ackers Adventure Activity Centre Golden Hillock Road, Small Heath, Birmingham B11 2PY (0121 772 5111; www.ackers-adventure.co.uk). Alongside the Grand Union canal at Small Heath. This non-profit making charity, run for the benefit of the community, offers a wide range of outdoor activities for all ages and abilities – everything from skiing and snowboarding to climbing, canoeing, archery and operating four-wheel-drive vehicles. Also a nature area. Charge. Telephone for further details.

Aston Hall Trinity Road, Aston, Birmingham B6 6JD (0121 348 8100; www.birminghammuseums.org.uk/aston). Built between 1618 and 1635, this one of the last great houses to be constructed in the spectacular Jacobean style and is decorated and furnished to reflect the lifestyle of a wealthy gentleman. There is the 136' Long Gallery and a magnificent carved oak staircase. It has been home to Charles I (albeit for a single night) and James Watt junior, son of the famous steam engineer. Drinks, snacks and souvenirs. *Open Tue-Sun & B Hol Mon 11.00-16.00.* *Closed 23rd Dec-2nd Jan.* Garden and grounds free. House charge.

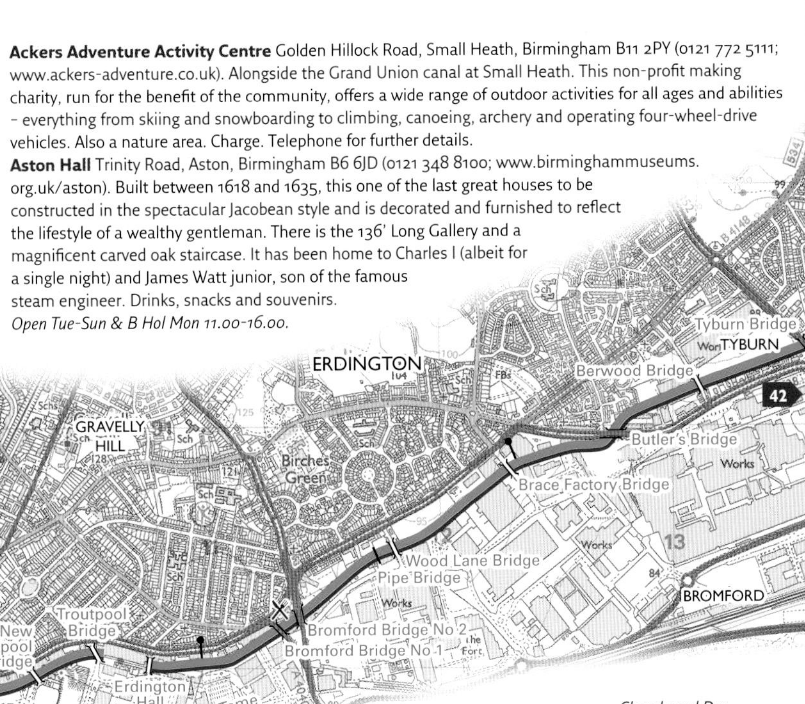

Aston Villa Stadium Tours Aston Villa Football Club, Villa Park, Birmingham B6 6HE (0333 323 1874; www.avfc.co.uk). A chance to take a look behind the scenes of one of the world's oldest football clubs. Tours take place throughout the week – telephone for further details.

Barber Institute of Fine Arts The University of Birmingham, Edgbaston, Birmingham B15 2TS (0121 414 7333; www.barber.org.uk). A fine collection, donated to the university complete with the impressive gallery building, and embracing works of art from Old Masters through to modern paintings, drawings and sculpture, including major works by Bellini, Poussin, Rubens, Gainsborough, Rossetti, Monet, Degas and Magritte. There really is something here for everyone. Also a regular programme of exhibitions, concerts, lectures and events. *Open Mon-Fri 10.00-17.00 & Sat-Sun 11.00-17.00.* Free (donations welcome).

BBC Birmingham Level 10, The Mailbox, Birmingham B1 1RF (0370 901 1227; www.bbc.co.uk/showsand tours). A chance to visit the BBC's Birmingham home and see where famous radio and television programmes are made. Home to *The Archers* and *Gardeners' World* to name but two. Take a peek into the television production gallery and a trip down memory lane with the Time Tunnel. Hands-on displays and exhibits. Shop. Visitor Centre *open daily 10.00-17.00 (Sun 11.00)*. Free. Pre-booked *1½ hr* tours available *Tue-Wed & Sat 10.30-13.00* – telephone 0121 567 6888. Charge.

Pubs and Restaurants

1 The Flapper Cambrian Wharf, Kingston Row, Birmingham B1 2NU (0121 236 2421; www.theflapper.co.uk). Student-type pub majoring on bottled beers, cocktails and music. Canalside terrace seating. *Open Mon-Thu & Sun 16.00-23.00 and Fri-Sat 12.00-01.00.*

2 The Malt House 75 King Edwards Road, Brindley Place B1 2NX (0121 633 4171; www.greeneking-pubs.co.uk/pub/malt-house-birmingham/p0937). Overlooking Deep Cuttings Junction, this pub serves real ale and food *12.00-21.00 daily.* Children welcome, outside seating. Sports TV and Wi-Fi. *Open 11.00-23.00 (Fri-Sat 00.00).*

Curdworth

Most of the factories on this section ignore the canal, although the Cincinnati works are a laudable exception: landscaped lawns and gardens run down from the buildings to the water's edge. Minworth Locks (anti-vandal - aka handcuff - key needed) start the descent towards Fazeley, and gradually the canal loses the industry that has accompanied it from Birmingham. Curdworth is passed in a tree-lined cutting: the church tower here has been visible for some time. The cutting continues beyond Curdworth Bridge, and enters a short tunnel (57yds), with the towpath alongside. From now until Fazeley the navigation used to make its way in complete isolation, through empty fields. However, today the roar of the motorway seems to dominate everything, until well beyond the bottom lock of the 11-lock Curdworth flight. The top lock was moved westwards and the lock cottage demolished to accommodate the M6 Toll. The lack of hedges in this area is very noticeable and only those by the towpath seem to have survived. As the canal swings north, hedges and trees thankfully reappear, and after Bodymoor Heath trees line the canal on both sidesfor two miles. Flooded gravel pits, and the bird life they attract, now constitute the Kingsbury Water Park - the Visitor Centre is east of Bodymoor Heath Bridge, across the motorway.

Tyburn
Warwicks. PO, tel, stores, off-licence, garage. A mixture of factories and houses.

Minworth
Warwicks. Tel, stores, off-licence, garage. A mainly residential area on the city outskirts, totally dominated by roads. There is a handy transport café close to Hansons Bridge, together with a *24hr* superstore *(weekdays)* which includes a chemist, just north of Dicken's Bridge. To the south of Minworth Green Bridge there is a useful cycle repair shop - F G Mansell 18 Water Orton Lane B76 9BU (0121 351 1047).

Curdworth
Warwicks. PO, tel, stores, off-licence, garage. Now set in the shadow of the motorway, and not far from the sewage works, Curdworth still manages to cling to a village identity. The squat church is partly Norman, c. 1170; note the finely carved Norman font, with images of standing men, a monster and a lamb The store (01675 470259) is *open Mon-Sat 06.30-18.00 (Sat 18.30) & Sun 07.00-12.30.*

Bodymoor Heath
Warwicks. Tel. A scattered village which has found a new lease of life with the creation of Kingsbury Water Park. Occasional 18th-C buildings survive as a memory of the pre-industrial Midlands, with the Dog & Doublet being one such fine example.

Kingsbury Water Park Bodymoor Heath Lane, Bodymoor Heath, Sutton Coldfield B76 0DY (01827 872660; countryparks.warwickshire.gov.uk/country-parks/kingsbury-water-park). A 600-acre landscaped park containing 30 lakes and pools, created from gravel pits worked over the last 50 years. Walks, nature trails, fishing, horse riding, sailing, power-boating and windsurfing, and exciting children's play area. Visitor Centre and coffee shop. Excellent programme of events *Apr-Sep* (modest charge per event). Cycle hire.

Broomey Croft Children's Farm Bodymoor Heath Lane, Bodymoor Heath B78 0EE (01827 873844; www.broomeycroftfarm.co.uk). Children's farm with goats, sheep and ponies. Tearoom and gift shop. *Open 08.00-17.00 in summer and 08.00-16.00 in winter.* Charge.

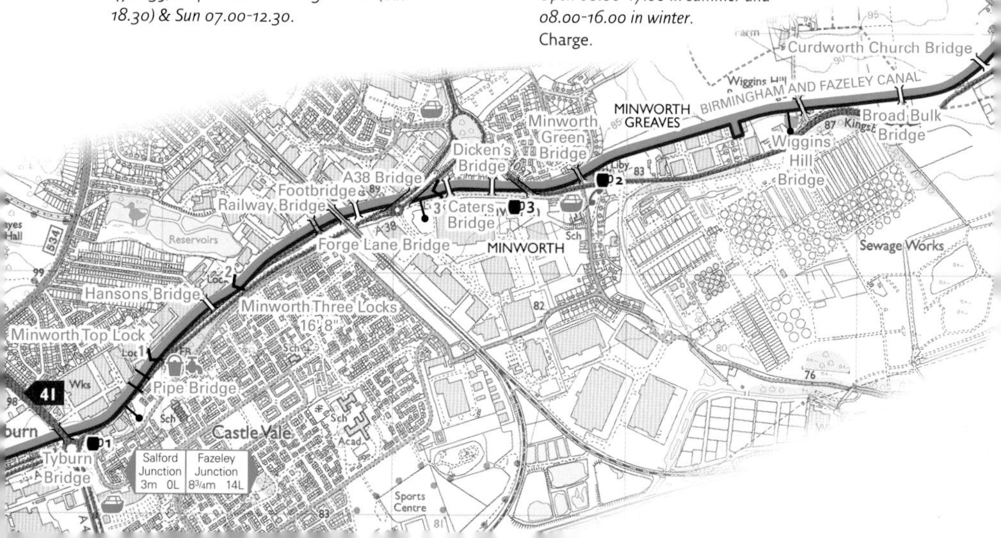

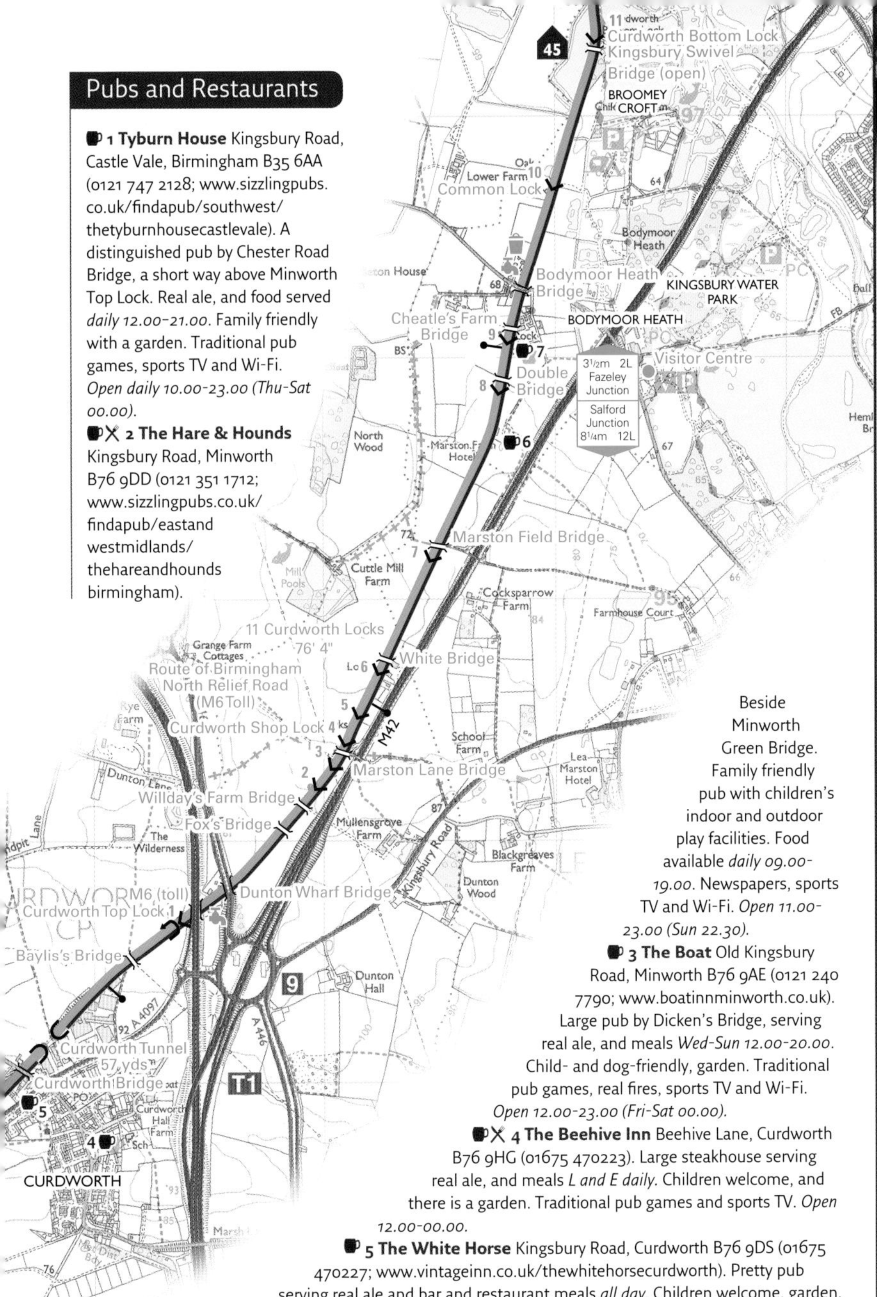

Pubs and Restaurants

1 Tyburn House Kingsbury Road, Castle Vale, Birmingham B35 6AA (0121 747 2128; www.sizzlingpubs.co.uk/findapub/southwest/thetyburnhousecastlevale). A distinguished pub by Chester Road Bridge, a short way above Minworth Top Lock. Real ale, and food served *daily 12.00-21.00*. Family friendly with a garden. Traditional pub games, sports TV and Wi-Fi. *Open daily 10.00-23.00 (Thu-Sat 00.00).*

2 The Hare & Hounds Kingsbury Road, Minworth B76 9DD (0121 351 1712; www.sizzlingpubs.co.uk/findapub/eastandwestmidlands/thehareandhoundsbirmingham). Beside Minworth Green Bridge. Family friendly pub with children's indoor and outdoor play facilities. Food available *daily 09.00-19.00*. Newspapers, sports TV and Wi-Fi. *Open 11.00-23.00 (Sun 22.30).*

3 The Boat Old Kingsbury Road, Minworth B76 9AE (0121 240 7790; www.boatinnminworth.co.uk). Large pub by Dicken's Bridge, serving real ale, and meals *Wed-Sun 12.00-20.00*. Child- and dog-friendly, garden. Traditional pub games, real fires, sports TV and Wi-Fi. *Open 12.00-23.00 (Fri-Sat 00.00).*

4 The Beehive Inn Beehive Lane, Curdworth B76 9HG (01675 470223). Large steakhouse serving real ale, and meals *L and E daily*. Children welcome, and there is a garden. Traditional pub games and sports TV. *Open 12.00-00.00.*

5 The White Horse Kingsbury Road, Curdworth B76 9DS (01675 470227; www.vintageinn.co.uk/thewhitehorsecurdworth). Pretty pub serving real ale and bar and restaurant meals *all day*. Children welcome, garden. Real fires, sports TV and Wi-Fi. *Open 12.00-23.00 (Sun 22.30).*

6 Marston Farm Hotel Dog Lane, Bodymoor Heath B76 9JD (01827 872133; www.marstonfarm-hotel.co.uk/en). A 17th-C hotel where you can enjoy a meal *L and E & afternoon* tea. Children welcome. Pleasant courtyard and tennis courts for hire. B&B. *Open all day.*

7 The Dog & Doublet Dog Lane, Bodymoor Heath B76 9JD (01827 872374). Smart and handsome red-brick canalside pub by Cheatles Farm Bridge, serving real ale. Varied menu and specials *L and E*. Children welcome. Canalside garden with good views, and a barbecue. Mooring. B&B. Look out for George, the 'car park ghost'. *Open 11.00-23.00.*

Fazeley

Continuing north, the canal runs through quiet and attractive open farmland, flanked on both sides by oak trees, their roots often projecting into the water. The isolation of the canal ends at Drayton Bassett where the A4091 swings in to run parallel as far as Fazeley. By Drayton Bassett is a curious footbridge, a marvellous folly, and immediately after it a second, swing bridge which is chained open. The countryside then gives way to the outskirts of Fazeley (*see* page 59) which are quickly followed by a handsome mill building and the junction with the Coventry Canal, overlooked by an imposing canal house. The Birmingham & Fazeley Canal continues to the north west, although its route is subsumed as part of the Coventry Canal. Under an arrangement with CRT, are available free to passing boaters 09.00-17.00 daily at Fazeley Mill Marina.

- **Drayton Bassett**

Staffs. Tel. The village is set ½ mile to the west of the canal. The best feature is the charming and totally unexpected Gothic-style footbridge over the canal. Its twin battlemented towers would look quite commanding but for their ridiculously small size. This bridge is unique, and there seems to be no explanation for its eccentricity, thus greatly increasing its attraction.

Drayton Manor Family Theme Park B78 3TW. Alongside the canal, off the A4091 at Drayton Manor Bridge (0844 472 1950; www.draytonmanor.co.uk). Formerly the site of the house of Sir Robert Peel's father, built 1820-35. The now-vanished house was designed by Sir Robert Smirke and the garden, 15 acres of wood and parkland, was originally laid out by William Gilpin. It has an extensive series of exciting rides, including Storm Force Ten, and amusements. *Open late Mar-Oct, 10.00-late afternoon.* Charge. Caravan and camping site.

- **Fazeley**

Staffs. PO, tel, stores, chemist, off-licence, takeaways, fish & chips, garage. Its importance as a road and canal junction determines the character of Fazeley; it is a small, industrial centre that has grown up around the communication network. From the canal the town appears more attractive than it really is. Useful as a supply centre.

- **Fazeley Junction**

Staffs. The Birmingham & Fazeley Canal joins the Coventry Canal here. Originally the Coventry Canal was to continue westwards to meet the Trent & Mersey Canal at Fradley; however, the Coventry company ran out of money at Fazeley, and so the Birmingham & Fazeley Canal continued on to Whittington (this section is covered within the Coventry Canal, for continuity). The Trent & Mersey Company then built a linking arm from Fradley to Whittington, which was later bought by the Coventry Company, thus becoming a detached section of their canal. The junction has been tastefully restored, with good moorings and a canalside seat made from a balance beam, overlooked by a fine navigation office. It was at Fazeley, in the 1790s, that Robert Peel, father of the prime minister, in partnership with Joseph Wilkes, transformed the area, building mills and wharves, chapels and watercourses, and making it a centre of industry that was to last until the depression of the mid-19th C. Just to the south of the canal junction is the Bourne Brook Cut, which has its source in reservoirs to the north of Watling Street and originally supplied the bleach and dye works here. A little further south of the junction, by the Birmingham & Fazeley Canal, is Fazeley Mill, built in 1886 as a tape mill, and remaining largely unaltered until its closure in the 1970s. Just beyond the next bridge, on the opposite side of the canal, is one of the best surviving mills of the Richard Arkwright pattern, built in 1791 with three storeys and 19 bays.

In Coleshill Street a fine terrace of 20 workers' houses can still be seen.

Boatyards

Ⓑ**Fazeley Mill Marina** Coleshill Road, Fazeley, Tamworth B78 3SE (01827 261138; www.canalmarinas.com/fazeley-mill). **D** Pump out, gas, overnight and long-term mooring, toilets and showers, solid fuel.

Ⓑ**Debbie's Day Boats Ltd, Drayton Boat Services, Drayton Narrowboat Hire** The Wharf, Coleshill Road, Fazeley, Tamworth B78 3RY (01827 262042/07504 135580; www.debbies-day-boats.co.uk/contact_debbies_canal_boats.html). Gas, solid fuel, day boat hire, narrowboat rentals, long-term mooring, boat and engine sales and repairs, welding, fabrication, GRP repairs, wooden boat building, DIY facilities.

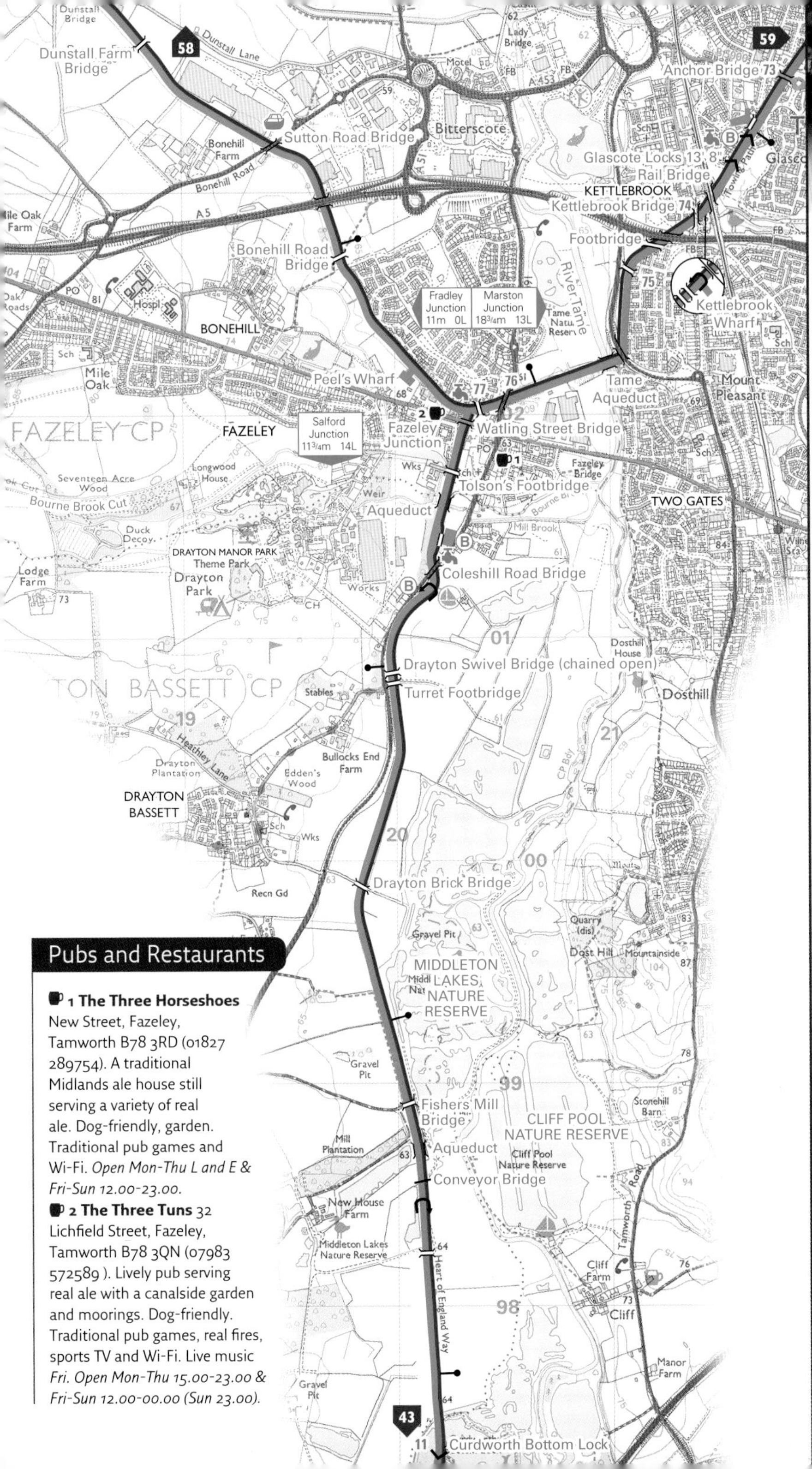

Pubs and Restaurants

1 The Three Horseshoes New Street, Fazeley, Tamworth B78 3RD (01827 289754). A traditional Midlands ale house still serving a variety of real ale. Dog-friendly, garden. Traditional pub games and Wi-Fi. *Open Mon-Thu L and E & Fri-Sun 12.00-23.00.*

2 The Three Tuns 32 Lichfield Street, Fazeley, Tamworth B78 3QN (07983 572589). Lively pub serving real ale with a canalside garden and moorings. Dog-friendly. Traditional pub games, real fires, sports TV and Wi-Fi. Live music Fri. *Open Mon-Thu 15.00-23.00 & Fri-Sun 12.00-00.00 (Sun 23.00).*

Statue of James Brindley, the canal engineer, at Coventry Canal Basin

COVENTRY CANAL

MAXIMUM DIMENSIONS

Length: 72'
Beam: 7'
Headroom: 6' 6"

MILEAGE

COVENTRY BASIN to:
HAWKESBURY JUNCTION (Oxford Canal): 5½ miles
MARSTON JUNCTION (Ashby Canal): 8¼ miles
Boot Wharf, Nuneaton: 10½ miles
Hartshill: 14 miles
Atherstone Top Lock: 16½ miles
Polesworth: 21½ miles
Alvecote Priory: 23¼ miles
Glascote Bottom Lock: 25½ miles
FAZELEY JUNCTION (Birmingham & Fazeley Canal): 27 miles
Hopwas: 29¾ miles
Whittington Brook: 32½ miles
Huddlesford Junction: 34 miles
FRADLEY JUNCTION (Trent & Mersey Canal): 38 miles

Locks: 13

MANAGER

0303 040 4040
enquiries.westmidlands@canalrivertrust.org.uk

The Coventry Canal, whose enabling Act of Parliament was passed in 1768, was promoted by pit owners such as the Parrotts of Hawkesbury and the Newdigates of Arbury with two main objectives: to connect the fast-growing town of Coventry with the new trade route called the Grand Trunk, now the Trent & Mersey Canal; and to provide Coventry with cheap coal from Bedworth coalfield, 10 miles to the north.

The first, long-term objective was not achieved for some years until the company had overcome financial difficulties, but – wisely – the stretch between Coventry and Bedworth was completed early on, so that the profitable carriage of local coal was quickly established along the canal, in 1769.

By the time the canal reached Atherstone in 1771, all the authorised capital had been spent and James Brindley, the original engineer of the canal, had been sacked. For these reasons – and because of the interminable wrangle with the Oxford Canal Company, whose scheme to link Coventry with southern England had followed hard upon the original Coventry scheme – the Coventry Canal did not reach Fazeley, nearly 12 miles short of its intended terminus at Fradley, until 1790.

By this time, the Birmingham & Fazeley Canal had been built, extending along the Coventry Canal's original proposed line to Whittington Brook, from where the Grand Trunk Canal Company carried it north to Fradley. The Coventry Company later bought this section back, which explains the fact that there is now a detached portion of the Coventry Canal from Whittington Brook to Fradley Junction (look out for the marker stone).

In 1790, the Oxford Canal was also completed through to Oxford and thus to London via the Thames. The profits of the Coventry Canal rose quickly, and rose even higher when the Grand Junction Canal was completed in 1799, shortening the route to London by 60 miles. Other adjoining canals contributed to the Coventry Canal's prosperity: the Ashby, the Wyrley & Essington and the Trent & Mersey. The extension of the Grand Junction Canal via Warwick to Birmingham naturally dismayed the Coventry, but the numerous locks – and high tolls on the stretch of the Oxford Canal between Braunston and Napton Junctions – ensured that a lot of traffic to and from Birmingham still used the slightly longer route via the Coventry and Birmingham & Fazeley Canals, especially after the Oxford Canal was shortened by 14 miles between Braunston and Longford.

The continuous financial success of the Coventry Canal could be attributed both to its being part of so many long-distance routes and to the continued prosperity of the coal mines along its way. Extensive landscaping and reclamation, along with on-going rebuilding, have made this an extremely attractive and interesting route.

Coventry

The Coventry Canal begins at the large Bishop Street Basin, opened in 1769, near the town centre. It is an interesting situation on the side of a hill, overlooked by tall buildings and attractive old wooden canal warehouses; the warehouses date from 1914, although there were, of course, earlier such buildings on the site. They once stored grain, food and cement, and were well restored in 1984. The old Weighbridge Office, beside the entrance gates, still looks out over the basin towards the Vaults, which were used to store coal. The canal leaves the terminus through bridge 1, a tiny structure designed to be easily closed with a wooden beam each evening: indeed at one time no boats were allowed to stay in the basin overnight (it is now an excellent *mooring*). There was once a toll house here. To the west of this bridge is Canal House, built for the local trader Alderman Clarke. The canal company purchased the house in 1809 and it was used for successive canal managers until 1947, when the last manager of the Coventry Canal, John Kaye, purchased it upon his retirement. It is now owned by the City Council. The canal now begins to wind through what were busy industrial areas towards Hawkesbury: it is in places quite narrow, and often flanked by buildings. Just beyond bridge 2 are 'Cash's Hundred Houses', an elegant row of weavers' houses, where the living accommodation was on the lower two floors, with the top storey being occupied by looms, driven by a single shaft from a steam engine. There never were 100 houses: only 48 were built, and of these only 37 remain. The canal then, after various contortions, continues towards Hawkesbury, passing through the outskirts of Coventry. Before it ducks under the motorway, just beyond bridge 10, you will notice that the canal is wider: this was the site of the original junction between the Oxford and Coventry Canals. It was known as Longford Junction. Hawkesbury Junction (aka Sutton Stop) their present meeting, contains all the elements expected of such a notable place: plenty of traditional boats, interesting buildings including a fine engine house, a splendid *pub* and useful *facilities* for boaters. To the east of the junction is Hawkesbury Hall (private), at one time the home of mine owner and sponsor of the Coventry Canal, Richard Parrott. The towpath between Coventry and Hawkesbury is decorated with some excellent sculptures, as the Canal Art Trail.

Coventry

West Midlands. All Services. Recorded as Couentrev in the Domesday Book, Coventry's modern history begins with the foundation of a Benedictine priory by Leofric and his wife Godgyfu in 1043, but its fame came with Lady Godiva, who in legend rode naked through the streets, to divert Leofric's anger from the town. This episode is first recorded in the *Flores Historiarum* of 1235. Following the Norman invasion, the town became second in commercial importance to London. Largely destroyed during World War II, it is today a modern and well-planned city, although a restored row of medieval buildings can be visited in Spon Street, in the west of the city centre. The origin of the popular phrase 'to send to Coventry', meaning to cold-shoulder or ignore, is uncertain, but there is no reason to connect it with the present population, who seem generally warm and friendly. Coventry was the world's first twin city when it forged a relationship with the Russian city of Stalingrad.

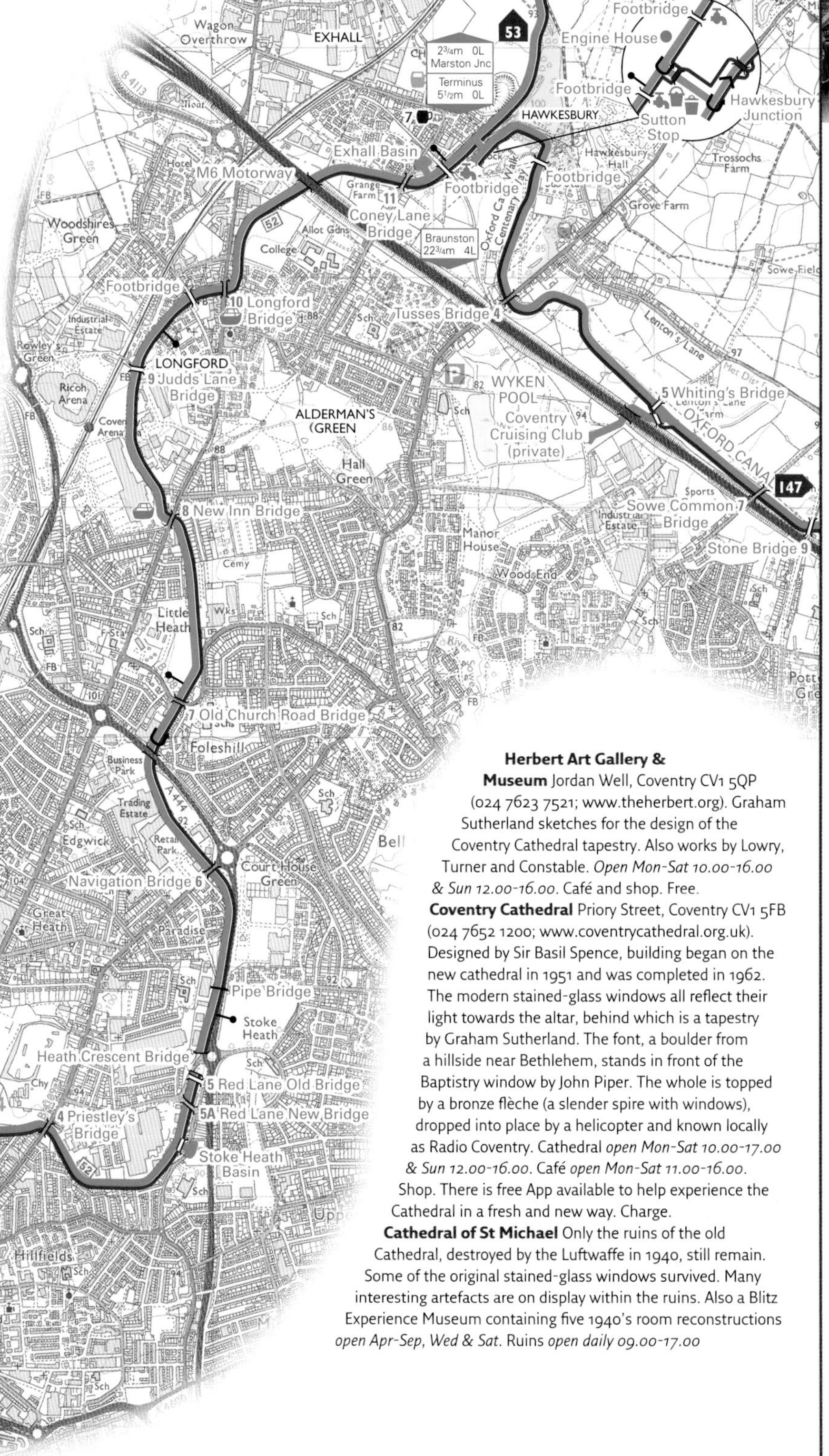

Herbert Art Gallery & Museum Jordan Well, Coventry CV1 5QP (024 7623 7521; www.theherbert.org). Graham Sutherland sketches for the design of the Coventry Cathedral tapestry. Also works by Lowry, Turner and Constable. *Open Mon-Sat 10.00-16.00 & Sun 12.00-16.00*. Café and shop. Free.

Coventry Cathedral Priory Street, Coventry CV1 5FB (024 7652 1200; www.coventrycathedral.org.uk). Designed by Sir Basil Spence, building began on the new cathedral in 1951 and was completed in 1962. The modern stained-glass windows all reflect their light towards the altar, behind which is a tapestry by Graham Sutherland. The font, a boulder from a hillside near Bethlehem, stands in front of the Baptistry window by John Piper. The whole is topped by a bronze flèche (a slender spire with windows), dropped into place by a helicopter and known locally as Radio Coventry. Cathedral *open Mon-Sat 10.00-17.00 & Sun 12.00-16.00*. Café *open Mon-Sat 11.00-16.00*. Shop. There is free App available to help experience the Cathedral in a fresh and new way. Charge.

Cathedral of St Michael Only the ruins of the old Cathedral, destroyed by the Luftwaffe in 1940, still remain. Some of the original stained-glass windows survived. Many interesting artefacts are on display within the ruins. Also a Blitz Experience Museum containing five 1940's room reconstructions *open Apr-Sep, Wed & Sat*. Ruins *open daily 09.00-17.00*

Coventry Transport Museum Millennium Place, Hales Street, Coventry CV1 1JD (024 7623 4270, www.transport-museum.com). Walk south from the canal basin. Reputedly the largest display of British-made transport in the world, with over 200 cars, 90 motorbikes and 230 cycles on view. There are also period street scenes, royal vehicles and the Blitz Experience. You can also see the awesome *Thrust SSC*, world land-speed record holder, and take an audio-visual run at over 600 mph. *Open daily 10.00-17.00. Closed Xmas and New Year.* Café with free Wi-Fi. Shop. Free.

Tourist Information Centre Jordan Well, Coventry CV1 5QP (024 7623 4284; www.coventrycitycentre.co.uk/directory/experience/tourist-information-centre). *Open Mon-Sun 10.00-16.00 (Sun 12.00).*

● **Longford Bridge**

West Midlands. PO box, tel, stores, off-licence, takeaways. It was here, between 1769 and 1865, that members of the nearby Salem Baptist Chapel were baptised in the canal. The nearby Ricoh Arena is a ready source of eateries and entertainment.

● **Hawkesbury Junction**

Hawkesbury Junction is also known as Sutton Stop, after the name of the toll clerks here. It was always a busy canal centre, and remains so today, with plenty of narrowboats permanently moored at the junction. There are also other things to see: a fine canal pub, a stop lock and a disused engine house. The latter used to pump water up into the canal from a well. Its engine was installed in 1821, having been previously employed for nearly 100 years at Griff Colliery, a few miles up the canal towards Nuneaton. This Newcomen-type atmospheric steam engine, called Lady Godiva, is now in Dartmouth Museum. It ceased work in 1913. Sephtons House and Boatyard once faced the junction: it was here, in 1924, that *nb Friendship* was built. This boat can now be seen at the Boat Museum, Ellesmere Port. The western side of the canal has subsequently been engulfed in a vast area of housing.

BOAT TRIPS

Nb Coventrian is a 38-seater boat based at Swan Lane Wharf, Swan Lane, Coventry CV2 4QN and used as a floating classroom for local children and special events. Also available for private charter, for parties and trips. Details from 024 7630 8244/07747 448572; covsf.com/coventrian.

WALKING AND CYCLING

The towpath is in good condition for walkers throughout, and the stretch between Coventry and Hawkesbury is now enlivened as the Canal Art Trail. Cyclists will find parts of the towpath bumpy.

Pubs and Restaurants (pages 48-49)

X 1 **Country Crust Tearooms** Canal Basin, St Nicholas Street, Coventry CV1 4LY (024 7663 3477). Excellent cooked breakfasts, light meals, coffee and tea. Outside seating. *Open Mon-Fri 09.30-16.30.*

X 2 **The Flying Standard** 2-10 Trinity Street, Coventry CV1 1FL (024 7655 5723; www.jdwetherspoon.com/pubs/all-pubs/england/west-midlands/the-flying-standard-coventry). The name of this pub recalls a fondly remembered motor car, part of a range of models made in Coventry, from 1903 until the 1960s. This city centre pub serves real ales and ciders, together with breakfast *from 08.00*. Food is available *all day* and children welcome. Outside seating. Sports TV and Wi-Fi. *Open daily 08.00-00.00.*

3 **The Gatehouse Tavern** 44-46 Hill Street, Coventry CV1 4AN (024 7663 0140; www.gatehousetavern.com). A traditional family pub in the centre of the city, with a large beer garden, serving real ales and ciders. Large portions of reasonably priced, homemade food are available *Mon-Sat L and E (not Sat E)*. Children welcome *until 21.00*, sports TV and Wi-Fi. *Open Mon-Sun 10.00-23.00 (Sun 12.00).*

4 **The Old Windmill** 22-23 Spon Street, Coventry CV1 3BA (024 7625 1717; www.old-windmill-inn.co.uk). Situated in medieval Spon Street, this is one of the oldest pubs in the city and it still retains a redundant brewing vessel in one of its back rooms. There are a good selection of real ales and real cider available. Dog-friendly, real fires and Wi-Fi. *Open Mon E & Tue-Sun 12.00-23.30.*

5 **The Town Wall Tavern** Bond Street, Coventry CV1 4AH (024 7622 0963). Renown for its excellent food served *Tue-Sat 12.00-20.00 (Fri-Sat 19.00) & Sun 12.30-15.30* and made from fresh local produce. Real ales, real cider and real fires. Patio, dog-friendly and sports TV. *Open Mon-Sat 12.00-23.00 (Fri-Sat 00.00) & Sun 12.00-22.00.*

6 **The Town Crier** Corporation Street, Coventry CV1 1PB (024 7663 2317; towncriercoventry.co.uk). Modern city-centre pub, popular with shoppers and workers alike, serving real ales and real cider. Excellent food is available *daily 12.00-21.00 (Sun 16.00)*. Courtyard seating, sports TV and Wi-Fi. Live music *Sat. Open Mon-Fri 11.00-23.00 (Thu-Fri 01.00) Sat 10.00-01.00 & Sun 11.30-18.00.*

See also **Pubs and Restaurants** on page 130.

Hawkesbury Junction (Sutton Stop)

Nuneaton

Leaving Hawkesbury Junction, the canal passes through Bedworth in a long cutting: the town seems to be composed mainly of vast housing estates, but these make little impression upon the canal. At Marston Junction the Ashby Canal (*see* page 16) branches to the east through pleasant countryside, while the Coventry Canal bends due west for a short way before resuming its course towards Nuneaton to the north. There is a pleasant short stretch of open fields, giving a welcome breathing space, before the canal once again enters the suburbs, this time of Nuneaton. There are good *moorings* and easy access to *facilities* by Boot Bridge (bridge 20). The canal takes a route around the town, marked by a succession of housing estates and well-tended allotments.

● **Nuneaton**
Warwicks. All services. A typical Midlands town. On the site of the Griff Colliery canal arm are the hollows said to be the origin of the Red Deeps in the *Mill on the Floss* by George Eliot, who was born here in 1819.

Nuneaton Museum & Art Gallery Riversley Park, 227 Coton Road, Nuneaton CV11 5TU (024 7635 0720; www.nuneatonandbedworth.gov.uk). Archaeological specimens of Nuneaton from prehistoric to medieval times, and also items from the local earthenware industry. Geological and mining relics, ethnography from Africa, Asia, America and Oceania. Paintings, prints and watercolours. Personalia collection of the novelist George Eliot. *Open Tue-Sat 10.30-16.30, Sun 14.00-16.30. Closed Mon except B Hols.* Tearoom and shop. Free.

Arbury Hall Griff Lane, Arbury Estate, Nuneaton CV10 7PT (024 7638 2804; www.arburyestate.co.uk). Two miles south west of the canal off B4102. Originally an Elizabethan house, it was gothicised by Sir Roger Newdigate in 1750-1800 under the direction of Sanderson Miller, Henry Keene and Couchman of Warwick. Fine pictures, furniture, china and glass. The Hall is in a beautiful park setting. Hall, gardens and tearoom *open Apr-Aug B Hol Sun & Mon 13.00-18.00.* Telephone for tour details. Charge.

Tourist Information Centre Nuneaton Library, Church Street, Nuneaton CV11 4AD (0300 555 8171; www.warwickshire.gov.uk/nuneatonlibrary).

● **Chilvers Coton**
Warwicks. PO box, tel, stores, off-licence, chemist, takeaway, butcher. A suburb of Nuneaton. Its church dates from 1946 and was designed by H. N. Jepson and built by German prisoners-of-war.

● **Bedworth**
Warwicks. All services. The most impressive parts of this town are its church by Bodley and Garner, 1888-90, and the almshouses built in 1840. Good shops.

Pubs and Restaurants (pages 53 and 55)

1 **The Horseshoes** 2 Heath End Road, Nuneaton CV10 7JQ (024 7767 5066). 300yds west of Boot Bridge 20. This Edwardian-style Everards pub serves a wide range of real ales together with real cider. Homemade food is available *L and E.* Dog- and family-friendly, garden. Newspapers, real fires and Wi-Fi. Quiz *Wed. Open 12.00-23.00 (Fri-Sat 00.00).*

2 **The Felix Holt** 3 Stratford Street, Nuneaton CV11 5BS (024 7634 7785; www.jdwetherspoon.com/pubs/all-pubs/england/warwickshire/the-felix-holt-nuneaton). Taking its name from the George Eliot novel, which is reflected in its décor of books, pictures and local history, this pub serves a wide range of real ale and real cider. Food is available *all day from 08.00.* Children welcome and Wi-Fi. *Open 08.00 'til late.*

3 **The Crown** 10 Bond Street, Nuneaton CV11 4BX (024 7637 3343). Busy town hostelry, 'twixt the railway and bus stations, serving up to 10 real ales. Also a good selection of foreign beers, cider and malt whiskies. Beer garden and live music *Sat. Sun L 12.00-16.00.* Garden, real fires, sports TV and Wi-Fi. *Open 12.00-23.00 (Fri-Sat 00.00).*

BIRD LIFE

The *Nuthatch* is recognised by its rounded, short-tailed appearance and its habit of descending tree trunks head-downwards, a trait unique in Britain to this species. The Nuthatch has blue-grey upperparts, a black eyestripe, white cheeks and orange-buff underparts. The chisel-like bill is used to prise insects from tree bark and to hammer open acorns wedged in bark crevices. This woodland species has a falcon-like call. It nests in tree holes, often plastering the entrance with mud to reduce its diameter.

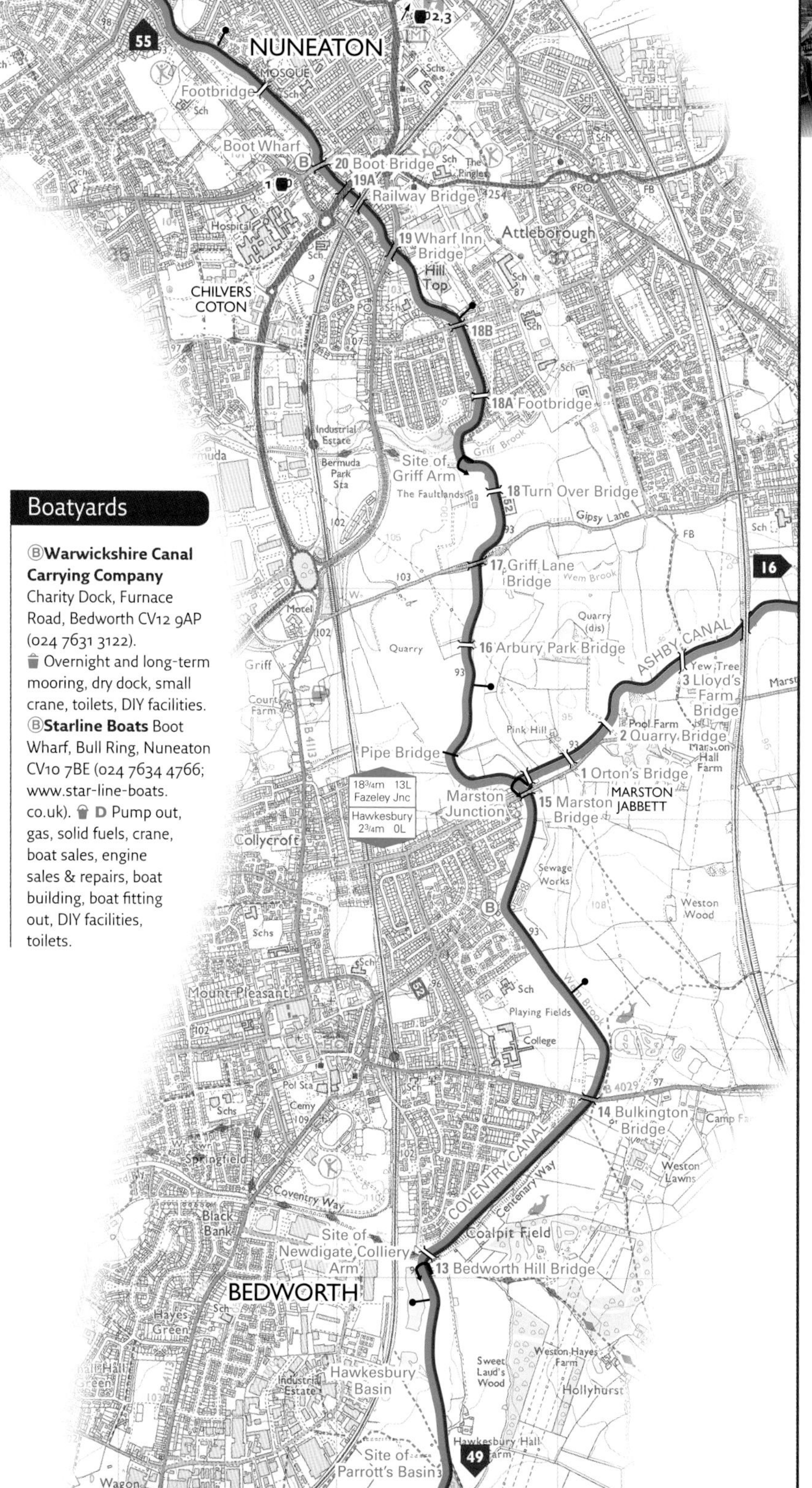

Boatyards

Ⓑ**Warwickshire Canal Carrying Company** Charity Dock, Furnace Road, Bedworth CV12 9AP (024 7631 3122). Overnight and long-term mooring, dry dock, small crane, toilets, DIY facilities.

Ⓑ**Starline Boats** Boot Wharf, Bull Ring, Nuneaton CV10 7BE (024 7634 4766; www.star-line-boats.co.uk). **D** Pump out, gas, solid fuels, crane, boat sales, engine sales & repairs, boat building, boat fitting out, DIY facilities, toilets.

Hartshill

Continuing north west out of Nuneaton, the canal winds along the side of a hill into a landscape which is curiously exciting. What were once quarries and spoil heaps are now landscaped, with many transformed into nature reserves. The largest mountain of waste, built with spoil from the old Judkins Quarry, is known as Mount Judd, or locally 'Jees'. This distinctly man-made landscape is broken up with unexpected stretches of open countryside, with fine views away to the north across the Anker valley. The canal passes below the town of Hartshill: the attractive buildings in the Canal & River Trust yard are crowned by a splendid clock tower, and those travelling on the canal will want to slow right down to enjoy the mellow architecture and old dock. The canal then continues towards Mancetter, leaving the quarry belt and moving into open rolling country backed by thick woods to the west. The railway closes from the east as the canal approaches Atherstone.

WALKING AND CYCLING
From Hartshill Yard you can walk south west to the Fox & Hounds, through Hartshill Hayes Country Park, then north by Mancetter Quarries, Quarry Farm, Purley Park and The Outwoods to Atherstone. After refreshment in the pub it is an easy return along the canal.

Hartshill
Warwicks. PO, tel, stores, chemist, takeaways. Once a mining community, Hartshill has now been swallowed up by Nuneaton, and as such its interest lies mainly in its past. The Romans recognised its strategic importance. There is evidence that they settled here, as both kilns and fragments of pottery have been unearthed. Hugh de Hardreshull chose it as a site for his castle in 1125, the view from the ridge enabling him to see as far as the distant peaks of Derbyshire on a clear day. Below, on the plains, can be counted the towers and steeples of 40 churches. Hartshill's most famous claim is that it was the birthplace of the poet Drayton in 1563, a friend of both Ben Johnson and Shakespeare. Drayton's greatest work was *Polyolbion*, a survey of the country with a son for each county. He died in 1631 and was buried in Westminster. There are fine walks over Hartshill Green to Oldbury Camp, a Bronze Age hill-fort covering 7 acres. Hartshill's shops are a 15-minute walk from the canal. There is a useful parade of *shops* at Chapel End.

Hartshill Yard Hartshill, Nuneaton. Part of the yard contains a 19th-C carpenters' workshop and blacksmiths' forge.

Mancetter
Warwicks. PO, tel, stores. About ½ mile east of bridge 36. The church dates from the 13th C, but its best feature is the large collection of 18th-C slate tombstones displaying all the elegance of Georgian incised lettering. There are some almshouses of 1728 in the churchyard, and across the road another row with pretty Victorian Gothic details. The manor, south of the church, is rather over-restored. It was from this house, in 1555, that Robert Glover was led when the Bishop of Lichfield ordered his arrest. A victim of the reign of Mary Tudor, he was seized and taken to the stake, where he was executed alongside a poor cap-maker from Coventry.

Pubs and Restaurants

4 The Anchor Inn Hartshill, Nuneaton CV10 0RT (024 7639 3444; www.theanchorinnhartshill.co.uk). Traditional pub serving real ale and food *daily 12.00–21.00 (Sun 18.00* – carvery). Dog- and child-friendly, garden. Real fires. *Open Mon–Sat 12.00–22.00 (Fri–Sat 23.00) & Sun 12.00–20.00.*

5 The Stag & Pheasant The Green, Hartshill, Nuneaton CV10 0SW (024 7639 6352). Overlooking the village green, this pub serves real ale and food *Wed–Sat E & Sun L.* Dog- and family-friendly, garden. Traditional pub games. *Open Mon–Fri E & Sat–Sun 12.00–00.00 (Sun 22.30).*

6 The Blue Boar Watling Street, Mancetter CV9 1NE (01827 716166; www.blueboarmancetter.co.uk). 1940s rebuild of an earlier pub of the same name serving real ales and food *Sun–Fri L and E & Sat 12.00–21.00.* Family-friendly. Traditional pub games and sports TV. *Open 12.00–23.00.*

Also try: **7 Maid of the Mill** 85 Coleshill Road, Atherstone CV9 2AB (01827 716517) and **8 The Royal Oak** Oldbury Road, Hartshill CV10 0TD (024 7639 6442; www.theroyaloakhartshill.co.uk).

Boatyards

Ⓑ **Springwood Haven Marina** Springwood Haven, Mancetter Road, Nuneaton CV10 0RZ (024 7639 3676; www.springwoodhaven.co.uk).
DE Pump out, gas, boat hire, overnight and long-term mooring, narrowboat slipway, boat and engine sales and repairs, welding, fabrication, painting, boat fitting out, chandlery, toilets, solid fuel, Wi-Fi. Also to be found at Springwood Haven Marina is **Onboard Energy** (024 7639 3676; www.onboardenergy.co.uk). A specialist company supplying electrical power systems for leisure craft.

CRT Hartshill Yard Clock Hill, Hartshill (0303 040 4040).

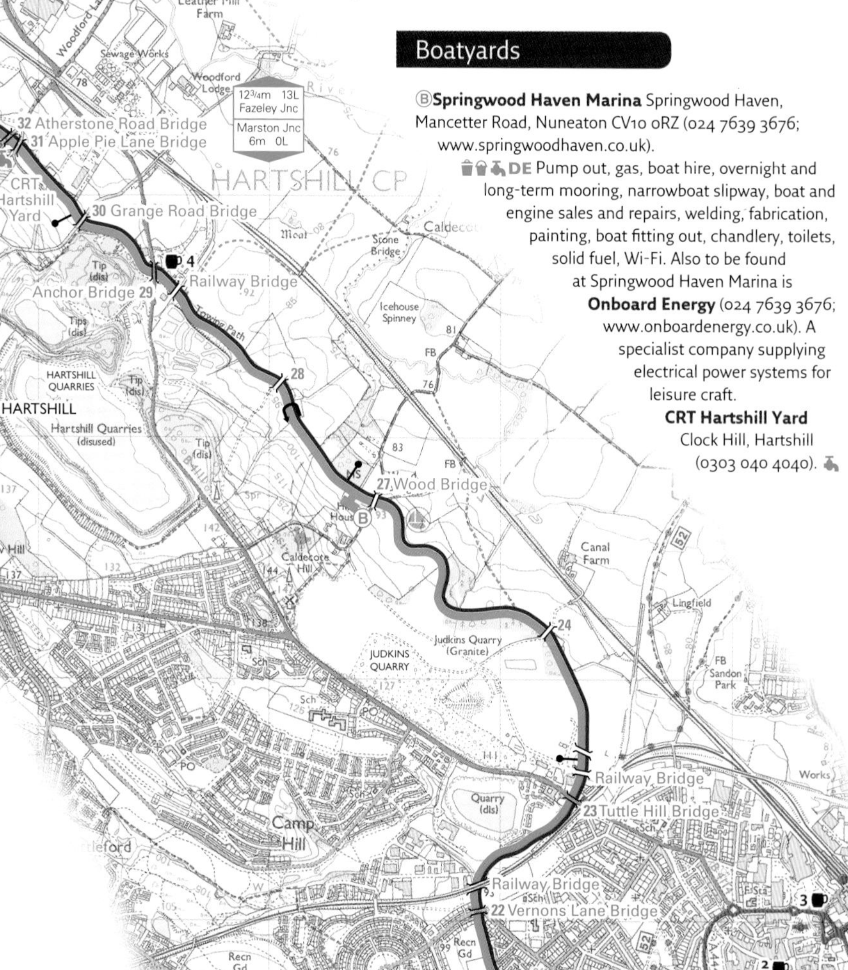

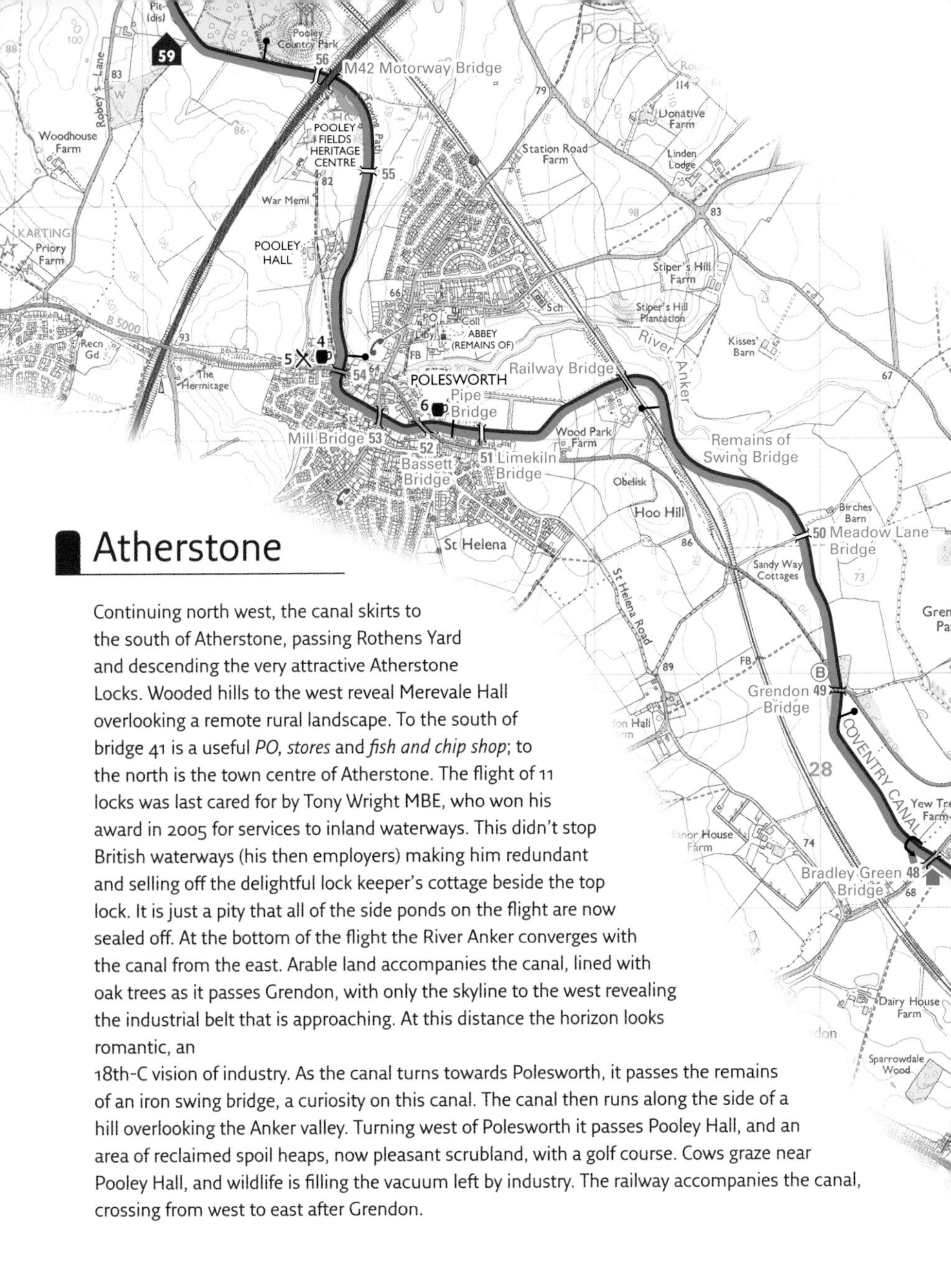

Atherstone

Continuing north west, the canal skirts to the south of Atherstone, passing Rothens Yard and descending the very attractive Atherstone Locks. Wooded hills to the west reveal Merevale Hall overlooking a remote rural landscape. To the south of bridge 41 is a useful *PO, stores* and *fish and chip shop*; to the north is the town centre of Atherstone. The flight of 11 locks was last cared for by Tony Wright MBE, who won his award in 2005 for services to inland waterways. This didn't stop British waterways (his then employers) making him redundant and selling off the delightful lock keeper's cottage beside the top lock. It is just a pity that all of the side ponds on the flight are now sealed off. At the bottom of the flight the River Anker converges with the canal from the east. Arable land accompanies the canal, lined with oak trees as it passes Grendon, with only the skyline to the west revealing the industrial belt that is approaching. At this distance the horizon looks romantic, an 18th-C vision of industry. As the canal turns towards Polesworth, it passes the remains of an iron swing bridge, a curiosity on this canal. The canal then runs along the side of a hill overlooking the Anker valley. Turning west of Polesworth it passes Pooley Hall, and an area of reclaimed spoil heaps, now pleasant scrubland, with a golf course. Cows graze near Pooley Hall, and wildlife is filling the vacuum left by industry. The railway accompanies the canal, crossing from west to east after Grendon.

- **Atherstone**
  Warwicks. All services. A pleasant town, with a strong 18th-C feeling, especially in the open market place in front of the church.
  Merevale Atherstone CV9 2HG. A large battlemented house, high to the west, is Merevale Hall, an early 19th-C mock Tudor mansion. To the west are the remains of the 12th-C abbey and the very pretty 13th-C church which contains fine stained glass, monuments and brasses.
- **Grendon**
  Warwicks. 1/2 mile north east of bridge 48. Grendon is just a small church set in beautiful parkland. The woods and rolling fields are a last refuge before the industrial landscape that precedes Tamworth.
- **Polesworth**
  Warwicks. PO, tel, stores, chemist, butchers, hardware, greengrocer, takeaways, fish & chips, off-licence, garage. The splendid gatehouse and the clerestory are all that remain of the 10th-C abbey, where Egbert, first Saxon King of England, built a nunnery.

Pubs and Restaurants

1 The Atherstone Red Lion Hotel 99 Long Street, Atherstone CV9 1BB (01827 713156; www.atherstoneredlion.co.uk). Friendly residential hotel serving real ale. Food available *daily 12.00-21.00, Sun* carvery. Conservatory, library and sports TV. Children welcome. B&B. *Open daily 10.00-23.00 (Fri-Sat 00.00).*

2 The Kings Head Grendon Terrace, Watling Street, Atherstone CV9 2PA (01827 712078; www.thekingsheadatherstone.co.uk). Beside Bridge 43. Real ale, along with bar and à la carte meals *L and E.* Dog- and family-friendly, outside seating. Traditional pub games, real fires and sports TV. Mooring. *Open daily 12.00-23.00 (Sun 22.30).*

3 The Market Tavern 21 Market Street, Atherstone CV9 1ET (01926 450747; www.warwickshirebeer.co.uk/market-tavern-atherstone). 16th-C pub located in the historic market square. At least six real ales can be enjoyed here together with filled rolls, snacks, tea and coffee. Dog-friendly, outside seating. Real fires and sports TV. *Open Mon-Thu 16.00-23.00 & Fri-Sun (12.00-23.00).*

4 The Bulls Head Tamworth Road, Polesworth, Tamworth B78 1JH (01827 893022). West of Bridge 54. Friendly, community pub serving real ale. Traditional pub games, sports TV and Wi-Fi. *Open daily 11.00-00.00 (Sun 23.30).*

5 India Garden Tamworth Road, Polesworth B78 1JH (01827 894112). Above the Bulls Head, this popular restaurant serves excellent Asian food and is always happy to pop downstairs for your favourite pint. Takeaway service. *Open daily 17.30-00.00.*

6 The Royal Oak Grendon Road, Polesworth, Tamworth B78 1NU (01827 892378; www.royaloakpolesworth.co.uk). Beside Bridge 52. Traditional, community pub, serving real ale. *Weekend* live music. Traditional pub games, sports TV and Wi-Fi. *Open daily 12.00-23.00 (Fri-Sat 00.00).*

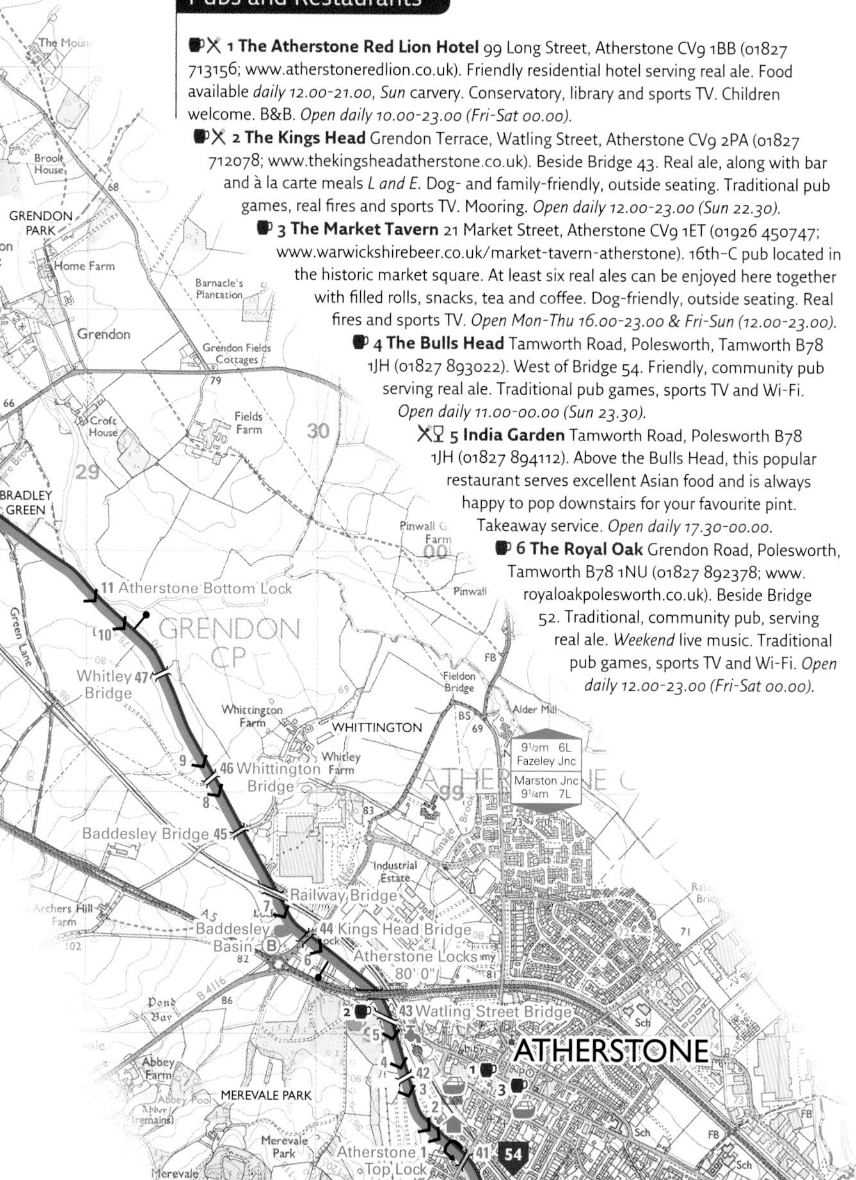

Tamworth

At Alvecote Priory the tree-surrounded ruins provide a sudden glimpse of history, while across the canal is Pooley Field Nature Reserve, firm evidence that the canal has now shed its industrial past. The canal then widens by two boatyards. Reaching Tamworth the canal runs through suburban housing, turning in a wide sweep south west past Tamworth towards Fazeley Junction, through the only locks on this stretch, at Glascote. Houses and factories flank the canal as it passes Kettlebrook Wharf, and then it moves briefly into more open country, crossing the River Tame on an impressive aqueduct. There are useful *stores* south of bridge 76. At Fazeley Junction the Coventry Canal meets the Birmingham & Fazeley Canal (*see* page 45), and then continues north west towards Fradley Junction, initially on the Birmingham & Fazeley Canal – the named bridges being an obvious clue. Much housing has been built around Fazeley Junction, and a short arm with a crane, Peel's Wharf, surrounded by dwellings, completes an attractive urban scene. This all soon gives way to lightly wooded open fields towards Hopwas Hill as the canal follows the course of the River Tame very closely, passing below Hopwas village. Just beyond here there is a delightful wooded stretch that covers the side of the hill. Landing is forbidden because these are the Whittington Firing Ranges. After the wood the canal continues in a side cut embankment with a view of Tamworth away to the east.

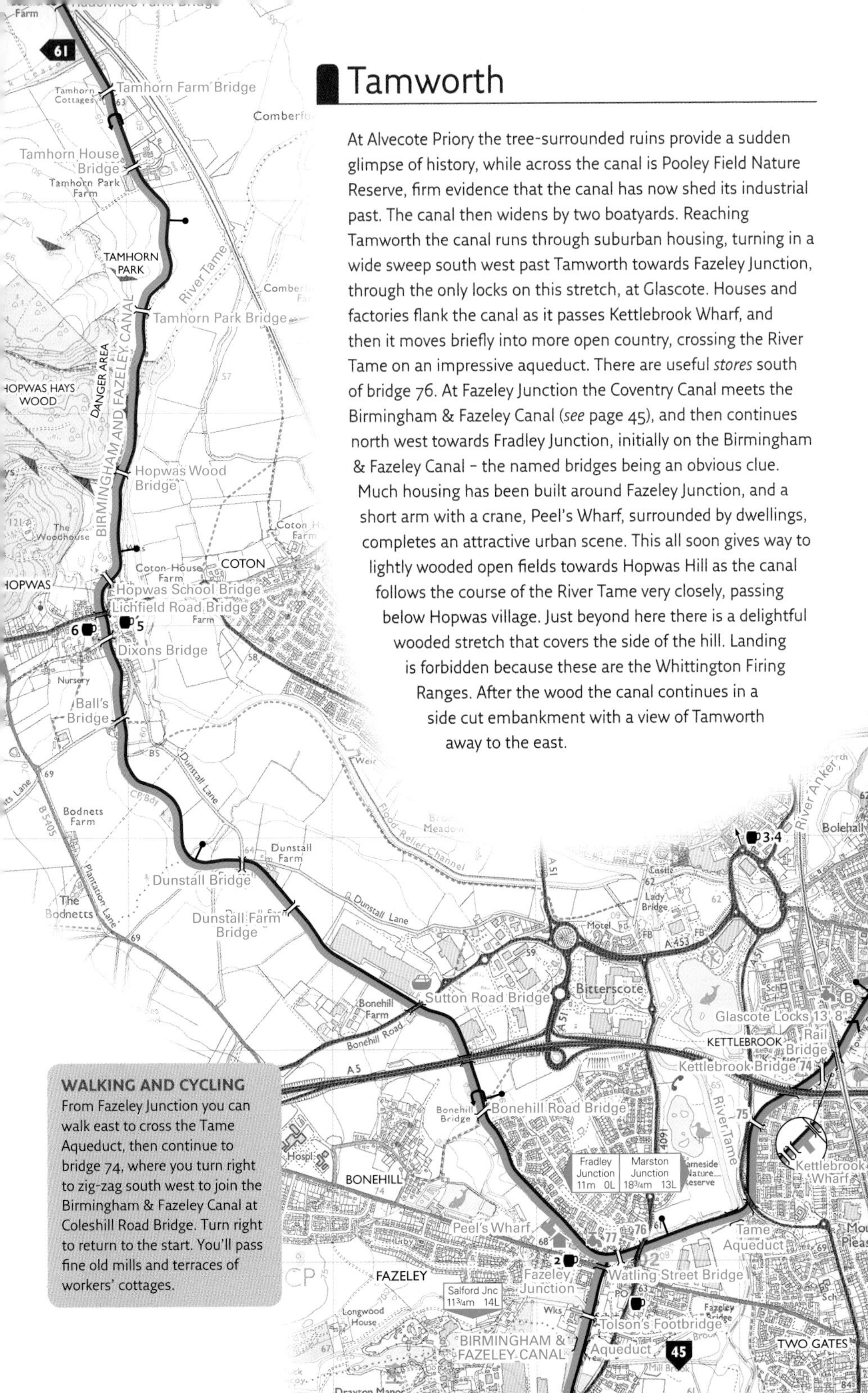

WALKING AND CYCLING

From Fazeley Junction you can walk east to cross the Tame Aqueduct, then continue to bridge 74, where you turn right to zig-zag south west to join the Birmingham & Fazeley Canal at Coleshill Road Bridge. Turn right to return to the start. You'll pass fine old mills and terraces of workers' cottages.

● **Amington**
Staffs. PO, tel, stores, takeaway, off-licence, chemist, fish & chips. The village, now an indistinguishable suburb of Tamworth, was once the focus of Amington Hall, an early 19th-C Grade II*, listed country house.

● **Tamworth**
Staffs. All services. Tamworth was originally a Saxon settlement, although only earthworks survive from this period.

Tamworth Castle The Holloway (off Castle Street), Tamworth B79 7NA (01827 709626; www.tamworthcastle.co.uk). With a Norman motte, an Elizabethan timbered hall and Jacobean apartments, it is a splendid mélange of styles. *Open Apr-Oct, Tue-Sun 11.30-16.00 & Nov-Mar, Sat-Sun 12.00-16.00. Also Mon B Hols and summer school Hols.* Charge.

Tourist Information Centre Marmion House, Lichfield Street, Tamworth B79 7BZ (01827 709581; www.tamworth.gov.uk/tamworth-information-centre). *Open Mon-Fri 8.45-17.00 & Sat 09.00-15.30.*

● **Fazeley Junction**
Staffs. PO, tel, stores, chemist, takeaways, fish & chips, off-licence, garage in Fazeley.

● **Hopwas**
Staffs. PO box, tel. A pretty and tidy village with a green, built on the side of a hill. Anyone walking should look out for the danger flags for Whittington Firing Ranges.

Boatyards

Ⓑ **Alvecote Marina and Narrowcraft** Grendon Dock, Robey's Lane, Alvecote B78 1AS (01827 898585; www.narrowboat.co.uk). D Pump out, gas, overnight and long-term mooring, winter storage, boat sales, boat and engine repairs, dry dock, welding and fabrication, bottom blacking, painting, Boat Safety Scheme, chandlery, solid fuel, books, maps and gifts. Boatyard *open Tue-Sat 08.30-17.30* and **The Samuel Barlow** *open Tue-Sun 12.00-23.00.* Food available *L and E.*

Ⓑ **Norton Canes Boatbuilders** Glascote Basin, Basin Lane, Glascote, Tamworth B77 2AH (01827 311317/07793 026669; www.nortoncanesboatbuilders.co.uk). D Pump out, gas, solid fuel, slipway, short- and long-term moorings, winter storage, self-storage, boat and engine sales and repairs, boat building and restoration, carpentry, small chandlery, dry dock, paint dock, boat blacking, welding, fabrication, DIY facilities.

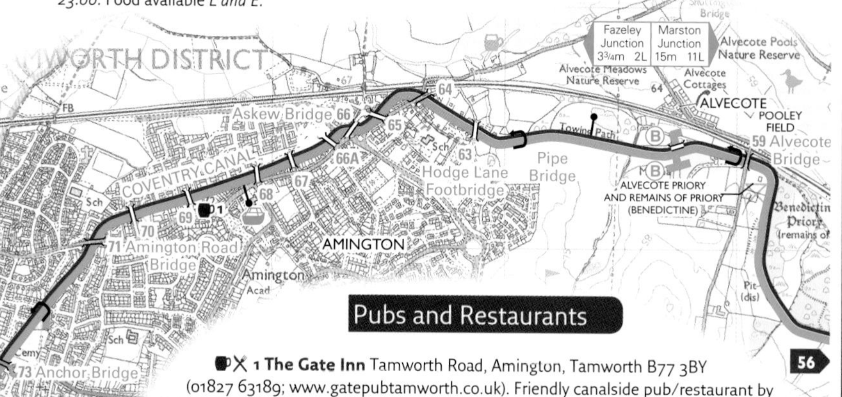

Pubs and Restaurants

1 The Gate Inn Tamworth Road, Amington, Tamworth B77 3BY (01827 63189; www.gatepubtamworth.co.uk). Friendly canalside pub/restaurant by bridge 69, serving real ale and food *daily 12.00-21.00 (Sun 17.00).* Child- and dog-friendly, garden and play area. Sports TV and Wi-Fi. Moorings. *Open 11.00-23.00 (Fri-Sat 23.30).*

2 The Three Tuns 32 Lichfield Street, Fazeley, Tamworth B78 3QN (07983 572589; www.threetunsfazeley.com/index). Lively canalside pub serving real ale. Dog-friendly, garden. Traditional pub games, real fires, sports TV and Wi-Fi. Live music *Fri.* Moorings. *Open Mon-Thu 15.00-23.00 & Fri-Sun 12.00-00.00 (Sun 23.00).*

3 The Globe Inn Lower Gungate, Tamworth B79 7AT (01827 60455; www.theglobetamworth.com). Selling a range of real ales, often from local micro-breweries, this hotel bar also offers, meals *Mon-Fri L and E, Sat 11.00-21.00 & Sun 12.00-16.00.* Family-friendly. Traditional pub games, sports TV and Wi-Fi. B&B. *Open Mon-Sat 11.00-23.00 (Fri-Sat 00.00) & Sun 12.00-23.00.*

4 The Sir Robert Peel 13-15 Lower Gungate, Tamworth B79 7BA (01827 300910). Award-winning CAMRA pub serving an ever-changing range of real ales and ciders. National micro-breweries are usually well represented. Dog-friendly, beer terrace and Wi-Fi. *Open Mon-Fri 14.00-23.00 (Tue 16.00) & Sat-Sun 12.00-23.00.*

5 The Tame Otter Litchfield Road, Hopwas B78 3AF (01827 53361; www.vintageinn.co.uk/thetameotterhopwastamworth). Canalside pub serving real ale. Food *all day, every day.* Children welcome. Garden and Moorings. *Open 12.00-23.00 (Sun 22.30).*

6 The Red Lion Litchfield Road, Hopwas B78 3AF (01827 62514). A canalside pub with an extensive garden, offering real ale. Serving a range of meals and snacks *Mon-Sat 10.00-21.00 (Fri-Sat 21.30) & Sun 10.00-19.00.* Family-friendly and garden. Traditional pub games, real fires, sports TV and Wi-Fi. *Open daily 10.00-23.00.*

Whittington and Fradley Junction

Between Whittington Bridge and Bridge 78 the canal changes from being the Birmingham & Fazeley Canal to the Coventry Canal (*see* Introduction, page 47). A stone marks the actual point. At Huddlesford the remains of the eastern end of the Wyrley & Essington Canal, now referred to as the Lichfield Canal and presently used only for moorings, branches to the south west. This route, which extends west to Ogley Junction on the Anglesey Branch of the BCN, is the subject of an energetic and effective restoration campaign. Problems of obstruction by the new M6 Toll road have been overcome with the installation of an aqueduct and there is increasing restoration activity in the area. The Coventry Canal then runs northwards through flat, open country towards Fradley Junction. Once an airfield, this is now a vast modern industrial estate. There are no locks, but a swing bridge announces your arrival at Fradley. Here the Coventry Canal meets the Trent & Mersey Canal, overlooked by The Swan, a famous canal landmark.

- **Fisherwick**
  Staffs. Tel. A small hamlet overlooking the canal.
- **Whittington**
  Staffs. PO, tel, stores, chemist, takeaway, off-licence. The village centre is to the west of Whittington Bridge; shops are best approached from bridge 78.
- **Lichfield**
  Staffs. All services. Two miles south west along the A38. Although not on the canal, Lichfield is well worth a visit for its three-spired, medieval cathedral alone.
  St Mary's Heritage Centre Market Square, Lichfield WS13 6LG (01543 256611; www.lichfieldheritage.org.uk). Formed from a redundant church (although worship is still very much alive in the adjoining Dyott Chapel and Chancel) to serve the community in a number of imaginative ways, this is the place to visit to learn about the city and its surroundings. There is something to appeal to all ages including the Staffordshire Millennium Embroidery Gallery and a tower viewing platform. Undergoing redevelopment so telephone for visiting details.
  Tourist Information Centre The Friary, Litchfield WS13 6QG (01543 308924; www.visitlichfield.co.uk). *Open Mon-Sat 09.30-15.30.*
- **Huddlesford**
  Staffs. PO box. At Huddlesford Junction the Wyrley & Essington Canal used to join the Coventry. Long abandoned, the first 1/4 mile is used for moorings and the remainder is scheduled for restoration, with much work already done.
- **Fradley**
  Staffs. PO, tel, stores, chemist, takeaway, fish & chips, off-licence. A small village set to the east of the canal, and well away from the junction. It owed its prosperity to the airfield which is not used as such any more.
- **Fradley Junction**
  Staffs. PO box, tel. A long- established canal centre where the Coventry Canal joins the Trent & Mersey Canal. There is a boatyard, a Canal & River Trust Information Centre and café (01283 792508), moorings, a boat club and a popular pub - all in the middle of a five-lock flight.

Boatyards

Ⓑ**Kings Orchard Marina** Broad Lane, Huddlesford, Lichfield WS13 8SP (01543 433608; www.canalmarinas.com/kings-orchard). D Pump out, gas, coal, long- and short-term moorings, books, maps, toilets, showers, laundry, shop, camping.

Ⓑ**Streethay Wharf** Streethay Wharf, Streethay, Lichfield WS13 8RJ (07824 848444; 217.199.187.59/streethaywharf.co.uk/narrowboats). D Pump out, gas, day-hire craft, overnight and long-term mooring, winter storage, wet dock, slipway, crane, boat and engine sales and repairs, boat building, telephone, toilets, showers, chandlery, solid fuel, laundrette, DIY facilities. *Emergency call out.*

Ⓑ**Tom's Moorings** Streethay Basin, Streethay, Lichfield WS13 8RJ (01840 770128/07860 729522; www.bargemovers.com). Pump out, gas, overnight and long-term mooring.

Ⓑ**CRT Fradley Junction** Alrewas, Burton-on-Trent DE13 7DN (0303 040 4040; www.canalrivertrust.org.uk). Overnight mooring, long-term mooring, toilets.

Ⓑ**Fradley Marine Services** Fradley Junction, Alrewas, Burton-on-Trent DE13 7DN (01283 790332). D Pump out, gas, solid fuel, overnight and long-term mooring, DIY facilities, boat repairs, gift shop, chandlery, provisions, gallery of artists and crafters, tearoom. Can issue CRT boat licences.

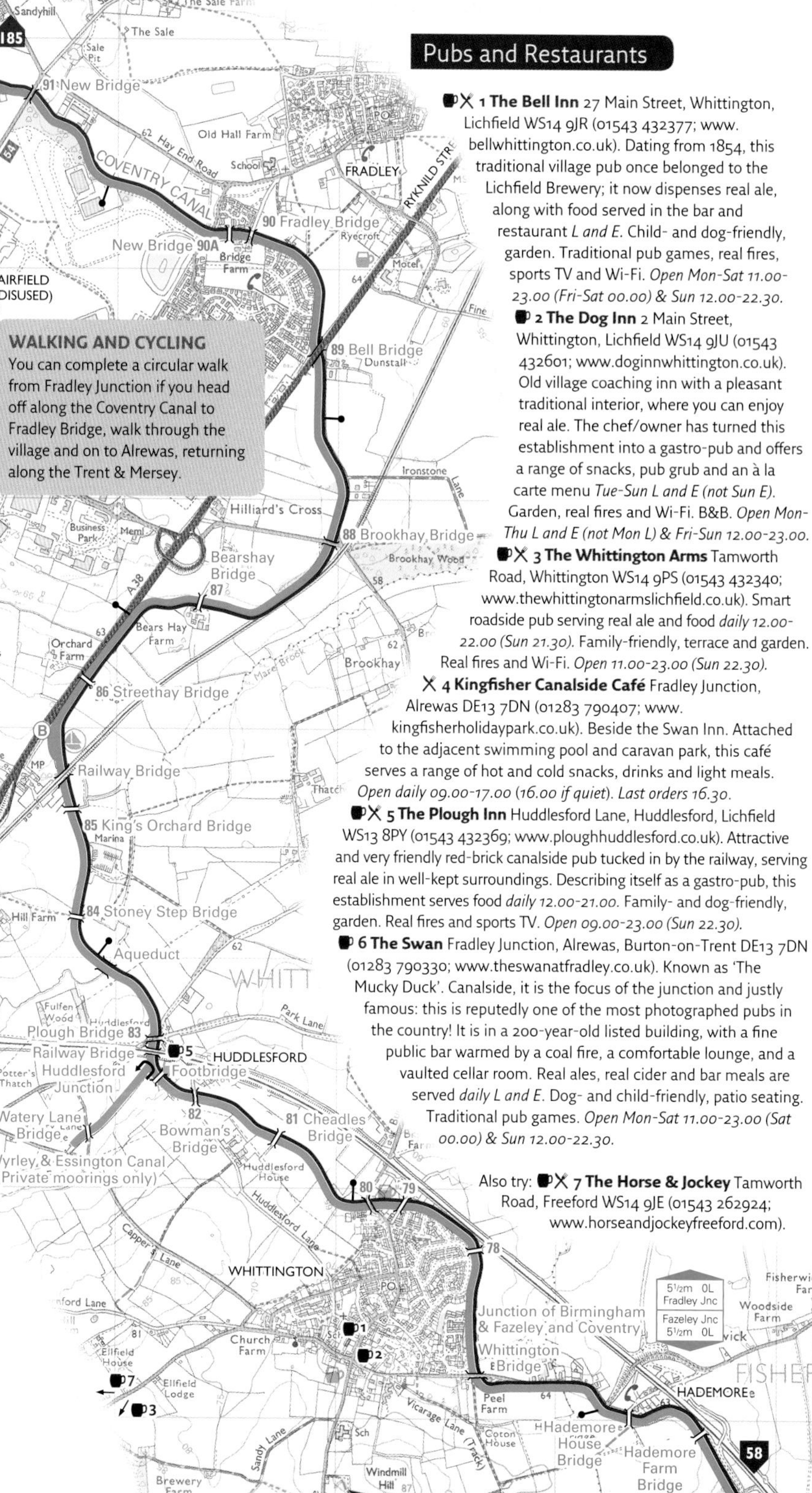

Pubs and Restaurants

1 The Bell Inn 27 Main Street, Whittington, Lichfield WS14 9JR (01543 432377; www.bellwhittington.co.uk). Dating from 1854, this traditional village pub once belonged to the Lichfield Brewery; it now dispenses real ale, along with food served in the bar and restaurant *L and E*. Child- and dog-friendly, garden. Traditional pub games, real fires, sports TV and Wi-Fi. *Open Mon-Sat 11.00-23.00 (Fri-Sat 00.00) & Sun 12.00-22.30.*

2 The Dog Inn 2 Main Street, Whittington, Lichfield WS14 9JU (01543 432601; www.doginnwhittington.co.uk). Old village coaching inn with a pleasant traditional interior, where you can enjoy real ale. The chef/owner has turned this establishment into a gastro-pub and offers a range of snacks, pub grub and an à la carte menu *Tue-Sun L and E (not Sun E)*. Garden, real fires and Wi-Fi. B&B. *Open Mon-Thu L and E (not Mon L) & Fri-Sun 12.00-23.00.*

3 The Whittington Arms Tamworth Road, Whittington WS14 9PS (01543 432340; www.thewhittingtonarmslichfield.co.uk). Smart roadside pub serving real ale and food *daily 12.00-22.00 (Sun 21.30)*. Family-friendly, terrace and garden. Real fires and Wi-Fi. *Open 11.00-23.00 (Sun 22.30).*

4 Kingfisher Canalside Café Fradley Junction, Alrewas DE13 7DN (01283 790407; www.kingfisherholidaypark.co.uk). Beside the Swan Inn. Attached to the adjacent swimming pool and caravan park, this café serves a range of hot and cold snacks, drinks and light meals. *Open daily 09.00-17.00 (16.00 if quiet). Last orders 16.30.*

5 The Plough Inn Huddlesford Lane, Huddlesford, Lichfield WS13 8PY (01543 432369; www.ploughhuddlesford.co.uk). Attractive and very friendly red-brick canalside pub tucked in by the railway, serving real ale in well-kept surroundings. Describing itself as a gastro-pub, this establishment serves food *daily 12.00-21.00*. Family- and dog-friendly, garden. Real fires and sports TV. *Open 09.00-23.00 (Sun 22.30).*

6 The Swan Fradley Junction, Alrewas, Burton-on-Trent DE13 7DN (01283 790330; www.theswanatfradley.co.uk). Known as 'The Mucky Duck'. Canalside, it is the focus of the junction and justly famous: this is reputedly one of the most photographed pubs in the country! It is in a 200-year-old listed building, with a fine public bar warmed by a coal fire, a comfortable lounge, and a vaulted cellar room. Real ales, real cider and bar meals are served *daily L and E*. Dog- and child-friendly, patio seating. Traditional pub games. *Open Mon-Sat 11.00-23.00 (Sat 00.00) & Sun 12.00-22.30.*

Also try: **7 The Horse & Jockey** Tamworth Road, Freeford WS14 9JE (01543 262924; www.horseandjockeyfreeford.com).

WALKING AND CYCLING

You can complete a circular walk from Fradley Junction if you head off along the Coventry Canal to Fradley Bridge, walk through the village and on to Alrewas, returning along the Trent & Mersey.

CROMFORD CANAL

MAXIMUM DIMENSIONS (AS BUILT)

From Langley Mill to the east end of Butterley Tunnel and Pinxton:
Length: 78' 6"
Beam: 14' 0"
Draught: 3' 0"
Headroom: 8' 0"

From the east end of Butterley Tunnel to Cromford and Lea:
Length: 78' 0"
Beam: 7' 0"
Draught: 3' 0"
Headroom: 8' 0"

MILEAGE

GREAT NORTHERN BASIN junction with the Erewash Canal to:
Codnor Park: 4 miles
Butterley Tunnel west portal: 6½ miles
Ambergate: 9 miles
CROMFORD WHARF: 14½ miles, 14 locks

Pinxton Branch: 2¼ miles, no locks

FRIENDS OF THE CROMFORD CANAL

Weighbridge Office, Gothic Warehouse, Mill Road, Cromford DE4 3RQ
07552 055455
sales@cromfordcanal.info
www.cromfordcanal.info/sales/sales.htm

General Note: With a waterway that was abandoned almost 75 years ago it would be surprising, indeed, if all the bridges, locks and associated infrastructure remained intact. In many cases structures marked on the map are no longer extant so it is the site of such features that has been recorded, hopefully to be replaced in the course of future restoration.

Construction of the Cromford Canal was viewed, in general, as a logical development of the recently realised vision of James Brindley's Grand Cross and, specifically, as an extension of the Erewash Canal.

Coal mining was prolific along the proposed route, while leadworks at Lea (and more widely in the Wirksworth area) together with an ironworks at Alderwasley would ensure reliable sources of traffic. However, being water-powered, it's unlikely that Arwright's Cromford cotton mills were seen as beneficiaries and there is little evidence that cotton (either in its raw or processed form) was ever carried.

The enabling Act was passed on 15th July 1789 and William Jessop was appointed as principal engineer, with Benjamin Outram as superintendent of works. The canal was opened to Pinxton in June 1792, although the challenges attached to the construction of Butterley Tunnel and the aqueducts at Bullbridge and Leawood conspired to delay the waterway's full opening until August 1794, with the private Leawood Arm connecting to lead smelters, mills and quarries finally finished in 1802. Throughout Wheatcroft & Sons were the principal long-distance carriers.

Traffic peaked at 300,000 tons per annum which was maintained pretty much until the 1850s, by which time the inevitable railway competition had begun to bite. The canal company responded by lowering rates with the outcome that toll income more or less halved, as did share dividends.

In 1852 the canal was sold to the Manchester, Buxton, Matlock & Midlands Junction Railway which only accelerated decline so that by 1870 trade was also halved and, in 1888, stood at a mere 46,000 tons, with more and more trade becoming local. The Butterley Tunnel collapse of 1889 exacerbated this trend and, although re-opened four years later, the final collapse in 1900 ensured that the remaining, isolated traffic, was predominantly coal from Pinxton onto the connected canal system,

Nightingale Arm

along with limestone (Bullbridge) and coal (Hartshay Pit) cargoes criss-crossing along the western section.

The navigation was finally abandoned in 1944 and restoration is now in the capable hands of the Friends of the Cromford Canal, who are working from both ends to revive the waterway for future generations of walkers and boaters to enjoy.

WALKING AND CYCLING

To get the most out of walking along the route of the Cromford Canal, and in the general area of the waterway, A Walker's Guide to the Cromford Canal – published by The Friends of The Cromford Canal – is a must. For a fascinating and highly illustrated insight into the waterway, Hugh Potter's the Cromford Canal is essential reading. Both can be purchased by visiting www.cromfordcanal.info/sales/books.htm.

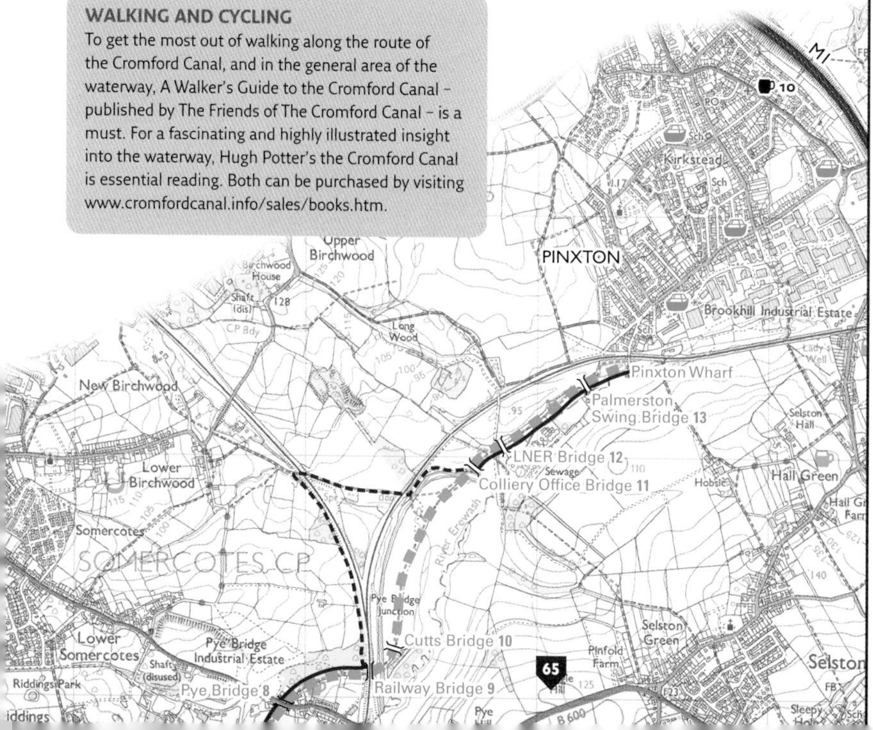

Ironville

A route has been identified to take the waterway under, and to the east of, the A610 trunk road using a redundant railway bridge so that it can re-join its original course near Stoney Lane, south of the flashes caused by mining subsidence. It will again cross the Erewash on an aqueduct beside the steel footbridge – where evidence of its predecessor is just visible in the form of masonry at water level on each bank – before making a beeline across the fields to Boat Lane at Stoneyford. Not only has the landscape been affected by deep-mining subsidence, the whole area has also been the subject of open-cast activity, so it is with some relief that a recognisable towpath and reed-filled channel are finally reached above Butterley Lock No 8. From here the substantial evidence of the navigation, with its lock flight more or less intact, is heart-warming, making light of the ascent to Codnor Park Reservoir and an onward perambulation to either Pinxton or the eastern portal of Butterley Tunnel.

- **Brinsley**
  Notts. PO, tel, stores, off-licence, takeaway, fish & chips. A major mining community, its past commemorated by the recently re-erected headstocks, following their sojourn in a local museum.
  Butterley Company Founded by Benjamin Outram in 1790 (and taken over by William Jessop Junior upon his death in 1805) this company grew to become one of the world's foremost iron founders, well known for the vast array of iron and steel structures produced over two centuries. These include London's Vauxhall Bridge and the trainshed of St Pancras Station, a multitude of canal bridges erected throughout Britain, together with their swan song boatlift, the Falkirk Wheel. Coal mining, limestone quarrying and brick making were also developed in tandem. Sadly, the company was placed in administration on 5th March 2009.
- **Codnor**
  Derbs. PO, tel, stores, chemist, delicatessen, off-licence, takeaway, fish & chips. Sitting aside the busy A610, the village was once a thriving mining community. Today it is notable for its ruined castle. Originally a Norman motte and bailey structure, it was replaced by a 13th-C stone construction held by the powerful de Grey family. In 2008 the ruin was the subject of a fascinating Channel 4, Time Team investigation.
- **Heanor**
  Derbs. PO, tel, stores, chemist, bank, baker, off-licence, takeaway. Set above the Erewash Valley, its name derived from the Old English meaning a high ridge, the village was once a mix of iron and coal workings, together with the manufacture of silk and cotton goods, predominantly hosiery.
- **Ironville**
  Derbs. PO, tel, stores, off-licence. Built by the Butterley Company as a model village in the 1830s to house its workers, many of the houses – notable for their spacious gardens – were demolished by the Local Authority in the late 20th C.
- **Jacksdale**
  Notts. PO, tel, stores, chemist, off-licence, hardware, takeaways, fish & chips, butcher, library. Another member of the Nottinghamshire Coalfield with the first pit sunk by James Oakes & Co in 1874. Pye Hill pit was the final coalmine to close in 1985 with the spoil heaps landscaped to form a nature reserve.
- **Langley Mill**
  Derbs. PO, tel, stores, chemist, off-licence, takeaways, garage, station. Set at the junction of the Erewash, Nottingham and Cromford Canals, this once industrial village was the home of Aristoc: manufacturer of silk stockings and, during the Second World War, parachutes and inflatable dinghies. The factory has long since disappeared under housing. See also page 84.
- **Pinxton**
  Derbs. PO, tel, stores, off-licence, delicatessen, chemist, butcher, takeaways, laundrette.

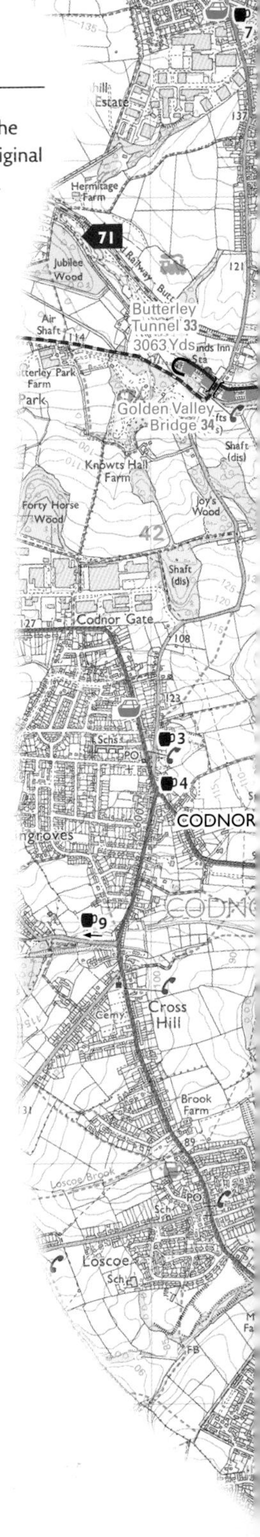

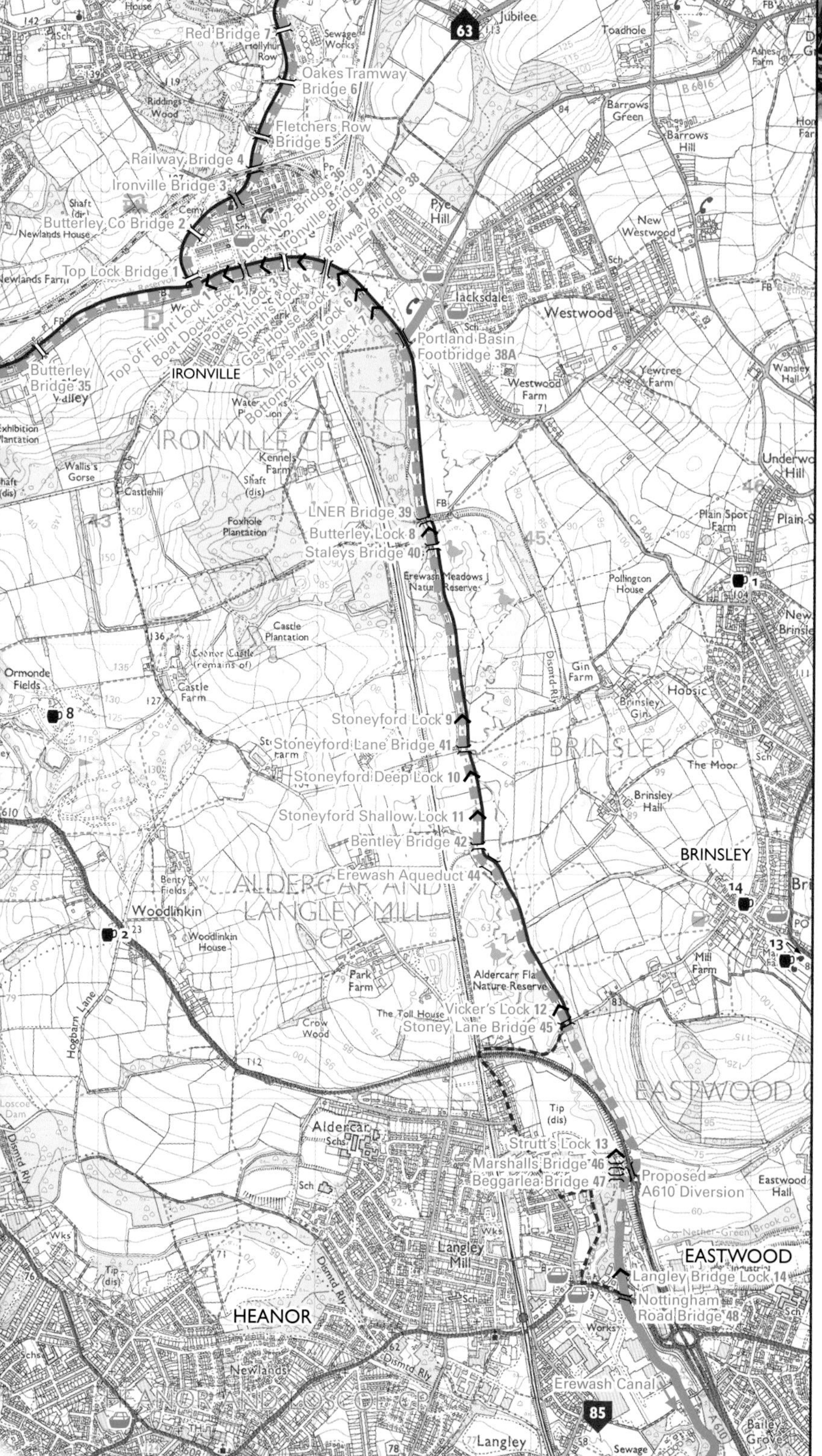
Red Bridge 7
Oakes Tramway Bridge 6
Fletchers Row Bridge 5
Railway Bridge 4
Ironville Bridge 3
Butterley Co Bridge 2
Top Lock Bridge 1
Lock No2 Bridge 36
Ironville Bridge 37
Railway Bridge 38
Top of Flight Lock 1
Boat Dock Lock 2
Pottery Lock 3
Smith's Lock 4
Gas House Lock 5
Marshalls Lock 6
Bottom of Flight Lock 7
Portland Basin Footbridge 38A
Butterley Bridge 35
IRONVILLE
IRONVILLE CP
LNER Bridge 39
Butterley Lock 8
Staleys Bridge 40
Erewash Meadows Nature Reserve
Stoneyford Lock 9
Stoneyford Lane Bridge 41
Stoneyford Deep Lock 10
Stoneyford Shallow Lock 11
Bentley Bridge 42
Erewash Aqueduct 44
ALDERCAR AND LANGLEY MILL CP
Aldercarr Flash Nature Reserve
The Toll House
Vicker's Lock 12
Stoney Lane Bridge 45
Strutt's Lock 13
Marshalls Bridge 46
Beggarlea Bridge 47
Proposed A610 Diversion
Langley Bridge Lock 14
Nottingham Road Bridge 48
Erewash Canal
Jubilee
Toadhole
Barrows Green
Barrows Hill
Pye Hill
Jacksdale
Westwood
New Westwood
Westwood Farm
Yewtree Farm
Wansley Hall
Underwood Hill
Plain Spot Farm
Pollington House
Gin Farm
Brinsley Gin
Hobsic
BRINSLEY CP
The Moor
Brinsley Hall
BRINSLEY
Mill Farm
EASTWOOD
Eastwood Hall
Codnor Castle (remains of)
Castle Farm
Castle Plantation
Foxhole Plantation
Kennels Farm
Castlehill
Wallis's Gorse
Exhibition Plantation
Newlands Farm
Newlands House
Riddings House
Riddings Wood
Ormonde Fields
Woodlinkin
Woodlinkin House
Park Farm
Crow Wood
Aldercar
Langley Mill
HEANOR
Newlands
Langley
Hogbarn Lane
Sewage Works

The long established deep mining of coal really took off in the village in the early 19th C with the coming of the Cromford Canal, and later the railway. There were also lime kilns, coke ovens and a china works.

Riddings

Derbs. PO, tel, stores, off-licence, takeaway. Its name meaning 'a clearing in the wood', the village originally developed around local, small-scale, coal and ironstone mining. The arrival of the Cromford Canal gave impetus to the establishment of iron furnaces and by-products - namely tar, sulphuric acid and various other chemicals - from the local gasworks contributed to the economy. Locally dug clay was used in the manufacture of bricks and pipes.

Riddings Pottery Greenhill Lane, Riddings DE55 4AY (01773 603181; www.riddingspottery.co.uk). The pottery has built its own gas-fired kiln, digs its clay locally and holds regular exhibitions. *Open to visitors whenever working.*

Travel A one-way expedition along the line of the waterway, returning by public transport, is relatively easy to accomplish using a mix of local buses and trains. Buses serve nearly all the towns, villages and hamlets along the route, although sometimes it is necessary to 'triangulate' the return trip: for example, following a walk from Langley Mill to Pinxton, the No 9.3 bus is caught back to Ripley and then the No 1 to Langley Mill. A regular train service runs along the Derwent Valley, from Derby to Matlock, with intermediate stops at Belper, Ambergate, Whatstandwell, Cromford and Matlock Bath. For further details contact Traveline (0871 200 22 33; www.traveline.info/about-traveline/traveline-services) or National Rail Enquires (03457 484950; www.nationalrail.co.uk).

Well Dressing In the Peak District and Derbyshire, from *May-Sep*, the ancient custom of Well Dressing takes place - a custom that celebrates water and the life it brings. Well dressings are pictures that are made from growing things (flower petals, bark, wool, fir cones, leaves, seeds and berries) constructed on a bed of soft clay which is spread over a wooden board, erected at the site of a well. Many villages have revived this tradition and a full list of dates are available by visiting www.visitpeakdistrict.com or by contacting a Tourist Information Centre.

Tourist Information Centre The Assembly Rooms, Market Place, Derby DE1 3AH (01332 643411; www,visitderby.co.uk/tourist-information-centre). *Open Mon-Sat 09.30-20.00.*

Birdswood at Cromford Wharf (see *page 77)*

WALKING AND CYCLING

For the intrepid cyclist, the route of the Cromford Canal is just about do-able with a few creative diversions. However, far more pleasure and overall insight into this lapsed waterway can be derived from walking the route, for which A Walker's Guide to the Cromford Canal is an essential companion (see Introduction on page 63 for more details).

It is currently impossible to follow the initial line of the waterway north out of Great Northern Basin so take the main A608 west towards Langley Mill for 150yds to the diminutive River Erewash. Turn right along the footpath on its west bank swinging left to join Cromford Road and turn right, continuing straight ahead up Plumptre Road where Cromford Road bends left. Passing under the A610 bypass bridge, follow the stone track round to the right, re-crossing the Erewash after some 400yds. After a further 150yds turn left across a field to follow the footpath signed to Brinsley Hill and Jacksdale. Follow this footpath across three fields, bearing left at the stile to re-cross the Erewash by a steel footbridge. Walk up the centre of the next three fields remaining approximately equidistant between the river and the railway line (using the stiles to cross the hedge lines) to join the recognisable line of the canal at Boat Lane beside the kennels.

Pubs and Restaurants (pages 62-65)

1 **The Durham** Ox 7 High Street, Brinsley NG16 5BN (01773 531052). Well patronised, community local dispensing real ales, real cider and bar snacks *daily 14.00-00.00 (Sat-Sun 12.00)*. Dog- and family-friendly *(until 21.00)* garden. Newspapers, real fires, sports TV and Wi-Fi. B&B. *Open Mon-Fri 16.00-00.00 (Fri 14.00) & Sat-Sun 12.00-00.00.*

2 **The Thorn Tree** 246 Nottingham Road, Woodlinkin NG16 4HG (01773 768675; www.thethorntreeinn.co.uk). Popular eatery serving real ales and excellent value food *Mon-Sun 11.30-21.30 (Sun 21.00)*. Terrace seating, children welcome. Incorporates George's takeaway fish and chip bar. Pub *open Mon-Sat 11.30-22.30 (Fri-Sat 23.00) & Sun 11.30-22.00*

3 **The Poet & Castle** 2 Alfreton Road, Codnor DE5 9QY (01773 744150; www.thepoetandcastle.co.uk) Recently refurbished pub dispensing a wide range of real ales, real cider and food *L and E*. Dog-friendly, garden and camping. Traditional pub games, newspapers, real fires and Wi-Fi. *Open Mon-Sat 12.00-23.00 Fri-Sat 00.00) and Sun 12.00-22.30.*

4 **The French Horn** Market Place, Codnor DE5 9SY (01773 742776). Friendly pub, with a packed weekly calendar of events, serving real ales and food *Tue-Sun 12.00-19.00 (Sun 15.00)*. Garden and children's play area. Traditional pub games, real fires and sports TV. *Open Mon 15.00-23.00 & Tue-Sun 12.00-23.00.*

5 **The Birdcage Tearooms** 43 Main Road, Leabrooks DE55 1LA (07926 587413). Lovely, quaint and quirky establishment, with attentive proprietors, serving breakfast, teas, coffee, sandwiches, nibbles, cakes and light lunches. Gluten-free options. Themed bistro nights. *Open Mon-Tue & Thu-Sat 09.00-16.00.*

6 **The Red Lion** 150 Greenhill Lane, Riddings DE55 4EX (01773 528172; www.redlionriddings.com). Lively, sports oriented community pub, serving real ales. Dog- and family-friendly, outside seating. Traditional pub games, sports TV and real fires. *Open Mon-Fri 17.00-00.00 (Fri 15.00) & Sat-Sun 12.00-00.00.*

7 **The Greenhill Tavern** Greenhill Lane, Riddings DE55 4AS (01773 602878; www.greenhilltavern.com). Friendly, welcoming pub serving real ale and real cider. Dog- and family-friendly *(until 19.00)*. Traditional pub games, sports TV and Wi-Fi. Quiz *Sun*. *Open daily 12.00-23.00;* 13 **The Brinsley Lodge Inn** 56a Mansfield Road, Brinsley NG16 5AE (01773 764053). Food-oriented hostelry serving real ale and food *daily 11.00-21.30 (Fri-Sat 22.30)*. Large garden and children's play area. Wi-Fi. *Open 11.00-23.00 (Sun 22.30);* 14 **The Lion at Brinsley** Hall Lane, Brinsley NG16 5AH (01773 714328). Open-plan pub serving real ale and food *Mon-Thu L and E (not Mon E) & Fri-Sun 12.00-21.00 (Sun 18.00)*. Dog- and family-friendly, large garden. Sports TV and Wi-Fi. *Open 12.00-23.00 (Sun 21.00).*

Also try: 8 **The Codnor** Castle Inn Nottingham Road, Codnor DE5 9RL (01773 744157; codnorcastleinn.co.uk; 9 **The Thorn Tree Inn** 161 Church Street, Waingroves, Ripley DE5 9TE (07929 620473); 10 **The Three Horseshoes** 78 Town Street, Pinxton NG16 6HN (01773 811803); 11 **Mayflower** 22 Birchwood Ln, Somercotes, Alfreton DE55 4LZ (011773 602372) and 12 **The Devonshire Arms** 241 Somercotes Hill, Somercotes DE55 4HX (01773 602808).

See also page 70

Ambergate

The walk along the old coach road, more or less following the route of Butterley Tunnel deep below, allows time for reflection on the three or so hours required to leg a fully-laden boat from one end to the other, before descending to Butterley Reservoir and the site of the closed engineering works. Two trunk roads intersect the line of the canal: the A38 on an extension to the tunnel and the A610 in a culvert, posing a significant challenge to restoration. There is a certain charm attached to the cottages lining the canal in Lower Hartshay, which is shared by the area surrounding the nearby Starvehimvalley Bridge, with the waterway widen to form a fishing lake. Passing through the car park of the Excavator pub, and behind the cottages strung out along Ripley Road in Sawmill village, the site of the demolished Bullbridge Aqueduct is reached, which once spanned road, railway and river. A further challenge to restoration is soon encountered at the cleared site of Stevenson's Dyeworks, with another immediately beyond Hag Tunnel in the form of the old Transco Works. At least the bridge here, carrying the water main from the Derwent Valley to Nottingham across the line of the navigation will, at a clearly labelled height of 10' 6", provide more that adequate air draught for future boaters' needs!

- **Ambergate**
  Derbs. Tel, PO box, takeaway, fish & chips, station. Situated within the Derwent Valley Mills UNESCO World Heritage Site, Ambergate is a relatively new name for the settlement which, until the early 19th C, went under the somewhat less attractive appellation of 'Toadmoor'. In 1966 the world's first fully electronic TXE2 telephone exchange opened in the village. From the beginning of the 19th C it was an important centre for lime burning and in 1876 a wire works opened beside the river.
- **Belper**
  Derbs. All services. A centre for nail making since medieval times, this fascinating and attractive town became well-known for its textile industry, following the Industrial Revolution. Surrounded by coal deposits and their associated ironstone seams, laid down in clay substrates, the settlement also became a focus for mining, brick making and iron working: Park Foundry, a forerunner in the solid fuel central heating boom of the 1960s and 70s, was established in the town. Perhaps lesser well known is the invention in 1938, by A B Williamson, of a substance for conditioning silk stockings. Made obsolete almost immediately by the arrival of nylon, it re-invented itself as a hand cleaner, later to be marketed as Swarfega!
- **Bullbridge**
  Derbs. PO box, tel. Location of the demolished canal aqueduct crossing of the main Ripley road, Midland Railway and River Amber. Limestone delivered from quarries in Crich was loaded onto barges for Butterley Ironworks here and James Stevenson established his main dye works alongside the waterway in 1908.
- **Crich**
  Derbs. PO, tel, stores, off-licence, takeaway, butcher, fish & chips, baker, delicatessen. Now home to the National Tramway Museum (see below) the village has seen limestone quarrying since Roman times. With the opening of the Butterley Company in 1790, production escalated and the local Hilt's and Cliff Quarries went on to supply vast quantities of carboniferous limestone, via a gravity tramway to Bullbridge, where some of the material was also burnt for local agricultural use. Crich Stand (01773 852350; www.crich-memorial.org.uk) a local landmark providing views over eight counties, was constructed in 1923 as a memorial to the Sherwood Foresters Regiment.

  Crich Tramway Village Crich DE4 5DP (01773 854321; www.tramway.co.uk). Vintage trams transport the visitor along a traditional village street out into open countryside. There are ever-changing exhibitions, a chance to watch expert craftsmen maintain and repair trams, together with the Stephenson Discovery and Learning Centre where you can view an audio visual presentation on the development of transport and the tram and how this impacted on people's changing lives. Café and shops, play areas, talks and tours, together with unlimited electric tram rides. *Open Mid Mar-Oct, daily 10.00-17.30.* Charge.

  Denby Pottery Village Derby Road, Denby DE5 8NX (01773 740799; www.denbypotteryvillage.co.uk). Museum, factory tour, Craft Room experience, regular events, farm shop and restaurant. Village *open Mon-Sat 09.30-17.30 (Sat 09.00) & Sun 11.00-17.00.* Bookable factory tours *Mon-Thu 11.00 & 13.00* (charge) and Craft Room experience *Fri-Sun 11.00 & 13.00* (charge).
- **Heage**
  Derbs. Tel, stores, off-licence. Probably best known for its six-sailed windmill built from local sandstone. Construction commenced in 1791 and there are records of it working in 1797. Each of its six sails weighs approximately one ton. Heage is also recognised as the site of Derbyshire's first coke-fired blast furnaces: the original erected in 1780 and the

second in 1818. Both closed in 1874 but remain in evidence in Morley Park.

Heage Windmill Chesterfield Rd, Belper DE56 2BH (01773 853579; www.heagewindmill.org.uk). Completed in 1797 and restored in 2002, this is the only working six-sailed, stone tower windmill in England and, as such, is Grade II* listed. Tours are available from guides in costume. Interpretation centre and shop selling souvenirs and light refreshments. *Open Apr-Oct, weekends and B Hols 11.00-16.00.* Charge.

- **Leabrooks**

Derbs. Tel, stores, chemist, butcher, off-licence, takeaway, fish & chips. Pretty much indistinguishable from Riddings, Leabrooks is notable for the manufacture of the Parker Knoll furniture range.

- **Lower Hartshay**

Derbs. Tel, PO box. Although Ripley is little more than a mile away (the distance recorded on an unusual milestone with the destinations written sideways on) hidden behind a low range of hills, there is little to disturb this settlement's pleasing mix of mellow red brick and whitewashed cottages. Especially since the colliery closed down in 1935.

Midland Railway Butterley Station, Ripley DE5 3QZ (01773 570140; www.midlandrailway-butterley.co.uk). Short, restored line setting out, via static and working museums, to commemorate the Derby-based Midland Railway Company, its predecessors and its successors. Train rides, footplate experience, catering services and guided tours. Country Park. Visit the website for further details and *opening times.* Charge.

- **Ripley**

Derbs. PO, tel, stores, chemists, baker, butcher, hardware, banks, off-licence, greengrocer, takeaway, fish & chips, library. Focus for much of the Butterley Company's three-pronged output, namely engineering, brick and aggregates. Although operating as three entirely separate entities, the company was a significant presence in the immediate area. The town was also an important centre for coal mining with around a dozen pits in the vicinity, several owned by the Butterley Company before Nationalisation.

- **Sawmills**

Derbs. Tel, PO, stores. A linear settlement sandwiched amidst the canal, road, railway and River Amber.

- **Swanwick**

Derbs. PO, tel, stores, chemist, butcher, fish & chips, takeaway, baker, off-licence, delicatessen, garage. Another centre for coalmining, initially on a small scale followed, in the 20th C, by a large pit which was sunk to the north of the settlement, closing in the 1960s. The site is now an industrial estate, home to Thornton's confectionary. The 'big house', Swanwick Hayes, was a World War II prisoner of war camp.

Strutt's North Mill Museum A chance to discover how Jedediah Strutt was instrumental in sparking the Industrial Revolution in the Derwent Valley, turning Belper into one of the world's foremost cotton mill towns. A living, industrial heritage museum, that explores the factory system's social impact on ordinary working people's lives through displays and changing exhibitions. Gift and book shop. Light refreshments. *Open Mar-Oct, Wed-Sun and B Hols & Nov and Feb, Sat-Sun 11.00-16.00.* Charge.

Tourist Information Centre Derwent valley Visitor Centre, Strutt's North Mill, Bridgefoot, Belper DE56 1YD (01773 880474; www.visitambervalley.co.uk). *Open as per Strutt's Mill.* Also at De Bradelei Stores, Chapel Street, Belper DE56 1AR (01773 827455; www.fashionfactoryoutlets.co.uk). *Open throughout the year, Mon-Sat 09.00-17.30 & Sun 10.00-17.00.*

WALKING AND CYCLING

It is worth following the line of the canal all the way through to the eastern end of Butterley Tunnel to view the portal, before retracing your steps and turning right along Newlands Road, taking the next right up Coach Road which parallels the tunnel to the closed Butterley Works and a T junction. Turn left and at the next bend walk straight ahead down Butterley Lane, following round to the right to cross under the A38 and immediately take the signed footpath on the left over the stile, dropping downhill beside the scrapyard to the western tunnel portal.

The line of the Pinxton Branch can be followed as far as the former Smotherfly opencast coal site - visible beyond the blue brick, twin-arched railway bridge - which necessitates a diversion. Turn left immediately before this bridge and follow a path for ½ mile, fenced off along the boundaries of two fields with the railway on the right, turning right where it meets the stone track. Follow this, under the railway, for approximately 500yds passing under a second railway line, and turn immediately left to follow the line for another 500yds before the path bears off to the right, away from the railway, to re-join the recognisable bed of the canal into Pinxton itself.

The Derwent Valley Heritage Way: the 55-mile route follows the River Derwent from Ladybower Reservoir to its mouth near Shardlow where it joins the River Trent, following paths, tracks, and some sections of road, waymarked with Purple discs. A guide book - The Derwent Valley Heritage Way (Jarrold Publishing - ISBN: 0711729581) gives complete OS maps of the route in 10 sections, with easy to follow directions and description of the key sights and features along the walk.

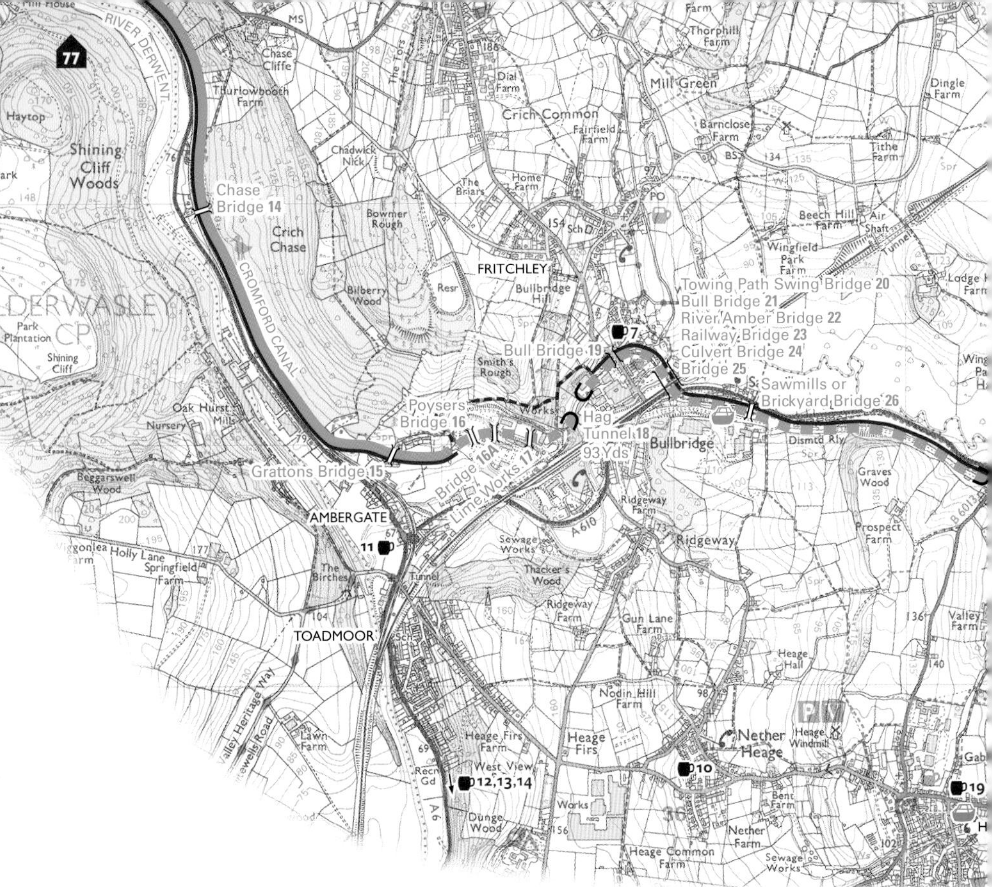

Pubs and Restaurants

1 The Gate Inn 9 The Delves, Swanwick DE55 1AQ (01773 605000). A pub with a friendly atmosphere serving real ales, snacks, and pork pies together with *Sun L*. Beer garden, traditional pub games, sports TV and Wi-Fi. *Open Mon-Fri 16.00-00.00 (Fri 01.00) & Sat-Sun 12.00-01.00 (Sun 00.00).*

2 The Steam Packet Inn Derby Road, Swanwick DE55 1AB (01773 607771). Lively hostelry with a warm welcome together with a wide range of real ales and real ciders. *Regular* quizzes and live music. Dog- and family-friendly. Traditional pub games, newspapers, real fires, sports TV and Wi-Fi. *Open Mon-Fri 14.00-23.00 (Fri 00.00) & Sat-Sun 12.00-00.00 (Sun 23.00).*

3 The Pantry 81 Derby Rd, Swanwick DE55 1BG (01773 602223; www.thepantryinswanwick.co.uk/tearoom.htm). Relaxed, traditional tearoom serving breakfast, lunches, soup, paninis, tea, coffee, cheese and cream teas. *Open Mon-Sat 09.00-16.00.*

4 The Salt Pot The Green, Swanwick DE55 1BL (01773 607056; www.valleycids.co.uk/salt-pot-community-café). Welcoming community café, run largely by volunteers, serving wholesome food at low prices in a friendly relaxed atmosphere. *Open Mon-Fri 10.00-15.00.*

5 The George Inn 56 Main Rd, Lower Hartshay DE5 3RP (01773 742597). Two-roomed pub, run by the same landlord for approaching 20 years, serving real ales and bar meals *E*. Family-friendly and traditional pub games. *Open Mon-Fri E & Sat-Sun L and E.*

6 The Excavator Buckland Hollow, Sawmills DE56 2HS (01773 744400). Heralded by the mini-digger parked outside, this pub serves real ale and food *Mon-Fri 12.00-17.00*. Dog- and child-friendly, beer garden. Wi-Fi. *Open daily 12.00-23.00.*

7 The Canal Inn 30 Bull Bridge Hill, Bullbridge DE56 2EW (01773 852739). Friendly local, close to the site of Bullbridge Aqueduct, serving real ale, real cider and bar snacks. Family-friendly, garden. *Open Tue-Fri 17.00-23.00 & Sat-Sun 12.00-23.00.*

8 The Red Lion Market Place, Ripley DE5 3BS (01773 512875; www.jdwetherspoon.com/pubs/all-pubs/england/derbyshire/the-red-lion-ripley). 1960s building, adorned on the outside with a lion rampant, serving real ales and food. Family-friendly, outside seating and Wi-Fi. *Open 08.00-00.00 (Fri-Sat 01.00).*

9 The Pear Tree 4 Derby Road, Ripley DE5 3HR (01773 741650). Busy, town-centre

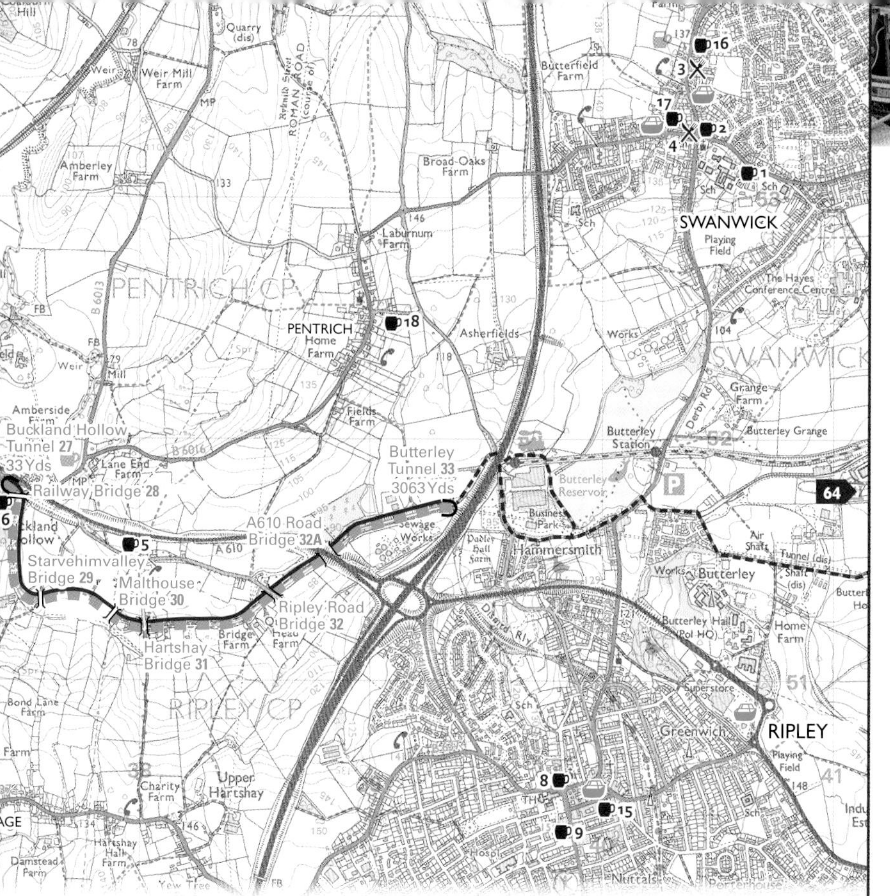

local dispensing real ales and a warm welcome. Dog- and child-friendly, garden. Traditional pub games, newspapers and real fires. *Open daily 11.00-00.00 (Sun 12.00).*

10 The Spanker Inn Spanker Lane, Belper DE56 2AT (01773 853222; thespankerpub.co.uk). Friendly, family-run, hostelry serving real ale and food *L and E (not Mon-Fri L)*. Dog- and child-friendly, garden. Traditional pub games, real fires and Wi-Fi. *Open Mon-Fri 17.00-23.00 & Sat-Sun 12.00-00.00 (Sun 23.0).*

11 The Hurt Arms Derby Road, Ambergate DE56 2EJ (01773 852006/0330 113 8779; www.hurtarmsambergate.co.uk). Large, imposing roadside pub serving real ale and food *daily 12.00-20.30 (Sun 17.00)*. Family-friendly, large garden. Wi-Fi. *Open*

12 Angels Micro Pub 30 Market Place, Belper DE56 1FZ. Friendly, quirky micro-pub serving up to 16 real ales (gradually decreasing as Sunday approaches and they are drunk) real cider, wines and gin, together with pork pies and cheese cobs. Dog-friendly, *Sun* live music. *Open Thu-Sun 12.00-22.00.*

13 Arkwright's Real Ale Bar 6 Campbell Street, Belper DE56 1AP (01773 823117; www.arkwrightsbar.com). Popular, town-centre pub serving real ales, real cider and perry together with bar snacks. Dog-friendly, beer garden. Traditional pub games, newspapers, sports TV and Wi-Fi. Live music *Tue & Sun. Open Mon-Fri 16.00-23.00 & Sat-Sun 12.00-23.00.*

14 The White Hart Sandbed Lane, Belper DE56 0JA (01773 827397). Friendly, CAMRA award-winning pub, serving real ales and bar snacks. Dog- and child-friendly, garden. Traditional pub games and real fires. *Open Mon-Fri 17.00-23.00 (Fri 15.00) & Sat-Sun 12.00-23.00.*

Also try: **15 Ripley's Little Alehouse** 55 Oxford Street, Ripley DE5 3AH (07918 659363); **16 The Cross Keys** Derby Road, Swanwick DE55 1BG (01773 602996); **17 The Boot & Slipper** The Green. Swanwick DE55 1BL (07870 780326); **18 The Dog Inn** Main Road, Pentrich DE5 3RE (01773 513360; www.thedogatpentrich.co.uk) and **19 The Eagle Tavern** 94 Ripley Road, Heage DE56 2HU (01773 436732).

Cromford

The final section of canal from Ambergate through to Cromford is designated a SSSI and sits comfortably in the Derwent Valley: now an easily recognisable waterway merged into a scene of considerable beauty which not even the attendant A6 road can ruffle. Both the river and the railway are never far away the latter, if anything, serving to enhance the outlook with its regular, though relaxed, passage of trains. Whatstandwell is charming whether beside the canal or lower down beside the Derwent, and both the short Gregory Tunnel and the aqueduct over the railway add interest. The beautifully painted cottage beside the Nightingale Arm awaits restoration, the Wigwell Aqueduct - spanning the Derwent - is breathtaking in its execution and the Leawood Pump House is maintained in an excellent state of repair. Passing the transhipment shed of the High Peak Railway, followed by its workshop complex, the canal makes a beeline for Cromford Wharf allowing the walker brief sojourn to absorb the cornucopia of industrial heritage encountered in a mere quarter of a mile of waterway.

● **Bonsall**
Derbs. PO box, tel, store, butcher, off-licence, delicatessen. Focus for lead mining reputed to date back to Roman times, more recently the village was the hub of the area's 18th- and 19th-C frame-knitting workshops (originally pre-dating Richard Arkwright's development of the local textile industry). A more recent attraction is the annual World Championship Hen race centred on the Barley Mow.

● **Cromford**
Derbs. PO, tel, stores, butcher, chocolatier, off-licence, fish & chips, station. Not a particularly pretty village in the accepted sense but, nonetheless, possessing a charm of its own, the settlement is a true heavy weight when it comes to an examination of its industrial heritage. Richard Arkwright's development of the water-powered spinning frame, designed to create cotton thread automatically - spinning 128 threads at a time with great consistency - was the backbone of the output from his cotton mill. The arrival of the Cromford Canal in August 1794 ensured that the prosperity of the village was secured.

Cromford Mills and Visitor Gateway Mill Road, Cromford, Matlock DE4 3RQ (01629 823256; www.cromfordmills.org.uk). The first water-powered cotton spinning mill developed by Richard Arkwright in 1771 and now hosting exhibitions, tours, a restaurant, shops and galleries. *Open daily 09.00-17.00.* Visitor Centre *open daily 10.30-16.00.*

Derwent Valley Mills World Heritage Site In December 2001 a 15-mile corridor from Masson Mill in Matlock Bath to the Silk Mill in Derby and including the mills in Cromford, Milford, Belper and Darley Abbey was declared the Derwent Valley Mills World Heritage Site after the Government's nomination of the area to UNESCO for World Heritage status was approved in Helsinki. The Arkwright Society began the campaign for the award, which recognises the part played during the Industrial Revolution with its far-reaching impact echoing around the world.

Ecclesbourne Valley Railway Wirksworth Station, Coldwell Street, Wirksworth DE4 4FB (01629 823076; www.e-v-r.com/contact). A 13-mile, restored line running from Duffield to Ravenstor, via Winksworth. Timetable operates *Feb-Nov with Dec* Santa Specials. Telephone the booking office - *open Tue-Sun 09.30-17.00* - for further details. Many special events and the opportunity for footplate experience. Charge.

Gulliver's Theme Park Temple Walk, Matlock Bath DE4 3PG (01925 444888; www.gulliversfun.co.uk/gullivers-kingdom-matlock-bath). More than 50 different rides and attractions in a theme park aimed at children 3-13. Café and restaurant. *Open daily 10.30-17.00.* Charge.

Heights of Abraham Dale Road, Matlock DE4 3NT (01629 582365; www.heightsofabraham.com). Hilltop park accessed by cable car offering walking trails, fossil exhibitions and cavern tours. Café. *Open Feb-Oct 10.00-16.30.* Charge.

High Peak and Tissington Trails (01335 343156; www.peakdistrict.gov.uk/visiting/accessible-places-to-visit/access4all-sites/hptt). Former railway lines converted to recreational routes for walkers, cyclists and horse-riders. The High Peak Trail runs for 17 miles from near Buxton to High Peak Junction, on the Cromford Canal and the Tissington Trail runs 13 miles from Parsley Hay to Ashbourne. The trails are generally level, have a variety of surfacing materials - mostly compacted stone - and are reasonably firm. They provide easy walking conditions for all abilities and are suitable for wheelchair users. *See* Walking and Cycling page 76 for details of cycle hire.

High Peak Junction Workshops Cromford DE4 5HN (01629 533105; www.derbyshire.gov.uk/leisure/countryside/countryside_sites/visitor_centres/high_peak_junction/default.asp?VD=highpeakjunction). A variety of buildings from the former Cromford and High Peak Railway: one of the first long distance railways which was built on canal principles and operated by a mix of endless-chain inclined planes and standard gauge railway, originally horse-drawn. The 17-mile track connected with Whalley Bridge on the Peak Forest Canal. *Open Easter-Oct 10.00-17.00 & Nov-Easter 10.30-16.00*. Visitor Centre and refreshments. Books, maps and gifts. Free (but small charge for audio tour).

Leawood Pump House High Peak Junction, Cromford DE4 5HW (01629 533287/533298; www.derbyshire.gov.uk/leisure/countryside/countryside_sites/wildlife_amenity/leawood_pumphouse/default.asp). Built in 1849, to pump water from the River Derwent into the Cromford Canal, and still in pristine working order thanks to the dedication of the Middleton Top and Leawood Pump Volunteer Group. The chance to experience the power of this great steam engine as it pumps four tons of water into the canal with each piston stroke. *Open Easter-Oct, one weekend per month* - visit website for details. Free (but donations gratefully accepted).

Masson Mills Working Textile Museum Derby Road, Matlock Bath, Matlock DE4 3PY (01629 581001; www.massonmills.co.uk). Built in 1783, these are reputed to be Sir Richard Arkwright's finest surviving and best-preserved example of a cotton mill. Working textile museum, shopping village, restaurant and riverside picnic area. *Open Feb-Nov, Mon-Sat 10.00-16.00 (Sun 11.00). Limited Jan opening*. Shopping Village *open Mon-Sat 10.00-17.30 & Sun 11.00-17.00*. Charge.

● **Matlock**

Derbs. All services. The town grew up at the confluence of the Derwent and Bentley Brook on the flatter ground of the valley bottom, its prosperity founded on hydrotherapy and cloth mills. At its peak, there were 20 hydros in the area. The underlying geology is both interesting and complex, being the meeting point of the limestone of the south west and the gritstones and sandstones of the north east; with igneous intrusions giving rise to valuable minerals such as the lead in the Bonsall area.

Matlock Farm Park Jaggers Lane, Matlock DE4 5LH (01246 590200; matlockfarmpark.co.uk). From ferrets to meerkats, ponies to pigs - all small people's small animal pre-occupations catered for! Also shop, go-karts, café and play equipment. Pony trekking. *Open daily 10.00-16.30*. Charge.

● **Matlock Bath**

Derbs. Tel, stores, off-licence, takeaway, fish & chips, station. With the discovery of warm springs in 1698, the settlement grew as a spa town although development was severely hampered by the steep hillsides. Over the decades Ruskin, Byron, Darwin and Josiah Wedgwood were all drawn to indulge in its soothing waters. Today motorcyclists flock into the town during warm summer weekends and holidays.

High Peak Junction Workshops

Peak District Lead Mining Museum The Pavilion, 196 South Parade, Matlock Bath DE4 3NR (01629 583834; www.peakdistrictleadminingmuseum.co.uk). Featuring a mock-up of a lead mine in which children can safely experience and explore how the miners - and in particular how children - were used in this dangerous aspect of England's industrial past. *Opening hours vary* so telephone for details.
St Mary's Church Mill Road, Cromford DE4 3RQ (01629 583924/822710; st-marys-cromford.co.uk). Grade I listed parish church, built by Sir Richard Arkwright and opened in 1797. The interior is decorated with striking wall paintings and the stained glass is by the Victorian artist A. O. Hemming. *Open May-Sep, Sat 11.00-13.00 and by prior telephone arrangement.*

Whatstandwell

Derbs. PO box, tel, station. Nestling peacefully in the Derwent Valley, the hamlet is believed to derive its name from one Walter Stonewall who, in the 14th C, lived in a cottage adjoining the river bridge. It also elicits a mention in D H Lawrence's *Sons and Lovers.*

Wirksworth

Derbs. PO (distant) tel, stores, chemist, butcher, bank, baker, greengrocer, delicatessen, off-licence, takeaways, fish & chips, cinema. An attractive market town developed around lead mining and stone quarrying. Richard Arwright's cotton spinning empire spilled over into the settlement in the late 18th C, only to morph into weaving tape when his son sold off spinning interests, upon deciding to move the business into banking. It was said that a week's output would comfortably girdle the globe, while one wag observed (with some degree of truth) that Wirksworth was the primary producer of red tape for Whitehall.
Tourist Information Centre The Pavilion, Matlock Bath DE4 3NR (01629 583834; www.visitpeakdistrict.com/visitor-information/matlock-bath-information-point-p685531). *Open summer 10.00-17.00 & winter 11.00-15.00.*

Pubs and Restaurants (pages 76-77)

1 The Royal Oak North End, Wirksworth DE4 4FG (01629 823000). Historic, stone-built pub serving a good range of real ale. Cobs usually available. Dog- and child-friendly, garden. Boules and Wi-Fi. *Open daily 20.00-23.30 (Fri-Sun 00.00) & Sun 12.00-16.00.*

2 The Family Tree Derby Road, Whatstandwell DE4 5HG (01773 425915; www.thefamilytreederbyshire.co.uk). Coffee lounge and restaurant serving breakfast, lunch and afternoon teas together with homemade cakes. B&B. *Open 09.00-18.00.*

3 Oakford Cottage Tearooms Oakford Cottage, Robin Hood, Whatstandwell DE4 5HF (01773 852400/07899 990612; www.oakfordcottage.co.uk). Offering superb views over the Derwent Valley, this cosy tearoom provides indoor and outdoor seating and tasty snacks, teas, homemade cakes and coffee. B&B. *Open Thu-Sun 09.00-17.00.*

4 The Black Swan 6 Bowns Hill, Crich DE4 5DG (01773 856405). Impressive, mock-tudor hostelry serving a wide range of real ale and real ciders. Family-friendly, garden and camping. Traditional pub games and real fires. *Open 12.00-23.00 (Fri-Sat 23.30).*

5 The Cliff Inn Town End, Crich DE4 5DP (01773 852444). Traditional grit-stone free house, close to the Tramway Museum, serving real ales and food *Tue-Fri E & Sat-Sun L.* Dog- and family-friendly, garden and camping. Traditional pub games, real fires and Wi-Fi. *Open Mon-Fri 17.00-00.00 (Mon 19.00) & Sat-Sun 12.00-00.00.*

6 Wheatcroft's Wharf 2 Mill Road, Cromford DE4 3RQ (01629 823256; www.cromfordmills.org.uk/wheatcrofts-wharf-dining). Picturesque canalside café serving delicious home-cooked food with a smile: breakfast, lunch and tea with homemade cakes. *Evening meals Thu-Sat (seasonal* - booking recommended). *Open daily 09.00-17.45 (reduced in winter).*

7 The Bell Inn 47 The Hill, Cromford DE4 3RF (01629 822102). A truly local pub, with a friendly atmosphere, dispensing real ale. Camping, traditional pub games, real fires and sports TV. *Open Mon-Fri 15.00-23.00 (Fri 00.00) & Sat-Sun 12.00-00.00 (Sun 23.00).*

8 The Boat Inn Scarthin, Cromford DE4 3QF (01629 258083; www.the-boat-inn.co.uk). Beamed ceilings and exposed stone walls contribute to a cosy feel in a pub that serves real ales and food *daily 12.00-21.00.* Live music *Fri & Sat,* Quiz *Thu.* Dog- and child-friendly, beer garden overlooking the mill pond. Newspapers, real fires, sports TV and Wi-Fi. *Open 12.00-00.00 (Sun 23.30).*

9 The Kings Head 62 Yeoman Street, Bonsall DE4 2AA (01629 822703; www.kingsheadbonsall.co.uk/index). Cosy, old, two-roomed pub - popular with walkers - serving real ale and home-cooked food. Garden, traditional pub games and real fires. *Open Mon 18.00-00.00, 17.30-00.00, Wed-Fri L and E & Sat-Sun 12.00-00.00.*

10 The Twenty Ten Matlock 16 Dale Road, Matlock DE4 3LT (07710 427442; twentytenmatlock.co.uk). Café/bar by day and a pub by night dispensing real ales. Food available *Tue-Sun 12.00-19.00.* Dog- and child-friendly, outside seating. Live music *Fri & Sat.* Newspapers and Wi-Fi. *Open Tue-Sun 12.00-22.00 (Fri-Sat 01.00).*

11 The Thorn Tree Inn Matlock 48 Jackson Road, Matlock DE4 3JQ (01629 580295; www.thorntreeatmatlock.co.uk) Perched high above the town, presenting commanding views, this pub serves real ale and bar snacks whilst *open.* Also *Mon-Fri L, Sun L 17.00-18.00 & Wed* Pie Night *(18.00-20.00).* Dogs and children welcome, heated terrace. Traditional pub games and Wi-Fi. *Open L and E Mon-Thu (not Mon L) & Fri-Sun 12.00-00.00 (Sun 23.30).*

Taking up the slack

Also try: **12 The Loaf** Victoria House, The Common, Crich DE4 5BH (01773 857074; www.theloaf.co.uk) ; **13 The Malt Shovel Tavern** Oakerthorpe Road, Bolehill, Matlock DE4 4GU (01629 822427; themaltshovel wirksworth.weebly.com); **14 The Greyhound** Market Place, Cromford DE4 3QE (01629 823172; www.thegreyhoundatcromford.co.uk); **15 The Market House Restaurant & Tapas Bar** 16/18 The Market Place, Cromford DE4 3QE (01629 822444; www.marketplacerestaurant.co.uk) and **16 The Barley Mow** The Dale, Bonsall, Matlock DE4 2AY (01629 825685; www.barleymowbonsall.co.uk).

WALKING AND CYCLING

For the most part the walker is able to follow the line of the canal fairly faithfully through to Bullbridge, crossing the A610 in Sawmills and the adjacent railway via the footbridge and thence taking the left fork up the steps to the original canal level. This is where the Bullbridge Aqueduct used to be. To negotiate the final two major obstacles blocking the canal and towpath – the demolished Stevenson's dyeworks and the National Grid Headquarters – leave the towpath at the foot of the 94 steps ascending into the woods on the right. At the top, turn right and then left through a small gate in the wall, following the path downhill, swinging gradually left skirting the perimeter fence of the National Grid HQ, to finally meet the canal (now in water) at an overflow weir. Five and a half miles of recognisable towpath and waterway, perched above the River Derwent, now wind their way (unhampered) into Cromford!

To explore the High Peak and Tissington Trails (and further afield) any manner of variation on the bicycle (together with all-terrain mobility scooters) can be hired by visiting www.peakdistrict.gov.uk/cyclehire who have bases at Parsley Hay (01298 84493) Ashbourne (01335 343156) and Fairholmes (01433 651261). *Open daily, Mar-Oct from 09.30 with limited opening Nov-Feb.*

BOAT TRIPS

Birdswood runs powered boat trips between Cromford Wharf DE4 3RQ and Leawood Pump House DE4 5HN *Mar-Oct Wed, Sat-Sun,* departing promptly at *11.00 & 14.00 and Apr-Sep, Thu 11.00 & 14.00.* Also horse-drawn days *two-three times per month Apr-Oct.* Charters and school trips. On-board refreshments. Visit www.birdswood.org or telephone 07552 055455 *(09.00-18.00)* to book.

Matlock Bath Rowing Boats Derby Road, Matlock Bath DE4 3NR (07971 982834). Rowing boats for hire on the River Derwent. *Open weekends Easter-May and Sep-Oct & daily Jun-Aug* river levels and weather permitting.

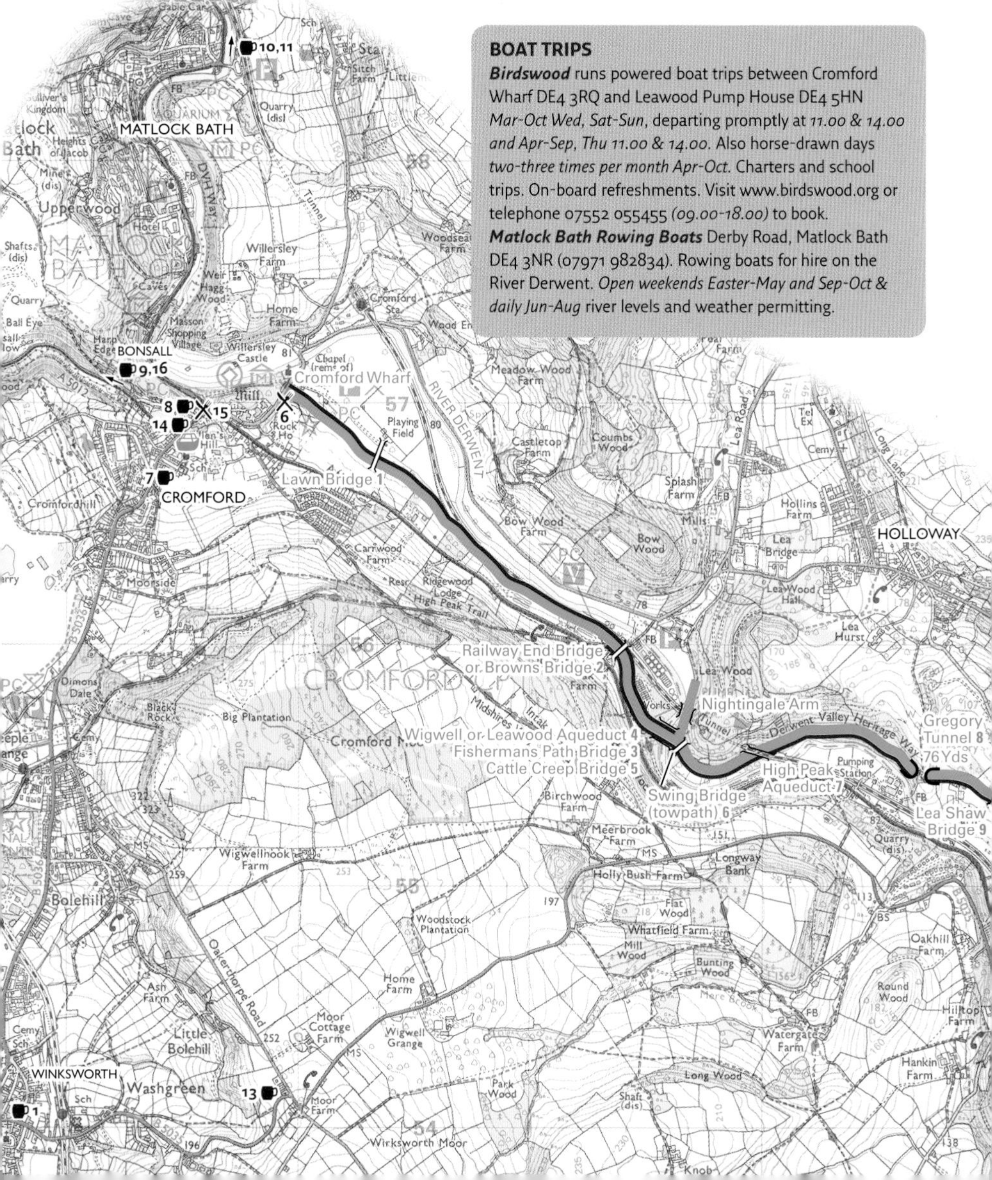

Leawood Pumphouse

EREWASH CANAL

MAXIMUM DIMENSIONS
Length: 72'
Beam: 10' 6"
Draught: 2' 6"
Headroom: 7' 4"

MILEAGE
TRENT LOCK to:
Sandiacre Lock: 3¼ miles
Hallam Fields Lock: 5½ miles
LANGLEY MILL: 11¾ miles
Locks: 15

MANAGER
0303 040 4040
enquiries.eastmidlands@canalrivertrust.org.uk.

The Erewash Canal is one of five canals built towards the end of the 18th C to carry coal from the pits of the Nottinghamshire/Derbyshire coalfield to the towns of the East Midlands. The construction of the canal was supported by local merchants and landowners who were keen to profit from the coal deposits of the Erewash Valley, as were the local colliery owners who could see the financial benefits of widening their markets. Completed in 1779 at a cost of £21,000 by the engineer John Varley, the canal involved the construction of 14 locks which took the navigation up 109ft from Trent Lock to Langley Mill. Begun in 1778, its 11¾ mile course was open to navigation by the following summer. As £23,000 had been raised in £100 shares in order to finance the project, the capital outlay was low. Abundant trade from local collieries, brickworks and ironworks made the canal one of the most prosperous in the country. The monopoly that the company had over transport in the area along with the high demand for coal meant that the £100 shares had risen to an incredible £1300. The enormous success of the Erewash Canal encouraged the promotion and construction, during the following decade, of the Cromford, Nottingham, Derby and Nutbrook canals. However, by 1834 the Canal Company was in trouble. High tolls plus the competition presented by the railways were taking trade away from the navigation. The Company reduced its tolls in an attempt to regain trade, but the railway system was expanding rapidly in the area and the Canal Company was unable to compete. The surrounding canals were bought up by the railway companies which further added to the problems of the Erewash Canal. The railway companies were happy to see these neighbouring waterways fall into disuse, thus putting an end to through traffic. By 1932 the Erewash Canal Company admitted defeat and was bought up by the Grand Union Canal Company. Having also bought the Loughborough and Leicester navigations, it was their intention to revitalise the network by creating a through navigation from the coalfields of Derbyshire to London. Sadly their attempts failed.

Nationalisation of the canals in 1947 brought the Erewash Canal under the administration of the British Transport Commission and in 1962 this body closed to navigation the upper section from Gallows Inn to Langley Mill. The need to supply water to the lower section for navigation and industry, however, meant that the upper section had still to be maintained and boats were allowed to navigate it upon application to the Commission and subsequently to its successor, the British Waterways Board. With the cessation of narrowboat carrying in 1963, such boats had been few, but the growing interest in pleasure boating resulted in more and more craft venturing up the canal from the popular River Trent. With increased use the canal gradually improved and the news that the major portion of it was to be designated a remainder waterway in the impending 1968 Transport Act was received locally with dismay. A public meeting led to the formation of the Erewash Canal Preservation and Development Association (ECPDA), a body consisting of representatives of boating and fishing interests, residents and local authorities. The need to convince local authorities of the value of the canal as an amenity was recognised at a very early stage and the association's efforts eventually met with success when, in 1972, Derbyshire and Nottinghamshire County Councils agreed to share the cost, with the then British Waterways Board, of the restoration of the canal to cruising waterway standards. This ambition was achieved in February 1983 when the canal was upgraded and boaters can now enjoy the entire course of the waterway. Further improvements are already afoot due to the continued involvement of the Erewash Initiative, a joint project involving Canal & River Trust, Erewash Borough Council and Groundwork Erewash.

Erewash Canal near Sandiacre

Long Eaton

The Erewash Canal leaves the Trent Navigation at Trent Lock. There is a useful *supermarket* just above Dockholme Lock, on the offside. North of the big concrete bridge carrying the A52 at Sandiacre is a delightfully landscaped free overnight *mooring*. There are public *toilets* at Bridge 9.

NAVIGATIONAL NOTES

1 Trent Lock should always be left *full*, with the top gates open, except when there is much traffic about. This will ensure that any flotsam coming down the canal is able to escape over the bottom gates.

2 The sanitary station at Sawley Locks should only be accessed from the backwater moorings on the river below the Lock.

Trent Lock
An important waterway junction and a long-established boating centre. Boats navigating the Trent in this rather complicated area should beware of straying too near Thrumpton Weir.

Long Eaton
Derbs. All services.
West Park Leisure Centre Wilsthorpe Road, Long Eaton NG10 4AA (0115 946 1400; www.erewash.gov.uk). Swimming pool, gym and sauna. *Open Mon-Fri 06.15-22.30 (Fri 22.00) Sat 06.30-19.30 & Sun 07.30-22.00.* Charge.

Lock Cottage Lock Lane, off Longmoor Lane, Sandiacre NG10 5LA (0115 854 3306/07809 252441; www.erewashcanalpreservationanddevelopmentassoc.org.uk). The last remaining toll house on the Erewash Canal, complete with unchanged, period interior. *Usually open one Sun in the month and B Hol Mon 13.30-16.30.* Telephone to confirm before visiting.

Derby Canal
The closure of the Derby Canal ended Derby's link with the navigable waterways which dated back to the time when the Danes sailed up the River Derwent to found the settlement of Deoraby.

WALKING AND CYCLING

The towpath is in excellent condition throughout the whole navigation and is suitable for both walking and cycling. The Nutbrook Trail is an off-road cycleway that runs from Long Eaton to Shipley and makes use of both canal towpath and abandoned railway track.

Pubs and Restaurants

1 Lock House Tea Rooms Lock Lane, Trent Lock, Long Eaton NG10 2FY (0115 972 2288). Chintzy tea rooms with a twist, offering a wide variety of teas and homemade food. Outside seating overlooking the lock. Dogs welcome. *Open Wed-Sun from 10.00; closing times vary from 16.00 to 18.00 depending on the day and season.*

2 The Trent Lock Lock Lane, Long Eaton NG10 2FY (0115 972 5159; www.vintageinn.co.uk). Formerly the Navigation Inn. Large, popular, family pub with a garden and play area. Real ales and a wide range of reasonably priced food available *L and E, daily.* Moorings. *Open 11.00.*

3 The Steamboat Inn Lock Lane, Long Eaton NG10 2FY. (0115 946 0356; www.steamboattrentlock.co.uk). On the Erewash Canal. Built by the canal company in 1791, when it was called the Erewash Navigation Inn, it is now an upmarket canalside pub and restaurant. Real ale available. Food served *L and E*. Dog- and child-friendly, garden. Traditional pub games and camping nearby. *Open 11.00.*

4 The Barge Inn 177 Tamworth Road, Long Eaton NG10 1DH (0115 972 5559). Formerly the Old Ale house, this pub still serves real ales and real cider. *Weekend* live music. Dog-friendly, outside seating. Traditional pub games. *Open Mon-Thu 14.00-23.30 & Fri-Sun 12.00-00.00 (Sun 23.30).*

5 The Hole in the Wall Regent Street, Long Eaton NG10 1JX (0115 973 4920). Real ales and cider. Dog-friendly, outside seating. Traditional pub games, newspapers and sports TV. *Open Mon-Thu 14.00-23.30, Fri-Sat 11.00-00.30 & Sun 12.00-23.30.*

6 The Stumble Inn 37 Tamworth Road, Long Eaton NG10 1JF (0115 972 4529). Popular, family-run, pub serving real ales and real cider with an on-site micro-brewery. Dog- and family-friendly, courtyard seating. Traditional pub games, real fires, sports TV and Wi-Fi. Quiz *Sun. Open Mon-Wed 14.00-23.30 & Thu-Sun 12.00-00.00.*

7 The Twitchel Inn Howitt Street, Long Eaton NG10 1ED (0115 972 2197). Decorated with photos of the local area, this pub dispenses real ales and real cider together with food *L and E*. Wi-Fi. *Open daily 08.00-23.00.*

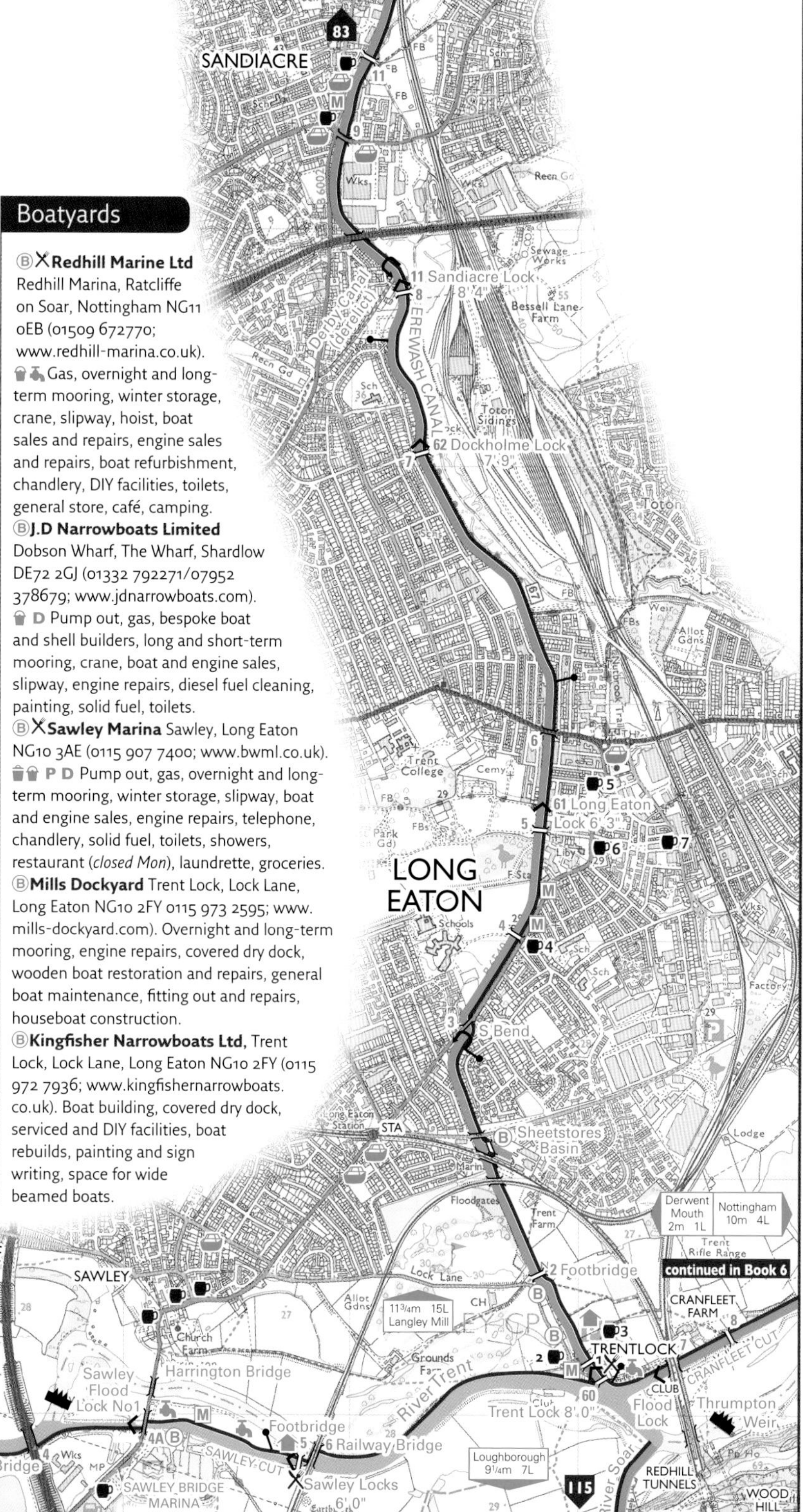

Boatyards

Ⓑ✕ **Redhill Marine Ltd** Redhill Marina, Ratcliffe on Soar, Nottingham NG11 0EB (01509 672770; www.redhill-marina.co.uk). Gas, overnight and long-term mooring, winter storage, crane, slipway, hoist, boat sales and repairs, engine sales and repairs, boat refurbishment, chandlery, DIY facilities, toilets, general store, café, camping.

Ⓑ **J.D Narrowboats Limited** Dobson Wharf, The Wharf, Shardlow DE72 2GJ (01332 792271/07952 378679; www.jdnarrowboats.com). D Pump out, gas, bespoke boat and shell builders, long and short-term mooring, crane, boat and engine sales, slipway, engine repairs, diesel fuel cleaning, painting, solid fuel, toilets.

Ⓑ✕ **Sawley Marina** Sawley, Long Eaton NG10 3AE (0115 907 7400; www.bwml.co.uk). P D Pump out, gas, overnight and long-term mooring, winter storage, slipway, boat and engine sales, engine repairs, telephone, chandlery, solid fuel, toilets, showers, restaurant (*closed Mon*), laundrette, groceries.

Ⓑ **Mills Dockyard** Trent Lock, Lock Lane, Long Eaton NG10 2FY 0115 973 2595; www.mills-dockyard.com). Overnight and long-term mooring, engine repairs, covered dry dock, wooden boat restoration and repairs, general boat maintenance, fitting out and repairs, houseboat construction.

Ⓑ **Kingfisher Narrowboats Ltd,** Trent Lock, Lock Lane, Long Eaton NG10 2FY (0115 972 7936; www.kingfishernarrowboats.co.uk). Boat building, covered dry dock, serviced and DIY facilities, boat rebuilds, painting and sign writing, space for wide beamed boats.

Ilkeston

At Stanton Gate the M1 motorway looms up and then crosses the canal on its way to Leeds and points north. The outskirts of Ilkeston appear on the left side while, across the shallow Erewash valley, the course of the disused Nottingham Canal appears from the east, twisting along the contours of the hillside. Like the Erewash Canal, its course is generally northerly, but the two waterways do not meet until Langley Mill. Meanwhile the Erewash Canal passes extensive low-lying playing fields before reaching the pub at Gallows Inn Lock with *PO, stores, takeaway, off-licence and garage* to the west of the navigation. North of Gallows Inn Lock, the canal passes housing estates on one side and water meadows and a main line railway on the other. The town of Ilkeston is on the hillside on the west side of the canal. In spite of its proximity to these built-up areas, the canal is relatively unspoiled and surprisingly rural. There are public *toilets* at bridge 17.

- **Sandiacre**
Derby. Tel, stores, butcher, hardware, takeaway, fish & chips, off-licence. Services are all conveniently near the canal, but there is not much of interest in these outskirts, apart from the handsome Springfield Mill by the canal and the church, which is set on a rise called Stoney Clouds (clearly visible from the canal at Pasture Lock). The mill was built by Ernest Terah Hooley of Risley Hall in 1888. It houses four separate spiral staircase towers, each catering for an individual lace company. The canal was used for the transportation of the raw materials needed by the lace industry and for the finished articles. There are fine views over the industrial valley from the church which features some original Norman work inside, including carvings. Outside is an old tombstone bearing a skull and crossbones. The font is 600 years old.

- **Ilkeston**
Derbs. All services. A market and textile town, with a compact main square. Pedestrianised areas make this a pleasant place to stroll. The parish church of St Mary dates from 1150 and has an unusual 14th-C stone screen. The annual three-day funfair is held in the Market Place in *Oct.*
Erewash Museum High Street, off East Street, Ilkeston DE7 5JA (0115 907 1141; www.erewashmuseum.co.uk). Set in a late 18th-C house, the museum tells the story of the local and social history of the Erewash area as well as housing permanent displays of an Edwardian period kitchen and wash house and an exhibition of children's toys. Tea room *(open 11.00-15.00)* gardens and children's play area. *Open Mon-Sat 10.00-16.00 during school holidays but closed Mon & Wed during term time.* Free.

- **Cossall**
Notts. Tel. Cossall is a refreshing contrast to Ilkeston, an attractive village built on top of a hill, spreading gently down to the Nottingham Canal. D.H. Lawrence used it as his background for Cossethay in *The Rainbow*. A narrow street winds among the houses, all of which seem to be surrounded by pretty gardens. The little church contains an oak screen made by village craftsmen; in the churchyard is a memorial to a soldier killed at Waterloo. Next to the church is Church Cottage, once the home of Louie Burrows to whom Lawrence was engaged. She was the model for the character of Ursula Brangwen.

- **Nutbrook Canal**
This little branch off the Erewash Canal used to lead for 4½ miles almost parallel to the Erewash Canal and slightly west of it. It still flows into the Erewash Canal upstream from Stanton Lock and parts of it are in water. The canal opened in 1795 at a cost of £22,800. Colliery owners Edward Miller-Mundy and Sir Henry Hunloke employed Benjamin Outram as engineer. It was in fact mining subsidence which caused much of the canal to be derelict by 1895 when it fell into disuse. Two of the three reservoirs which supplied the canal with water are still in evidence at Shipley. The short section that used to pass through the old Stanton Ironworks was filled in in 1962 and is now quite untraceable.

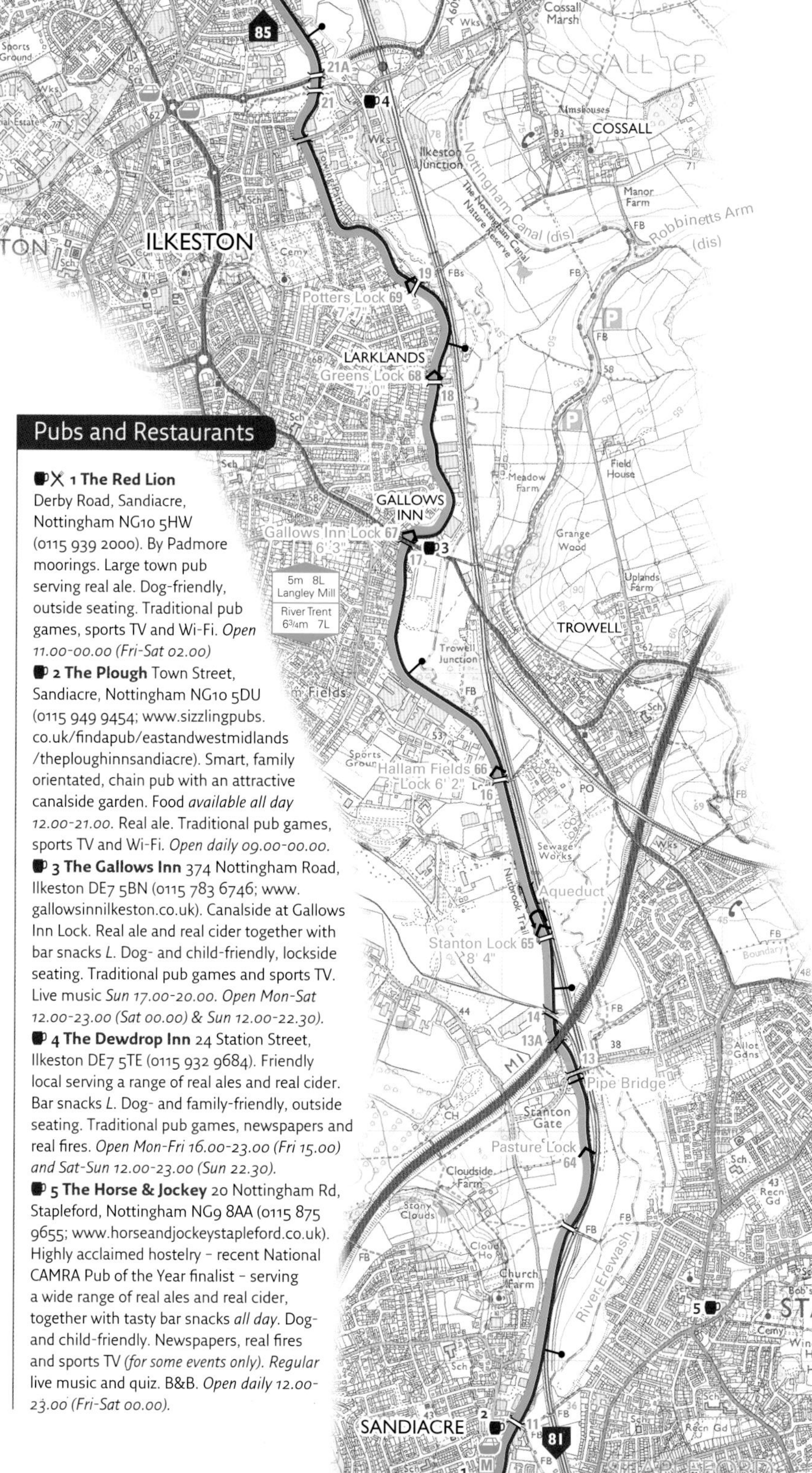

Pubs and Restaurants

1 The Red Lion Derby Road, Sandiacre, Nottingham NG10 5HW (0115 939 2000). By Padmore moorings. Large town pub serving real ale. Dog-friendly, outside seating. Traditional pub games, sports TV and Wi-Fi. *Open 11.00-00.00 (Fri-Sat 02.00)*

2 The Plough Town Street, Sandiacre, Nottingham NG10 5DU (0115 949 9454; www.sizzlingpubs.co.uk/findapub/eastandwestmidlands/theploughinnsandiacre). Smart, family orientated, chain pub with an attractive canalside garden. Food *available all day 12.00-21.00*. Real ale. Traditional pub games, sports TV and Wi-Fi. *Open daily 09.00-00.00.*

3 The Gallows Inn 374 Nottingham Road, Ilkeston DE7 5BN (0115 783 6746; www.gallowsinnilkeston.co.uk). Canalside at Gallows Inn Lock. Real ale and real cider together with bar snacks *L*. Dog- and child-friendly, lockside seating. Traditional pub games and sports TV. Live music *Sun 17.00-20.00. Open Mon-Sat 12.00-23.00 (Sat 00.00) & Sun 12.00-22.30).*

4 The Dewdrop Inn 24 Station Street, Ilkeston DE7 5TE (0115 932 9684). Friendly local serving a range of real ales and real cider. Bar snacks *L*. Dog- and family-friendly, outside seating. Traditional pub games, newspapers and real fires. *Open Mon-Fri 16.00-23.00 (Fri 15.00) and Sat-Sun 12.00-23.00 (Sun 22.30).*

5 The Horse & Jockey 20 Nottingham Rd, Stapleford, Nottingham NG9 8AA (0115 875 9655; www.horseandjockeystapleford.co.uk). Highly acclaimed hostelry – recent National CAMRA Pub of the Year finalist – serving a wide range of real ales and real cider, together with tasty bar snacks *all day*. Dog- and child-friendly. Newspapers, real fires and sports TV *(for some events only). Regular* live music and quiz. B&B. *Open daily 12.00-23.00 (Fri-Sat 00.00).*

Langley Mill

The northernmost section of the Erewash Canal is more isolated than the rest, and is definitely more rural and attractive. There are two splendid old canal buildings beside Shipley Lock – one was a stable and the other a slaughterhouse for worn-out canal horses. Just above the lock, the River Erewash creeps under the canal, which is carried above it on a very small aqueduct. Beyond the next pleasant rural stretch is Langley Mill, where the canal terminates at the Great Northern Basin beyond the final lock. Boatmen who have navigated the whole of the Erewash to this point are able to obtain a head of navigation plaque from the very helpful Langley Mill Boatyard.

Great Northern Basin
This restored basin, officially reopened in 1973, once formed the junction of the Erewash, Cromford and Nottingham canals. A feeder enters here from Moorgreen Reservoir. Since it passed through a coalfield on its way to the basin, it brought down a lot of coal silt – which over the years filled up the Great Northern Basin. Now the Erewash Canal Preservation & Development Association (ECPDA) has restored the basin and lock, so that boats may reach a good mooring site with an enjoyable pub beside it. The Nottingham canal can never be restored here, for its closure was necessitated by mining subsidence – although lengths of the waterway are still in water, away from Langley Mill. The Cromford Canal, however, has nudged onto the CRT priority list for restoration promoted by The Friends of the Cromford Canal (www. cromfordcanal.info). It was originally engineered by William Jessop and Benjamin Outram, its 14½ mile length being completed in 1793. One of its chief instigators had been Richard Arkwright who had come to Cromford in 1771 and built the world's first successful water-powered cotton spinning mill. The canal was used for transporting limestone, coal, iron, lead and building stone, (see page 62 for full coverage). Jessop was joined by James Green in engineering the Nottingham Canal. Running from Langley Mill to the River Trent at Nottingham, it involved 20 locks including a flight of 14 at Wollaton. The stretch from Langley Mill to Lenton had to be abandoned in 1937 but the remaining section through to the River Trent is still in use. Both canals pass through an interesting mixture of heavily industrial surroundings and quiet open countryside. The northern 5 miles of the Cromford Canal, from Ambergate to Cromford (a length still in water) is strongly recommended to all walkers, country lovers and especially industrial archaeologists. Explorers will find all kinds of exciting things, including two aqueducts and a fine old pumping station, regularly in steam.

Langley Mill
Derbs. PO, tel, stores, chemist, off-licence, takeaways, garage, station. Near the head of the Erewash Canal, with the little Erewash river going past it.

Eastwood
Notts. PO, tel, stores, banks, takeaways, farm shop, chemist, off-licence, fish & chips. Up on the hill east of the Great Northern Basin, this mining town is best known as the childhood home of D.H. Lawrence. He was born at 8a Victoria Street, and the early part of *Sons and Lovers* is set in the town. The cemetery contains the Lawrence family graves. Lawrence's own headstone was brought from Vence in France and is now on display in the local library. A meeting at the Sun Inn in 1843, between local coal owners and iron masters, led to the construction of the Midland Railway.

D.H. Lawrence Birthplace Museum 8a Victoria Street, Eastwood NG16 3AW (0115 917 3824; www.liberty-leisure.org.uk/d-h-lawrence-birthplace-museum). Birthplace of the novelist, poet and playwright, David Herbert Lawrence. The house has been restored to reflect the lifestyle of a working-class Victorian family. There is also a video presentation of the author's Eastwood days. Also available from the museum is a leaflet entitled *The Blue Line Trail* which guides you around Eastwood's Lawrentian connections. *Open Tue-Sat 10.00-16.00.* Entry by timed tours only. Charge.

Durban House Heritage Centre Mansfield Road, Eastwood NG16 3DZ (01773 717353; www.lawrenceseastwood.co.uk/durbanhouse.htm). Set in the mining company offices where Lawrence would have collected his wages. The displays tell you about Lawrence himself, the social history of the area and its changing community. *Telephone for opening times.* Excellent restaurant *open from 10.00.* Charge.

Eastwood Library Wellington Place, Nottingham Road, Eastwood NG16 3GB (01773 712209; www.inspireculture.org.uk/reading-information/find-a-library/eastwood-library). The library houses a display of letters, books and first editions connected with D.H. Lawrence. *Open Mon & Thu 09.00-18.00; Tue & Sat 09.00-13.00 & Fri 09.00-14.00.*

Tourist Information Centre Centre Assembly Rooms, Market Place, Derby DE1 3AH (01332 643411; www.visitderby.co.uk/tourist-information-centre). *Open Mon-Sat 09.30-20.00.* The Tourist Information Centre sells an excellent guide to the Cromford Canal featuring both a complete walk along its 14½-mile course, from the Great Northern Basin to its terminus at Cromford, and shorter circular walks taking in specific highlights. There is much of interest to visit in the Amber valley, to the north west of Langley Mill, all of which is very accessible by bus or train. So before navigating the waterway contact the TIC for their comprehensive information pack.

Boatyards

Ⓑ**Langley Mill Boatyard Ltd** Great Northern Basin, Derby Road, Langley Mill NG16 4AA (01773 760758). Pump out, gas, overnight mooring, Long-term mooring (by arrangement), dry dock, DIY facilities, end of navigation plaques.

Ⓑ**ECP and DA** Great Northern Basin, Derby Road, Langley Mill NG16 4AA (0115 854 4155; www.erewashcanal preservation anddevelopmentassoc.org.uk). The ECP and DA offer limited moorings in Great Northern Basin, primarily for members of the Association of Waterways Cruising Clubs (AWCC). Mooring space is generally only available in the summer months and must be pre-booked. Telephone for further details on 0115 854 4155.

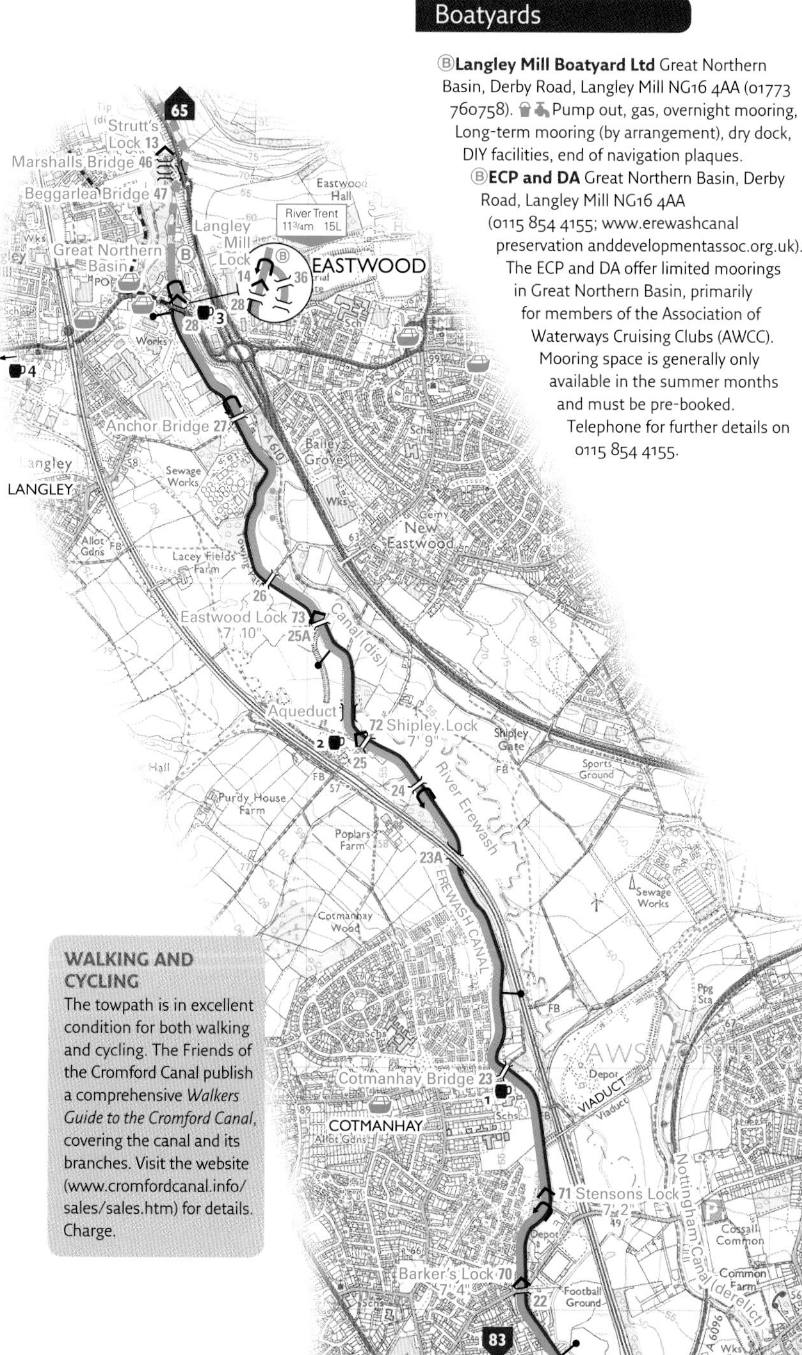

WALKING AND CYCLING
The towpath is in excellent condition for both walking and cycling. The Friends of the Cromford Canal publish a comprehensive *Walkers Guide to the Cromford Canal*, covering the canal and its branches. Visit the website (www.cromfordcanal.info/sales/sales.htm) for details. Charge.

Pubs and Restaurants (page 85)

1 The Bridge Inn Bridge Street, Cotmanhay DE7 8RD (0115 930 0596/07825 616807). Small, friendly canalside local serving real ales, real cider and food *Tue-Sun L and E (not Tue L or Sun E)* together with *all day breakfasts*. Dog- and child-friendly, canalside garden. Traditional pub games, *regular* live music and real fires. *Open Mon-Thu 12.00-23.00 & Fri-Sun 10.00-00.00 (Sun 23.00).*

2 MFN Shipley Gate, Eastwood NG16 3JE (01773 530313; www.mfn-club.co.uk). Advertising itself as being 'Miles from Nowhere' this eclectic mix of bikers, music and classic cars, trucks and motorbikes is, in fact, rather close to Shipley Lock. Diner-style café and *opening hours* to match its car/truck, biker *(Wed-Thu)* and music *(Wed)* events, usually *from 18.00 onwards.*

3 The Great Northern 134 Derby Road, Langley Mill NG16 4AA (01773 719886; www.pubpeople.com/greatnorthern). At Great Northern Basin (the railway company was once owner of the canal). An excellent local pub serving real ale, real cider and traditional pub food *daily L and E*. Dog- and family-friendly, outside seating. Wi-Fi. *Open Mon-Fri 12.00-23.00 (Fri 01.00) & Sat-Sun 12.00-00.00 (Sun 22.30).*

4 The Redemption Alehouse Ray Street, Heanor DE75 7GE (07887 568576). A micro-pub with a serious interest in dispensing real ales (up to 10 at any time) and real cider (nearer 12). Bar snacks available *whenever open*. Outside seating, dogs welcome. No under 18s. Wi-Fi. *Open Thu-Sun 12.00-22.00 (Fri-Sat 22.30).*

GERMANS COTTON ON

Before the arrival of Richard Arkwright and his partners in August 1771, the area around Cromford was a scattered community of families who earned their livings in the lead mines. By Christmas of that year Arkwright was already utilising the waters of a local lead mine drain, the Cromford Sough, and of the Bonsall Brook, to power what was soon to become the world's first successful water-powered cotton spinning mill. By 1777 there were two mills in Cromford and further developments were soon to take place in Derby and Matlock Bath. New housing built to accommodate the workers in Cromford featured an additional upper storey which acted as a workroom. Visiting industrialists from New England were entertained in the new Greyhound Hotel. So impressed were they with the developments in Cromford that they returned to America and used Sir Richard's mills as a model for their own. By 1783 continental Europe was catching up with the rest of the world when its first water-powered cotton spinning mill was erected near Ratingen, Germany. Johann Gottfried Brägelmann created his very own cotton new town and named it Cromford in recognition of Arkwright's innovation.

Langley Mill Lock near the end of navigation on the Erewash Canal

GRAND UNION CANAL LEICESTER SECTION AND THE RIVER SOAR

MAXIMUM DIMENSIONS

Norton Junction to Foxton Junction
Length: 72'
Beam: 7'
Headroom: 7'

Market Harborough to Leicester
Length: 72'
Beam: 13'
Headroom: 7'

Leicester West Bridge to River Trent
Length: 72'
Beam: 14' 4"
Headroom: 7' 6"

MILEAGE

NORTON JUNCTION to:
Crick: 5 miles
Welford Arm: 15½ miles
Market Harborough Arm: 23¼ miles
Blaby: 36 miles
Leicester West Bridge: 41¼ miles
Cossington Lock: 49 miles
Barrow upon Soar: 53¼ miles
Loughborough Basin: 57¼ miles
Zouch Lock: 60½ miles
RIVER TRENT: 66¼ miles

Locks: 59

MANAGER

0303 040 4040

Norton Junction to Bridge 82, Turnover Bridge (including the Welford Arm and the Market Harborough Arm): enquiries.southeast@canalrivertrust.org.uk
Bridge 82, Turnover Bridge to the Trent: enquiries.eastmidlands@canalrivertrust.org.uk

The River Soar is a tributary of the River Trent and is approximately 40 miles long. It runs mainly through Leicestershire, rising at Smockington Hollow on the Warwickshire border. For most of the way from Aylestone (just south of Leicester) to the Trent, the Soar forms the Leicester section of the Grand Union Canal.

In 1634 Thomas Skipworth of Cotes attempted to make the River 'portable for barges and boats up to the town of Leicester' by means of a grant from King Charles I in return for 10 per cent of the profits. This scheme was a failure. But, after several other attempts, prominent citizens of Loughborough secured an Act of Parliament in 1776, and the River Soar Navigation (Loughborough Canal) was opened two years later, bringing great prosperity to the town. The continuation of the navigation up to Leicester (the Leicester Canal) was built under an Act passed in 1791. Its opening was marked by the arrival in Leicester of two boats loaded with provisions from Gainsborough on 21 February 1794. The engineers concerned with construction of the River Soar Navigation were John Smith and John May (Loughborough Canal) and William Jessop (Leicester Canal). With the completion of the Grand Junction Canal between Brentford and Braunston, a connection was soon established between this and the River Soar Navigation, built to the narrow gauge, thwarting the Grand Junction's scheme for a system of wide canals.

The Loughborough Navigation was one of the most prosperous canals in England, by virtue of its position in relation to the Nottinghamshire/Derbyshire coalfield and the Erewash Canal. However, railway competition took its usual toll, and although trade revived when the Grand Union Canal purchased the Loughborough and Leicester navigations in 1931, the improvement proved temporary. It remains a pretty, rural river and is much enjoyed by those on pleasure craft.

Norton Junction

Leaving Norton Junction *(sanitary station and toilets)* there is a quiet, meandering mile through light woods and rolling fields before the motorway and railway take over; the canal passes the back door of the Watford Gap service area. The noise and bustle of the motorway and main railway line intrude, accentuating the sedate pace of those using the original of the three transport systems. The Watford Gap motorway service station (south of bridge 6) is by no means inaccessible from the towpath and could provide the boater with *24hr* sustenance and provisions. Otherwise the Leicester Section of the Grand Union Canal is very attractive, quiet and in no hurry to reach Foxton. It wanders through rolling, hilly country, riverlike with constant changes of direction that guide it gently north eastwards. It avoids villages and civilisation generally; only the old wharves serve as a reminder of the canal's function. The slow course of the navigation, its relative emptiness and its original plan combine to make it very narrow in places; reeds, overhanging trees and shallow banks quite often do not allow two boats to pass. After negotiating Watford Locks and reaching the summit level of 412ft there is nothing strenuous to look forward to, as this level continues for the next 20½ miles. Four of these locks form a staircase – adopt a 'one up, one down' procedure, and use both ground and side paddles when going either up or down. At Watford the waterway swings east away from the M1 for good. The locks and Crick Tunnel with its wooded approaches offer canal excitement to contrast with the quiet of the landscape.

NAVIGATIONAL NOTES

1 Watford locks are open *daily*. The locks open *from 08.00* but the time of the last boat through depends on the time of year. From *end Apr–end Sep, last boat into lock is 18.15; during Oct and mid-Mar–end Apr 16.15; from Nov–mid Mar 14.45*. The exact times are variable depending when Easter falls, therefore, it is advisable to contact the lock keeper.

2 Local branches of the IWA have produced a guide to the Leicester Arm obtainable from various lockside positions (using a Watermate key) or from the IWA's Northampton Branch website (http://northampton.waterways.org.uk and select 'Local Links').

Welton

Northants. PO box, tel. The village climbs up the side of a steep, winding hill, which makes it compact and attractive, especially around the church.

Watford

Northants. PO box, tel. Set in the middle of wooded parkland, Watford gives the impression of being a private village. The church and Watford Court dominate, and luckily the M1 has made no impact. The 13th-C church contains some interesting monuments. The Court is partly 17th-C, although there are Victorian additions. The rich brown stone used throughout the village adds to the feeling of unity.

Crick Tunnel

1528yds long, the tunnel was opened in 1814. All tunnels built in this area suffered great problems in construction. Quicksands caused the route of the tunnel to be changed and greatly affected work. Stephenson found similar difficulties when building the nearby Kilsby Tunnel for the London to Birmingham railway.

Pubs and Restaurants

1 The New Inn Watling Street, Buckby Wharf, Long Buckby NN6 7PW (01327 844747; thenewinnbuckbywharf.co.uk). Canalside, at Buckby Top Lock. Cosy alcoved free house, serving real ale and a range of inexpensive meals and snacks *Mon-Sat L and E & Sun 12.00-19.00*. Child- and dog-friendly, patio and canalside seating. Traditional pub games and real fires. *Open daily12.00-23.00 (Sun 22.30).*

2 The White Horse High Street, Welton NN11 2JP (01327 702820; www.thewhitehorsewelton.co.uk). Delightful, 17th-C country pub serving real ales, real cider and excellent food *Wed-Sun L and E (not Sun E)*. Dog- and family-friendly, patio and garden. Traditional pub games, real fires and Wi-Fi. *Open Mon-Thu L and E (not Mon-Tue L) & Fri-Sun 12.00-00.00 (Sun 23.00).*

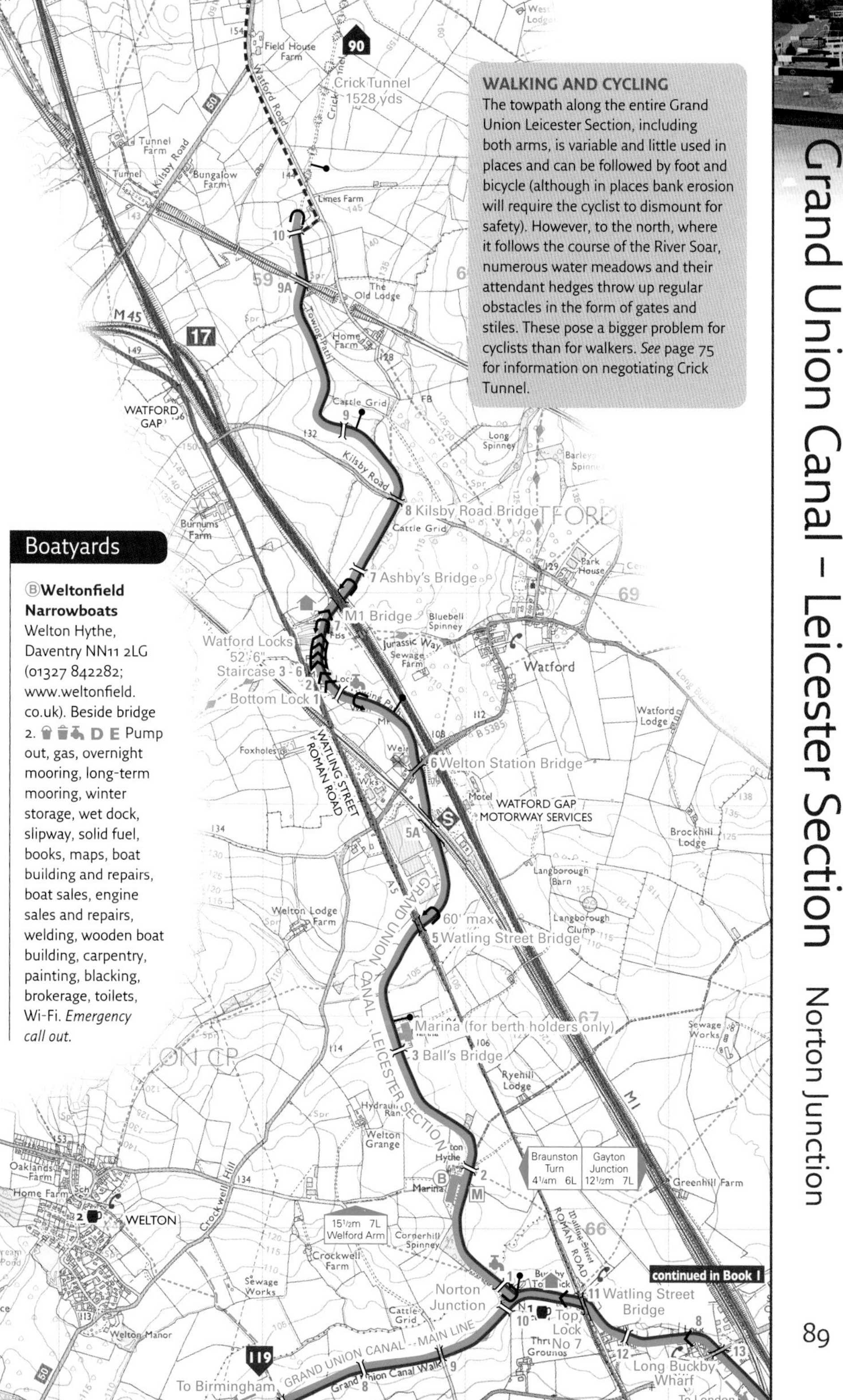

WALKING AND CYCLING

The towpath along the entire Grand Union Leicester Section, including both arms, is variable and little used in places and can be followed by foot and bicycle (although in places bank erosion will require the cyclist to dismount for safety). However, to the north, where it follows the course of the River Soar, numerous water meadows and their attendant hedges throw up regular obstacles in the form of gates and stiles. These pose a bigger problem for cyclists than for walkers. *See* page 75 for information on negotiating Crick Tunnel.

Boatyards

Ⓑ**Weltonfield Narrowboats** Welton Hythe, Daventry NN11 2LG (01327 842282; www.weltonfield.co.uk). Beside bridge 2. D E Pump out, gas, overnight mooring, long-term mooring, winter storage, wet dock, slipway, solid fuel, books, maps, boat building and repairs, boat sales, engine sales and repairs, welding, wooden boat building, carpentry, painting, blacking, brokerage, toilets, Wi-Fi. *Emergency call out.*

Yelvertoft

Leaving Crick Tunnel the navigation dodges the village and passes the site of an old wharf, followed by a large *marina*. After skirting Crack's Hill, a curious tree-topped mound, the canal wanders to the east in a series of loops which cause it to miss both Yelvertoft and Winwick, the only villages in the section. Hills surround the course of the canal, encouraging its meandering. At one point it passes under the same road three times in under a mile. Occasional woods add to the pleasure of the isolation. After Winwick, a vague north east course is resumed, passing the long-abandoned village of Elkington. There are no locks, but a regular procession of brick-arched bridges serves as a reminder that it is still a canal.

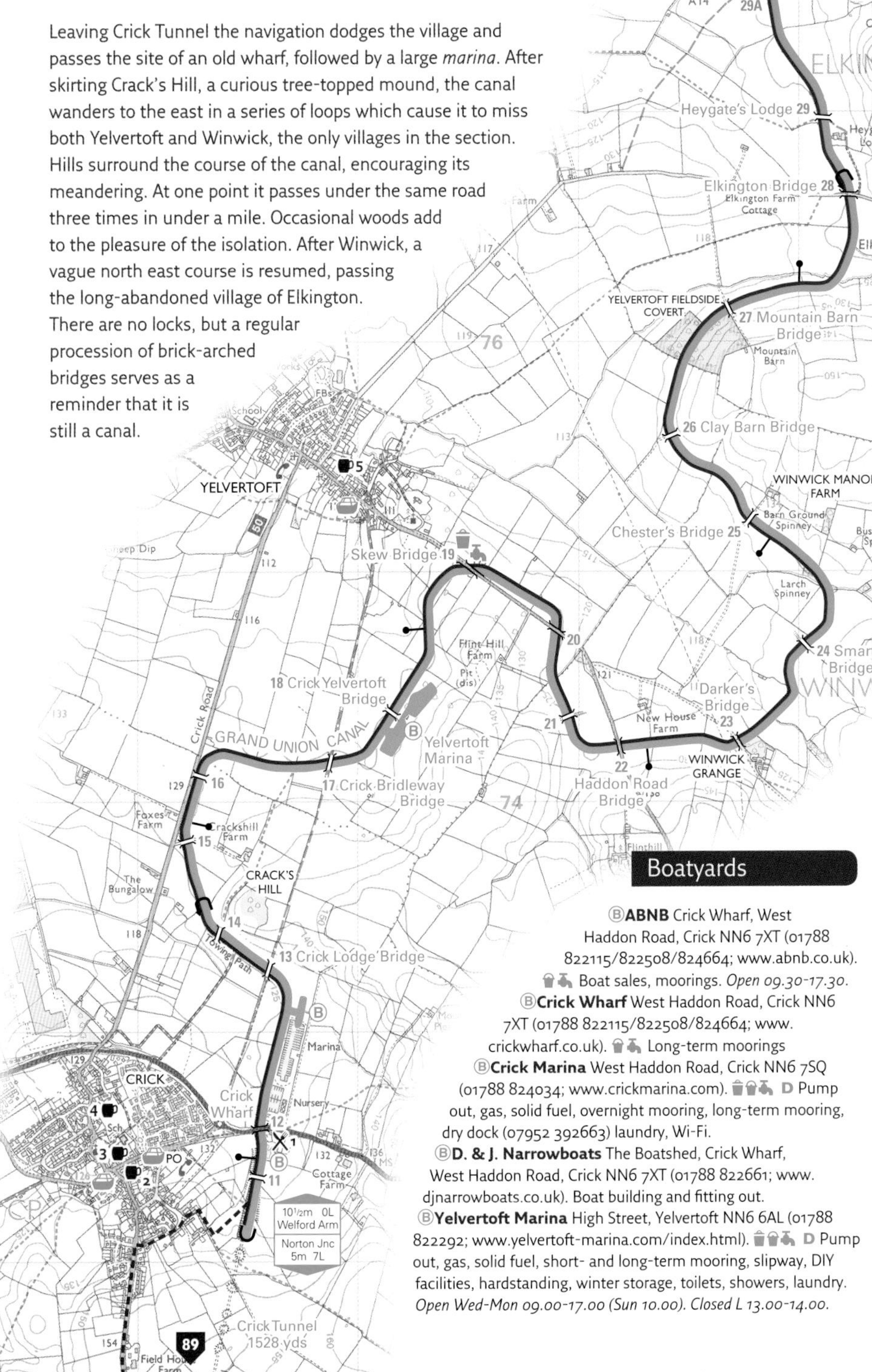

Boatyards

Ⓑ **ABNB** Crick Wharf, West Haddon Road, Crick NN6 7XT (01788 822115/822508/824664; www.abnb.co.uk). Boat sales, moorings. *Open 09.30-17.30.*

Ⓑ **Crick Wharf** West Haddon Road, Crick NN6 7XT (01788 822115/822508/824664; www.crickwharf.co.uk). Long-term moorings

Ⓑ **Crick Marina** West Haddon Road, Crick NN6 7SQ (01788 824034; www.crickmarina.com). D Pump out, gas, solid fuel, overnight mooring, long-term mooring, dry dock (07952 392663) laundry, Wi-Fi.

Ⓑ **D. & J. Narrowboats** The Boatshed, Crick Wharf, West Haddon Road, Crick NN6 7XT (01788 822661; www.djnarrowboats.co.uk). Boat building and fitting out.

Ⓑ **Yelvertoft Marina** High Street, Yelvertoft NN6 6AL (01788 822292; www.yelvertoft-marina.com/index.html). D Pump out, gas, solid fuel, short- and long-term mooring, slipway, DIY facilities, hardstanding, winter storage, toilets, showers, laundry. *Open Wed-Mon 09.00-17.00 (Sun 10.00). Closed L 13.00-14.00.*

- **Crick**
  Northants. PO, tel, stores, off-licence. A large village built around the junction of two roads. There are several attractive stone houses, and the large church has managed to escape restoration. It contains much decorative stonework and a circular Norman font.
- **Yelvertoft**
  Northants. Tel, stores, delicatessen. Set back from the canal, the village is built round a wide main street, terminated in the east by the church. Sadly, many of the original thatched roofs have been replaced.
- **Winwick**
  Northants. Tel. One mile south east of bridge 23. The 16th-C Manor House, built of richly decorated brick and with an ornamental Tudor gateway, is the major building in this neat, sleepy, village.

WALKING AND CYCLING

Walkers and cyclists bypassing Crick Tunnel need to take the short track on the right of the tunnel mouth and, on joining the minor road, turn left. Follow this into the village and turn right down Boathorse Lane. When the road bends sharply to the left walkers may follow the footpath straight ahead (signposted to West Haddon), cross a field along the hedgerow (still following the waymarking to West Haddon) and, having negotiated the stile, bear left diagonally, downhill across the next field following the line of the drainage pits to the sign in the hedge, which is immediately above the northern tunnel cutting. Cyclists are advised to follow the road through the village, bearing right and rejoining the canal at bridge 12.

Pubs and Restaurants

1 **The Moorings** West Haddon Road, Crick NN6 7SQ (01788 822517; www.themooringscrick.co.uk). Beside bridge 12. Restaurant and coffee house offering a wide-ranging menu from inexpensive snacks *L* through to a mouth-watering à la carte selection, available *Mon-Sun L and E (not Mon & Sun E)*. Tea, coffee, cake, etc available *throughout the day*. Everything homemade, including the bread. Excellent wine list.

2 **The Red Lion** 52 Main Street, Crick NN6 7TX (01788 822342). Real ale dispensed in a cosy, unadulterated pub with low ceilings and coal fires. Excellent home-cooked meals served with fresh vegetables *L and E (not Sun E)*. Children *L only*. Dogs welcome. Patio seating. *Open daily L and E.*

3 **The Wheatsheaf** 15 Main Road, Crick NN6 7TU (01788 823824). 18th-C, oak-beamed hostelry serving real ales and home-cooked food (sourced from local ingredients wherever possible) *Mon-Sat 12.00-21.00 (Fri-Sat 21.30) & Sun 12.00-20.00*. Children and dogs welcome, garden. Traditional pub games and real fires. Quiz *Tue*. B&B. *Open Mon-Sat 12.00-23.00 (Fri-Sat 00.00) & Sun 12.00-22.30.*

4 **The Royal Oak** 22 Church Street, Crick NN6 7TP (01788 822340; www.theroyaloakcrick.co.uk). Attractive old village local serving real ales and food *daily 16.00-22.00*. Dog- and child-friendly, garden. Traditional pub games, real fires, sports TV and Wi-Fi. Live music *Sun*. *Open Mon-Fri 15.00-00.00 & Sat-Sun 12.00-00.00.*

5 **The Knightley Arms** 49 High Street, Yelvertoft NN6 6LF (01788 823555). Traditional village pub, offering a warm welcome and a good range of real ales and a real cider. Home-cooked food available *L and E*. Children and dogs welcome, garden. Traditional pub games, real fires and sports TV. *Open Mon-Thu (not Mon-Tue L) & Fri-Sun 12.00-23.00.*

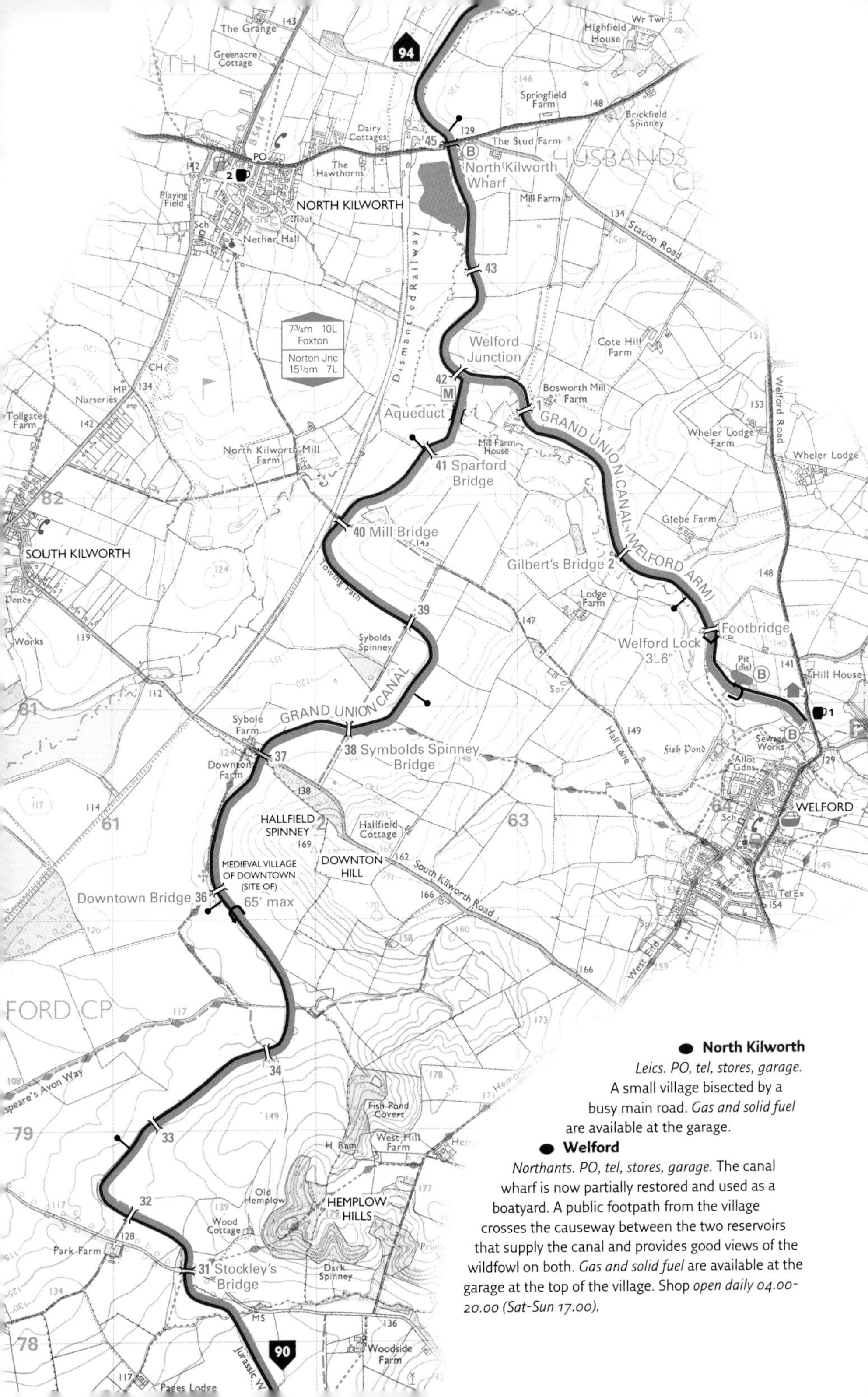

North Kilworth

Leics. PO, tel, stores, garage. A small village bisected by a busy main road. *Gas and solid fuel* are available at the garage.

Welford

Northants. PO, tel, stores, garage. The canal wharf is now partially restored and used as a boatyard. A public footpath from the village crosses the causeway between the two reservoirs that supply the canal and provides good views of the wildfowl on both. *Gas and solid fuel* are available at the garage at the top of the village. Shop *open daily 04.00-20.00 (Sat-Sun 17.00).*

Welford

Continuing north east the canal wanders on through open fields, backed by wooded hills to the east. To the west there are splendid views over the Avon valley. The river passes under the canal before the Welford Arm. Beyond the valley the spires of South and North Kilworth churches can be seen for several miles. The Welford Arm, which was completed in 1814, branches away to the south east for $1\frac{1}{4}$ miles, linking the canal with the Welford and Sulby reservoirs, and reaches its terminus in a small basin; there is one shallow lock on the arm. Otherwise it is quiet and tree-lined, following closely the path of the Avon, whose source is just east of Welford. The arm was reopened to navigation in 1969, having been derelict for some years. The main line continues, entering the wooded cutting that announces Husbands Bosworth Tunnel. There are no locks, but many of the bridges are original, fine faded red brick, echoing the seclusion of the canal.

Battle of Naseby 1645 2 miles east of Welford. Here Fairfax's New Model Army routed the Royalists under King Charles I, ensuring the end of the Civil War.

Stanford Hall Lutterworth LE17 6DH (01788 860250; stanfordhall.co.uk/events-activities.php). Two miles west of bridge 31. A William and Mary brick mansion (the south elevation is in stone), built in 1697-1700, with a Georgian stable block. Furniture, paintings, costume and a replica of the experimental flying machine built by Percy Pilcher in 1898. Walled rose garden and nature trail. Open *on select days throughout the year*, hosting a number of public events and car rallies throughout the summer season. Visit the website for details.

Boatyards

Ⓑ**Welford Marina /Narrowboats** Canal Wharf, Welford NN6 6JQ (01858 575995). Pump out, overnight mooring, long-term mooring, boat and engine repairs, boat fitting out, wet dock, dry dock, boat sales, DIY facilities, solid fuel, toilets.

Ⓑ**North Kilworth Wharf Ltd** Station Road, North Kilworth, Lutterworth LE17 6JB (01858 881723; www.northkilworthwharf.com). By bridge 45. D E Pump out. *Open Mon-Sun 09.00-17.00 (Sun 16.00).*

Ⓑ**North Kilworth Marina** Station Road, North Kilworth LE17 6HY (01858 450550; www.northkilworthmarina.co.uk). Long- and short-term moorings. At the time of going to press this marina was still under construction so telephone for details of the full boater facilities.

Pubs and Restaurants

1 The Wharf Inn Canal Wharf, Welford NN6 6JQ (01858 575075). Warm, friendly pub over 200 years old, popular with the locals, dispensing real ale, real cider and food *Mon-Sat L and E & Sun 12.00-20.00*. Children and dogs welcome, large garden. Newspapers, real fires and Wi-Fi. B&B. *Open 12.00-23.00.*

2 The White Lion Lutterworth Road, North Kilworth LE17 6EP (01858 882112; www.whitelionnorthkilworth.co.uk). Almost lost to housing development, this welcoming pub was saved by the developer himself and now lives on to serve real ale and an imaginative menu *Tue-Wed E and Thu-Sun L and E (not Sun E)*. Family-friendly and outside seating. Wi-Fi. *Open Tue-Wed E, Thu-Sat L and E & Sun 12.00-20.00.*

Husbands Bosworth

Continuing north east, the canal enters a remote, but attractive stretch. There are no villages on the canal here, Husbands Bosworth being hidden by the tunnel. The A50 crosses over the tunnel and meets the A427 in Husbands Bosworth. The canal runs north east through fields to the top of Foxton Locks. It then falls 75ft to join the former Leicester & Northampton Union Canal. At the bottom of the locks the 5½ mile Market Harborough Arm branches off to the east.

NAVIGATIONAL NOTES

Foxton Locks are open daily as per Watford Locks, *see* page 68.

Husbands Bosworth
Leics. PO, tel, stores (www.husbandsbosworth.info). Access from canal: walk up the lane from bridge 46. Shop *open daily 06.00-22.00.*
Husbands Bosworth Tunnel 1166yds long, the tunnel was opened in 1813.
Foxton Locks Gumley Road, Foxton, Market Harborough LE16 7RA (www.foxtonlocks.com). The Foxton staircase was opened in 1812. There are two staircases of five locks each with a passing pound in the middle. Check each flight of five is clear before you enter.
Foxton Inclined Plane Foxton, Market Harborough LE16 7RA. In 1900 an inclined plane was opened to bypass Foxton Locks. Two caissons carrying either two narrowboats or one barge moved sideways on rails up and down the plane. A steam-driven winch pulling an endless cable was used to start the caissons moving. The journey time was reduced from 70 to 12 minutes. Mechanical problems and high running costs, plus the fact that the planned widening of the Watford flight never took place, soon made the plane a white elephant. The cut leading to the bottom of the plane is still navigable, and the plane itself can still be traced, running at right angles to the east of the locks. Exploratory trail and museum. *Open Apr-Oct, Mon-Sun 10.00-17.00 (Sat-Sun 11.00) & Nov-Mar, Sat-Sun 11.00-16.00.* Charge. Restoration is in the hands of **Foxton Inclined Plane Trust** Middle Lock, Foxton Locks, Foxton, Market Harborough LE16 7RA (0116 279 2657; www.fipt.org.uk). There is a picnic site, car park and toilets (including disabled) at bridge 60, beside the Gumley Road. Charge.

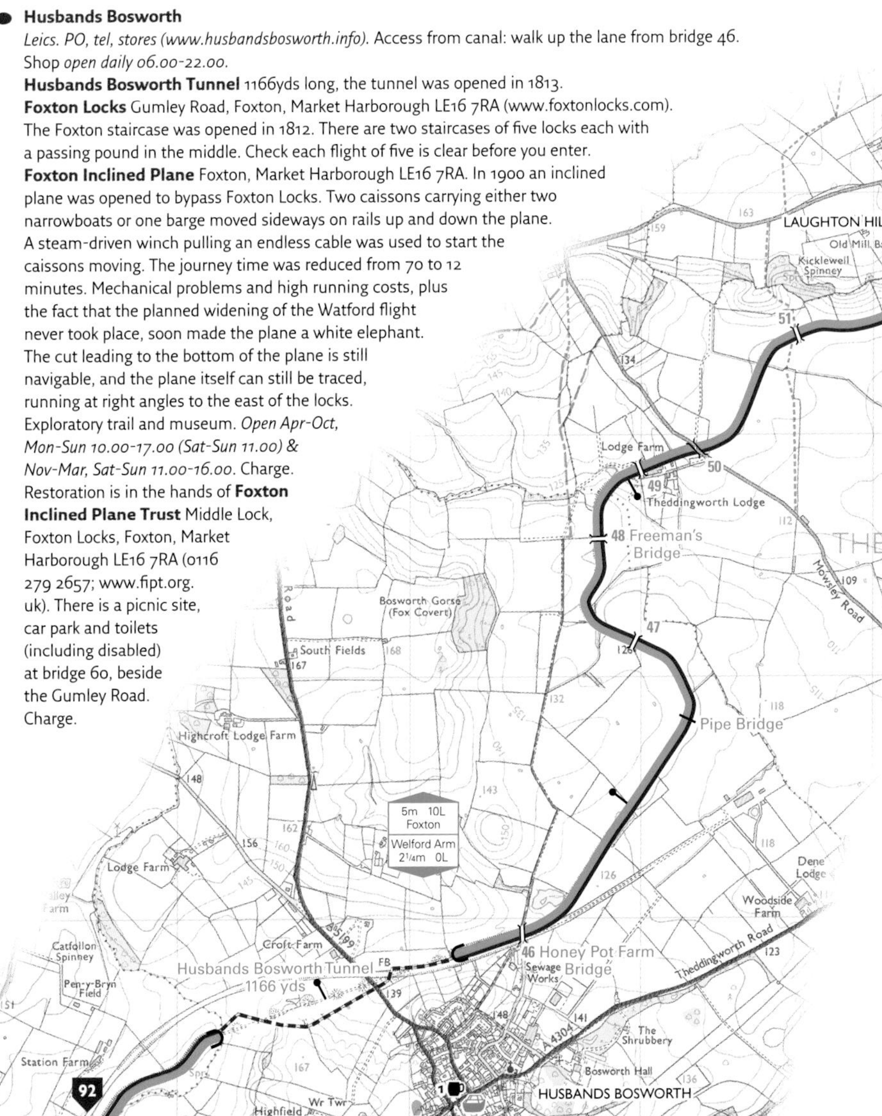

Boatyards

Ⓑ**Foxton Boat Services** Bottom Lock, Foxton, Market Harborough LE16 7RA (0116 279 2285; www.foxtonboats.co.uk). Gas, day-craft hire, chandlery, boat repairs, engine sales and repairs, toilets, showers, groceries, tearoom, laundrette, solid fuel, books, maps and gifts. Commercial boat hire. *Emergency call-out.*

Ⓑ**Union Wharf Narrowboats** The Canal Basin, Leicester Road, Market Harborough LE16 7AY (01858 432123; www.unionwharfmarina.com). Narrowboat hire, day boat hire, boat sales, online chandlery.

WALKING AND CYCLING

Walkers and cyclists confronted with Husbands Bosworth Tunnel should take the track climbing up to the left of the tunnel mouth and follow it over the hill to the road on the outskirts of the village (A50). Cross this road and follow the track over the disused railway line, down a tree-lined glade, rejoining the waterway at the eastern tunnel portal. The towpath is becoming seriously eroded and potentially dangerous on the Welford to Foxton stretch, especially in the Husbands Bosworth area, so exercise caution especially in the summer months when undergrowth potentially masks the hazards.

Pubs and Restaurants

1 The Bell Inn 2 Kilworth Road, Husbands Bosworth LE17 6JZ (01858 880246). Real ale and food available *Tue-Wed E, Thu-Fri L and E & Sat-Sun 12.00-21.00*. Dog- and child-friendly, garden. Traditional pub games, real fires, sports TV and Wi-Fi. *Open Mon-Fri L and E & Sat-Sun 12.00-00.00 (Sun 22.00).*

2 The Bell Inn Main Street, Gumley LE16 7RU (0116 279 0126; www.thebellinngumley.co.uk). Friendly, old village local serving real ale and real cider. Food available *L and E*. Child- and dog-friendly, garden. Traditional pub games, real fires, sports TV and Wi-Fi. *Open Mon-Fri L and E & Sat-Sun 12.00-23.00 (Sat 21.00).*

3 Bridge 61 Bottom Lock, Foxton, Market Harborough LE16 7RA (0116 279 2285; www.foxtonboats.co.uk). Small, popular pub serving real ale, coffees, teas and bar snacks *all day from 09.00*. Children and dogs welcome, canalside seating. Real fires. *Open daily 09.00-23.00.*

4 The Foxton Locks Inn Bottom Lock, Foxton, Market Harborough LE16 7RA (0116 279 1515; www.restaurantfoxtonlocks.co.uk). At the foot of the famous Foxton Locks. Pub garden overlooking the canal. Real ales, real cider and food available *Mon-Sun 12.00-20.45 (Sun 19.45)*. Dog- and child-friendly, garden and fully enclosed heated terrace. Wi-Fi. *Open 11.00-23.00.*

5 Lock Keepers Cottage Café Top Lock, Foxton, Market Harborough LE16 7RA (07789 817397). *Open as per Foxton Locks opening times.* Coffee tea, breakfasts, various hot rolls and cream teas. Souvenirs.

BOAT TRIPS

Vagabond Foxton Boat Services, Bottom Lock, Foxton, Market Harborough LE16 7RA (0116 279 2285; www.foxtonboats.co.uk). Canal trips for casual visitors *on summer weekends, B Hols, and school holiday weekday afternoons* from Foxton bottom lock; available for charter by parties any other day. Dogs go free.

Market Harborough

The Market Harborough Arm runs along the side of the hills which dominate the landscape to the south. The original plan was to build a canal to Northampton but this was abandoned due to lack of funds, leaving a 5½-mile branch. In the terminal basin there are *visitor moorings* with *electrical hook-ups* together with *showers, toilets and pump out* (by appointment – telephone 01858 432123). The site of the inclined plane, beside Foxton Locks, is well worth exploring (see page 95) and progress is being made towards partial restoration with a grant of £1.78m from the Heritage Lottery Fund.

● **Foxton**
Leics. PO, tel, stores. A village built on the side of a hill, either side of the canal, in pretty countryside. There is an excellent information leaflet and village trail available from Foxton Boat Services and Market Harborough Tourist Information Centre. The village stores (07837 734010; www.foxtonvillagestore.co.uk) operates a grocery box system and provides good, old-fashioned service. *Open Mon-Sat 09.00-17.00.*

● **Market Harborough**
Leics. All services (except cinema). Established as a market town by 1203, Market Harborough still retains much of its rural elegance and local importance. There are various markets *Tue-Sat 08.00-17.00* and an antiques and collectors market *Sun 10.00-16.00* (01858 465206/07773 058933; www.harboroughmarket.co.uk).

Traveline (0871 200 22 33; www.traveline.info) for details on bus travel.

Frank Haynes Gallery 50 Station Road, Great Bowden, Market Harborough LE16 7HN (01858 464862). 3/4 mile north of the station. Two galleries with paintings and pottery from the region. Cards, etc. *Open Thu-Sun 10.00-17.00.* Free.

Harborough Leisure Centre Northampton Road, Market Harborough LE16 9HF (01858 410115; www.harboroughleisurecentre.co.uk). The usual mix of swimming pool, child-enticing water features, fitness room, etc. Also bar, bistro and crèche.

Harborough Museum The Symington Building Adam and Eve Street, Market Harborough LE16 7LT (0116 305 3627; www.harboroughmuseum.org.uk). Contains the Civic Society's own collection and illustrates local life from the earliest times. Relics of the Battle of Naseby, a reconstructed bootmaker's workshop and the Symington Collection of corsetry. *Open Tue-Sat 10.00-18.00 (Sat 16.00).* Free.

Harborough Theatre Church Square, Market Harborough LE16 7NB (01858 463673; www.harboroughtheatre.com).

Market Harborough Canal Basin Significant as the site of the first Inland Waterways Association campaigning rally held in 1950 which, arguably, laid the foundations for a resurgence in canal interest that could easily be taken for granted by the contemporary pleasure boater. The canal basin – or Union Wharf – has been extended and the surrounding area developed with apartments, a time-share base and small business units, making it completely unrecognisable from the wharfs and timber storage sheds that used to predominate.

Parish Church of St Dionysius High Street, Market Harborough LE16 7NB (www.harborough-anglican.org.uk). Built in the 14thC by Scropes and enlarged a century later.

Old Grammar School High Street, Market Harborough LE16. Founded by Robert Smyth. It stands on wooden carved pillars, and behind the arches was held the ancient butter market. The building was used as the grammar school until 1892 and is now a meeting hall.

Tourist Information Centre Millers House, Roman Way, Market Harborough LE16 7PQ (01858 828282; www.harborough.gov.uk). *Open Mon–Fri 08.45–17.00, Sat 09.30–12.30.*

NAVIGATIONAL NOTES

A Watermate key is required to operate Foxton Swing Bridge No 4.

WALKING AND CYCLING

Brampton Valley Way runs for 14 miles along an old railway track and links Market Harborough with the northern outskirts of Northampton. It makes use of two old tunnels and passes a selection of old steam locomotives at Chapel Brampton.

Pubs and Restaurants

1 **The Waterfront** Union Wharf, Market Harborough LE16 7UW (01858 434702; waterfrontharborough.co.uk). Canalside bar, fish and grill restaurant, bereft of real ale. Upstairs gin bar *Wed-Sat from 17.00 & Sun 12.00-20.00*. Canalside seating. *Open Mon-Sun 11.00-23.00 (Sun 20.00).*

2 **The Black Horse** Main Street, Foxton, Market Harborough LE16 7RD (01858 545250). Real ales and lovely gardens. An excellent selection of home-made food available *L and E, daily (not Sun E)*. (Bookings available *Tue-Sun L and E (not Sun E)*. Children and dogs welcome. Traditional pub games and real fires. *Open Mon-Fri L and E, Sat 12.00-23.00 & Sun 12.00-18.00.*

3 **The Shoulder of Mutton** Main Street, Foxton, Market Harborough LE16 7RB (01858 545964). Real ales and a wide variety of steaks are the staple of this hostelry close to Foxton Locks. Children welcome. Large garden and patio seating. Wi-Fi. B&B. *Open Mon-Thu 17.00-23.00 & Fri-Sun 12.00-23.00.*

4 **The Angel Hotel** 37 High Street, Market Harborough LE16 7AF (01858 462702; www.theangel-hotel.co.uk). Hotel serving food from full à la carte restaurant menu through to bar meals *L and E*. Real ales. Real fires, newspapers, sports TV and Wi-Fi. B&B. *Open 11.00-23.00 (Sun 22.30).*

5 **The Three Swans Hotel** 21 High Street, Market Harborough LE16 7NJ (01858 466644; www.bw-threeswanshotel.co.uk). Real ales and a comprehensive range of bar and restaurant food *09.00-18.00 daily*. Dog- and family-friendly, courtyard seating. Real fires, newspapers, sports TV and Wi-Fi. *Open 10.00-23.00 (Fri-Sat 00.00).*

6 **The Red Cow** 59-60 High Street, Market Harborough LE16 7AF (01858 461635; www.theredcowmarketharborough.co.uk). A selection of real ales and bottled beers available *Mon-Sat 09.00-00.00 (Fri-Sat 01.00) & Sun 10.00-00.00*. Dogs welcome. Traditional pub games, newspapers and sports TV.

Smeeton Westerby

From Foxton the canal continues north and swings north west towards Leicester. Shortly before the tunnel an unnavigable feeder joins the canal from Saddington Reservoir. It is a quiet, empty landscape, all villages set back from the canal, leaving it to pursue a vague course through open fields and occasional trees. No locks, and a curious mixture of bridges, some original, some rebuilt in the 19th C in red brick, some more modern. The A6 and the railway pass beyond the hills to the east, parallel to the canal.

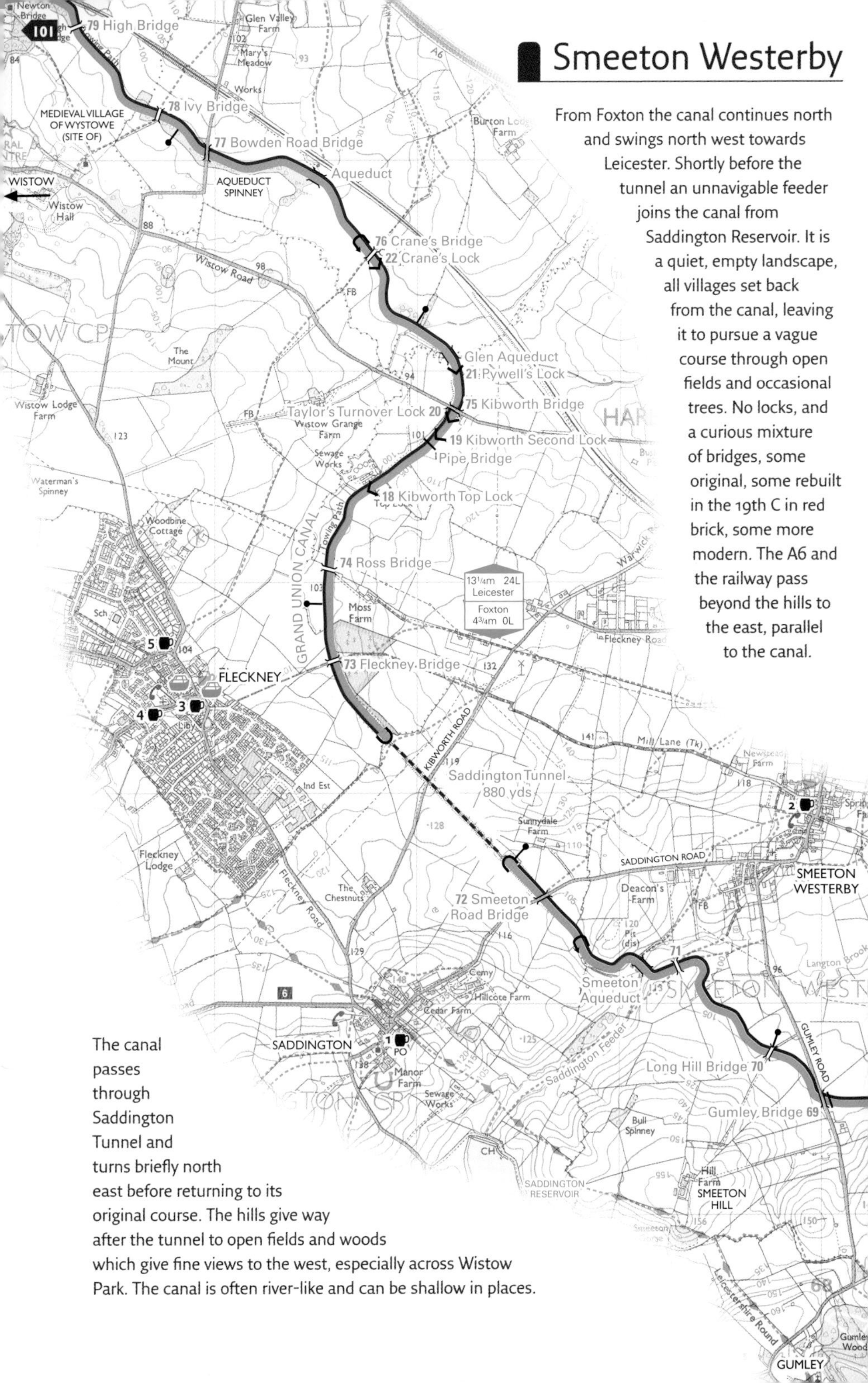

The canal passes through Saddington Tunnel and turns briefly north east before returning to its original course. The hills give way after the tunnel to open fields and woods which give fine views to the west, especially across Wistow Park. The canal is often river-like and can be shallow in places.

- **Gumley**
  Leics. PO box, tel. 1/2 mile west of bridge 63. Small village scattered among trees, set on a hillside high above the canal. The Italianate tower of Gumley Hall rises above the trees, overlooking the valley.
- **Saddington**
  Leics. PO box, tel, farm shop. Small village set back from the canal, with only the church tower breaking the skyline. There is a *farm shop*, selling a range of fresh local produce at the Queens Head *open daily 09.00-14.00 and you can ask a member of the pub staff for service outside these hours.*
- **Smeeton Westerby**
  Leics. Tel. The village undulates over the hills to the east of the canal, built along the sides of the main street.

Saddington Tunnel 880yds long, the tunnel was completed in 1797, after great difficulties owing to its being built crooked. Naturalists enthuse about the bats that nowadays live in the tunnel.

- **Fleckney**
  Leics. PO, tel, stores, off-licence, chemist, butcher, takeaway, library. An industrial village just 10 minutes' walk from the canal. Shop *open Mon-Sat 08.00-21.00 & Sun 09.00-16.00.*
- **Wistow**
  Leics. For a while the canal runs through woods and parkland to the west adjoining Wistow Park. Wistow itself has a church and a Hall, the church with Norman work but mostly 18th-C, including fine monuments. The Hall is Jacobean in principle but was largely rebuilt in the 19th C. For amusement there is a maize maze.

Pubs and Restaurants

1 The Queens Head Main Street, Saddington LE8 0QH (0116 240 2536; www.queensheadsaddington.co.uk). A village centre pub with attractive gardens and a cosy restaurant, set in a tasteful extension with superb views over Saddington Reservoir. Real ales and real cider. A wide range of food is available in the bar or à la carte restaurant *Mon-Fri L and E, Sat 12.00-21.30 & Sun 12.00-18.00.* Booking advisable *especially at weekends.* Dog- and child-friendly. Real fires and Wi-Fi. *Open Mon-Tue L and E & Wed-Sun 12.00-23.00 (Sun 22.00).* Farm shop *open daily 09.00-14.00.*

2 The Kings Head 23 Main Street, Smeeton Westerby LE8 0QJ (0116 279 2676; smeetonwesterby.co.uk/kings-head.html). Unadulterated, village local offering a friendly welcome and real ale. Inexpensive food available *Tue-Sun 12.00-14.00 (Sun 14.30).* Children and dogs welcome. Small patio area. Darts. *Open Tue-Sun 12.00-23.00.*

3 The Old Crown 7 High Street, Fleckney LE8 8AJ (0116 240 2223; www.oldcrownfleckney.co.uk). West of bridge 73. Wide range of real ales and food served *daily* in this friendly, welcoming village pub. *Sun* carvery *12.00-15.00.* Children welcome. Large garden; pool, darts and cards. Real fires, sports TV and Wi-Fi. *Open daily L and E (not Mon L and Sun E).*

4 The Golden Shield 46 Main Street, Fleckney LE8 8AN (0116 240 2366; www.goldenshieldfleckney.co.uk). Cosy village local serving real ales and appetising food, prepared from locally sourced ingredients, *Wed-Sun L and E (not Sun E).* Child- and dog-friendly, garden. Traditional pub games, sports TV and Wi-Fi. *Open Mon-Thu 16.00-23.00, Wed-Thu 12.00-14.00 & Fri-Sun 12.00-00.00 (Sun 22.00).*

5 The Crown of India 6 Leicester Road, Fleckney LE8 8BF (0116 240 4580; the-crown-of-india.co.uk). Highly-regarded Indian takeaway happy to deliver to locations along the canal. Online ordering. *Open daily 17.30-22.45.*

Boatyards

Ⓑ **Debdale Wharf Marina**
Debdale Wharf, Kibworth LE8 0XA (0116 279 3034; www.debdalewharf.co.uk). D E Pump out, gas, overnight mooring, long-term mooring, winter storage, slipway, crane (32 tons), dry dock, wet dock, chandlery, boat lengthening, boat repairs, engine sales and repairs, boat building and boat fitting out, DIY facilities, books and maps, solid fuel, general fabrication, laundry. *Emergency call out.*

Wigston

Newton Harcourt breaks the unwritten rule of this navigation by being right beside it (other villages keep their distance). The tunnel, the bridges and the locks which begin the descent to Leicester provide plenty of canal interest although the amount of rubbish in the waterway begins to increase. The A6 and the main railway slowly encroach on the canal to the east. The navigation follows the north westerly course of the River Sence, bounded by low hills to east and west and still remote, until Kilby Bridge (*showers and toilets*) where indications of the city of Leicester begin with distant views of housing estates and factories. By Ervin's Lock at South Wigston the city seems, for a while, to take over. The locks continue the steady fall, giving the stretch its individuality. Immediately to the north west of Leicester Road Bridge (98) is the original site of Pickfords Canal Carriers, established when they transferred their activities from horse and cart to the newly burgeoning canals. A little further west, before the navigation swings north, are the disused clay pits and derelict brickyard, once owned by the Union Canal Company; they produced the materials used to construct its locks and bridges.

Boatyards

Ⓑ**CRT Kilby Bridge Yard** Pump out, moorings, showers.

NAVIGATIONAL NOTES

A CRT Watermate key is required to operate the water saving devices between Kilby Bridge and Aylestone Mill.

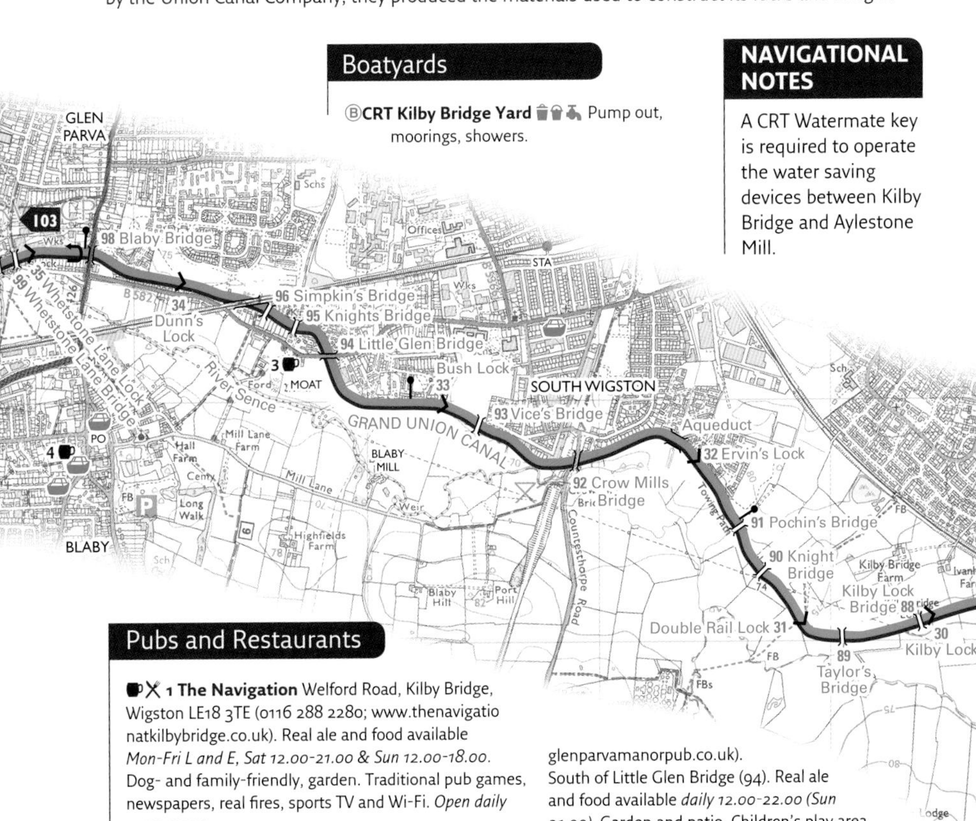

Pubs and Restaurants

1 The Navigation Welford Road, Kilby Bridge, Wigston LE18 3TE (0116 288 2280; www.thenavigationatkilbybridge.co.uk). Real ale and food available *Mon-Fri L and E, Sat 12.00-21.00 & Sun 12.00-18.00.* Dog- and family-friendly, garden. Traditional pub games, newspapers, real fires, sports TV and Wi-Fi. *Open daily 11.30-23.30.*

2 The Horse and Trumpet Bull Head Street, Wigston LE18 1PB (0116 288 6290; www.everards.co.uk/our-pubs/horse-trumpet-wigston). One mile north of Kilby Bridge on A5199. Real ale and inexpensive *Sun L* carvery, together with *Thu E* steak *night*. Dog- and child-friendly, courtyard seating. Traditional pub games. *Open Mon-Thu 17.00-23.00 & Fri-Sun 12.00-00.00 (Sun 23.00).*

3 Glen Parva Manor The Ford, Little Glen Road, Glen Parva LE2 9TL (0116 247 7604; www.glenparvamanorpub.co.uk). South of Little Glen Bridge (94). Real ale and food available *daily 12.00-22.00 (Sun 21.00)*. Garden and patio. Children's play area. Real fires and Wi-Fi. *Open 12.00-23.00 (Sun 22.30).*

4 The Baker's Arms The Green, Blaby LE8 4FQ (0116 278 7253; www.thebakersarms.com). A 15th-C, heavily beamed and thatched village local dispensing real ale and real cider in summer. Also an an 18th-C museum bakery to see. Food available *Tue-Sun L and E (not Sun E)*. Traditional *Sun L* and children's menu. Garden and real fires. Children and dogs welcome. *Open daily 12.00-23.00 (Fri-Sat 00.00).*

- **Newton Harcourt**
  Leics. Scattered village bisected by the railway in a cutting. The Hall is 17th-C, with later rebuilding; it has a fine gateway. Newton Harcourt is a well-known Leicester beauty spot, popular on *Sun afternoons.*
  Traveline (0871 200 22 33; www.traveline.info). For full details on bus travel to local (and not so local) attractions.
  Brocks Hill Country Park & Environment Centre Washbrook Lane, Oadby LE2 5JJ (0116 257 2888; www.oadby-wigston.gov.uk/pages/brocks_hill_visitor_centre_and_country_park). Unique environment centre built to demonstrate wind and solar power, photovoltaics, rainwater recycling and sewerage composting. Set in 67 acres of country park with woodland, meadowland and an Arboretum. Café open *daily 10.00-16.00.* Park *open all year* and Centre *open Mon-Fri 10.00-17.00; Sat, Sun and B Hols 10.00-16.00.* Free. Although a 2½ mile walk north along footpath from Clifton Bridge (85) and then via A5199 and B582, a visit to the centre makes a very worthwhile day out.
- **Kilby Bridge**
  Leics. PO, tel.
  Wistow Rural Centre Wistow, nr Great Glen LE8 0QF (www.wistow.com). Take the footpath south from Ivy Bridge (78) to the church. Acclaimed model village (setting for the children's storybook *Tales from Old Wistan*), 1/18th scale, mid-Victorian period. Village railway. Also craft shop, artists' studios, teashop serving lunches, teas and coffee, garden centre and village store. *Open Mon-Sat 09.00-17.00 & Sun 10.30-16.30.* Donations to Rainbow, a children's hospice charity. Also award-winning Wistow Maize Maze during the summer. Visit the website for more information.
- **South Wigston**
  Leics. PO, tel, stores, chemist, bakery, library, off-licence, fish & chips, takeaways, garage, station. Wigston is now part of Leicester, but traces of its earlier independence can still be found. Much of the handsome church dates from the 14th C, especially the interior, while the cottages in Spa Lane, with their long strips of upper window, indicate an old Leicester industry, stocking making. At Wigston Magna there is a tiny Norman church and a monument to the Roman town of Veronae. Unfortunately, only housing estates and a school can be seen from the canal, but exploration is worthwhile.
  Wigston Framework Knitters Museum 42-44 Bushloe End, Wigston LE18 2BA (0116 288 2637; www.wigstonframeworkknitters.co.uk). About ½ mile north of Kilby Bridge (87). Heritage award winning 18th-C knitters house and workshop. Demonstrations and tranquil Victorian garden open to visitors to the rear of the building. *Open every Sun and 1st Sat of the month 14.00-17.00. Also B Hol Mon. Closed Xmas.* Charge.
- **Blaby**
  Leics. PO, tel, stores, takeaways, butcher, banks, off-licence, fish & chips, chemist, garage. The church is partly 14th-C, with a fine 18th-C gallery unsuited to the Blaby of today. The shop is *open Mon-Sat 08.00-22.00 & Sun 10.00-16.00.*

WALKING AND CYCLING

The navigation from Blaby into Leicester runs through a linear country park and mostly parallels the off-road cycleway along the old Great Central trackbed. It is covered in three sections by a detailed series of leaflets, entitled *Discover Leicester's Riverside Park*, and available from Tourist Information Centres in the area. Both the towpath and the cycleway offer excellent walking and cycling opportunities. Throughout the city itself there is a series of well-marked cycle routes using coloured banding.

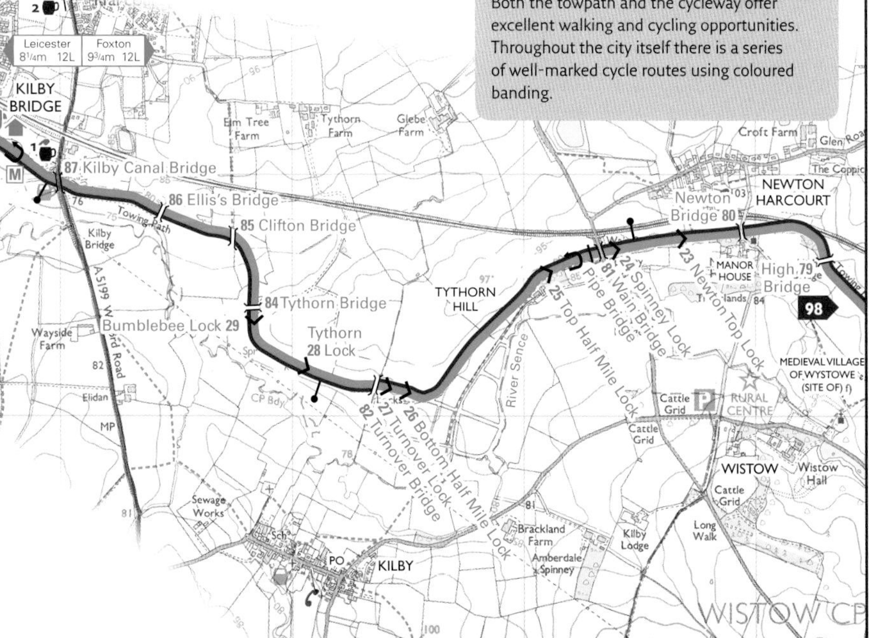

Aylestone

Following the River Sence to its junction with the Soar, the navigation makes a wide swing around Glen Parva and then flows north into Leicester along the Soar valley. After Glen Parva the buildings suddenly cease, and there follows a mile of pleasant rural waterway, lightly wooded to the east, and with the extensive water meadows of the Soar to the west. Sometimes the river and canal flow side by side separated only by the towpath; sometimes they share the same bed. Inevitably in winter this can cause flooding, *and anyone intending to navigate this stretch after heavy rainfall should check the state of the water before proceeding.* Only the pylons and the distant views of Braunston and Aylestone reveal the closeness of Leicester. Now, with the football ground in full view, the canal and the River Soar meet for the penultimate time above a huge weir; care is needed during times of flood. The canal enters Leicester along a pleasant cutting. A variety of buildings line the banks and there is a fine canalside walk under the ornamental bridges that lead straight into the town centre by West Bridge. These factors combine to make the canal entry to Leicester outstanding among large towns. The A46 and A426 run parallel to the canal, but the railway which follows it, the old Great Central line, has long been closed.

NAVIGATIONAL NOTES

1. Strong Stream Warning markers are fixed below all locks on the river sections between here and the River Trent. Boaters should check the readings and observe the warnings.
2. The canal and the River Soar meet just above Freeman's Meadow Lock, where there is an enormous unprotected weir. Care is needed, especially in time of flood. KEEP WELL OVER TO THE TOWPATH SIDE.

Glen Parva

Leics. Suburb of Leicester inseparable now from the main town. Curiously enough there was a Saxon cemetery in the town from which 6th-C grave ornaments have been excavated.

Aylestone

Leics. PO, tel, stores, takeaways, chemist, off-licence, fish & chips, garage. A Leicester suburb coming down to the east bank of the canal. The church contains an interesting stained-glass window of 1930. To the west of the canal the Soar is crossed by an old stone packhorse bridge of eight low arches, perhaps dating from the 15th C. This area still retains the feel of a country village, at least in the area sandwiched between the main Rugby road and the navigation. Narrow streets, bordered by pretty brick cottages, isolate the walker from the bustle of what is otherwise a busy suburb of Leicester. Aylestone Hall and its surrounding gardens and recreational park is a particular haven of peace. On the west of the waterway Aylestone Meadows is now a nature reserve stretching for 1½ miles along the canal and Great Central Way (once the route of the Great Central Railway and now a cycle route and footpath). There are waymarked circular walks along a network of paths together with excellent illustrated interpretation boards. The nature reserve is operated by Leicester City Council who employ rangers who patrol the riverside on motorcycles and can provide advice and assistance. Access for shops and the Union Inn is east from Freestone Bridge (106). There is also a useful *farm shop* between Packhorse Bridge (105) and the railway bridge.

Traveline (0871 200 22 33; www.traveline.info). For full details on bus travel to local (and not so local) attractions.

The National Gas Museum 195 Aylestone Road, Leicester LE2 7QJ(0116 250 3190/07557 612340; www.goleicestershire.com/thedms.aspx?dms=3&venue=2500498). Situated in the Victorian gatehouse of one of the city's gas works: the first museum to tell the story of the impact of gas on our lives from 19th-C lighting to a gas hairdryer and radio. *Open Tue-Thu 10.30-15.00 (closed Xmas-New Year's Day).* Free. Disabled access to ground floor.

Raw Dykes Ancient Monument Aylestone Road, Leicester (www.leicester.gov.uk). A large earthwork near to the canal and River Soar; presumed to be a Romano-British aqueduct. Viewing area *open at all times.*

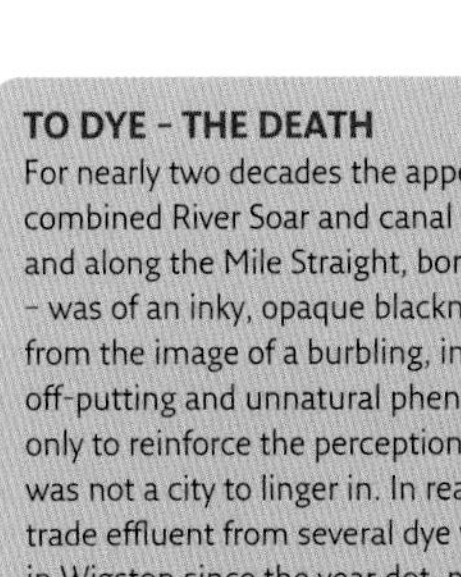

TO DYE – THE DEATH

For nearly two decades the appearance of the combined River Soar and canal skirting Aylestone – and along the Mile Straight, bordering the city itself – was of an inky, opaque blackness far removed from the image of a burbling, infant stream. This off-putting and unnatural phenomenon served only to reinforce the perception that Leicester was not a city to linger in. In reality the cause was trade effluent from several dye works, established in Wigston since the year dot, passing straight through the local sewerage treatment works. New legislation, however, imposed colour conditions on discharges amounting to full colour removal: a real challenge for the Environment Agency's hard-pressed chemists.

Yet what remained was the puzzle of the problem's relatively recent origins. One plausible explanation lay in the changing nature of the fashion industry. Once, ostensibly, buyer-led (we responded to the length of a skirt or the cut of a suit) our sartorial whims became firmly orchestrated by the industry itself, colour consistently being its key device. In unison went a definite movement towards man-made fibres and their reactive dye processes; bright colours predominated in wardrobes, their turgid residues lingered in rivers.

Pubs and Restaurants

1 Kings Lock Tearooms Kings Lock, Marsden Lane, Aylestone LE2 8LT (07722 542034). Cosy, welcoming tearooms in the delightful old lock keeper's cottage beside the lock serving cream teas, coffee, ices, baguettes and appetising daily specials all home-made. Outside seating. Dogs and children welcome. *Open Apr-Oct, Thu-Sun 10.30-15.30 (Sun 16.30) & B Hol Mon 11.00-17.00.* Live music *every 3rd Sun in month.*

2 The Union Inn 24 Middleton Street, Aylestone, Leicester LE2 8LU (0116 283 1796/07970 553424). Friendly, and often boisterous pub, serving real ale. Dog- and family-friendly, patio. Traditional pub games, newspapers, sports TV and Wi-Fi. *Open daily 11.00-23.00 (Sun 12.00).*

3 The Black Horse 65 Narrow Lane, off Sanvey Lane, Aylestone, Leicester LE2 8NA (0116 283 7225; www.blackhorse-aylestone.co.uk). East of Packhorse Bridge (105); fork left up Sanvey Lane, and then first left. A wide range of real ales and real ciders are available together with home-cooked food *daily 12.00-20.30 (Sun 17.30)*. Dog- and family-friendly, large beer garden. Traditional pub games, real fires and Wi-Fi. Quiz *Sun. Open 11.00-23.00 (Sun 12.00).*

Leicester

For almost all of its journey through the city of Leicester, the navigation pursues a course quite separate from the river, the navigation having been rebuilt towards the end of the 19th C as part of Leicester's flood prevention scheme. For more than ½ mile south of West Bridge, the navigation, a section known locally as the Mile Straight, is like a formal avenue, tree-lined and crossed by several ornamental iron bridges, but where it curves under the old Great Central Railway it begins to follow a less public course through the nether regions of Leicester. A combination of locks, once-derelict canal basins (some now restored for moorings), tall factory buildings and a substantial stretch of parkland adds up to a stretch of urban canal that offers a greater variety of interest than exists in most other cities. At Belgrave Lock the canal joins the Soar, which proceeds to meander carelessly through the city's outskirts. The city centre is remarkably compact, and there are some gems amongst the façades jostled together along its main thoroughfares, with everything surprisingly close to the secure *moorings* at Castle Gardens and Friars Mill (between Bridges 3 and 4). As in the case with all large towns, if you moor at an unprotected site make sure your boat is securely locked if you leave it unattended. Birstall provides a useful *mooring* and place to shop to the north of the city: tie up near the lock and walk up beside the White Horse.

NAVIGATIONAL NOTES

It is worth remembering that the River Soar may flood at any time, so boaters travelling after heavy rainfall should enquire about the navigational conditions in advance in order to avert the risk of running aground in the middle of a water meadow.

● **Leicester**
All services. A prosperous city with two universities. Fortunes were founded on the hosiery and the boot and shoe trades, but now a variety of light industries flourish in Leicester. There are a great many things to see, for this was the Roman town of Ratae and there is plenty of evidence of the Roman buildings, plus a castle that dates from 1088, with the delightful church of St Mary de Castro next to it. The travel agent Thomas Cook started business in Leicester; in 1841 he organised the first publicly advertised excursion by train. It was a great success, and Cook made the organising of such trips a regular occupation. Leicester has a particularly good selection of museums, and it is fortunate that most of these are near the Grand Union Canal which forms the western boundary of Castle Park. The city should be commended, both for the comprehensive manner in which it markets its copious wealth of attractions and for promoting its cultural diversity in such a positive fashion. The opportunities to sample Asian cuisine, produce, jewellery, cloth, faith and festivals must be second to none outside the Indian sub-continent and could, alone, fill this page. With the provision of secure visitor moorings at Castle Gardens and Friars Mill, boaters have no reason to ignore a city that has so much to offer.

Abbey Park Abbey Park Road, Leicester LE4 5AQ. All that remains of the abbey is a mansion built from the ruins and the old stone wall surrounding the grounds. Cardinal Wolsey was buried here in 1530. The park itself, very much in the Victorian mould, has a boating lake, Chinese garden, bandstand and riverside café and is the setting for music festivals and fairs. There is a landing stage in Abbey Park Basin. *Open daily.*

Abbey Pumping Station Corporation Road, Abbey Lane, Leicester LE4 5PX (0116 299 5111; www.abbeypumpingstation.org). Dating from 1891 this refurbished site features the Victorian steam-powered beam engines that used to pump the city's sewerage to the nearby treatment plant. Also a unique public health exhibition and the manager's house c. World War II. *Open Feb–Oct, daily, 11.00–16.30.* Free. Partial disabled access. Moorings.

Belgrave Hall and Gardens Church Road, Belgrave, Leicester LE4 5PE (0116 229 8181; www.leicester.gov.uk/leisure-and-culture/museums-and-galleries/museums-and-historic-venues/belgrave-hall). Three-storey Queen Anne house dating from 1709 with attractive period and botanical gardens, and 18th- and 19th-C room settings including kitchen, drawing room and nursery. The gardens are *open Apr–Sep, Wed & first full weekend in the month 11.00–16.30.* Hall *open to the public during some events* – visit website for further details. Partial Disabled access to gardens and ground floor only. Moorings.

Boatyards

Ⓑ **MGM Boats Ltd** 27 Mill Lane Boatyard, Thurmaston, Leicester LE4 8EF (0116 264 0009; www.mgmboats.co.uk). Slipway, gas, boat repairs, overnight and long-term mooring, winter storage, engine sales and repairs, boat building, boat fitting out, solid fuel, showers, toilets, laundrette.

Ⓑ **Leicester Marina** Pinfold Road, Thurmaston, Leicester LE4 8AS (0116 260 6166; www.leicestermarina.co.uk). D Pump out, gas, overnight mooring, long-term mooring, slipway, boat sales, solid fuel, laundrette, toilets, showers.

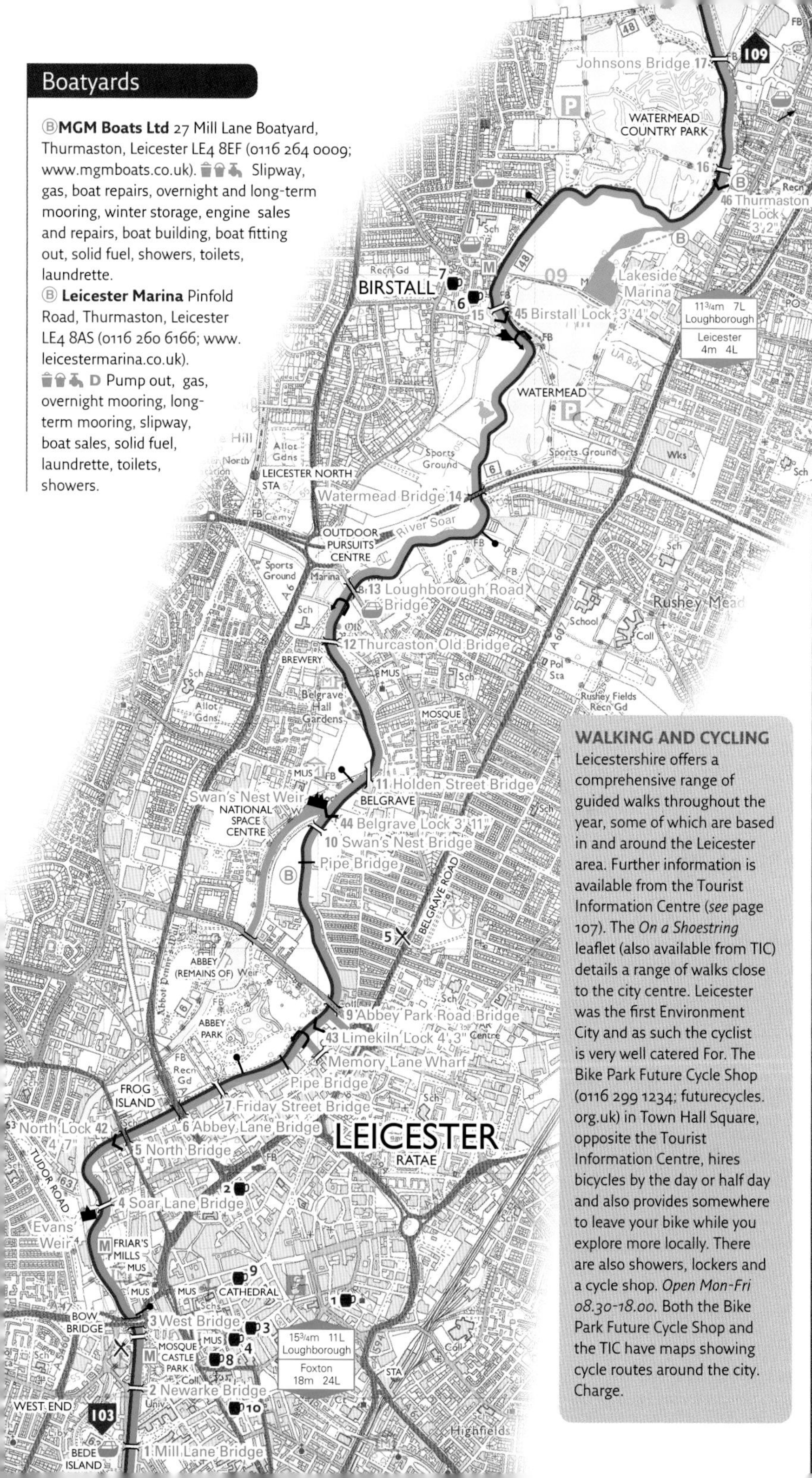

WALKING AND CYCLING

Leicestershire offers a comprehensive range of guided walks throughout the year, some of which are based in and around the Leicester area. Further information is available from the Tourist Information Centre (*see* page 107). The *On a Shoestring* leaflet (also available from TIC) details a range of walks close to the city centre. Leicester was the first Environment City and as such the cyclist is very well catered For. The Bike Park Future Cycle Shop (0116 299 1234; futurecycles.org.uk) in Town Hall Square, opposite the Tourist Information Centre, hires bicycles by the day or half day and also provides somewhere to leave your bike while you explore more locally. There are also showers, lockers and a cycle shop. *Open Mon-Fri 08.30-18.00*. Both the Bike Park Future Cycle Shop and the TIC have maps showing cycle routes around the city. Charge.

Castle Gardens & Castle Motte (www.leicester.gov.uk). Riverside between St Nicholas Circle and The Newarke. Once a low-lying marshy area of reeds and willows, it was drained in the late 19th C as part of the city's flood alleviation scheme and initially used as allotments. The public gardens were established in 1926. The raised mound, or motte, dates from the 11th C and would originally have been surmounted by a timber fortification. Garden *open daily during daylight hours and as an access for boaters to secure moorings.*
Cathedral 21 St Martins, Leicester LE1 5DE (0116 261 5200; www.cathedral.leicester.anglican.org). Originally the parish church of St Martin's, it was extended in the 14th and 15th C, restored in the 19th C and became the cathedral in 1927. *Open daily.* Donations. Disabled toilets.
Curve Theatre 60 Rutland Street, Leicester LE1 1SB (0116 242 3560; www.curveonline.co.uk). Venue for hit shows bound for the West End with the emphasis on musicals. Also hard hitting modern drama and the classics.
De Montfort Hall Granville Road, Leicester LE1 7RU (0116 233 3111; www.demontforthall.co.uk). Prime venue for touring opera and ballet companies and for orchestras and soloist alike.
Golden Mile An area centred on Belgrave Road, to the north of the city centre, where the focus lies on the superb range of Asian cultural delights and cuisine, reflecting Leicester's status as a truly cosmopolitan city. Excellent guide entitled *A Taste of Asia* available from Tourist Information Centre (*see* page 91). Free.
Guildhall 11-15 Guildhall Lane, Leicester LE1 5FQ (0116 253 2569). Built by the Guild of Corpus Christi and dating from the 14th C, it contains fine oak panelling and an elaborately carved chimney-piece from 1637. It includes the Old Town Library, 19th-C police cells and a Great Hall with civic murals. *Open daily 11.00-16.30. Closed G Fri, Xmas Day and Boxing Day.* Free. Disabled toilets.
Guru Nanak Sikh Museum 9 Holy Bones, Leicester LE1 4LJ (0116 262 8606; www.thesikhmuseum.com). An impressive Sikh Temple in a transformed hosiery factory. Also spectacular models of shrines, manuscripts, paintings, coins, photographic portrayal of the part played by Sikh soldiers in both World Wars in a museum depicting the history of the Sikh nation. *Open to devotees daily.* Museum *open Thu 13.00-16.00, Sat 19.00-20.30. Other times by appointment.* Free.
Jain Centre 32 Oxford Street, Leicester LE1 5XU (0116 254 1150; www.jaincentreleicester.com). A fine example of traditional Indian architecture in the western world and a place of pilgrimage for Jains. Shrines of white marble, hand-carved pillars, stained glass, mirror walls, a dome and ceilings in sandstone. *Open Mon-Fri 07.30-14.00 and 18.00-20.00, Sat 07.30-20.00 & Sun and B Hols 07.30-18.30.* Donations appreciated.
Jewry Wall Museum 156-160 St Nicholas Circle, Leicester LE1 4LB (0116 225 4971; www.leicester.gov.uk/ museums). Collection of the county's archaeology from early times through to the Middle Ages overlooking the Jewry Wall, a small portion of which remains. This is thought to have been part of a basilica or Roman baths dating from the 2nd C. Two Roman mosaic pavements can be seen *in situ. Open Feb-Oct, daily 11.00-16.30.* Free.
Little Theatre Dover Street, Leicester LE1 6PW (0116 255 1302; www.thelittletheatre.net). Amateur dramatics, social activities and theatre workshops.
Markets 2-4 Market Place South, Leicester LE1 5HB (0116 454 3185; www.leicestermarket.co.uk). The Food Hall, selling fresh meat, poultry, dairy produce and fish from all over the world, is *open Mon-Sat 09.00-17.00.* The retail market, composed of over 300 covered stalls, is *open Mon-Sat 07.00-18.00.*
New Walk Museum & Art Gallery 53 New Walk, Leicester LE1 7EA (0116 255 4900; www.leicester.gov.uk/leisure-and-culture/museums-and-galleries/museums-and-historic-venues/new-walk-museum-and-art-gallery). Italian, Spanish and Flemish old masters. 18th-20th C English paintings. Also French Impressionists and German Expressionists, ceramics, silver, archives, natural history and geology. Gift shop, coffee shop and Wi-Fi. *Open Mon-Sat 10.00-17.00, Sun 11.00-17.00. Closed G Fri, Xmas Day and Boxing Day.* Free.
National Space Centre Exploration Drive, Leicester LE4 5NS (0116 261 0261; spacecentre.co.uk). The opportunity to explore many facets of space travel, to meet the furthest reaches of our universe face to face and to interact with both science fact and science fiction. Boosters Restaurant and Satellite Bar. Full disabled facilities. *Open Mon-Sun 10.00-16.00 (Sun 17.00).* Charge. Frequent bus service (no 54) to Abbey Lane.
Newarke Houses Museum and Gardens The Newarke, Leicester LE2 7BY (0116 225 4980; www.leicester.gov.uk/leisure-and-culture/museums-and-galleries/museums-and-historic-venues/newarke-houses-museum). The social history of the area from 1500 to the present day. Locally made clocks and a clockmaker's workshop. Also shows the history of the hosiery, costume and lace industries. There is a reconstructed Victorian street scene. *Open Mon-Sat 10.00-17.00 & Sun 11.00-17.00.* Free
Phoenix Cinema and Art Centre 4 Midland Street, Leicester LE1 1TG (0116 242 2800; www.phoenix.org.uk). Cinema and live performances of contemporary dance, mime, jazz and folk. Café serving a varied and interesting menu *daily 09.00-23.00 (Sat-Sun 10.00).*
Highcross Shopping Centre Level 3, Management Suite, 5 Shires Lane, Leicester LE1 4AN (0116 242 8644; www.highcrossleicester.com). All the usual big name (and not so big) stores under one high, glass-arched roof plus cafés, pizzeria and gelateria. *Open Mon-Fri 09.30-20.00, Sat 09.00-19.00, Sun and B Hols 11.00-17.00.*
St Martins Square & Loseby Lane Between Cank Street and Silver Street, Leicester. Speciality shopping centre in the heart of the city. Food,

fashion, wine and flowers amongst which to browse placidly, take in some street entertainment or simply unwind. Most shops *open Mon-Sat 09.00-17.00.*

St Mary de Castro Castle Yard, Leicester LE1 5WN (0116 262 8727). Founded in 1107 with excellent examples of Norman glass, stone and wood carving. Henry VI was knighted here in 1426 and Geoffrey Chaucer was probably married here.

St Nicholas Church St Nicholas Circle, Leicester LE1 5LX. The oldest church in the city, dating back to Anglo-Saxon times, and retaining examples of Saxon construction and Roman brickwork in the tower. *Open for services.*

Wygston's House 12 Applegate, St Nicholas Circle, Leicester LE1 5LD. An attractive, timber-framed building originally constructed for Roger Wygston, a 15th-C merchant.

'Y' Theatre YMCA East Street, Leicester LE1 6EY (0116 255 7066; www.leicesterymca.co.uk). A mixed programme of largely local productions.

Tourist Information Centre 51 Gallowtree Gate, Leicester LE1 5AD (0116 299 4444; www.goleicestershire.com/tourist-information-centres.aspx). *Open Mon-Sat 09.30-17.30 & Sun and B Hols 10.00-16.00.* Leicestershire also offers a comprehensive range of guided walks throughout the year, some of which are based in the Leicester area. Contact the TIC for further details.

● **Thurmaston**

Leics. PO, tel, stores, chemist, takeaways, off-licence, garage. This unexciting suburb stretches along the Roman road, the old Fosse Way, now bypassed by a dual carriageway. However, the opportunity thus afforded to Thurmaston has not been exploited. Evidence of Roman habitation was discovered in 1955, when excavation of an Anglo-Saxon cemetery brought to light 95 urns dating from 50 years after Julius Caesar's invasion. There is a large retail park, including a *24hr* superstore *(chemist etc)* ½ mile due east of Johnsons Bridge 17, beside the A607.

● **Birstall**

Leics. PO, tel, stores, chemist, delicatessen, bakery, takeaways, fish & chips, off-licence, DIY shop, butcher, library. A quiet suburb of Leicester which, together with peaceful moorings, makes it a useful place to stop for supplies. The stores are *open Mon-Sat 08.00-20.00, Sun 10.00-16.00* and gas is available from the DIY shop.

Pubs and Restaurants (page 105)

In a large city such as Leicester there is a wide range of pubs and restaurants to choose from; those listed are within reach of the waterway.

1 The Ale Wagon 27 Rutland Street, Leicester LE1 1RE (0116 262 3330; www.alewagon.co.uk). Close to the Curve Theatre, this 1930's hostelry retains its central bar and tiled and parquet floors. Always a good range of real ales and real cider, together with real fires in *winter*, newspapers and traditional pub games. *Open Mon-Sat 11.00-23.00 & Sun 07.30-22.30.*

2 The Salmon 19 Butt Close Lane, Leicester LE1 4QA (0116 253 2301; www.blackcountryales.co.uk/the-pubs/the-salmon). Near to St Margaret's bus station, a friendly brewery pub serving real ale and food *Tue-Sun 12.00-19.00 (Sun 17.00).* Real ciders. Dog-friendly, outside seating. Traditional pub games, newspapers, real fires, sports TV and Wi-Fi. *Open Mon-Sat 11.00-23.00 (Fri-Sat 00.00) & Sun 12.00-23.00.*

3 The Blue Boar 16 Millstone Lane, Leicester LE1 5JN (0116 231 9230; www.blueboarleicester.co.uk). Named after the eponymous inn where Richard III stayed before the Battle of Bosworth, this micro pub serves a wide range of real ales and real ciders, together with vegan and gluten-free ales. Bar snacks. Dog-friendly, traditional pub games, newspapers and Wi-Fi. *Open daily 11.00-23.00.*

4 The Rutland & Derby 21 Millstone Lane, Leicester LE1 5JN (0116 262 3299; www.therutlandandderby.co.uk). Open plan, with a contemporary feel, this pub serves real ales, real cider and food *Mon-Sat 12.00-20.00 (Fri 21.00).* Dog- and child-friendly (when food is being served). Courtyard seating and rooftop terrace. Newspapers, sports TV and Wi-Fi. *Open Mon-Thu 12.00-23.00 & Fri-Sat 12.00-00.10.*

5 Golden Mile Consult *A Taste of Asia (see opposite under Golden Mile)* for a wide-ranging selection of excitingly different and authentic eating experiences. This is a detailed and comprehensive selection numbering nearly 30 establishments.

6 The White Horse White Horse Lane, Birstall LE4 4EF (0116 267 1038; www.thewhitehorsebirstall.co.uk). Large, friendly riverside pub serving real ale. Home cooked food using locally sourced produce served *Mon-Fri L and E & Sat-Sun 12.00-21.00 (Sun 18.00).* Dog- and child-friendly, garden. Traditional pub games and *regular* live music. *Open daily 12.00-23.00 (Sun 10.30).*

7 The Old Plough 18 Front Street, Birstall, Leicester LE4 4DP (0116 267 4836). Friendly village pub. Food served *Tue-Sun 12.00-20.00.* Child- and dog-friendly, garden. Traditional pub games and *regular* live music. *Open Tue-Sun 12.00-23.00.*

In Leicester also try; **8 The Criterion** 44 Millstone Lane LE1 5JN (0116 262 5418); **9 The Globe** 43 Silver Street LE1 5EU (0116 262 9819; www.eversosensible.com/globe/default.asp) and **10 The Bowling Green** 44 Oxford Street, Leicester LE1 5XW (0116 254 6496; www.greatukpubs.co.uk/thebowlinggreenleicester).

Mountsorrel

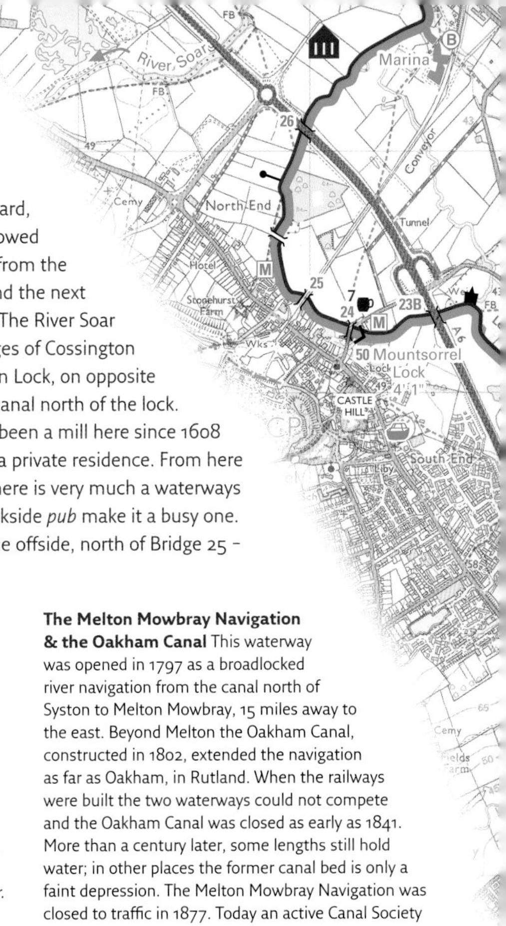

North of Thurmaston the canal leaves the river and heads north through an area scarred by busy gravel workings. Just beyond the boatyard, the River Wreake – once the course largely followed by The Melton Mowbray Navigation – flows in from the north east; the name of the nearby *boatyard* and the next lock hints at the significance of this little river. The River Soar rejoins the canal by Cossington Lock. The villages of Cossington and Rothley are one mile away from Cossington Lock, on opposite sides of the Soar. The Rothley Brook joins the canal north of the lock. At Sileby Lock is another water mill. There has been a mill here since 1608 and the present building has been restored as a private residence. From here it is a short distance to Mountsorrel. The lock here is very much a waterways showplace, and the extensive *moorings* and lockside *pub* make it a busy one. There are also limited moorings available on the offside, north of Bridge 25 – telephone 01509 425001for further details.

- **Cossington**
Leics. Tel. A mile east of Cossington Lock, this is a pretty village with wide, well-kept grass verges and plenty of trees.
- **Sileby**
Leics. PO, tel, stores, chemist, butcher, takeaways, hardware, delicatessen, fish & chips, bank, library, station. Once a thriving community based around hosiery manufacture, this large village is much swollen by dormitory housing for neighbouring Leicester and Loughborough. Shop *open 06.00–23.00.*
- **Mountsorrel**
Leics. PO, tel, stores, takeaways, chemist, library, butcher. It is but a few yards from the lock here to the centre of the village with its long main street. Late opening shop *open Mon–Sat 05.30– 17.30 (Wed & Sat 19.30) & Sun 05.30–12.30.*
- **Barrow-Upon-Soar**
Leics. PO, tel stores, chemist, takeaways, off-licence, fish & chips, library, garage, station. Busy village running up from the navigation useful for supplies. Shop *open Mon–Sat 08.00–19.00 & Sun 09.00–15.00.*

Traveline (0871 200 22 33; www.traveline.info). For full details on bus travel to local (and not so local) attractions.

The Melton Mowbray Navigation & the Oakham Canal This waterway was opened in 1797 as a broadlocked river navigation from the canal north of Syston to Melton Mowbray, 15 miles away to the east. Beyond Melton the Oakham Canal, constructed in 1802, extended the navigation as far as Oakham, in Rutland. When the railways were built the two waterways could not compete and the Oakham Canal was closed as early as 1841. More than a century later, some lengths still hold water; in other places the former canal bed is only a faint depression. The Melton Mowbray Navigation was closed to traffic in 1877. Today an active Canal Society (meltonwaterways.org.uk) is preserving and restoring the waterway.

Stonehurst Farm and Motor Museum Bond Lane, Mountsorrel LE12 7AA (01509 413216; www.stonehurstfarm.co.uk). A chance to see a working farm, a museum of memorabilia and old cars, and for children to cuddle and stroke small animals. Teashop serving light lunches and cream teas. Farm shop selling fresh produce, home-made bread and preserves. *Open daily 09.30–17.00.* Charge. Shop and tearoom *open all year.* Disabled visitors telephone for assistance.

Boatyards

Ⓑ**L.R. Harris & Son** Old Junction Boatyard, Meadow Lane, Syston LE7 1NR (0116 269 2135; www.lrharris.co.uk). (charge) Gas, overnight mooring, long-term mooring, chandlery and extensive spares, books, gifts and maps, slipway, winter storage, boat sales and repairs, inboard and outboard engines sales and repairs, welding specialists, fabrication, GRP repairs.

Ⓑ**Sileby Mill Boatyard** Mill Lane, Sileby, Loughborough LE12 7UX (01509 813583; www.silebymill.co.uk). D E Pump out, gas, narrowboat hire, day-craft hire, overnight mooring, long-term mooring, winter storage, slipway, boat sales and repairs, engineering, welding and structural repairs, wooden boat repair specialists, chandlery, engine sales and repairs, welding, fabrication, GRP repairs, DIY facilities, solid fuel, books, maps and gifts, ice creams, toilets.

Ⓑ**Meadow Farm Marina** Huston Close, Barrow-Upon-Soar, Loughborough LE12 8NB (01509 812215/816035) Pump out, gas, free visitor moorings, long-term mooring (20–60ft boats), slipway, crane, boat sales, toilets, showers. Private club for moorers. Disabled facilities.

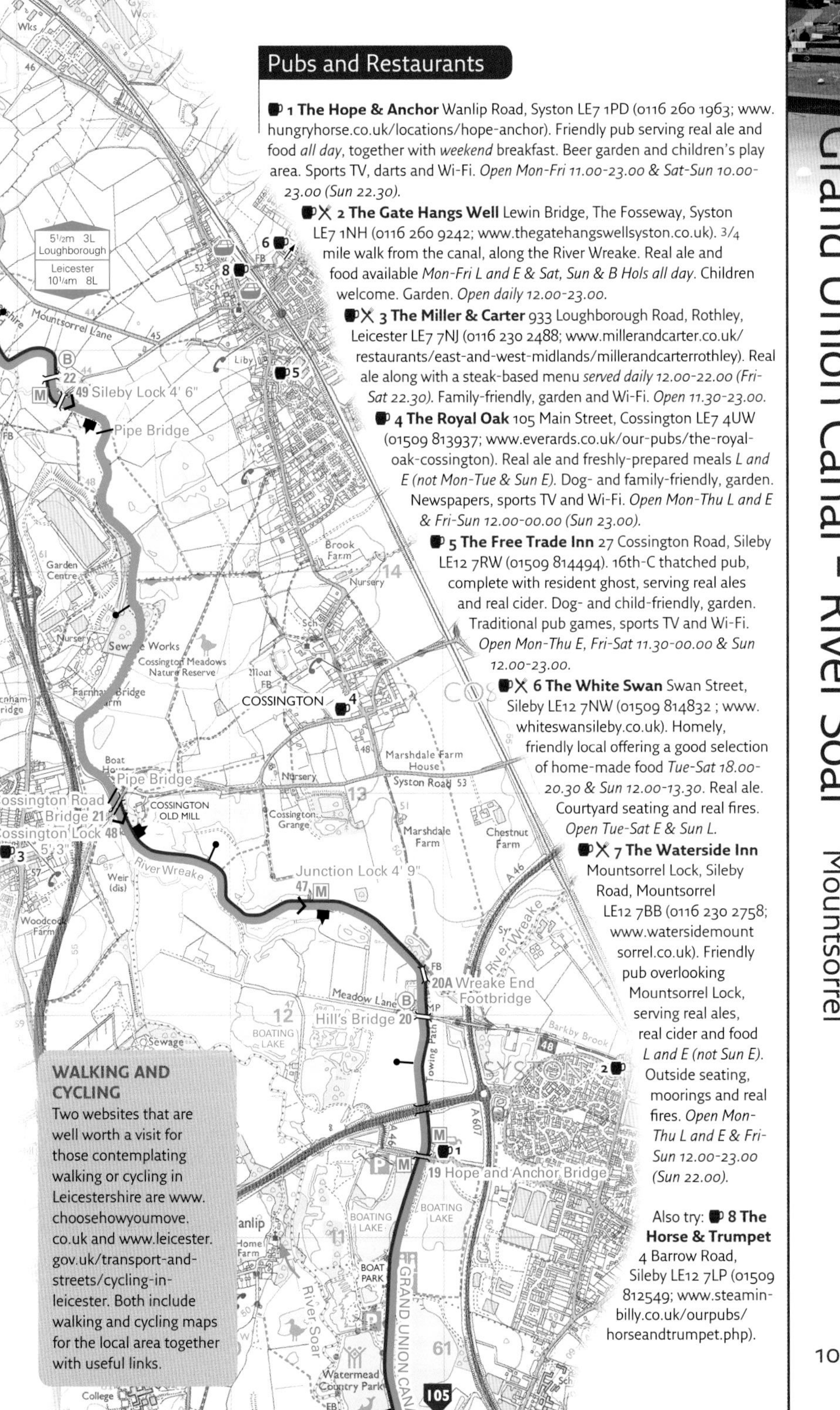

Pubs and Restaurants

1 The Hope & Anchor Wanlip Road, Syston LE7 1PD (0116 260 1963; www.hungryhorse.co.uk/locations/hope-anchor). Friendly pub serving real ale and food *all day*, together with *weekend* breakfast. Beer garden and children's play area. Sports TV, darts and Wi-Fi. *Open Mon-Fri 11.00-23.00 & Sat-Sun 10.00-23.00 (Sun 22.30).*

2 The Gate Hangs Well Lewin Bridge, The Fosseway, Syston LE7 1NH (0116 260 9242; www.thegatehangswellsyston.co.uk). 3/4 mile walk from the canal, along the River Wreake. Real ale and food available *Mon-Fri L and E & Sat, Sun & B Hols all day.* Children welcome. Garden. *Open daily 12.00-23.00.*

3 The Miller & Carter 933 Loughborough Road, Rothley, Leicester LE7 7NJ (0116 230 2488; www.millerandcarter.co.uk/restaurants/east-and-west-midlands/millerandcarterrothley). Real ale along with a steak-based menu *served daily 12.00-22.00 (Fri-Sat 22.30).* Family-friendly, garden and Wi-Fi. *Open 11.30-23.00.*

4 The Royal Oak 105 Main Street, Cossington LE7 4UW (01509 813937; www.everards.co.uk/our-pubs/the-royal-oak-cossington). Real ale and freshly-prepared meals *L and E (not Mon-Tue & Sun E).* Dog- and family-friendly, garden. Newspapers, sports TV and Wi-Fi. *Open Mon-Thu L and E & Fri-Sun 12.00-00.00 (Sun 23.00).*

5 The Free Trade Inn 27 Cossington Road, Sileby LE12 7RW (01509 814494). 16th-C thatched pub, complete with resident ghost, serving real ales and real cider. Dog- and child-friendly, garden. Traditional pub games, sports TV and Wi-Fi. *Open Mon-Thu E, Fri-Sat 11.30-00.00 & Sun 12.00-23.00.*

6 The White Swan Swan Street, Sileby LE12 7NW (01509 814832 ; www.whiteswansileby.co.uk). Homely, friendly local offering a good selection of home-made food *Tue-Sat 18.00-20.30 & Sun 12.00-13.30.* Real ale. Courtyard seating and real fires. *Open Tue-Sat E & Sun L.*

7 The Waterside Inn Mountsorrel Lock, Sileby Road, Mountsorrel LE12 7BB (0116 230 2758; www.watersidemountsorrel.co.uk). Friendly pub overlooking Mountsorrel Lock, serving real ales, real cider and food *L and E (not Sun E).* Outside seating, moorings and real fires. *Open Mon-Thu L and E & Fri-Sun 12.00-23.00 (Sun 22.00).*

Also try: **8 The Horse & Trumpet** 4 Barrow Road, Sileby LE12 7LP (01509 812549; www.steamin-billy.co.uk/ourpubs/horseandtrumpet.php).

WALKING AND CYCLING

Two websites that are well worth a visit for those contemplating walking or cycling in Leicestershire are www.choosehowyoumove.co.uk and www.leicester.gov.uk/transport-and-streets/cycling-in-leicester. Both include walking and cycling maps for the local area together with useful links.

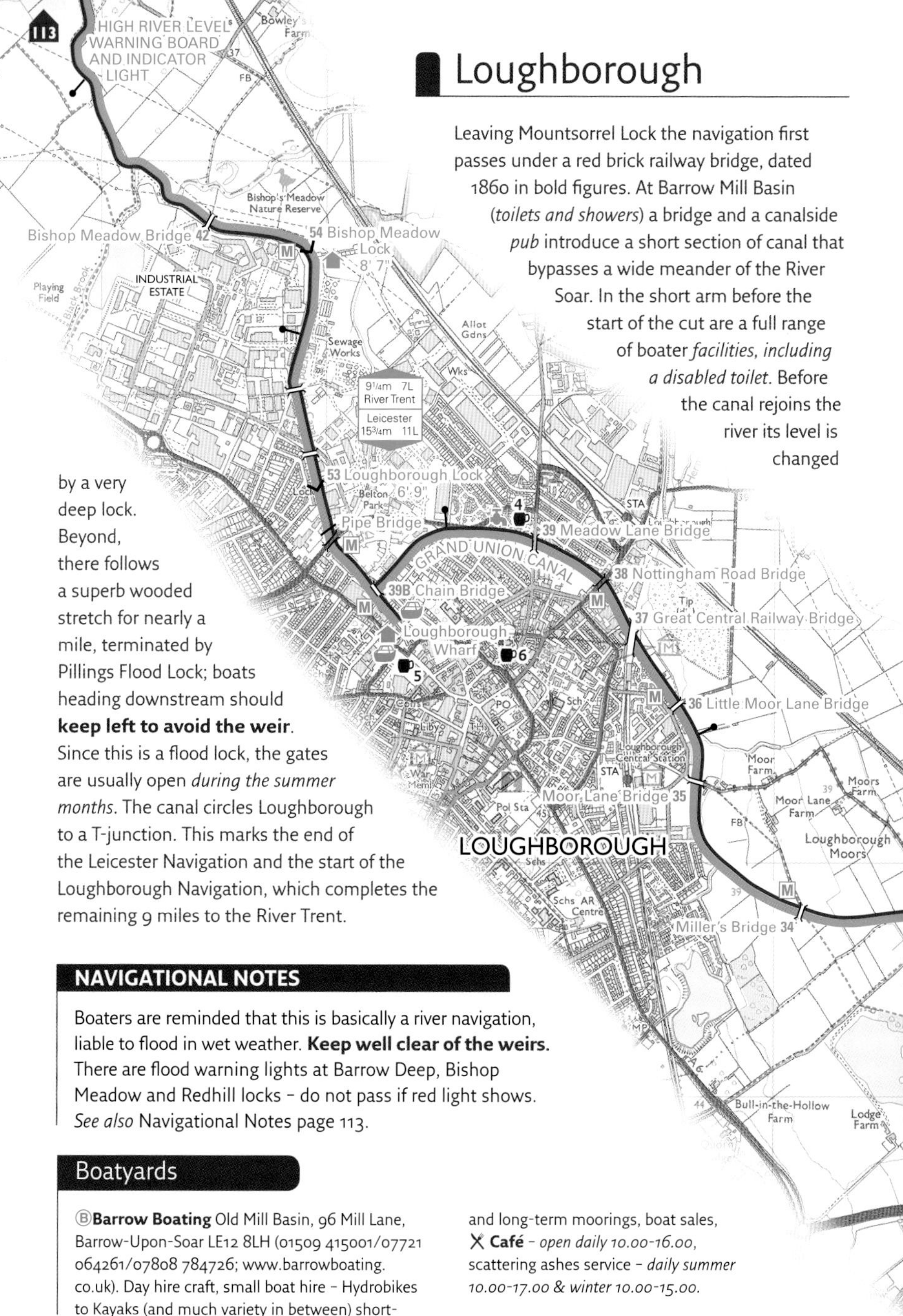

Loughborough

Leaving Mountsorrel Lock the navigation first passes under a red brick railway bridge, dated 1860 in bold figures. At Barrow Mill Basin (*toilets and showers*) a bridge and a canalside *pub* introduce a short section of canal that bypasses a wide meander of the River Soar. In the short arm before the start of the cut are a full range of boater *facilities, including a disabled toilet*. Before the canal rejoins the river its level is changed by a very deep lock. Beyond, there follows a superb wooded stretch for nearly a mile, terminated by Pillings Flood Lock; boats heading downstream should **keep left to avoid the weir**. Since this is a flood lock, the gates are usually open *during the summer months*. The canal circles Loughborough to a T-junction. This marks the end of the Leicester Navigation and the start of the Loughborough Navigation, which completes the remaining 9 miles to the River Trent.

NAVIGATIONAL NOTES

Boaters are reminded that this is basically a river navigation, liable to flood in wet weather. **Keep well clear of the weirs.** There are flood warning lights at Barrow Deep, Bishop Meadow and Redhill locks – do not pass if red light shows. *See also* Navigational Notes page 113.

Boatyards

Ⓑ**Barrow Boating** Old Mill Basin, 96 Mill Lane, Barrow-Upon-Soar LE12 8LH (01509 415001/07721 064261/07808 784726; www.barrowboating.co.uk). Day hire craft, small boat hire – Hydrobikes to Kayaks (and much variety in between) short- and long-term moorings, boat sales, ✕ **Café** – *open daily 10.00-16.00*, scattering ashes service – *daily summer 10.00-17.00 & winter 10.00-15.00.*

● **Loughborough**
Leics. All services (including laundrette). A busy industrial town. There is a bric-a-brac market held in the Queens Hall, Granby Street *every Fri.*

Carillon & War Memorial Queens Park, Loughborough LE11 3DU (01509 263370; www.loughboroughcarillon.com). *Open Good Fri-Sep, Tue-Sun 13.00-16.30.* Charge.

Charnwood Museum Queen's Park, Granby Street, Loughborough LE11 3DU (01509 233754; www.charnwood.gov.uk). Find out how different groups of people have contributed to life in Charnwood over the past 4000 years; discover more about the area's natural world; how the land has nurtured its inhabitants and how they, in turn, have earned a living. Gift shop and café (01509 233750) with outdoor patio. *Open Apr-Sep, Tue-Sat 10.00-16.30 & Sun 14.00-17.00 and Oct-Mar, Tue-Sat 10.00-15.00 & Sun 12.00-15.00.* Free.

Great Central Railway Great Central Road, Loughborough LE11 1RW (01509 632322; www.gcrailway.co.uk). South west of bridge 36. 8 miles of preserved main line taking you back to the days of express steam haulage. *Open weekends and B Hols throughout the year and some weekdays Jun-Sep.* Charge. Telephone for details of special events.

Tourist Information Centre Town Hall, Market Place, Loughborough LE11 3EB (01509 231914; www.leicestershire.gov.uk). *Open Mon-Sat 09.00-17.00 & Sun 11.00-15.00.*

Pubs and Restaurants

1 The Navigation Mill Lane, Barrow-Upon-Soar LE12 8LQ (01509 413611; www.navigationinn.info). Traditional canalside country pub serving real ales and food *L and E (not Sun E).* Dogs and children welcome, garden. Sports TV, Wi-Fi and moorings. *Open daily 12.00-23.00.*

2 The Soar Bridge Inn 29 Bridge Street, Barrow-Upon-Soar LE12 8PN (01509 412686; www.everards.co.uk/our-pubs/the-soar-bridge-inn-barrow-on-soar). Near Barrow Deep Lock. Real ale, real cider and food available *Tue-Sun L and E (not Sun E).* Floodlit petanque court. Dog- and child-friendly, garden. Traditional pub games, real fires and sports TV. Camping. *Open Mon 16.00-23.00 and Tue-Sun 12.00-23.00 (Sun 22.30).*

3 The Boat House at Barrow 14 Bridge Street Barrow-Upon-Soar LE12 8PN (01509 412260; www.theboathousebarrow.co.uk). Community pub serving real ale and real cider together with cobs and pizzas *daily 12.00-23.00.* Attached Chinese restaurant *open Thu-Tue L and E.* Child- and dog-friendly, garden. Traditional pub games, real fires, sports TV and Wi-Fi. *Open Sun-Thu 12.00-23.00 & Fri-Sat 11.00-00.00.*

4 The Boat Inn 47 Canal Bank, Meadow Lane, Loughborough LE11 1JN (01509 261565). Real ale and food served *daily 12.00-20.00.* Family-friendly, canalside seating. *Open 11.00-23.00.* Shops, takeaway, station and PO nearby.

5 The Swan in the Rushes 21 The Rushes, Loughborough LE11 5BE (01509 217014; www.castlerockbrewery.co.uk/pubs/swan-in-the-rushes). A drinkers' paradise dispensing a wide range of real ales, real cider, perry, craft beers and single malt whiskies. Home-cooked food available *Mon-Thu E, Fri L and E, Sat 12.00-20.00 & Sun 12.00-17.00.* Fresh cobs *outside these times.* Dog- and child-friendly, outside seating. Newspapers, real fires and Wi-Fi. *Open Mon-Sun 11.00-23.00 (Fri-Sat 00.00).*

6 The Three Nuns 30 Churchgate, Loughborough LE11 1UD (01509 611989). Warm, friendly traditional pub serving a range of real ales and home-made food *Mon-Fri L and E; Sat 09.00-15.00 & Sun 12.00-15.00.* Outside seating and traditional pub games. *Open 11.00-00.00.*

Boatyards

Ⓑ **Pilling's Lock Marina** Flesh Hovel Lane, Quorn LE12 8FE (01509 620990; www.pillingslock.com). DE Pump out, gas, overnight and long-term mooring, day and holiday boat hire, slipway, DIY facilities, welding, fabrication, GRP repairs, wooden boat building, boat sales and repairs, engine repairs, solid fuel. Facilities building includes showers, toilets and launderette with bar/restaurant. Wi-Fi.

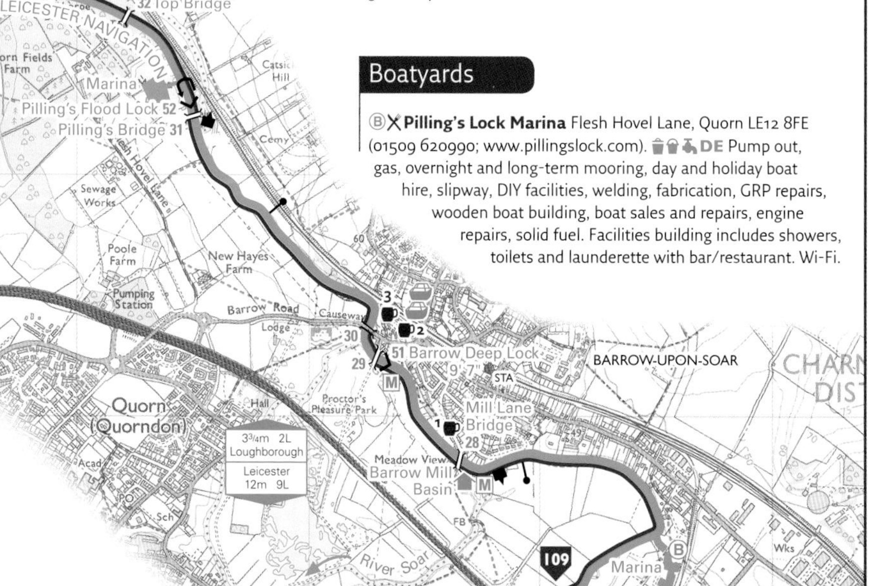

Kegworth

The Loughborough Navigation has the same physical characteristics as the Leicester Navigation. It continues the fall towards the Trent with a similar pattern of meandering river reaches and the occasional canal cut, with locks bypassing the weirs. Normanton on Soar is visible some way away because of its prominent church steeple; on approaching, one finds the church is only a matter of yards from the river bank. However the inhabitants of Normanton guard their waterfront jealously, making it extremely difficult to get ashore. Below Normanton is the settlement of Zouch which has a certain weary and less conventional charm, together with easier access. At Devil's Elbow boats heading downstream should keep right to stay in the main navigation channel. At the point where the A6 and the Soar almost touch there is a riverside *pub and a boatyard.* North of the *pub* a willow-lined reach leads to a stone mansion with spreading lawns where the channel divides. To the left (nearer Kegworth) is a maze of shallow and weedy backwaters, weirs and a water mill; boats should keep to the right for Kegworth Deep Lock where a lock has been constructed beside the old as part of a flood prevention scheme. After another sharp swing to the north the channel divides again, and northbound boats should once more bear right for Kegworth Shallow Lock: a flood lock usually left open *during the summer months.*

- **Whatton House**
  Long Whatton, Loughborough LE12 5BG (01509 270202; www.whattonhouseandgardens.co.uk). Visible from the river near the Devil's Elbow, this mansion was built about 1802, damaged by fire and restored in 1876. Its fine 15 acre gardens are *open Mar-Oct, Sun-Fri 11.00-16.00.* Charge.
- **Normanton on Soar**
  Notts. PO box, tel. A quiet and carefully preserved village with wide grass verges and some discreetly pretty buildings. The cruciform church has a central tower and spire, rare in so small a church. On the east wall of the nave there are some excellent stone carvings; the centre one is an elaborate coat of arms with a quizzical lion in the middle. The plain glass windows make the church enjoyably light. A ferry here once again links Nottinghamshire to Leicestershire.
- **Kegworth**
  Leics. PO, tel, stores, chemist, delicatessen, baker, fish & chips, off-licence, butchers, takeaways, garage.

  Kegworth has an attractive situation up on a wooded hill that is crowned by the church spire, but although it is close to the river, access is easy only from Kegworth Shallow Lock. The shop is *open Mon-Sat 07.00-22.00 & Sun 08.00-22.00.*

  Kegworth Village Association and Museum 52 High Street, Kegworth DE74 2DA (01509 670137; www.kegworthmuseum.org.uk). Award-winning displays include Victorian parlour, local school, saddlers, knitting industry, Royal British Legion war memorabilia and local transport history. *Open Easter-Sep Wed 14.00-17.00; Sat 10.00-13.00; Sun 13.00-16.00. Small charge.*
- **Kingston on Soar**
  Notts. Tel. Situated east of the railway embankment, this is a small quiet estate village which looks much as it must have done 100 years ago. The church, still very much the focus of the village, is a pretty building dating from 1900.

Boatyards

Ⓑ**East Midlands Boat Services** London Road, Kegworth DE74 2EY (01509 672385; eastmidlandsboatservices.com). **D** Pump out, gas, overnight mooring, long-term mooring, slipway, boat sales and repairs, engine sales and repairs, welding, GRP repairs, wooden boat building, chandlery, DIY facilities, solid fuel. Boat Safety (BSS) examinations.

Ⓑ**Kegworth Marine** 2 Kingston Lane, Kegworth DE74 2FS (01509 672300). **D** Gas, long-term mooring, covered slipway, boat and engine repairs, DIY facilities, wet dock (60ft).

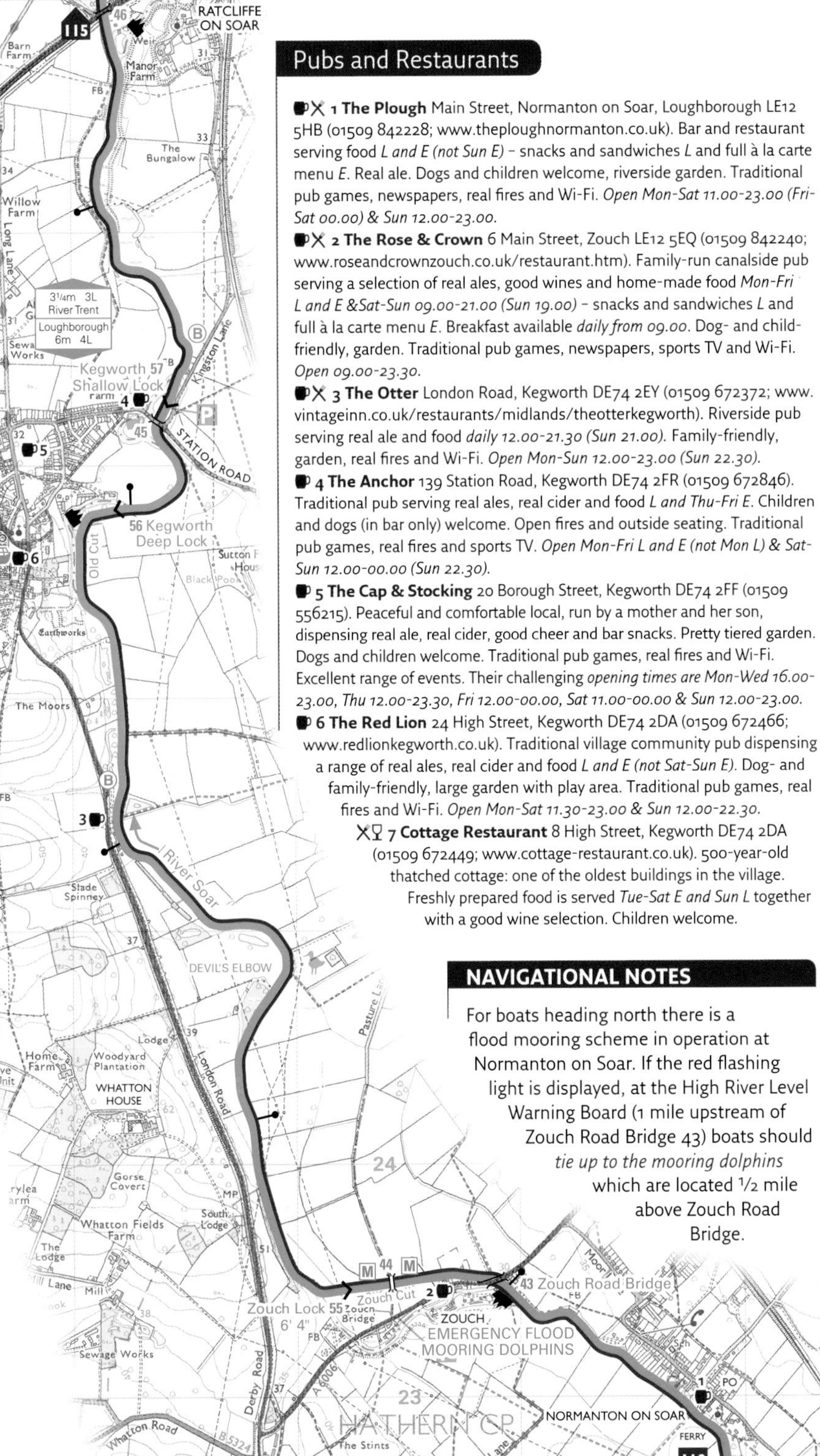

Pubs and Restaurants

1 The Plough Main Street, Normanton on Soar, Loughborough LE12 5HB (01509 842228; www.theploughnormanton.co.uk). Bar and restaurant serving food *L and E (not Sun E)* – snacks and sandwiches *L* and full à la carte menu *E*. Real ale. Dogs and children welcome, riverside garden. Traditional pub games, newspapers, real fires and Wi-Fi. *Open Mon-Sat 11.00-23.00 (Fri-Sat 00.00) & Sun 12.00-23.00.*

2 The Rose & Crown 6 Main Street, Zouch LE12 5EQ (01509 842240; www.roseandcrownzouch.co.uk/restaurant.htm). Family-run canalside pub serving a selection of real ales, good wines and home-made food *Mon-Fri L and E &Sat-Sun 09.00-21.00 (Sun 19.00)* – snacks and sandwiches *L* and full à la carte menu *E*. Breakfast available *daily from 09.00*. Dog- and child-friendly, garden. Traditional pub games, newspapers, sports TV and Wi-Fi. *Open 09.00-23.30.*

3 The Otter London Road, Kegworth DE74 2EY (01509 672372; www.vintageinn.co.uk/restaurants/midlands/theotterkegworth). Riverside pub serving real ale and food *daily 12.00-21.30 (Sun 21.00)*. Family-friendly, garden, real fires and Wi-Fi. *Open Mon-Sun 12.00-23.00 (Sun 22.30).*

4 The Anchor 139 Station Road, Kegworth DE74 2FR (01509 672846). Traditional pub serving real ales, real cider and food *L and Thu-Fri E*. Children and dogs (in bar only) welcome. Open fires and outside seating. Traditional pub games, real fires and sports TV. *Open Mon-Fri L and E (not Mon L) & Sat-Sun 12.00-00.00 (Sun 22.30).*

5 The Cap & Stocking 20 Borough Street, Kegworth DE74 2FF (01509 556215). Peaceful and comfortable local, run by a mother and her son, dispensing real ale, real cider, good cheer and bar snacks. Pretty tiered garden. Dogs and children welcome. Traditional pub games, real fires and Wi-Fi. Excellent range of events. Their challenging *opening times are Mon-Wed 16.00-23.00, Thu 12.00-23.30, Fri 12.00-00.00, Sat 11.00-00.00 & Sun 12.00-23.00.*

6 The Red Lion 24 High Street, Kegworth DE74 2DA (01509 672466; www.redlionkegworth.co.uk). Traditional village community pub dispensing a range of real ales, real cider and food *L and E (not Sat-Sun E)*. Dog- and family-friendly, large garden with play area. Traditional pub games, real fires and Wi-Fi. *Open Mon-Sat 11.30-23.00 & Sun 12.00-22.30.*

7 Cottage Restaurant 8 High Street, Kegworth DE74 2DA (01509 672449; www.cottage-restaurant.co.uk). 500-year-old thatched cottage: one of the oldest buildings in the village. Freshly prepared food is served *Tue-Sat E and Sun L* together with a good wine selection. Children welcome.

NAVIGATIONAL NOTES

For boats heading north there is a flood mooring scheme in operation at Normanton on Soar. If the red flashing light is displayed, at the High River Level Warning Board (1 mile upstream of Zouch Road Bridge 43) boats should *tie up to the mooring dolphins* which are located ½ mile above Zouch Road Bridge.

Ratcliffe on Soar

From Kegworth Shallow Lock to the Trent the navigation is somewhat more isolated, but two notable landmarks are the spire of Ratcliffe on Soar church and the eight cooling towers and vast chimney of the Ratcliffe Power Station that totally dominate the landscape for miles around. The navigation skirts round the west side of Red Hill. The last lock here has a well-painted bridge on which are shown the flood levels for 1955 and 1960, explaining the necessity for the flood prevention works. A few hundred yards below Red Hill Lock the Soar flows into the River Trent and loses its identity in this much bigger waterway.

NAVIGATIONAL NOTES

1 Boats negotiating the junction of the rivers Soar and Trent should keep well away from Thrumpton Weir, which is just east (downstream) of the big iron railway bridge. Navigators are reminded that the main line of the Trent Navigation is the Cranfleet Cut. This begins 200yds upstream of the mouth of the Soar, right by the large, wooden building which houses one of the many sailing clubs on the Trent. The entrance to the Erewash Canal is also here, marked by a lock and a cluster of buildings. **If the warning light at Redhill Lock shows red – *do not pass*.**

2 The sanitary station at Sawley Locks should only be accessed from the backwater moorings on the river below the Lock.

Ratcliffe on Soar
Notts. Tel. A tiny village with a spired church dating from the 13th C. The interior of the nave is pleasantly uncluttered and rather spartan. There is no stained glass to darken it, and the white-washed walls accentuate the bold and ancient arches. In the chancel, on the other hand, there is a profusion of stone effigies and wall memorials, many of them to the Sacheverell family.

Trent Lock
A busy and unusual boating centre at the southern terminus of the Erewash Canal (*see* page 65). There are two boatyards, two pubs and a delightful tearoom here.

Sawley
Notts. PO, tel, stores. The tall church spire attracts one across the river to Sawley, and in this respect the promise is fulfilled, for the medieval church is very beautiful and is approached by a formal avenue of lime trees leading to the 600-year-old doorway. But otherwise Sawley is an uninteresting main road village on the outskirts of Long Eaton.

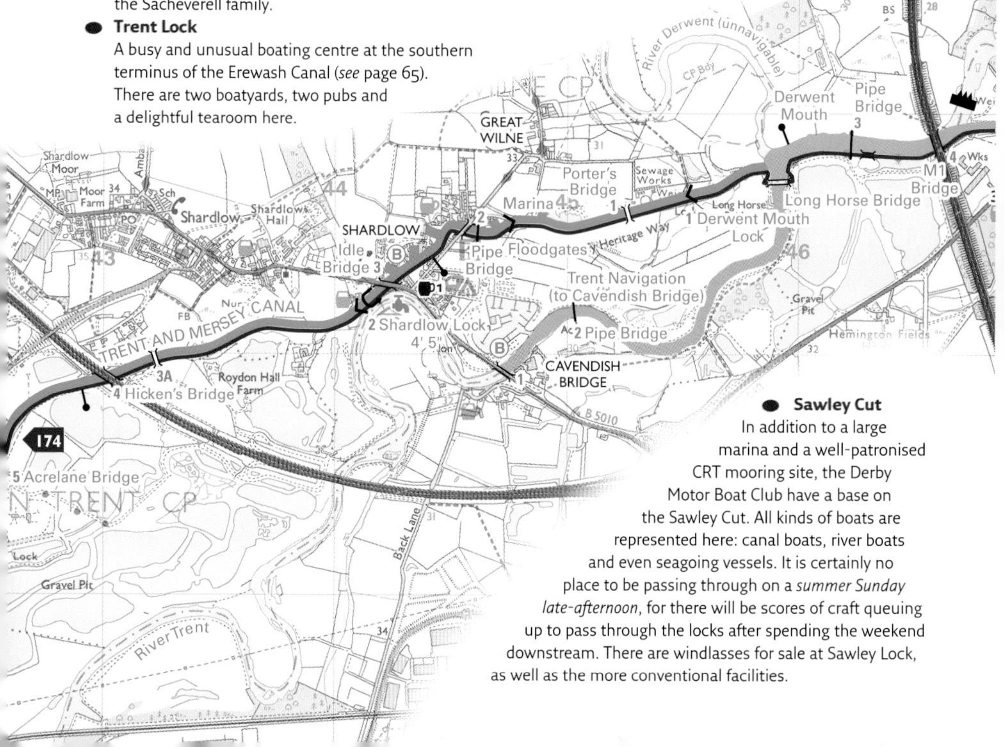

Sawley Cut
In addition to a large marina and a well-patronised CRT mooring site, the Derby Motor Boat Club have a base on the Sawley Cut. All kinds of boats are represented here: canal boats, river boats and even seagoing vessels. It is certainly no place to be passing through on a *summer Sunday late-afternoon*, for there will be scores of craft queuing up to pass through the locks after spending the weekend downstream. There are windlasses for sale at Sawley Lock, as well as the more conventional facilities.

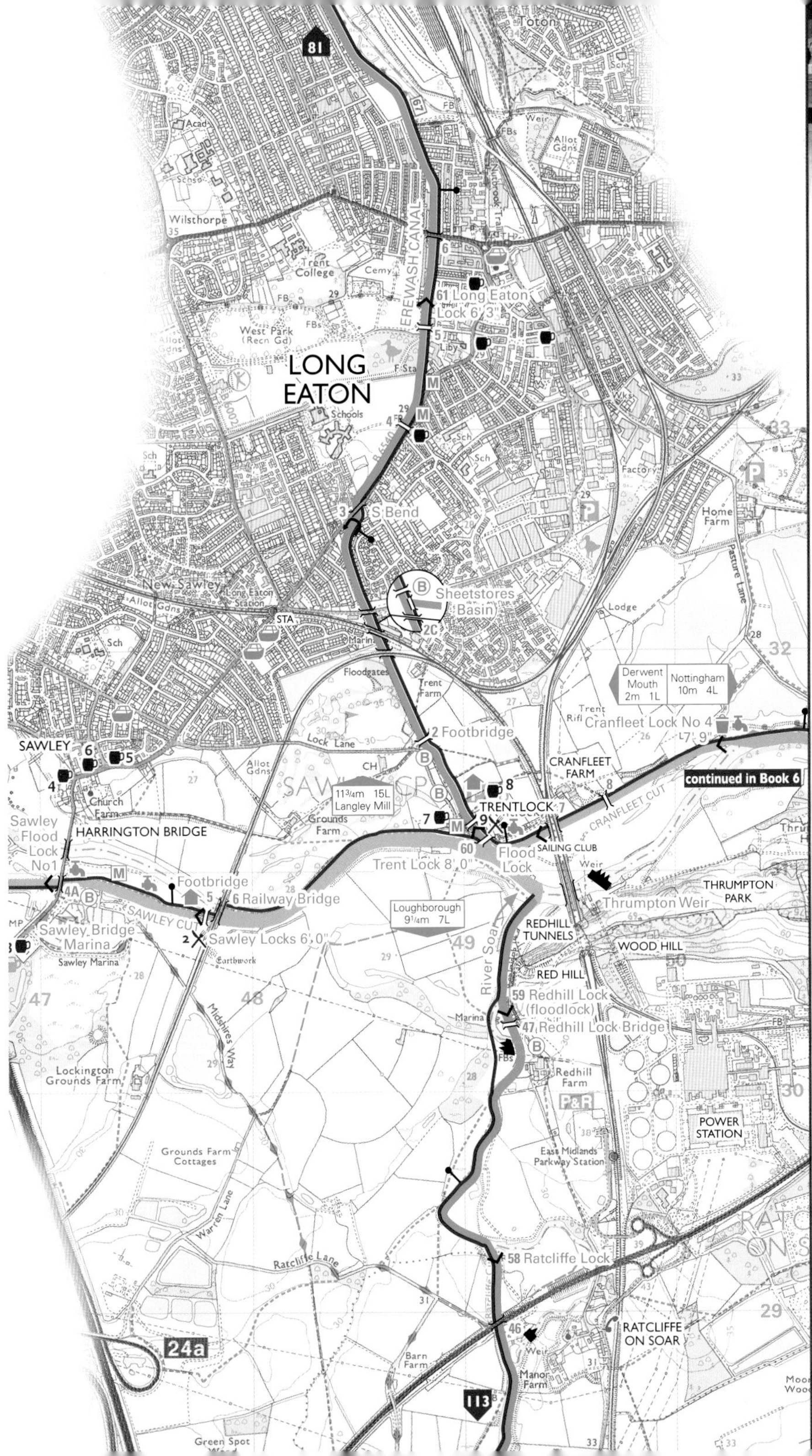

81
Toton
LONG EATON
ERREWASH CANAL
Wilsthorpe
Trent College
Cemy
West Park (Recn Gd)
6
61 Long Eaton Lock 6' 3"
5 Liby
4
3 S Bend
Sheetstores Basin
2C
New Sawley
Long Eaton Station
STA
Marina
Floodgates
Trent Farm
Lodge
Factory
Home Farm
Pasture Lane
2 Footbridge
Lock Lane
CH
Allot Gdns

Derwent Mouth 2m 1L	Nottingham 10m 4L

Cranfleet Lock No 4 7' 9"
CRANFLEET FARM
8
CRANFLEET CUT

continued in Book 6

SAWLEY
6
5
4
Church Farm
Sawley Flood Lock No1
HARRINGTON BRIDGE

11¾m 15L Langley Mill

Grounds Farm
7
9
TRENTLOCK 7
SAILING CLUB
60
Flood Lock
Trent Lock 8' 0"
Weir
THRUMPTON PARK
Thrumpton Weir
4A
Footbridge
5
6 Railway Bridge
SAWLEY CUT
Sawley Bridge Marina
Sawley Marina
2
Sawley Locks 6' 0"
Earthwork

Loughborough 9¼m 7L

River Soar
REDHILL TUNNELS
WOOD HILL
RED HILL
59 Redhill Lock (floodlock)
Marina
47 Redhill Lock Bridge
FBs
Redhill Farm
P&R
East Midlands Parkway Station
POWER STATION
Midshires Way
Lockington Grounds Farm
Grounds Farm Cottages
Warren Lane
Ratcliffe Lane
58 Ratcliffe Lock
46
Weir
RATCLIFFE ON SOAR
Barn Farm
Manor Farm
24a
113
Green Spot

Boatyards

Ⓑ**Redhill Marine Ltd** Redhill Marina, Ratcliffe on Soar, Nottingham NG11 0EB (01509 672770; www.redhill-marina.co.uk). Gas, overnight and long-term mooring, winter storage, crane, slipway, hoist, boat sales and repairs, engine sales and repairs, boat refurbishment, chandlery, DIY facilities, toilets, general store, café, camping.
Ⓑ**J.D Narrowboats Limited** Dobson Wharf, The Wharf, Shardlow DE72 2GJ (01332 792271/07952 378679; www.jdnarrowboats.com). D Pump out, gas, bespoke boat and shell builders, long and short-term mooring, crane, boat and engine sales, slipway, engine repairs, diesel fuel cleaning, painting, solid fuel, toilets.
Ⓑ✕**Sawley Marina** Sawley, Long Eaton NG10 3AE (0115 907 7400; www.bwml.co.uk). P D Pump out, gas, overnight and long-term mooring, winter storage, slipway, boat and engine sales, engine repairs, telephone, chandlery, solid fuel, toilets, showers, restaurant (*closed Mon*), laundrette, groceries.
Ⓑ**Mills Dockyard** Trent Lock, Lock Lane, Long Eaton NG10 2FY 0115 973 2595; www.mills-dockyard.com). Overnight and long-term mooring, engine repairs, covered dry dock, wooden boat restoration and repairs, general boat maintenance, fitting out and repairs, houseboat construction.
Ⓑ**Kingfisher Narrowboats Ltd,** Trent Lock, Lock Lane, Long Eaton NG10 2FY (0115 972 7936; www.kingfishernarrowboats.co.uk). Boat building, covered dry dock, serviced and DIY facilities, boat rebuilds, painting and sign writing, space for wide beamed boats.

WALKING AND CYCLING
Once the River Trent is reached the towpath comes to an abrupt halt and there is no right of way along the south bank of the river. Originally there would probably have been a bridge here; more recently there was certainly a ferry. Walkers and cyclists will have to retrace their steps and make a detour (1/4 mile north west of Ratcliffe Lock take the footpath south west and join the Midshires Way, meeting the Trent at Sawley Marina) if they wish to follow the waterways system further. This is a pity, as it is the only break in an otherwise continuous towpath linking London to Nottingham and the Humber estuary to the north east and Burton on Trent, and ultimately Manchester, in the north west.

Pubs and Restaurants (pages 114-115)

1 The Navigation Inn Cavendish Court, Shardlow DE72 2HJ (01332 792918). Beside the canal at Bridge 2, this friendly pub serves real ale and food *L and E*. Dog- and child-friendly, garden. Traditional pub games and *regular* live music. Camping nearby. *Open 12.00.*
✕ **2 The Coffee Kiosk** Sawley Lock House, Sawley NG10 3AD (0115 972 7551). Coffee with a view! Friendly service and a perfect location in which to enjoy tea, coffee, ice-creams, sandwiches and light meals. Dogs welcome. *Open Wed-Sat 11.00-16.30.*
✕ **3 Plank & Leggit** Tamworth Road, Sawley, Long Eaton NG10 3AD (0115 972 1515; www.hungryhorse.co.uk/locations/plank-leggit). 200yds south of Sawley Cut, behind the marina. Serving food *all day from 12.00*. Beer garden together with indoor and outdoor children's play areas. Dogs welcome in garden. Food available *Mon-Sat 12.00-22.00 & Sun 11.30-21.00. Open daily 11.00 (Sun 11.30).*
4 Harrington Arms 392 Tamworth Road, Sawley Long Eaton NG10 3AU (0115 973 2614; www.oldenglishinns.co.uk/our-locations/the-harrington-arms-long-eaton). North of the flood lock. 400-year-old, heavily beamed pub, 1/4 mile from Sawley Marina, serving an extensive selection of meals *available all day*. Excellent real ale selection. Children welcome, large garden. Newspapers and real fires. *Open L and E.*
5 The Nag's Head Wilne Road, Sawley, Long Eaton NG10 3AL (0115 973 2983). Village local serving real ale and good value, home-cooked food *L and E*. Dog- and family-friendly. Traditional pub games and newspapers. *Open 12.00.*
6 The White Lion 352 Tamworth Road, Sawley, Long Eaton NG10 3AT (0115 946 3061). North of the flood lock. Skittles, darts, pool, real ale and real cider. Children and dogs welcome, garden. No machines. Newspapers, real fires and Wi-Fi. *Open Mon-Thu 14.00 & Fri-Sun 12.00.*
7 The Trent Lock Lock Lane, Long Eaton NG10 2FY (0115 972 5159; www.vintageinn.co.uk). Formerly the Navigation Inn. Large, popular, family pub with a garden and play area. Real ales and a wide range of reasonably priced food available *L and E, daily*. Moorings. *Open 11.00.*
8 The Steamboat Inn Lock Lane, Long Eaton NG10 2FY. (0115 946 0356; www.steamboattrentlock.co.uk). On the Erewash Canal. Built by the canal company in 1791, when it was called the Erewash Navigation Inn, it is now an upmarket canalside pub and restaurant. Real ale available. Food served *L and E*. Dog- and child-friendly, garden. Traditional pub games and camping nearby. *Open 11.00.*
✕ **9 Lock House Tea Rooms** Lock Lane, Trent Lock, Long Eaton NG10 2FY (0115 972 2288). Chintzy tea rooms with a twist, offering a wide variety of teas and homemade food. Outside seating overlooking the lock. Dogs welcome. *Open Wed-Sun from 10.00; closing times vary from 16.00 to 18.00 depending on the day and season.*

GRAND UNION CANAL – MAIN LINE

MAXIMUM DIMENSIONS

Norton Junction to Camp Hill Top Lock (Birmingham)
Length: 72'
Beam: 7'
Headroom: 7' 6"
Craft up to 12' 6" beam are permitted between Norton Junction and Camp Hill but all craft of this size must seek advice before proceeding. Permission must be obtained from BW (01908 302500; enquiries.southeast@britishwaterways.co.uk) for passage through the tunnels.

Camp Hill to Aston Junction and Salford Junction
Length: 70'
Beam: 7'
Headroom: 6' 6"

MILEAGE

NORTON JUNCTION to:
Braunston Turn: 4¼ miles
Napton Junction: 9¼ miles
Kingswood Junction: 31 miles
Bordesley Junction: 45¼ miles
Salford Junction: 48 miles

Locks: 68

MANAGERS

0303 040 4040
Norton Junction to Radford Bottom Lock: enquiries.southeast@canalrivertrust.org.uk
Radford Bottom Lock to Salford Junction: enquiries.westmidlands@canalrivertrust.org.uk

The whole length of the Grand Union Canal is unique among English canals in being composed of at least eight separate canals, linking London with Birmingham, Leicester and Nottingham. Up to the 1920s all these canals were owned and operated by quite separate companies: five between London and Birmingham alone.

The original – and still the most important – part of the system was the Grand Junction Canal, constructed at the turn of the 18th C to provide a short cut between Braunston on the Oxford Canal and Brentford, west of London on the Thames. Previously, all London-bound traffic from the Midlands had to follow the Fazeley, Coventry and Oxford canals down to Oxford, there to tranship into lighters to make the 100-mile trip down river to Brentford and London. The new Grand Junction Canal cut this distance by fully 60 miles, and with its 14ft-wide locks and numerous branches to important towns rapidly became busy and profitable. The building of wide locks to take 70-ton barges was a brave attempt to persuade neighbouring canal companies – the Oxford, Coventry and the distant Trent & Mersey – to widen their navigations and establish a 70-ton barge standard throughout the waterways of the Midlands. Unfortunately, the other companies were deterred by the cost of widening, and to this day those same canals can only pass boats 7ft wide.

The mere proposal of the building of the Grand Junction Canal was enough to generate and justify plans for other canals linked to it. Before the Grand Junction itself was completed, independent canals were built linking it in a direct line to Warwick and Birmingham, and a little later a connection was established from the Grand Junction to Market Harborough and Leicester, and thence via the canalised River Soar to the Trent.

These canals made up the spine of southern England's transport system until the advent of the railways. When the Regent's Canal Company acquired the Grand Junction and others, the whole system was integrated as the Grand Union Canal Company in 1929. In 1932 the new company, aided by the Government, launched a massive programme of modernisation: widening the 52 locks from Braunston to Birmingham. But when the grant was all spent, the task was unfinished and broad beam boats never became common on the Grand Union Canal.

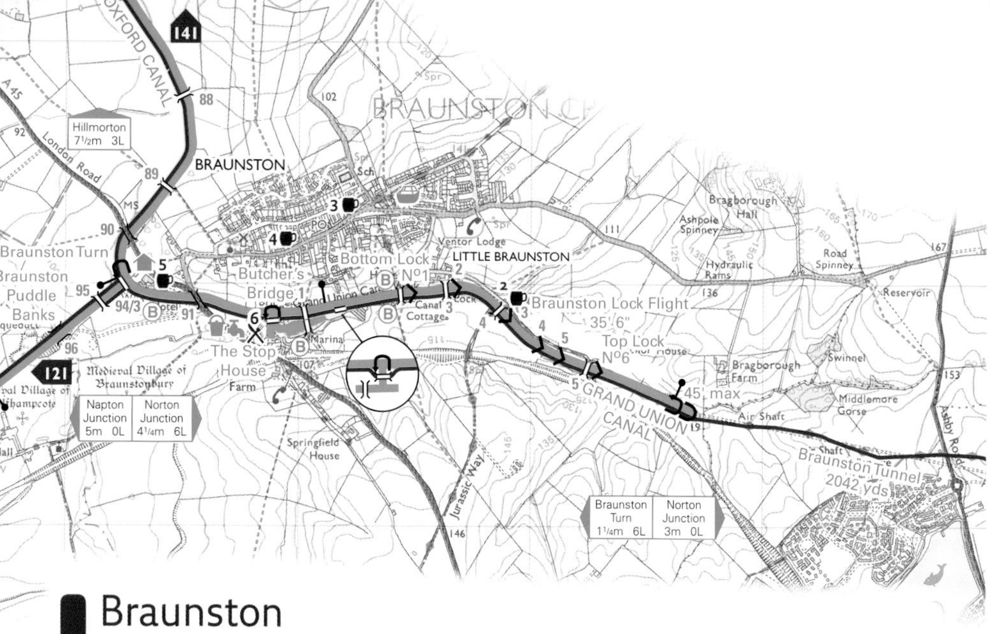

Braunston

From Norton Junction to Braunston the canal runs westward through hills and wooded country, then into a wooded cutting which leads to Braunston Tunnel. There is a good track over the top of the hill, which passes the brick tops of the ventilation shafts. A cutting follows the tunnel, and then the landscape opens out although the hills stay present on either side. Long rows of moored craft flank the canal, but there is usually plenty of space to moor, and a fine selection of old buildings at Braunston. Note especially the iron side-bridge and the 18th C dry dock. The arm in fact was part of the old route of the Oxford Canal before it was shortened by building a large embankment (Braunston Puddle Banks) across the Leam Valley to Braunston Turn. The entrance to this arm was thus the original Braunston Junction. The delightful building alongside, known as the Stop House, was originally the Toll Office between the Oxford Canal and the Grand Junction Canal.

Boatyards

Ⓑ**The Boat Shop** Bottom Lock, Dark Lane, Braunston NN11 7HJ (01788 891310; www.boatshopbraunston.co.uk). Started on board a boat moored at Braunston Turn, this is now a shop selling a comprehensive range of books, maps, gifts and provisions, including freshly-baked bread. *Open summer 08.00–19.00 and winter 08.00–17.00.*

Ⓑ**Braunston Boats** Bottom Lock, Braunston NN11 7HJ (01788 891079). Gas, solid fuel, slipway, hard standing/winter storage, short-term and long-term mooring, chandlery, boat repairs, engine sales and repairs, welding, fabrication, electrics, internal fit-outs, blacking, toilets.

Ⓑ**Wharf House Narrowboats** Braunston Boat Haven, Botton Lock, Dark Lane, Braunston NN11 7HJ (01788 899041; www.wharfhouse.co.uk). Boat building, fitting out and refits, electrics, chandlery, books, maps and gifts.

Ⓑ**Union Canal Carriers** Canalside at Braunston Pump House, Dark Lane, Little Braunston NN11 7HJ (01788 890784; www.unioncanalcarriers.co.uk). **D** Pump out, gas, narrowboat hire, day-boat hire, dry dock, engine sales, boat and engine repairs, blacking, painting. *24hr emergency call out.*

Ⓑ**Braunston Marina** The Wharf, Braunston NN11 7JH (01788 891373; www.braunstonmarina.co.uk). Through the fine bridge dated 1834 and into an historic canal wharf. **D E** Pump out, gas, overnight and long-term mooring, dry and wet dock, crane, boat building, sales and repairs, engine repairs, DIY facilities, welding, limited chandlery, toilets, showers, gift shop selling books and maps, laundrette, coal. There are also boatbuilders, fitters and fender makers at the marina.

Ⓑ**Midland Chandlers** London Road, Braunston NN11 7HB (01788 891401/02476 390111; www.midlandchandlers. co.uk) In operation for almost 30 years. A wide range of chandlery.

NAVIGATIONAL NOTES

Braunston Tunnel: two boats of 7ft beam can pass in this tunnel, but wide beam boats *must get permission from CRT* to arrange passage (0303 040 4040; enquiries.southeast@canalrivertrust.org.uk).

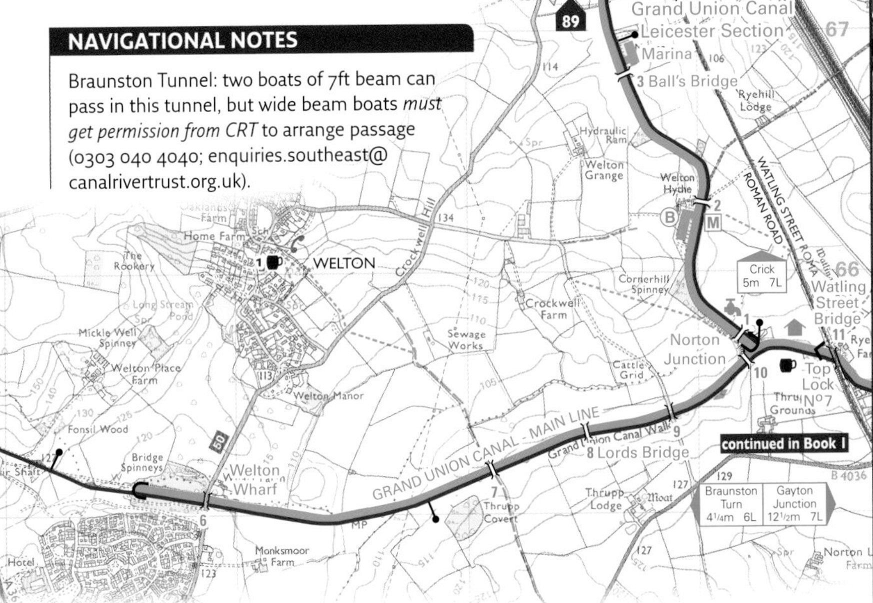

WALKING AND CYCLING

A footpath south west of bridge 91 crosses the sites of the medieval villages of Braunstonbury and Wolfhampcote.

- **Welton**
Northants. Tel. The village climbs up the side of a steep hill, which makes it compact and attractive, especially around the church.

- **Braunston Tunnel**
Opened in 1796 to bore through the Northamptonshire heights, the tunnel is 2042yds long. Its construction was hindered by quicksands, and a mistake in direction whilst building has given it a slight S bend.

- **Braunston**
Northants. PO, tel, stores, butcher, fish & chips, tea shop, gift shop. Set up on a hill to the north of the canal. The village is really a long main street a little separate from the canal, with houses of all periods. A well-known canal centre, it is no less significant today than when the Oxford and Grand Junction canals were first connected here.

Pubs and Restaurants

X 1 **The White Horse** High Street, Welton NN11 2JP (01327 702820). 3/4 mile from the canal at Bridge 6. A 400-year-old public house serving real ale. A wide range of bar and restaurant food is served *Wed-Sat L and E & Sun 12.00-16.00*. Family-friendly; large garden. Traditional pub games and real fires. *Open Mon-Tue E; Wed-Thu L and E & Sat-Sun 12.00.*

X 2 **The Admiral Nelson** Dark Lane, Braunston NN11 7HJ (01788 891900; www.theadmiralnelson.co.uk). Beside Lock 3. Canalside hostelry serving Food *L and E (not Sun E)*. Canalside seating and mooring. Child- and dog-friendly. Wi-Fi. *Open all day from 12.00 (winter opening may vary).*

X 3 **The Wheatsheaf** The Green, Braunston NN11 7HW (01788 890748). Small local pub, in the centre of the village, with a garden.

X 4 **The Old Plough** 82 High Street, Braunston NN11 7HS (01788 878126; www.theoldplough-braunston.co.uk). A fine village pub dating from 1672, with open fires and serving real ale. Good food *daily L and E (not Sun E)*. Garden; child- and dog-friendly. Traditional pub games. *Open 12.00.*

X 5 **The Boat House** London Road, Braunston NN11 7HB (01788 891734; www.boathousepub.co.uk). Once the Rose and Castle, it is now a welcoming restaurant and pub, serving real ale. Grills, *Sun* roasts, carvery meals *daily*. Children's room and fine canalside garden with swings. Overnight mooring for patrons. *Open all day.*

X 6 **The Gongoozler's Rest** Narrowboat café moored outside the Stop House NN11 7JQ (07940 973529; www.gongoozlersrest.wix.com/gongoozler). Breakfasts, sandwiches, omelettes, homemade cakes and a variety of good fare. Children's menu and takeaway service. *Open daily 09.00-14.00 (Jul-Aug 15.00).*

Napton Junction

The canal now passes through open countryside with a backdrop of hills, seeming very quiet and empty following all of the waterway activity around Braunston. The land is agricultural, with just a few houses in sight. There are initially no locks, no villages and the bridges are well spaced, making this a very pleasant rural stretch of canal running south west towards Napton Junction, on a length once used by both the Grand Junction Company and the Oxford Canal Company. As the Oxford Canal actually owned this stretch, they charged excessive toll rates in an attempt to get even with their rival, whose more direct route between London and the Midlands had attracted most of the traffic. At Napton Junction the Oxford Canal heads off to the south while the Grand Union Canal strikes off north towards Birmingham. The empty landscape rolls on towards Stockton, broken only by Calcutt Locks. The Windmill on Napton Hill, now almost hidden behind the trees, can still just be seen from Napton Junction.

Boatyards

Ⓑ**Wigrams Turn Marina** Shuckburgh Road, Napton, Southam CV47 8NL (01926 817175; www.castlemarinas.co.uk/marinas/wigrams-turn). D E Pump out, gas, solid fuel, short- and long-term mooring, narrowboat hire, boat sales and brokerage, toilets, showers, laundry, camping.

Ⓑ**Napton Narrowboats** Napton Marina, Tomlow Road, Stockton, Southam (01926 813644; www.napton-marina.co.uk). D Pump out, gas, narrowboat hire, overnight and long-term mooring, boatbuilding, boat and engine repairs, toilets, chandlery, gifts, dry dock, solid fuel, boat painting, bottom blacking, toilets. *Open daily 08.30-17.00.*

Ⓑ**Calcutt Boats** Tomlow Road, Stockton, Southam CV47 8HX (01926 813757; www.calcuttboats. com). D Pump out, gas, narrowboat hire, overnight mooring, long-term mooring, slipway, crane, dry dock, boat and engine sales and repairs, BMC engine specialists, marine engineering, boatbuilding and fitting out, chandlery, toilets, solid fuel, breakdown service.

Ⓑ**Ventnor Farm Marina** Calcutt Lane, Stockton, Rugby, Warwickshire CV23 8HY (01926 815023; www.castlemarinas.co.uk/marinas/ventnor). D E Pump out, short- and long-term mooring, dry dock, boat maintenance and repair, boat sales and brokerage, toilet, shower, laundry, members lounge. The facilities are for the use of moorers only.

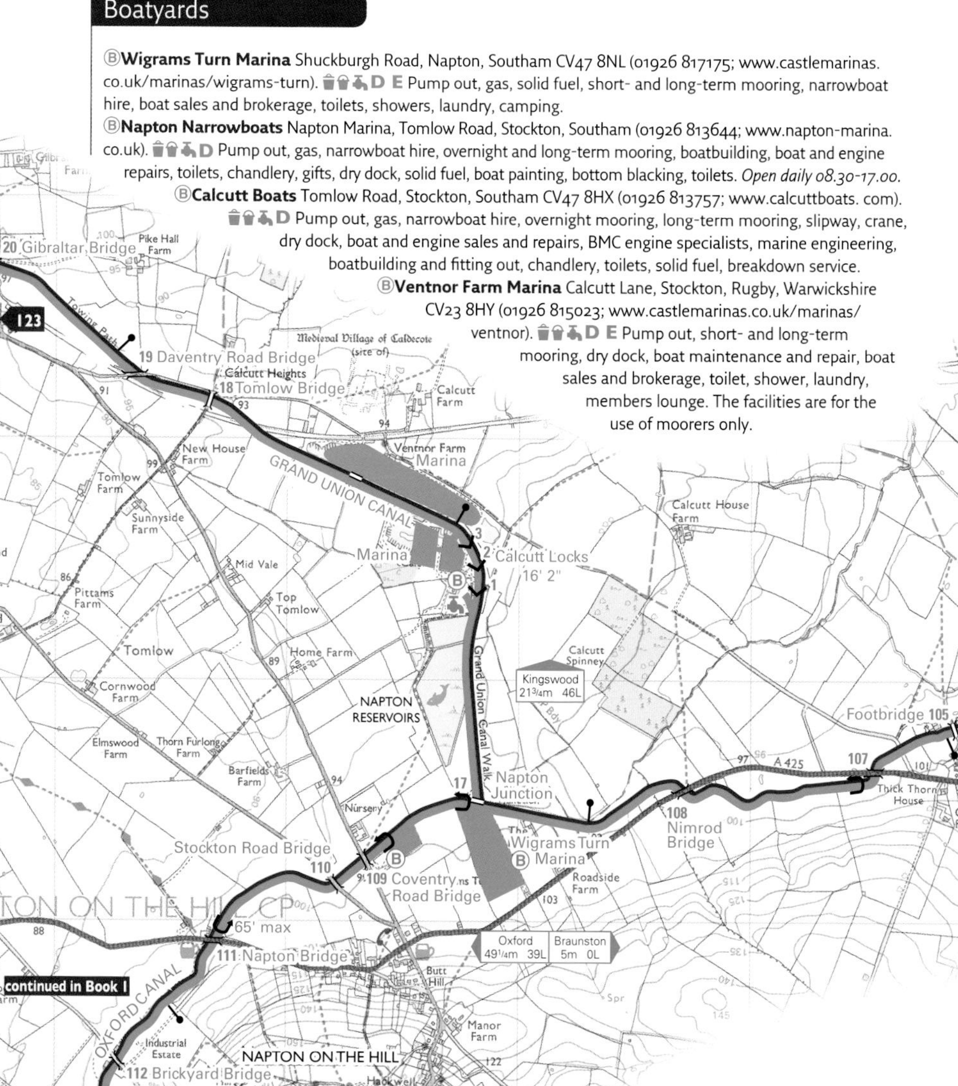

Pubs and Restaurants

1 Old Olive Bush Flecknoe CV23 8AT (01788 891134; www.theoldolivebush.co.uk). ¾ west of Bridge 102. A cosy village pub serving real ale and home-cooked meals *Wed-Sat E and Sun L (booking essential at weekends).* Delightful garden; family-friendly. Quiz *Thu.* Camping, traditional pub games and real fires. *Open Sat, Sun and B Hol Mon L and Tue-Sat E.*

Lower Shuckburgh
Warwicks. PO box. A tiny village along the main road. The church, built in 1864, is attractive in a Victorian way, with great use of contrasting brickwork inside.

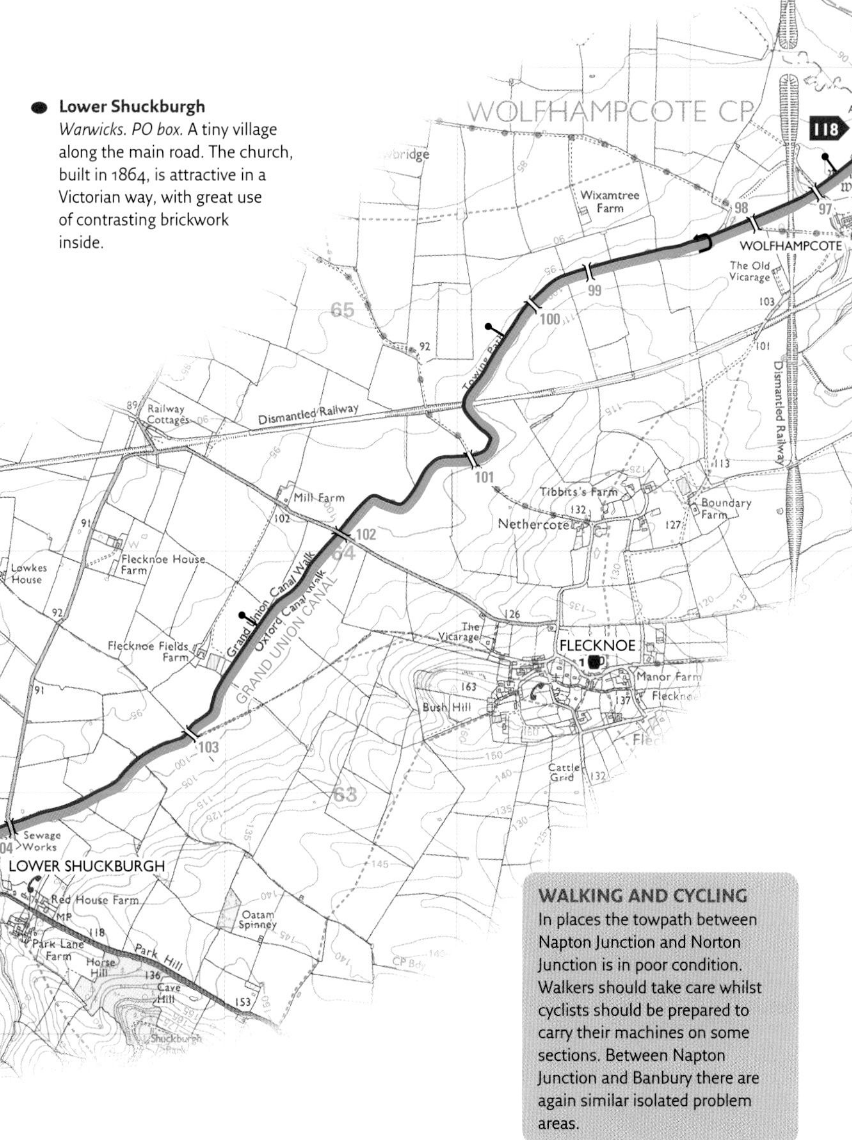

WALKING AND CYCLING
In places the towpath between Napton Junction and Norton Junction is in poor condition. Walkers should take care whilst cyclists should be prepared to carry their machines on some sections. Between Napton Junction and Banbury there are again similar isolated problem areas.

Stockton

Continuing west, the canal passes to the north of Stockton and descends Stockton Locks, where you will notice the remains of the old narrow locks beside the newer wide ones. Around here there is a change in landscape, with the hills coming much closer to the canal, broken by old quarries and thick woods along the south bank. The quarries produced blue lias, a local stone, and cement which was used in the construction of the Thames Embankment. Huge fossils have been found in the blue lias clay, which is the lowest layer from the Jurassic period. This section contrasts greatly with the open landscape that precedes and follows it. The canal passes Long Itchington, a village with a large number of pubs, including two on the canal, all the while flanked by open arable land backed on both sides by hills. This pleasant emptiness is broken only by further locks continuing the fall to Warwick. Of particular interest are the top two locks at Bascote, just beyond the pretty toll house, which form a staircase. Then the canal is once again in quiet, wooded, countryside.

- **Stockton**
  Warwicks. PO, tel, stores, takeaway. Stockton is a largely Victorian village in an area which has been dominated by the cement works to the west.
  St Michael's church is built of blue lias, quarried near Stockton Locks, although the tower is of red sandstone.
- **Long Itchington**
  Warwicks. PO, tel, stores, off-licence. A large housing estate flanks the busy A423; the village proper lies a short walk to the north west, and is very attractive. Apart from the proliferation of pubs there are houses of the 17th and 18th C, and impressive poplars around the village pond. St Wulfstan, who later became Bishop of Worcester, was born here in 1012.
  Holy Trinity A largely 13th-C church whose tall spire was blown down in a gale in 1762, and replaced with a stump. Parts of the south aisle date from the 12th C, although the 13th-C windows are perhaps the building's best feature.

Boatyards

Ⓑ**Willow Wren Training** Nelson's Wharf, Rugby Road, Stockton, Southam CV47 8AA (07970 770565; www.willowwrentraining.co.uk). Offering a range of training from RYA boat handling to the MCA Boatmaster certificate. Steam experience days. Visit the website for full details.

Ⓑ**Stockton Narrowboats** Stockton, Rugby Road CV47 8HN (01926 492968; www.kateboats.co.uk/stockton-narrowboats). At the top of Stockton Locks. **D** Pump out, gas, narrowboat hire, long-term mooring, slipway, toilets.

Ⓑ**Warwickshire Fly Boat Company** Stop Lock Cottage, Stockton CV47 8LD (01926 812093; www.wfbco.co.uk). By the Kayes Arm. Gas, long-term mooring, dry dock, boat sales, engine repairs, chandlery, telephone, toilets, showers, solid fuel, laundrette, books and maps. Painting undertaken by Bill Matthews 07798 575730.

Ⓑ**Stockton Dry Dock Company** Stop Lock Cottage, Stockton CV47 8LD (01926 814441). Boatbuilding and repairs. Dry dock.

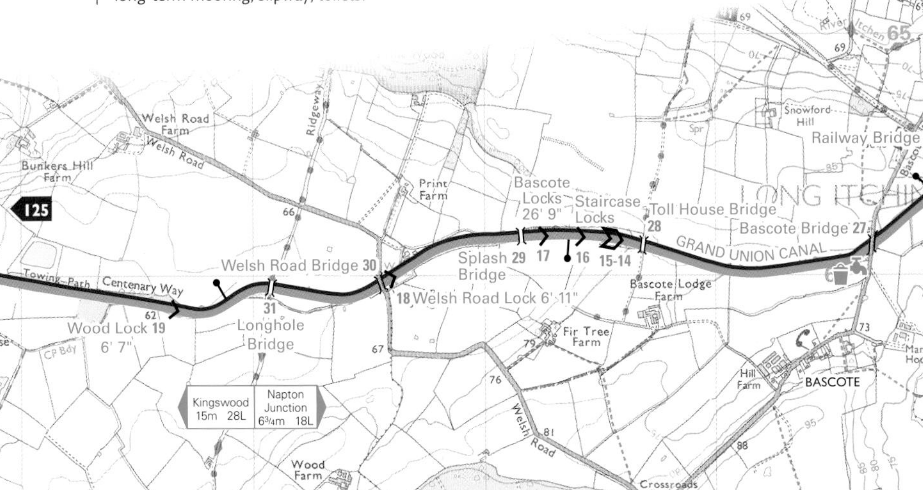

Pubs and Restaurants

1 The Crown 8 High Street, Stockton CV47 8JZ (01926 812255; www.crowninnstockton.com). A cosy, traditional village pub where bar meals are served in large portions *L and E (not Sun and Mon E)*. Real ales. Children welcome. Outside seating. Traditional pub games, live music and real fires. *Open 11.00 (Sun 12.00).*

2 The Boat Inn Birdingbury Wharf, Rugby Road CV23 8HQ (01926 812657; www.boatbirdingburywharf.com). Canalside at Bridge 21. A pleasant old pub with a fine map, painted by Dusty Miller, around the top of the bar. Real ale. Food available *Tue E and Wed-Sun 12.00-20.45*. Canalside patio, garden and play area. Children and dogs welcome. Traditional pub games, newspapers, real fires and Wi-Fi. *Open Tue E and Wed-Sun 12.00.*

3 The Blue Lias Inn Stockton Road, Stockton CV47 8LD (01926 812249; www.bluelias.com). Canalside at Bridge 23. A well-kept and attractive pub, with a pleasant canalside garden. Be prepared for the uneven interior brickwork, which may look straighter when you have enjoyed one of the real ales they regularly keep. Bar meals *L and E*. Dog- and family-friendly. Camping and real fires. *Open daily L and E.*

4 The Two Boats Inn Southam Road, Long Itchington CV47 9QZ (01926 812640; www.thetwoboats.co.uk). Canalside at Bridge 25. A good selection of real ale and real cider is available in this fine pub, built in 1743. At one time there was a forge and stables here for the boat horses. Food is available *Mon-Thu L and E; Fri-Sat 12.00-21.00 and Sun 12.00-17.00*. Children and dogs welcome. Towpath terrace. Real fires, sports TV and Wi-Fi. *Open 12.00.*

5 The Cuttle Inn Southam Road, Long Itchington CV47 9QZ (01926 812314; www.thecuttleinn.co.uk). Canalside at Bridge 25. Traditional locals' pub with outside seating and children's play area. Real ale and bar food *daily 12.00-21.00 (Sun 17.00)*. Live music *most weekends*; dog- and family-friendly. Traditional pub games, newspapers, real fires and Wi-Fi. *Open 12.00.*

6 The Duck on the Pond The Green, Long Itchington CV47 9QJ (01926 815876; www.theduckonthepondlongitchington.co.uk). Specialising in food, this pub overlooks the village green and pond. Queen Elizabeth I once stayed in the black and white timbered building opposite. Real ale, and a wide range of meals are served *Mon-Thu L and E & Fri-Sun 12.00-21.30 (Sun 19.30)*. Garden; children and dogs welcome. Traditional pub games, newspapers, real fires, Wi-Fi and live music. *Open 11.00.*

7 The Buck and Bell The Green, Long Itchington CV47 9PH (01926 811177; www.buckandbellpub.co.uk). Real ale. Appetising, locally-sourced food is available *Mon-Sat L and E & Sun 12.00-17.30*. Child- and dog-friendly; patio seating. Newspapers, real fires, sports TV and Wi-Fi. *Open 12.00.*

8 The Harvester Church Road, Long Itchington CV47 9PE (01926 812698; www.theharvesterinn.co.uk). Small, family-run village local serving real ale. Bar and restaurant meals, *L and E*. Children and dogs welcome. Beer garden, newspapers and Wi-Fi. *Open daily L and E.*

9 The Green Man Church Road, Long Itchington CV47 9PW (01926 812208; www.greenmanlongitchington.co.uk). Just past the church, this is a fine traditional community pub with a very low ceiling in the corridor. Real ale, family room and garden. Traditional pub games, newspapers, real fires, sports TV and Wi-Fi. Camping. *Open Mon-Fri E and Sat-Sun 12.00.*

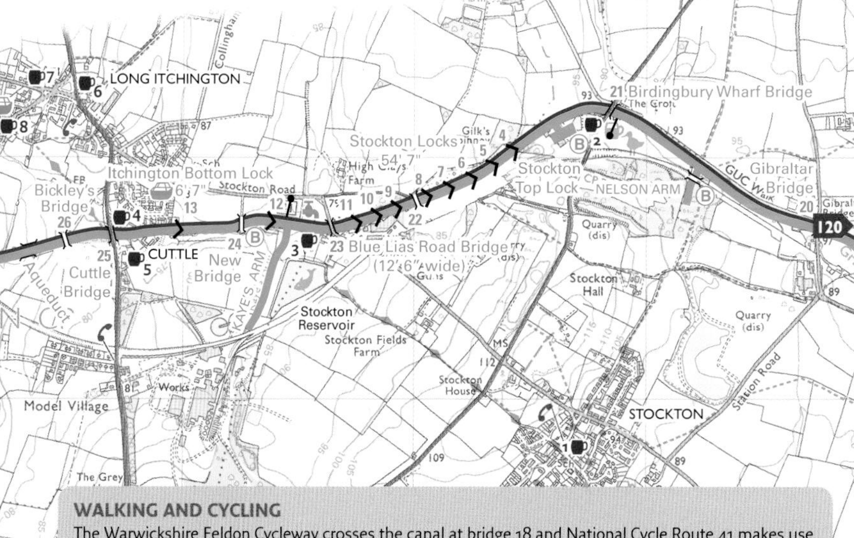

WALKING AND CYCLING

The Warwickshire Feldon Cycleway crosses the canal at bridge 18 and National Cycle Route 41 makes use of the towpath between bridge 21 and the disused railway bridge east of bridge 27. It re-joins at bridge 34, making its way into Leamington and offers an attractive alternative route.

Royal Leamington Spa

The waterway makes its descent through the quiet Fosse Locks and continues west through attractive and isolated country to pass to the north of Radford Semele, where there is a fine wooded cutting. Eggs and poultry (alive and dead) are available from the farm beside Bridge 34 and there is a *PO, stores, fish & chips, chemist, pub and a takeaway* at Bridge 37. Emerging from the cutting, the canal joins a busy road for a short while, then carves a fairly discreet course through Leamington. Midway through the town the canal enters a deep cutting that hides it from the adjacent main road and railway. Leaving Leamington the canal swings north west under a main road and crosses the railway and the River Avon on aqueducts, to immediately enter the outskirts of Warwick. There are good *moorings, shops* and two *Indian takeaways* close to Bridge 40.

Pubs and Restaurants

1 The Stag Welsh Road, Offchurch CV33 9AQ (01926 425801; www.thestagatoffchurch.com). A thatched 15th-C pub, serving real ale and food *L and E*. Children and dogs welcome. Garden, real fires and Wi-Fi. *Open 12.00.*

2 The White Lion 60 Southam Road, Kingshurst, Radford Semele CV31 1TE (01926 678573; www.chefandbrewer.com/pub/white-lion-radford-semele-leamington-spa/p1192). Real ale, and meals served *daily 12.00-22.00 (Sun 21.30)*. Child- and dog-friendly; garden. Real fires and Wi-Fi. *Open 11.30.*

3 The Procaffeinate Club 66 -68 Clemens Street, Leamington Spa CV31 2DN (01926 737006; procaffeinate.club). At Bridge 40, overlooking the canal. Unusual, inviting, coffee shop-cum-tearoom serving superb coffees and teas together with a enticing range of pastries and freshly-made light meals. *Open Mon-Sat 07.30-23.00 (Sat 09.00) & Sun 09.00-18.00.*

4 The Waterside Inn Queensway, Leamington Spa CV31 3JZ (01926 435139; www.watersideinn-leamingtonspa.co.uk). Large, modern, canalside pub serving real ale and food *daily 10.00-22.00* - breakfast is available *10.00-12.00*. Large garden; child- and dog-friendly. Live music, sports TV and Wi-Fi. Mooring. *Open 10.00.*

5 The Moorings Myton Road, Leamington Spa CV31 3NY (01926 425043; www.themoorings.co.uk). By Bridge 43. Real ale. Meals available *L and E, daily*. Children and dogs welcome. Canalside terrace. Newspapers, real fires and Wi-Fi. Mooring. *Open 10.30.*

6 The Fusilier Sydenham Drive, Leamington Spa CV31 1NJ (01926 257012; www.fusilierleamington.co.uk). Beside Bridge 37. 1970s estate pub serving real ale. Garden, children and dogs welcome. *Regular* live music. Traditional pub games, sports TV and Wi-Fi. *Open 12.00-23.00 (Fri-Sat 00.00).*

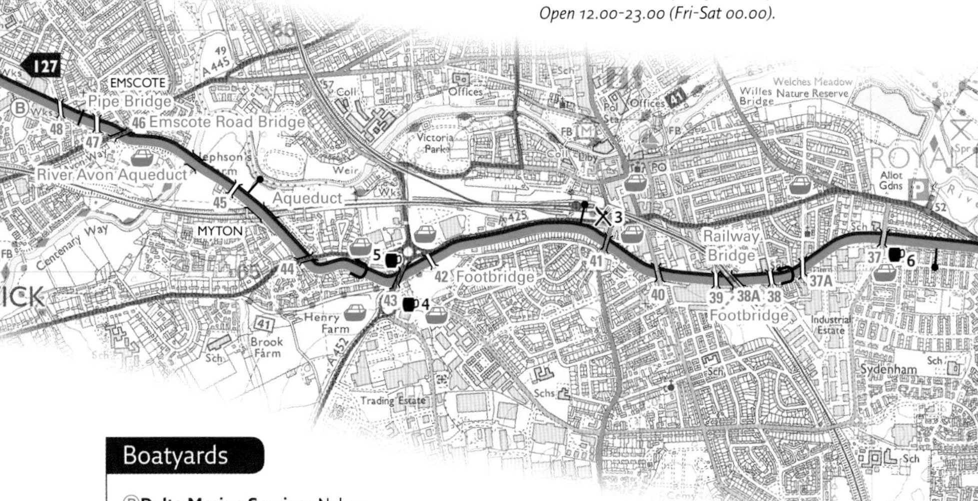

Boatyards

Ⓑ **Delta Marine Services** Nelson Wharf, Nelson Lane, Warwick CV34 5JB (01926 499337/07831 355543; www. delta-marineservices.co.uk). Canalside near Bridge 48. D Pump out, gas, long-term mooring, wet dock, boat and engine repairs, boat building, surveying, DIY facilities, toilets. *24hr emergency breakdown service.*

- **Offchurch** *Warwicks. Tel.* A scattered residential village reflecting the proximity of Leamington. It takes its name from Offa, the Saxon King of Mercia, reputedly buried near here. The church, with its tall grey stone tower, contains some Norman work. To the west lies Offchurch Bury, whose park runs almost to the canal. Originally this was a 17th-C house, but it has since been entirely rebuilt. The façade is now early 19th C Gothic.
- **Radford Semele**
Warwicks. PO, tel, stores, off-licence. A main road suburb of Leamington, Radford Semele takes no notice of the canal that runs below the village, alongside the River Leam and what was once the railway line to Rugby. Among the bungalows are some fine large houses, including Radford Hall, a reconstructed Jacobean building. The Victorian church of St Nicholas, recently completely gutted by fire and now rebuilt, is set curiously by itself, seeming to be in the middle of a field.
- **Royal Leamington Spa**
Warwicks. All services. During the 19th C the population of Leamington increased rapidly, due to the late 18th- and 19th C fashion for spas generally. As a result the town is largely Regency with later Victorian additions resulting in a most pleasingly spacious layout. Several hotels and churches were designed by J. Cundall, a local architect of some note who also built the brick and stone town hall. The long rows of villas, elegant houses in their own grounds spreading out from the centre, all express the Victorian love of exotic styles – Gothic, Classical, Jacobean, Renaissance, French and Greek are all mixed here with bold abandon. Since the Victorian era, however, much industrialisation has taken place.

Assembly Rooms, Art Gallery and Museum Royal Pump Rooms, The Parade CV32 4AA (01926 742700; www.warwickdc.gov.uk/royalpumprooms). British, Dutch and Flemish paintings of the 16th- and 17th-C. Also a collection of modern art, pottery and porcelain through the ages and a specialist series of 18th-C English drinking glasses. Victorian costumes and objects. Tea room. *Open Tue-Sat 10.30-17.00; Sun and B Hol 11.00-16.00.* Free.

All Saints' Church Bath Street CV33 9HA Begun in 1843 to the design of J. C. Jackson, who was greatly influenced by the then vicar, Dr John Craig. It is of Gothic style, apparently not always correct in detail. The north transept has a rose window patterned on Rouen Cathedral; the west window is by Kempe. The scale of the building is impressive, being fully 172ft long and 80ft high.

Jephson Gardens Alongside Newbold Terrace, north of Bridge 40, CV32 4AB. Beautiful ornamental gardens named after Dr Jephson (1798- 1878), the local practitioner who was largely responsible for the spa's high medical reputation.

Tourist Information Centre Royal Pump Rooms, The Parade CV32 4AB (01926 742762).Contact via info@visitleamingtonspa.info for details of *opening times* or visit the library in the same building.

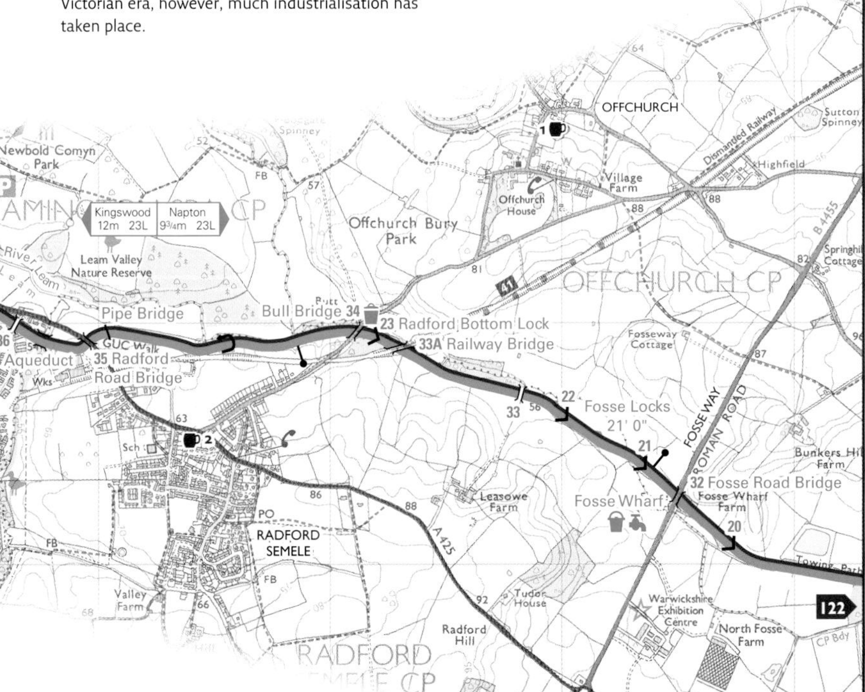

Warwick

The canal passes around the north side of central Warwick, so if you wish to visit the town centre, it is best to approach from Bridge 49 (walking to the south for a little over half a mile), or from the Saltisford Canal Centre (*see* below). After climbing the two Cape Locks, the canal swings south to Budbrooke Junction, where the old Warwick and Napton Canal joined the Warwick and Birmingham Canal. A short section of the arm to the east of the junction has been restored, and has a *winding hole, moorings, laundrette and other facilities*. To the west of the junction, beyond a large road bridge, is the first of the 21 locks of the Hatton flight, with distinctive paddle gear and gates stretching up the hill ahead, a daunting sight for even the most resilient boatman. Consolation is offered by the fine view of the spires of Warwick as you climb the flight. A fine pair of traditional working boats are sometimes moored in front of an old British Waterways van by the old Hatton Yard. On reaching the top, the canal turns to the north west, passing the wooded hills that conceal Hatton village and Hatton Park. It then enters the wooded cutting that leads to Shrewley Tunnel.

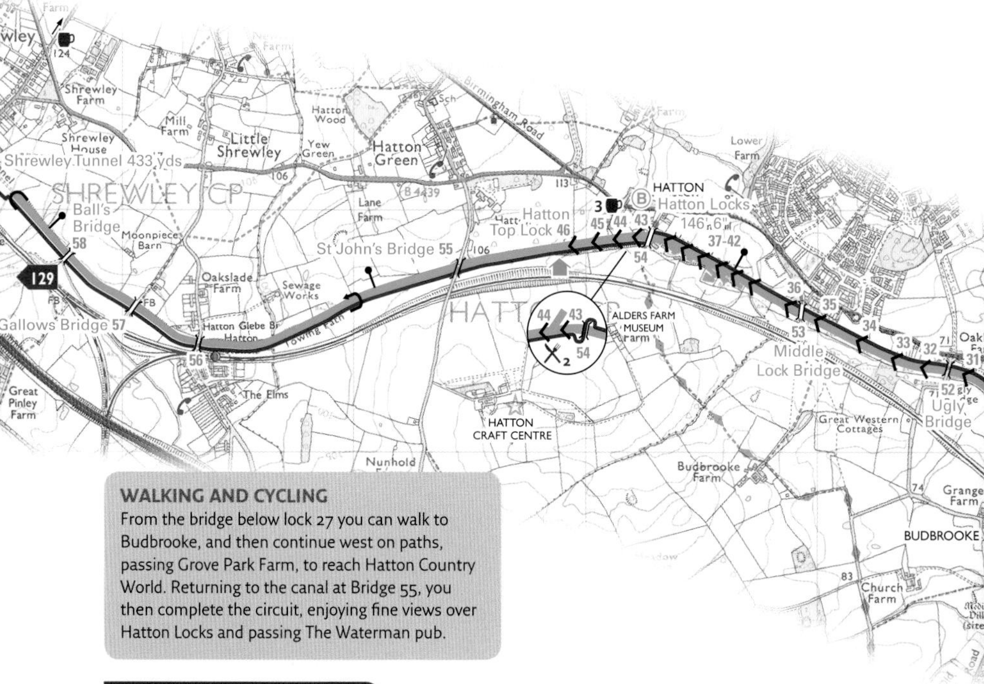

WALKING AND CYCLING

From the bridge below lock 27 you can walk to Budbrooke, and then continue west on paths, passing Grove Park Farm, to reach Hatton Country World. Returning to the canal at Bridge 55, you then complete the circuit, enjoying fine views over Hatton Locks and passing The Waterman pub.

Boatyards

Ⓑ**Saltisford Canal Centre** Budbrooke Road CV34 5RJ (01926 490006; www.saltisfordcanal.co.uk). E Gas, pump out, day-hire craft, overnight and long-term mooring, winter storage, small chandlery, telephone nearby, toilets, gifts, laundry. Gardens and picnic areas. Snacks available. An excellent place in its own right, with good access to Warwick.

Ⓑ**Warwick Narrowboats** The Boatyard, Nelson Lane Warwick CV34 5JB (01926 492968; www.kateboats.co.uk/warwick-narrowboats). D Pump out, gas, narrowboat hire, overnight and long-term mooring, boat and engine repairs, boatbuilding, chandlery, toilets, books.

Ⓑ**Get Knotted** Lower Cape CV34 5DP (01926 410588; www.getknotted.co.uk). Next door to the Cape of Good Hope pub. Rope fender-making specialist, plus general ropework and an expanding chandlery. Narrowboat graphics and vinyl wrapping.

Ⓑ**Stephen Goldsbrough Boats** Hatton CV47 2XD (01564 778210; www.knowlehallwharf.co.uk/dry-dock.html). Dry dock on the Hatton flight, boat painting and repairs, boat building, engine repairs, DIY facilities.

● **Warwick**
Warwicks. All services. Virtually destroyed by fire in 1694 the town rose again, with Queen Anne styles now mixed with the medieval buildings which survived the blaze.
Warwick Castle Castle Hill CV34 4QU (0871 265 2000; www.warwick-castle.com). Built on the site of a motte and bailey constructed by William the Conqueror in 1068, the present exterior is a famous example of a 14th C fortification, with the tall Caesar's Tower rising to a height of 147ft. The castle grounds were laid out by Capability Brown. *Open daily 10.00-18.00. Closed Xmas.* Charge. Programme of events *throughout the year.*
Collegiate Church of St Mary's Old Square, CV34 4RA Of Norman origin (01926 403940; www.stmaryswarwick.org.uk). The most striking feature of the rebuilt church is its pseudo-Gothic tower, built 1698–1704. Climb to the top to enjoy the view (*May–Sep, 10.00–16.00 weather permitting).* Church *open Apr-Sep, Mon-Sat 10.00-18.00; Oct-Mar, Mon-Sat 10.00-16.30 and all year Sun 12.30-16.30.* Free (charge for tower).
Market Hall Museum Market Place CV34 4SA (01926 412500/412501; www.warwickshire.gov.uk/museum). Housed in the Market Hall. Includes the Sheldon tapestry map of Warwickshire, which dates from 1588. *Open Tue-Sat and B Hols 10.00-17.00, Sun 11.30-17.00 Apr–Sept.* Free.
Lord Leycester Hospital 60 High Street CV34 4BH (01926 491422; www.lordleycester.com). A superbly preserved group of 14th-C timber-framed buildings. Chapel of St James, Great Hall and galleried courtyard. The Museum of the Queen's Own Hussars is also here. *Open Tue-Sun and B Hol Mon 10.00-17.00 (16.00 in winter).* The restored gardens are *open during the summer.* Charge.
Tourist Information Centre The Court House, Jury Street CV34 4EW (01926 492212; www.visitwarwick.co.uk). Guided walks are arranged from here *during the summer. Open Mon-Sat 9.30-16.30 (Sat 10.00) and Sun 10.00-16.00).*

● **Hatton**
Warwicks. A heavily wooded village.
Hatton Country World George's Farm, Hatton CV35 8XA (01926 843411; www.hattonworld.com). South of Bridge 55. Rare breeds, craft workshops and a children's play area. Arts and crafts shops. *Open daily 10.00-17.30 (closed Xmas).* Entrance to the craft village is free, but a charge is made for the Farm Park. Restaurant.

● **Shrewley**
Warwicks. Tel, PO, stores, off-licence. Best approached from the north western end of the Shrewley Tunnel, through an exciting, but slippery, towpath tunnel.
Shrewley Tunnel 433yds long, the tunnel was opened in 1799 with the completion of the Warwick and Birmingham Canal. *This tunnel allows two 7ft boats to pass: keep to the right.*

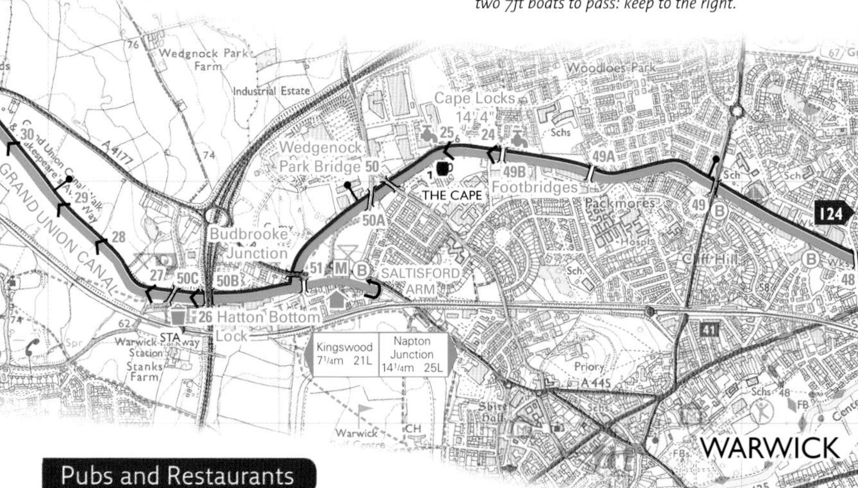

Pubs and Restaurants

1 The Cape of Good Hope 66 Lower Cape, Warwick CV34 5DP (01926 498138; www.thecapeofgoodhopepub.com). Beside Cape Lock 25. Friendly, canalside pub serving a wide range of real ales and food *daily 12.00-21.15 (reduced hours in winter).* Lockside seating; well-behaved children and dogs welcome. *Regular* live music. Traditional pub games, newspapers, real fires, sports TV and Wi-Fi. Mooring. *Open 12.00.*

X **2 Hatton Locks Café** Canal Road, Hatton, CV35 7JL (01926 409432). Friendly establishment serving breakfast, light meals, tea, coffee and cakes. *Open daily 09.00-17.00.*

X **3 The Hatton Arms** Birmingham Road (A4177), Hatton CV35 7JJ (01926 492427; www.hattonarms.com). An extensive bar menu is served *daily 12.00-21.00 (Sun 19.00)* together with a selection of real ales available in this country pub which has fine views over the Hatton flight. Family friendly with a large garden. Real fires. *Open 11.00 (Sun 12.00).*

Kingswood

After Shrewley Tunnel hills surround the canal on all sides as it travels through steep wooded folds. At Turner's Green a beautiful old beamed house stands by the canal; the waterway continues to Kingswood and the junction with the Stratford-upon-Avon Canal. There are plenty of facilities near at hand.

Pubs and Restaurants

1 The Durham Ox Shrewley Common, Shrewley CV35 7AY (01926 842283; www.oldenglishinns.co.uk/our-locations/durham-ox). Country pub and restaurant serving real and food *all day*. Garden, children welcome and Wi-Fi.

2 The Case is Altered Case Lane, just off Five Ways, Haseley Knob CV35 7JD (01926 484206). A brisk 45-minute walk from Bridge 62, but worth it to find this quiet old-fashioned ale house. Pass Rowington Hall, then north east past South Lawn. Real ale, but no children, food or dogs. Outside seating. Traditional pub games and real fires. *Open Mon-Sat L and E & Sun 12.00-19.30.*

3 Tom O' The Wood Finwood Road, Rowington CV35 7DH (01564 782252; www.tomothewood.co.uk). Traditional country pub serving real ale, and bar and restaurant meals *Mon-Sat L and E & Sun 12.00-16.00.* Canalside garden; child- and dog-friendly. Real fires and Wi-Fi. Mooring. *Open 11.00-23.00 (Sun 20.00).*

4 The Navigation Old Warwick Road, Lapworth B94 6NA (01564 783337; www.navigationlapworth.co.uk). Real ales, real cider and food available *Mon-Thu L and E & Fri-Sun 12.00-21.30 (Sun 20.00).* Breakfast *Sat-Sun from 10.00.* Family-friendly, canalside garden. Traditional pub games, real fires and Wi-Fi. Camping & Moorings. *Open 11.30-00.00.*

WALKING AND CYCLING

By walking west from the Tom o'the Wood pub and crossing Dick's Lane Bridge on the Stratford-upon-Avon Canal, you can follow paths past Ardenhill Farm to bring you to Bridge 31 on the Lapworth Flight. It is then an excellent and fascinating walk back, passing the locks and returning to the Grand Union via Kingswood Junction.

- **Rowington**
Warwicks. Near the canal the 13th C church retains some furnishings and a fine peal of bells.

- **Lapworth**
Warwicks. Tel, PO, stores, off-licence, garage, station. The village is scattered over a wide area from the Grand Union Canal to the Stratford-upon-Avon Canal. The centre is a mile to the west, around the ambitious 15th-C church.

Packwood House Packwood Lane, Lapworth B94 6AT (01564 782024; www.nationaltrust.org.uk/packwood-house). 1½ miles west of Bridge 66. Much restored timber-framed Tudor house. Cromwell's general, Henry Ireton, slept here before the Battle of Edgehill in 1642. Gardens with notable topiary; lakeside walk. Park *open all year*. House *open Feb-Oct, Tue-Sun and B Hols 11.00-17.00 but visit website to confirm details before visiting.* Shop and café. Charge.

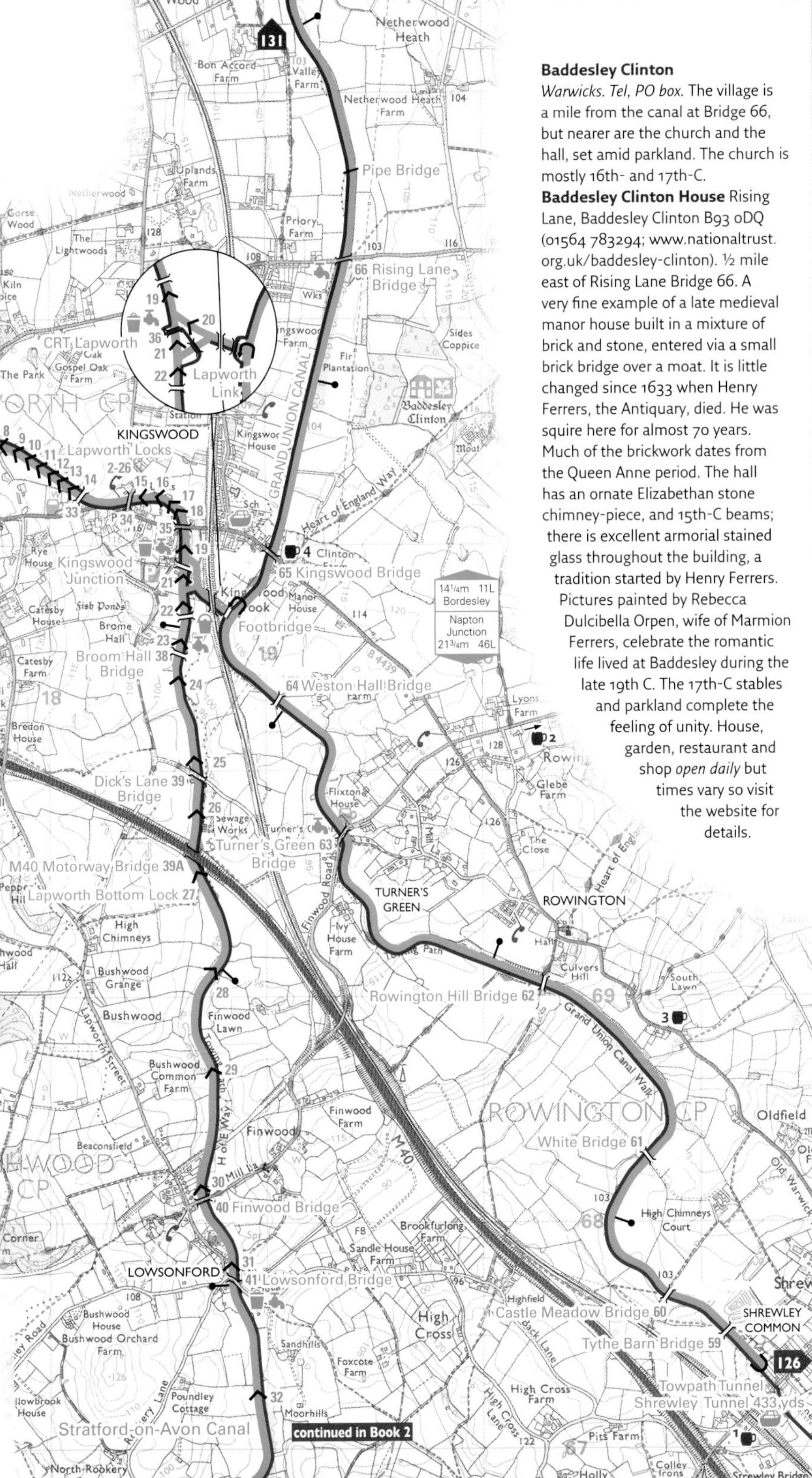

Baddesley Clinton
Warwicks. Tel, PO box. The village is a mile from the canal at Bridge 66, but nearer are the church and the hall, set amid parkland. The church is mostly 16th- and 17th-C.

Baddesley Clinton House Rising Lane, Baddesley Clinton B93 0DQ (01564 783294; www.nationaltrust.org.uk/baddesley-clinton). ½ mile east of Rising Lane Bridge 66. A very fine example of a late medieval manor house built in a mixture of brick and stone, entered via a small brick bridge over a moat. It is little changed since 1633 when Henry Ferrers, the Antiquary, died. He was squire here for almost 70 years. Much of the brickwork dates from the Queen Anne period. The hall has an ornate Elizabethan stone chimney-piece, and 15th-C beams; there is excellent armorial stained glass throughout the building, a tradition started by Henry Ferrers. Pictures painted by Rebecca Dulcibella Orpen, wife of Marmion Ferrers, celebrate the romantic life lived at Baddesley during the late 19th C. The 17th-C stables and parkland complete the feeling of unity. House, garden, restaurant and shop *open daily* but times vary so visit the website for details.

Knowle

The canal now continues its northerly route, passing through countryside which is surprisingly peaceful. Knowle Locks introduce more hilly countryside again, and this green and pleasant land continues right through to Solihull, concealing the nearness of Birmingham. The flight of five wide locks at Knowle used to be six narrow ones, until the 1930 improvements; the remains of the old locks can still be seen alongside the new, together with the side ponds (originally built to save water). The locks are comparatively deep, well maintained and pleasantly situated. They are also the northernmost wide locks for many miles now, since all the Birmingham canals have narrow locks. Knowle is set back from the canal, but warrants a visit, especially to see the church. Continuing north west through wooded country, the canal passes under the M42 motorway and crosses the River Blythe on a small aqueduct. The waterway is quite shallow between Knowle and Bordesley Junction.

Knowle
W. Midlands. All services. Despite its proximity to Birmingham, Knowle still survives as a village, albeit rather self-consciously. A number of old buildings thankfully remain, some dating from the Middle Ages and including such gems as Chester House (now the library), which illustrate the advances in timber-frame construction from the 13th to the 15th C. Have a look at the splendid knot garden around the back. Half-a-mile north of the village is Grimshaw Hall, a gabled 16th-C house noted for its decorative brickwork. There are good views of it from the canal.
Church of St John the Baptist, St Lawrence and St Anne Knowle B93 0LN. This remarkable church was built as a result of the efforts of Walter Cook, a wealthy man who founded a chapel here in 1396, and completed the present church in 1402. Prior to its building the parishioners of Knowle had to make a 6-mile round trip each Sunday to the church at Hampton-in-Arden. This involved crossing the River Blythe, an innocuous brook today, but in medieval times 'a greate and daungerous water' which 'noyther man nor beaste can passe wt. owte daunger of peryshing'. The church is built in the Perpendicular style, with a great deal of intricate stonework. There is much of interest to be seen inside, including the roof timbers, the original font and a medieval dug-out chest. Behind the church is the 3-acre 'Children's Field', given to the National Trust by the Reverend T. Downing 'to be used for games'.

WE ARE THE OVALTINE-EES . . .

Dr George Wander founded the company which was to manufacture Ovaltine in Switzerland in 1864. Finding a ready market in England, the company established a factory at Kings Langley, beside what is now the Grand Union Canal. In 1925 they decided to build their own fleet of narrowboats to bring coal to this factory from Warwickshire. Their boats were always immaculately maintained, with the words 'Drink delicious Ovaltine for Health' emblazoned in orange and yellow on a very dark blue background. The last boat arrived at Kings Langley on 17 April 1959.

Pubs and Restaurants

1 **The Black Boy** Warwick Road Knowle B93 0EB (01564 772655; www.theblackboyknowle.co.uk). Beside Bridge 69. Traditional family-owned pub, built in 1793, sporting a canalside garden with children's play area. Real ale and excellent bar meals with a wide choice of main courses served *L and E*. Children welcome *until 20.00*. *Open 11.00 (Sun 12.00).*

X 2 **The Wilsons Arms** High Street, Knowle B93 9AH (01564 772559; www.tobycarvery.co.uk/restaurants/midlands/knowlesolihull). Toby Carvery pub which dates from the 16th C. The older part still retains much of its character. Real ale, and fresh food and carvery *served all day*. Family-friendly and Wi-Fi. *Open 11.00*.

X 3 **Kings Arms** 2110 Warwick Road, B93 0EE (01564 771177; www.thekingsarmsknowle.co.uk). Canalside at Bridge 70. Attractive country pub serving real ale, and traditional seasonal food *daily 12.00-22.00 (Sun 21.30)*. Canalside garden. Mooring. B&B. *Open 12.00.*

4 **The Red Lion** 1672 High Street, Knowle B93 0LY (01564 771522; www.thekingsarmsknowle.co.uk). Large, 17th C, Grade II listed hostelry dispensing a good selection of real ales and food *daily 11.30-22.00*. Garden; family-friendly. *Occasional* live music. Sports TV and Wi-Fi. *Open 11.30*.

WALKING AND CYCLING
You can enjoy a circular walk from Bridge 70. Walk west to Knowle for a look at the splendid church, then continue on passing Grimshaw Hall to rejoin the canal at Bridge 73 and complete the circuit.

Boatyards

Ⓑ**Copt Heath Wharf**
309 Barston Lane, Solihull B91 2SX At Bridge 76 (0121 704 4464; www. coptheathwharf. co.uk). Pump out, gas, holiday- and day-hire craft, overnight and long-term mooring.

Ⓑ**Knowle Hall Wharf**
Knowle Hall Wharf, Kenilworth Road B93 0JJ (01564 778210; www. knowlehallwharf.co.uk). Gas, boat fitting and repairs, engine sales and repairs, surveys, moorings. *24hr emergency call out.*

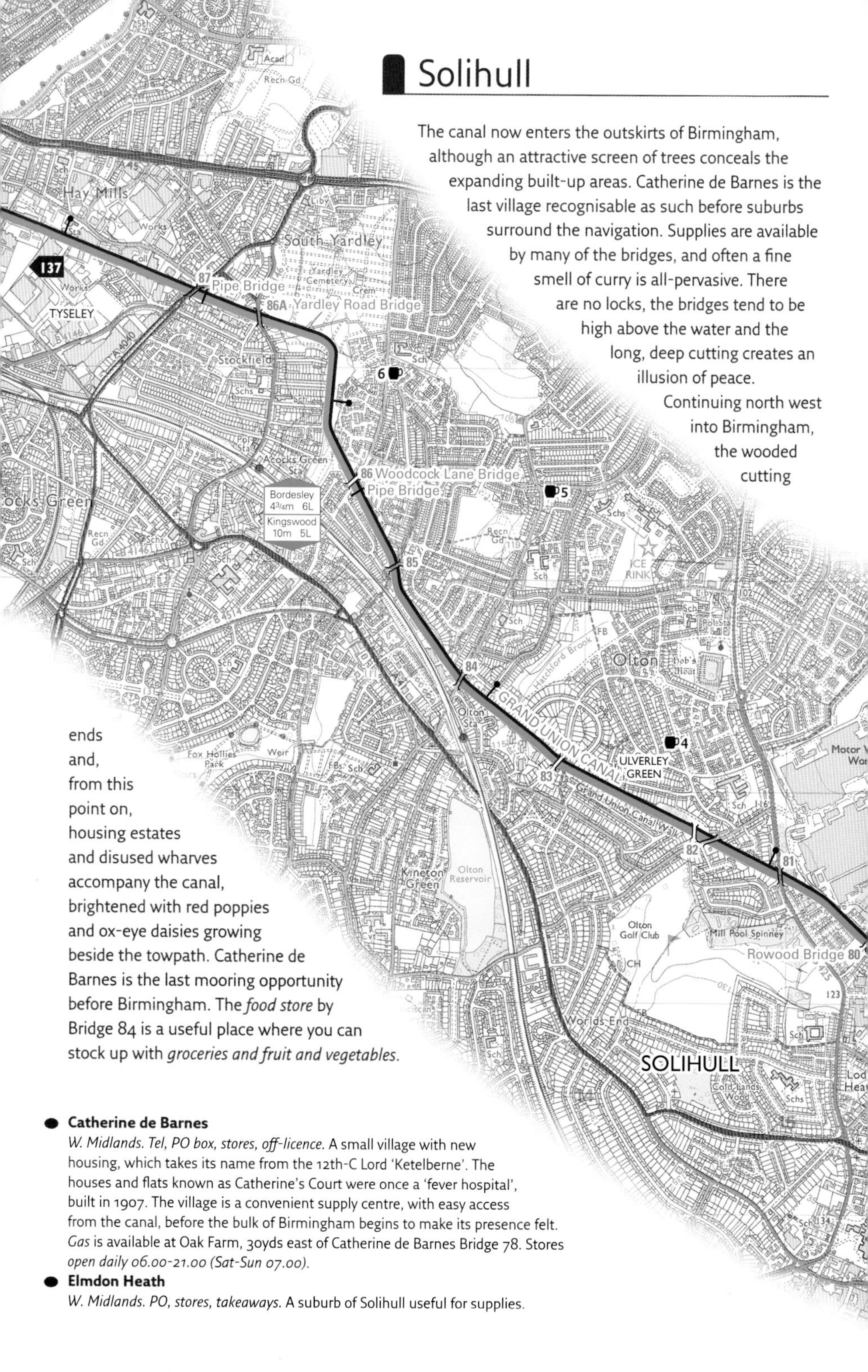

Solihull

The canal now enters the outskirts of Birmingham, although an attractive screen of trees conceals the expanding built-up areas. Catherine de Barnes is the last village recognisable as such before suburbs surround the navigation. Supplies are available by many of the bridges, and often a fine smell of curry is all-pervasive. There are no locks, the bridges tend to be high above the water and the long, deep cutting creates an illusion of peace.

Continuing north west into Birmingham, the wooded cutting ends and, from this point on, housing estates and disused wharves accompany the canal, brightened with red poppies and ox-eye daisies growing beside the towpath. Catherine de Barnes is the last mooring opportunity before Birmingham. The *food store* by Bridge 84 is a useful place where you can stock up with *groceries and fruit and vegetables*.

- **Catherine de Barnes**
  W. Midlands. Tel, PO box, stores, off-licence. A small village with new housing, which takes its name from the 12th-C Lord 'Ketelberne'. The houses and flats known as Catherine's Court were once a 'fever hospital', built in 1907. The village is a convenient supply centre, with easy access from the canal, before the bulk of Birmingham begins to make its presence felt. *Gas* is available at Oak Farm, 30yds east of Catherine de Barnes Bridge 78. Stores *open daily 06.00-21.00 (Sat-Sun 07.00).*
- **Elmdon Heath**
  W. Midlands. PO, stores, takeaways. A suburb of Solihull useful for supplies.

- **Solihull**
  W. Midlands. All services. A modern commuter development, with fine public buildings. What used to be the town centre, dominated by the tall spire of the parish church, is now a shopping area.

St Alphege Church Church Hill Road B91 3RQ. Built of red sandstone, it is almost all late 13th-C and early 14th-C. The lofty interior contains work of all periods, including a Jacobean pulpit, a 17th-C communion rail, 19th-C stained glass and a few notable monuments.

Pubs and Restaurants

1 The Boat Inn 222 Hampton Lane, Catherine de Barnes B91 2TJ (0121 705 0474; www.chefandbrewer.com/pub/boat-inn-catherine-de-barnes-solihull/p1485). A well-kept and friendly pub, offering real ale, together with food *daily 12.00-22.00 (Sun 21.30)*. Beer garden; children welcome. *Open 12.00.*

2 Longfellows English Restaurant 255 Hampton Lane, Catherine de Barnes B91 2TJ (0121 705 0547; www.long-fellows.co.uk). Cosy and intimate family-run restaurant serving fresh food, including game and seafood, *L Tue-Fri 12.00 until last orders 13.30; Sun L and E Mon-Sat from 18.00.* Specialist vegetarian menu and *daily* fixed price menus. Theme nights. Seating outside in landscaped garden.

3 The Greville Arms Cornyx Lane, Elmdon Heath, Solihull B91 2RB (0121 711 8031; www.sizzlingpubs.co.uk/findapub/wales/thegrevillearmssolihull). ¼ mile south of Elmdon Heath Bridge 79. Large suburban pub serving real ales and food *daily 12.00-21.00* (breakfast *09.00-12.00*). Patio, family-friendly. *Open 09.00. Chemist* nearby.

4 The Highwood Highwood Avenue, Olton, Solihull B92 8SX (0121 743 6154; www.facebook.com/pages/The-Highwood-Solihull/426006504133153). ¼ mile north of Bridge 82. Lively community local serving real ale and good cheer *from 12.00 daily*. Garden and sports TV. Children welcome *until 21.00*. Quiz *Mon* and live music *Sat*.

5 The Lyndon Barn Lane, Olton, Solihull B92 7LY (0121 743 2179; www.facebook.com/pages/The-Lyndon-Pub-Solihull/413909918788402). ½ mile north of Bridge 84. Large community local dispensing real ale and food *daily 12.00-20.00 (Sun 19.00)*. Garden; dog-and family-friendly. Live music *Sat*. Real fires and Wi-Fi. *Open 12.00.*

6 The Journeys End 262 Clay Lane, Yardley, Birmingham B26 1EH (0121 706 9656; www.sizzlingpubs.co.uk/findapub/wales/thejourneysendyardley). ¼ mile north of Woodcocks Lane Bridge 86. Imposing roadside pub serving food *daily 12.00-21.00*. Outside patio seating. *Open 11.30.*

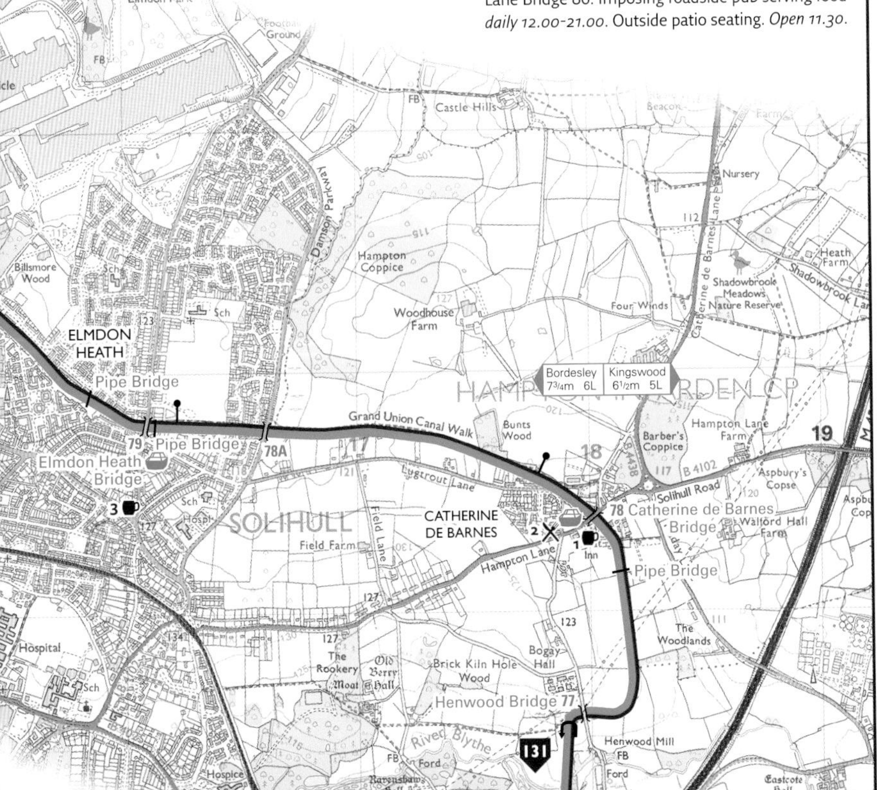

Hatton Locks

Birmingham

The canal curves past the large Energy from Waste plant and the Ackers Trust Basin before reaching Camp Hill Locks. These, and all the succeeding locks, are narrow. After passing through subterranean vaults formed by the criss-crossing of railway viaducts, Bordesley Junction is reached. Ahead, beyond the junction, the canal continues towards the Birmingham Canal Main Line, joining the Birmingham & Fazeley Canal at Aston Junction, passing a very fine collection of old wharf buildings on the way.

Heading north from Bordesley Junction, the Grand Union is accompanied by pleasantly transformed surroundings to join the Birmingham & Fazeley Canal at Salford Junction.

NAVIGATIONAL NOTES

Moor only at recognised sites in the city, such as Gas Street, Cambrian Wharf or boatyards (by arrangement). Contact the local Waterway Unit for advice if you are in doubt.

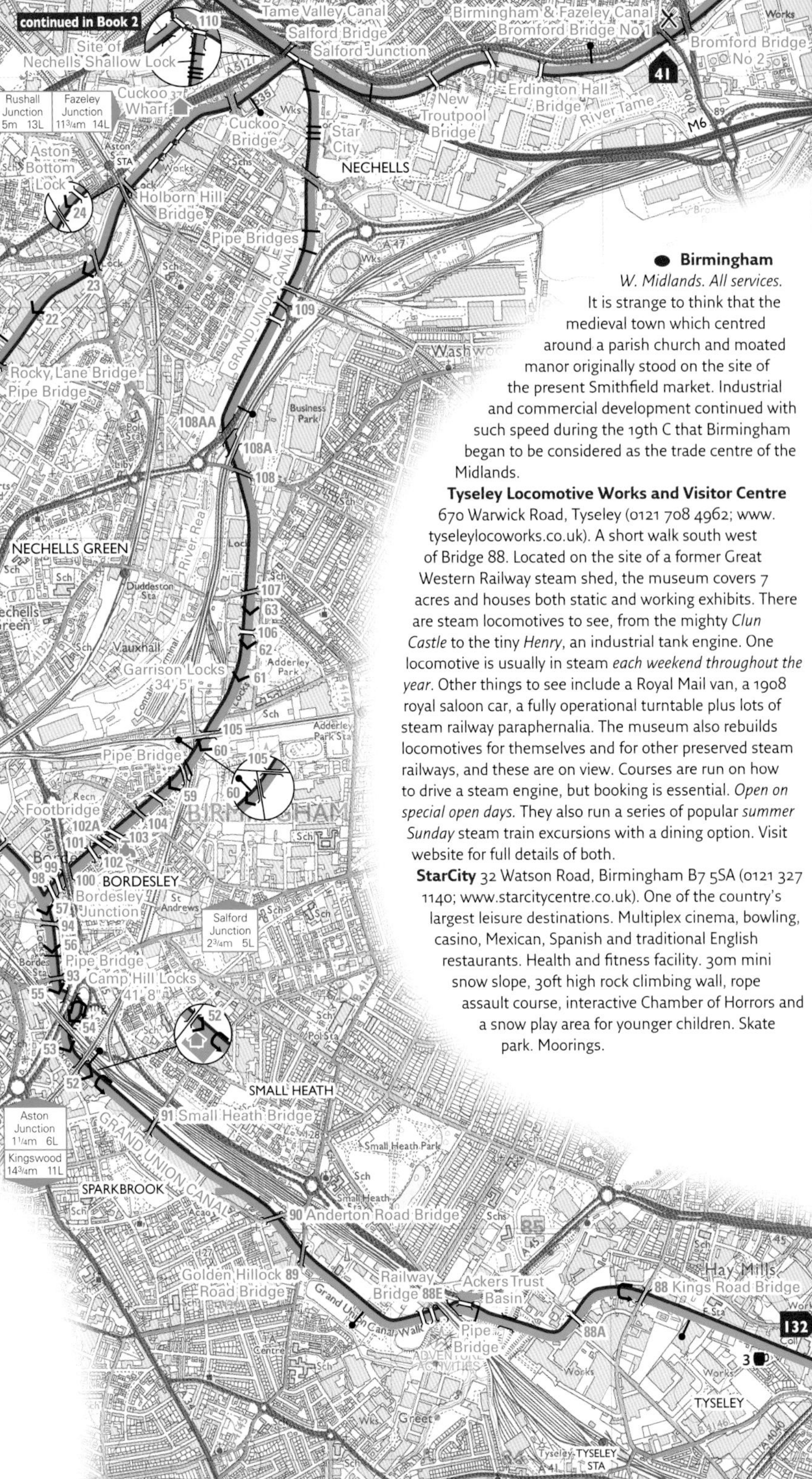

● **Birmingham**

W. Midlands. All services. It is strange to think that the medieval town which centred around a parish church and moated manor originally stood on the site of the present Smithfield market. Industrial and commercial development continued with such speed during the 19th C that Birmingham began to be considered as the trade centre of the Midlands.

Tyseley Locomotive Works and Visitor Centre 670 Warwick Road, Tyseley (0121 708 4962; www.tyseleylocoworks.co.uk). A short walk south west of Bridge 88. Located on the site of a former Great Western Railway steam shed, the museum covers 7 acres and houses both static and working exhibits. There are steam locomotives to see, from the mighty *Clun Castle* to the tiny *Henry*, an industrial tank engine. One locomotive is usually in steam *each weekend throughout the year*. Other things to see include a Royal Mail van, a 1908 royal saloon car, a fully operational turntable plus lots of steam railway paraphernalia. The museum also rebuilds locomotives for themselves and for other preserved steam railways, and these are on view. Courses are run on how to drive a steam engine, but booking is essential. *Open on special open days.* They also run a series of popular *summer Sunday* steam train excursions with a dining option. Visit website for full details of both.

StarCity 32 Watson Road, Birmingham B7 5SA (0121 327 1140; www.starcitycentre.co.uk). One of the country's largest leisure destinations. Multiplex cinema, bowling, casino, Mexican, Spanish and traditional English restaurants. Health and fitness facility. 30m mini snow slope, 30ft high rock climbing wall, rope assault course, interactive Chamber of Horrors and a snow play area for younger children. Skate park. Moorings.

Cruising through the trees on the Oxford Canal near Brinklow

OXFORD CANAL: NORTH

MAXIMUM DIMENSIONS
Length: 70'
Beam: 7'
Headroom: 6' 9"

MILEAGE
BRAUNSTON TURN to:
Hillmorton Bottom Lock: 7½
Rugby Wharf Arm: 10¼
Stretton Stop: 15¾
HAWKESBURY JUNCTION
(*Coventry Canal*): 22¾ miles

Locks: 4

MANAGER
0303 040 4040
enquiries.southeast@canalrivertrust.org.uk

The Oxford Canal was one of the earliest and, for many years, one of the most important canals in southern England. It was authorised in 1769, when the Coventry Canal was in the offing, and was intended to fetch coal southwards from the Warwickshire coalfield to Banbury and Oxford, at the same time giving access to the River Thames. James Brindley was appointed engineer: he built a winding contour canal 91 miles long which soon began to look thoroughly outdated and inefficient for the carriage of goods. Brindley died in 1772, and was replaced by Samuel Simcock: he completed the line from Longford, where a junction was made with the Coventry Canal, to Banbury, in 1778. After a long pause, the canal was finally brought into Oxford in 1790, and thereafter through-traffic flowed constantly along this important new trade route.

In 1780, however, the Grand Junction Canal opened (excepting the tunnel at Blisworth) from London to Braunston, and the Warwick & Napton and Warwick & Birmingham Canals completed the new short route from London to Birmingham. This had the natural - and intended - effect of drawing traffic off the Oxford Canal, especially south of Napton Junction, but the Oxford Company protected itself very effectively against this powerful opposition by charging outrageously high rates for their 5½-mile stretch between Braunston and Napton, which had become part of the new London-Birmingham through route. Thus the Oxford Canal maintained its revenue and very high dividends for many years to come.

By the late 1820s, however, the Oxford Canal had become conspicuously out of date with its extravagant winding course and, under the threat of various schemes for big new canals which, if built, would render the Oxford Canal almost redundant, the company decided to modernise the northern part of their navigation. Tremendous engineering works were executed which completely changed the face of the canal north of Braunston. Aqueducts, massive embankments and deep cuttings were built, carrying the canal in great sweeps through the countryside and cutting almost 14 miles off the original 36 miles between Braunston Junction and the Coventry Canal. Much of the old main line suddenly became a series of loops and branches leading nowhere, now crossed by elegant new towpath bridges inscribed Horseley Ironworks 1828.

This very expensive programme was well worthwhile. Although toll rates, and thus revenue, began to fall because of keen competition from the railways, dividends were kept at a high level for years - indeed a respectable profit was still shown right through to the 20th C.

Braunston and Willoughby

North of Braunston the Oxford Canal soon leaves behind the excitement and interest of the village to run through wide open country, backed by bare hills to the east. It is an ancient landscape, and by Bridge 87 medieval ridge and furrow field patterns are in evidence. These were created as villagers cleared forested land, and each ploughed strips throwing soil towards the centre. Gradually a collection of strips, all running parallel to each other, made up a furlong or cultura. This was then enclosed by a low bank and an access track (usually difficult to identify today) was created. Fields, consisting of dozens of furlongs, were then sometimes fenced. Skirting round Barby Hill, the canal swings north east towards Hillmorton and Rugby. The M45 makes a noisy crossing after Barby Hill.

Boatyards

The Boat Shop Bottom Lock, Dark Lane, Braunston NN11 7HJ (01788 891310; www.boatshopbraunston.co.uk). Started on board a boat moored at Braunston Turn, this is now a shop selling a comprehensive range of gifts and provisions, including fresh-baked bread. *Open summer 08.00-19.00 and winter 08.00-17.00.*

Ⓑ**Braunston Boats** Bottom Lock, Braunston NN11 7HJ (01788 891079). D Gas, boatbuilding, fitting-out, mooring, hull blacking, boat surveys, solid fuel.

Ⓑ**Wharf House Narrowboats** Braunston Boat Haven, Bottom Lock, Dark Lane, Braunston NN11 7HJ (01788 899041; www.wharfhouse.co.uk). Boat building, fitting out and refits, electrics, chandlery, books, maps and gifts.

Ⓑ**Union Canal Carriers** Canalside at Braunston Pump House, Dark Lane, Little Braunston NN11 7HJ (01788 890784; www.unioncanalcarriers.co.uk). D Pump out, gas, narrowboat hire, day-boat hire, dry dock, engine sales, boat and engine repairs. Surveys, gas installation, *24hr emergency call out.*

Ⓑ**Braunston Marina** The Wharf, Braunston NN11 7JH (01788 891373; www.braunstonmarina.co.uk). Through the fine bridge dated 1834 and into an historic canal wharf. D Pump out, gas, overnight and long-term mooring, dry and wet dock, boat building sales and repairs, engine repairs, limited chandlery, toilets, showers, gift shop selling books and maps, laundrette, coal. There are also boatbuilders, fitters and fender makers at the marina.

Ⓑ**Midland Chandlers** London Road, Braunston NN11 7HB (01788 891401/02476 390111; www.midlandchandlers. co.uk) in operation for over 30 years. A very wide range of chandlery.

Ⓑ**Barby Moorings** Barby Lane, Barby CV32 8UJ (01788 890486; www.barbymoorings.co.uk). D Pump out, gas, long- and short-term moorings, toilets, showers.

WALKING AND CYCLING

The towpath is passable for walkers, but very bumpy in places for cyclists.

Pubs and Restaurants

1 The Boat House London Road, Braunston NN11 7HB (01788 891734; www.boathousepub.co.uk). Once the Rose and Castle, it is now a welcoming restaurant and pub, serving real ale. Grills, *Sun* roasts, carvery meals *daily*. Children's room and fine canalside garden with swings. Overnight mooring for patrons. *Open all day.*

2 The Gongoozler's Rest Narrowboat café moored outside the Stop House NN11 7JQ (07940 973529; www.gongoozlersrest.wix.com/gongoozler). Breakfasts, sandwiches, omelettes, homemade cakes and a variety of good fare. Children's menu and takeaway service. *Open daily 09.00-14.00 (Jul-Aug 15.00).*

3 The Wheatsheaf The Green, Braunston NN11 7HW (01788 890748). Small local pub, in the centre of the village, with a garden.

4 The Old Plough 82 High Street,Braunston NN11 7HS (01788 878126; www.theoldplough-braunston.co.uk). A fine village pub dating from 1672, with open fires and serving real ale. Good food *daily L and E (not Sun E).* Garden; child- and dog-friendly. Traditional pub games. *Open 12.00.*

5 The Admiral Nelson Dark Lane, Braunston NN11 7HJ (01788 891900; www.theadmiralnelson.co.uk). Beside Lock 3. Canalside hosteling serving food *L and E (not Sun E).* Canalside seating and mooring. Child- and dog-friendly. Wi-Fi. *Open all day from 12.00 (winter opening may vary).*

6 The Rose Inn Main Street, Willoughby CV23 8BH (01788 891180; www.therosecountrypub.co.uk). Attractively maintained thatched village pub, offering real ale and food *L and E Tue-Sun (not Sun E).* Outside seating with children's play area. Real fires. *Open Tue-Sat L and E and Sun 12.00-16.00.*

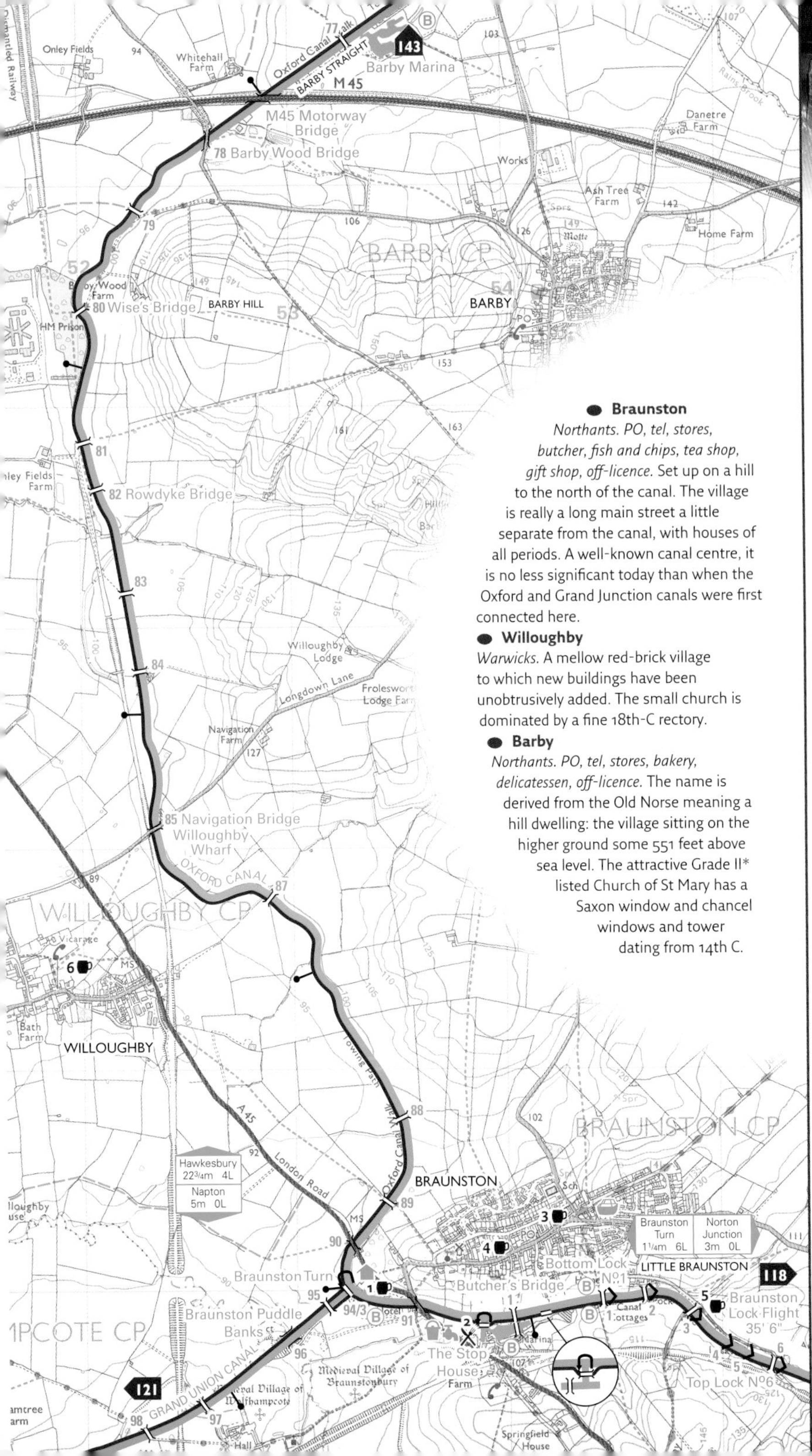

● Braunston
Northants. PO, tel, stores, butcher, fish and chips, tea shop, gift shop, off-licence. Set up on a hill to the north of the canal. The village is really a long main street a little separate from the canal, with houses of all periods. A well-known canal centre, it is no less significant today than when the Oxford and Grand Junction canals were first connected here.

● Willoughby
Warwicks. A mellow red-brick village to which new buildings have been unobtrusively added. The small church is dominated by a fine 18th-C rectory.

● Barby
Northants. PO, tel, stores, bakery, delicatessen, off-licence. The name is derived from the Old Norse meaning a hill dwelling: the village sitting on the higher ground some 551 feet above sea level. The attractive Grade II* listed Church of St Mary has a Saxon window and chancel windows and tower dating from 14th C.

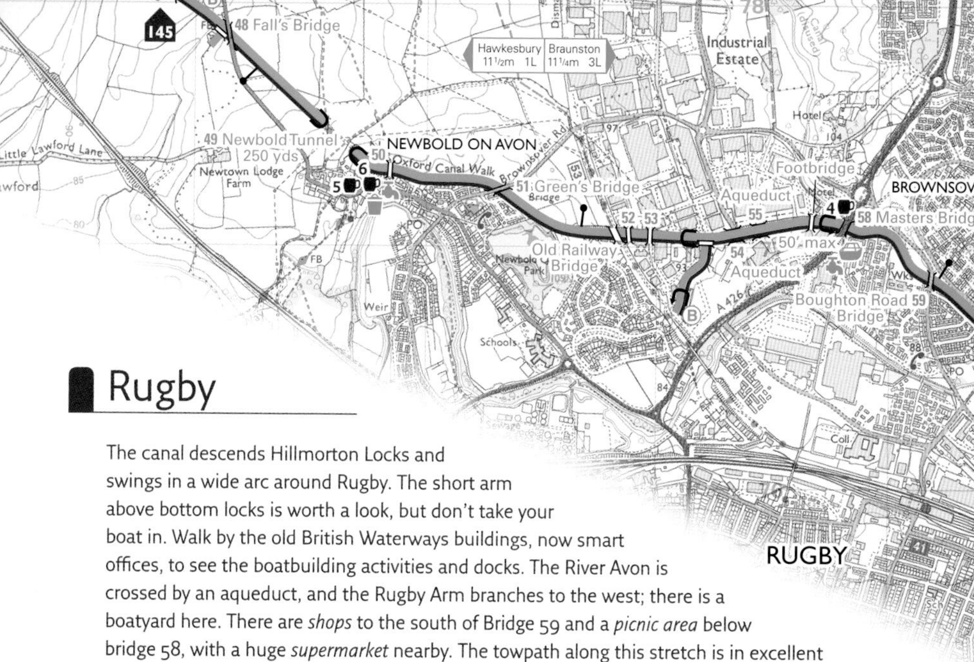

Rugby

The canal descends Hillmorton Locks and swings in a wide arc around Rugby. The short arm above bottom locks is worth a look, but don't take your boat in. Walk by the old British Waterways buildings, now smart offices, to see the boatbuilding activities and docks. The River Avon is crossed by an aqueduct, and the Rugby Arm branches to the west; there is a boatyard here. There are *shops* to the south of Bridge 59 and a *picnic area* below bridge 58, with a huge *supermarket* nearby. The towpath along this stretch is in excellent condition. Moorings at Newbold Tunnel make a pleasant stop, with a choice of pubs close by.

Boatyards

Ⓑ**The Canal Shop** Hillmorton Wharf, Crick Road, Rugby CV21 4PW (01788 542169; www.canalshoponline.co.uk). D Gas, long- and short-term moorings, solid fuel, chandlery, groceries, off-licence, re-cycling, Eco Toilets (01327 844442; www.eco-toilets.co.uk). *Open Mon-Sat 09.00-17.30 (winter 17.00) and Sun 10.00-16.30 (winter 16.00).*

Ⓑ**Steve's Boat Painting Services** The Canal Shop, Hillmorton Wharf, Crick Road, Rugby CV21 4PW (01788 542169/07715 842947). Wet dock, boat painting, boat maintenance.

Ⓑ**Hillmorton Wharf Marina** Hillmorton Wharf, Crick Road, Rugby CV21 4PW (01788 540149; www.hillmortonwharf.com). Long-term mooring.

Ⓑ**Grantham Bridge Boat Services** The Locks, Hillmorton CV21 4PP (01788 578661/07812 039110; www.canalbreaks.com). D Wet dock and dry dock, pump out, gas, boat hire, boatbuilding, boat and engine repairs, DIY facilities, books and maps, solid fuel, Russell Newbery engine manufacture, boat painting. *24hr emergency breakdown call out.*

Ⓑ**Clifton Cruisers** Clifton Wharf, Vicarage Hill, Clifton on Dunsmore CV23 0DG (01788 543570; www.cliftoncruisers.com). D Pump out, gas, narrowboat hire, overnight mooring, long-term mooring, winter storage, engine sales, boat and engine repairs, boatbuilding, chandlery, solid fuel, painting and signwriting, crane, bottom blacking, boat sales, gifts, laundry.

Ⓑ**Willow Wren Hire Cruisers** Rugby Wharf, off Consul Road, Rugby CV21 1PB (01788 562183/569153; www.willowwren.co.uk). D Pump out, gas, narrowboat hire, overnight and long-term mooring (by prior arrangement), wet dock, boat repairs, engine repairs, toilets, books and maps, DIY facilities.

- **Hillmorton**
  Warwicks. PO, stores, garage, takeaways, but all a fair distance from the canal.
- **Rugby**
  Warwicks. All Services. There is a pedestrianised shopping centre, a leisure centre and an open market with a town crier. Look out for the tiny shop in Chapel Street, which has stood for over 500 years and is reputedly the oldest building in the town.

Rugby Art Gallery and Museum Little Elborow Street, Rugby CV21 3BZ (01788 533201; www.ragm.org.uk). Contemporary visual art and crafts; museum includes Roman artifacts and social history gallery. *Open Tue-Fri 10.00-17.00 and Sat 10.00-16.00, B Hols 12.00-16.00*

Webb Ellis Rugby Football Museum 5-6 St Matthews Street, Rugby CV21 3BY (01788 567777; www.rugbyfootballhistory.com/WebbEllisMuseum.html). The museum is housed opposite Rugby School in the original building where James Gilbert, boot-maker, made the first rugby footballs in 1842. *Open Mon-Sat 09.00-17.00.*

Tourist Information Centre Located in the foyer of the Art Gallery and Museum (01788 533217; www.enjoyrugby.co.uk/enjoyrugby/site/index.php). *Open Mon-Sat 10.00-16.00 and B Hols 12.00-16.00.*

Pubs and Restaurants

1 **The Old Royal Oak** Crick Road, Hillmorton Wharf CV21 4PW (01788 561401; www.hungryhorse.co.uk/locations/old-royal-oak). Canalside at Bridge 73. Real ale and bar meals *all day*, in a family dining pub. Children's room and play area. Large garden. Mooring for patrons. Wi-Fi. *Open 12.00 (Sat-Sun 10.00).*

2 **Canalchef** Badsey's Wharf, The Locks, Hillmorton CV21 4PP (01788 567600; www.canalchef.co.uk). Lockside café serving an appetising range of hot food, snacks, sandwiches, hot and cold drinks, cakes and scones. *Open daily Mar-Oct 09.00-17.00 and Fri E. Last orders for hot food 14.00.*

3 **The Jolly Brewers** 343 Clifton Road, Rugby CV21 3QZ (01788 542338; www.warwickshirebeer.co.uk/jolly-brewers-rugby). South of Bridge 66. Friendly pub serving real ale and bar snacks. Traditional pub games, sports TV, Wi-Fi and outside seating. Takeaway service for beers from their own microbrewery.

4 **The Bell and Barge** Brownsover Road, Rugby CV21 1DG (01788 569466; www.harvester.co.uk/restaurants/eastandwestmidlands/thebellandbargerugby). Large pub serving real ale and food *daily 11.30-22.00* (breakfast *09.00-11.00; Sat-Sun 08.00)*. Dog- and family-friendly. B&B. *Open 09.00 (Sat-Sun 08.00).*

5 **The Boat Inn** 62 Main Street, Newbold-on-Avon CV21 1HN (01788 832608). By Bridge 50. Real ale, and homemade food *L*. Pleasant garden and moorings. *Open 12.00.*

6 **The Barley Mow** 64 Main Street, Newbold- on-Avon CV21 1HW (01788 544174; www.barleymow-newbold.co.uk). Country-style canalside pub serving real ale. Bar and restaurant meals available *L and E*. Children and dogs welcome. Play area and canalside garden. Traditional pub games. Bathroom hire and laundry service. B&B. *Open 12.00.*

Try also: **The Squirrel** Inn 33 Church Street, Rugby CV21 3PU (01788 578527); **The Bell** High Street, Hillmorton, Rugby CV21 4HD (01788 544465); **The Paddox** 360 Hillmorton Road, Rugby CV22 5EY (01788 542748).

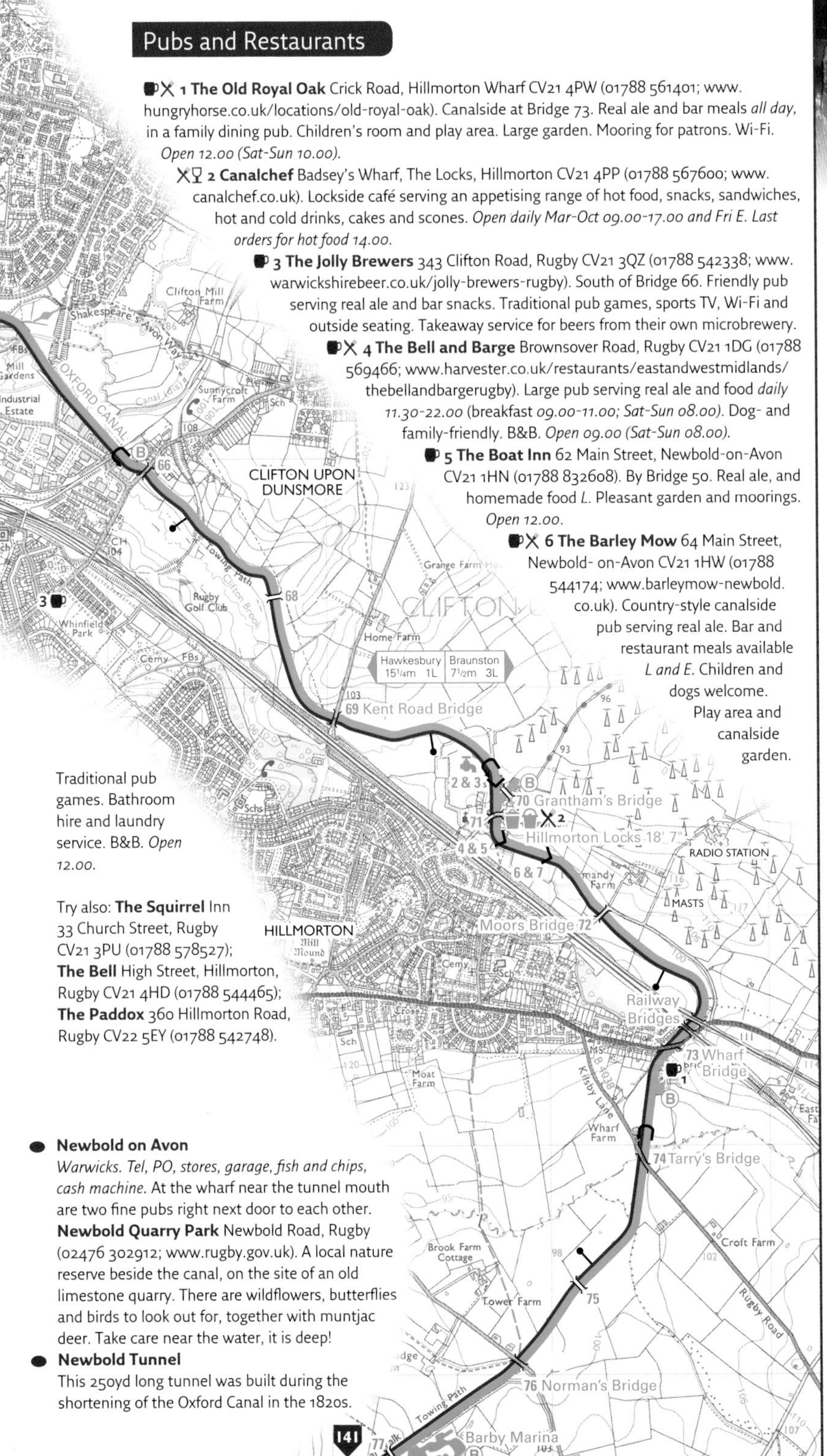

- **Newbold on Avon**
Warwicks. Tel, PO, stores, garage, fish and chips, cash machine. At the wharf near the tunnel mouth are two fine pubs right next door to each other.
Newbold Quarry Park Newbold Road, Rugby (02476 302912; www.rugby.gov.uk). A local nature reserve beside the canal, on the site of an old limestone quarry. There are wildflowers, butterflies and birds to look out for, together with muntjac deer. Take care near the water, it is deep!
- **Newbold Tunnel**
This 250yd long tunnel was built during the shortening of the Oxford Canal in the 1820s.

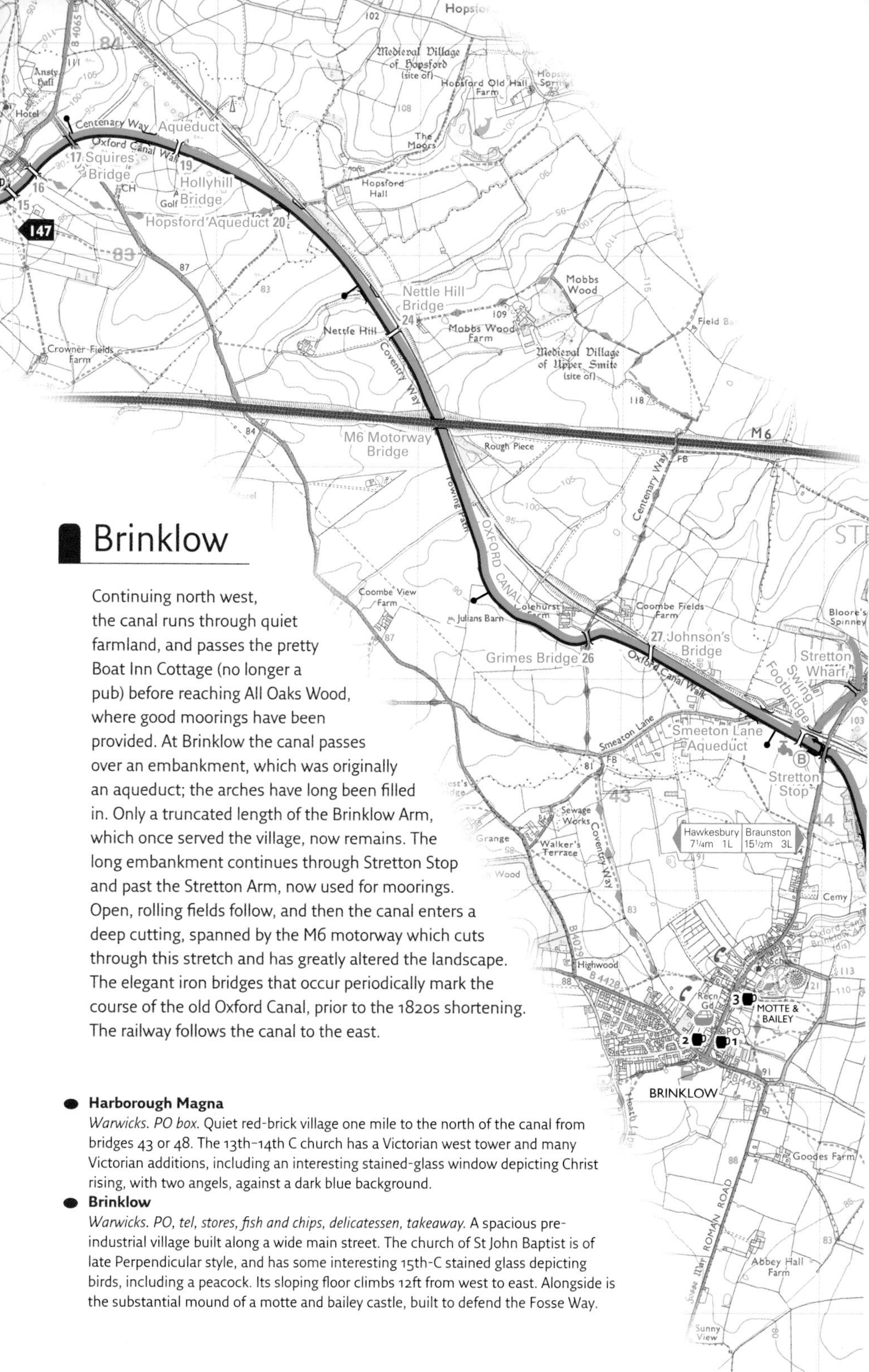

Brinklow

Continuing north west, the canal runs through quiet farmland, and passes the pretty Boat Inn Cottage (no longer a pub) before reaching All Oaks Wood, where good moorings have been provided. At Brinklow the canal passes over an embankment, which was originally an aqueduct; the arches have long been filled in. Only a truncated length of the Brinklow Arm, which once served the village, now remains. The long embankment continues through Stretton Stop and past the Stretton Arm, now used for moorings. Open, rolling fields follow, and then the canal enters a deep cutting, spanned by the M6 motorway which cuts through this stretch and has greatly altered the landscape. The elegant iron bridges that occur periodically mark the course of the old Oxford Canal, prior to the 1820s shortening. The railway follows the canal to the east.

- **Harborough Magna**
  Warwicks. PO box. Quiet red-brick village one mile to the north of the canal from bridges 43 or 48. The 13th–14th C church has a Victorian west tower and many Victorian additions, including an interesting stained-glass window depicting Christ rising, with two angels, against a dark blue background.
- **Brinklow**
  Warwicks. PO, tel, stores, fish and chips, delicatessen, takeaway. A spacious pre-industrial village built along a wide main street. The church of St John Baptist is of late Perpendicular style, and has some interesting 15th-C stained glass depicting birds, including a peacock. Its sloping floor climbs 12ft from west to east. Alongside is the substantial mound of a motte and bailey castle, built to defend the Fosse Way.

Boatyards

Brinklow Boat Services Units 2 and 4, The Wharf, Smeaton Lane, Stretton under Fosse, Rugby, CV23 0PR (01788 833331/833789/ 07921 636247; www.brinklowboatservices.com). Boat building and repairs, classic boat restoration and replica construction, boat fitting out, boat painting (07977 504766), modern and vintage engine installation, dry dock, hull blacking, surveys.

Rose Narrowboats Fosse Way, Stretton under Fosse, Rugby CV23 0PU (01788 832449; www.rose-narrowboats.co.uk). D Pump out, gas, narrowboat hire, day-hire craft, long-term mooring, boat and engine repairs, engine sales, boatbuilding, chandlery, toilets, solid fuel. Gift shop selling books and maps, and an art gallery. *Open 09.00-17.00 (Sun 12.00).*

Brinklow Marina Cathiron Lane, Cathiron, Brinklow, Rugby, CV23 0JH (01788 832600/07711 803430; www.brinklowmarina.com). D Pump out, gas, solid fuel, long-term mooring.

Lime Farm Marina Cathiron, Rugby CV23 0JH (01788 570131/07973 423707; www. limefarmmarina. co.uk). D Located in one of the old loops that were created in 1828 when the canal was re-routed to a straighter, shorter route. Gas, pump out, solid fuel, day boat hire, mooring, boat building and fitting out, engineering services, carpentry, hull blacking, surveys.

Pubs and Restaurants

1 The White Lion Broad Street, Brinklow CV23 0LN (01788 834650). Traditional coaching inn with an old-fashioned bar, serving real ale and food *L Mon-Sat (also E by prior arrangement).* Children welcome. Delightful garden with a play area. Skittles, pool and darts. Camping. B&B.

2 The Bulls Head Coventry Road, Brinklow CV23 0NE (01788 832355; www.bullsheadbrinklow.co.uk). A smartly furnished family pub. Good food served *daily.* Children welcome, indoor and outdoor play areas. Garden and real fires. B&B. *Open Mon-Sat 18.00 and Sun 12.00.*

3 The Raven 68 Broad Street, Brinklow CV23 0LN (01788 832655). Friendly family pub at the top of the village, where real ale is served. Bar meals *L and E (not Sun E)* Children welcome, garden.

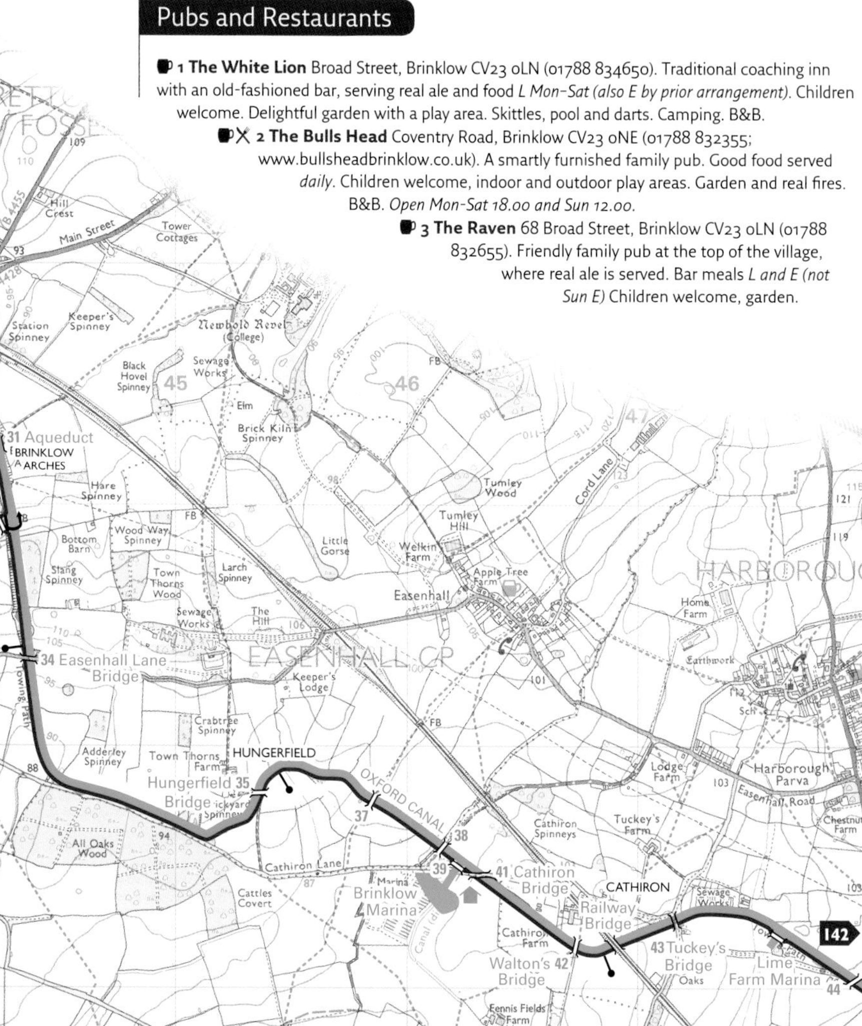

Hawkesbury Junction

The open landscape continues beyond Ansty, although the motorway is never far away. Soon the first signs of Coventry appear, with views of pylons and housing estates. The new Wyken Colliery Arm leaves to the west: it was built to replace the old one eaten up by the motorway which comes alongside the canal at this point: it is now used by the Coventry Cruising Club. Sharp bends then lead to the stop lock before Hawkesbury Junction, the end of the Oxford Canal where it joins the Coventry Canal. This last stretch of the Oxford Canal is characterised by the 1820s shortenings: straight cuttings and embankments date from this period, while the cast-iron bridges mark the old route.

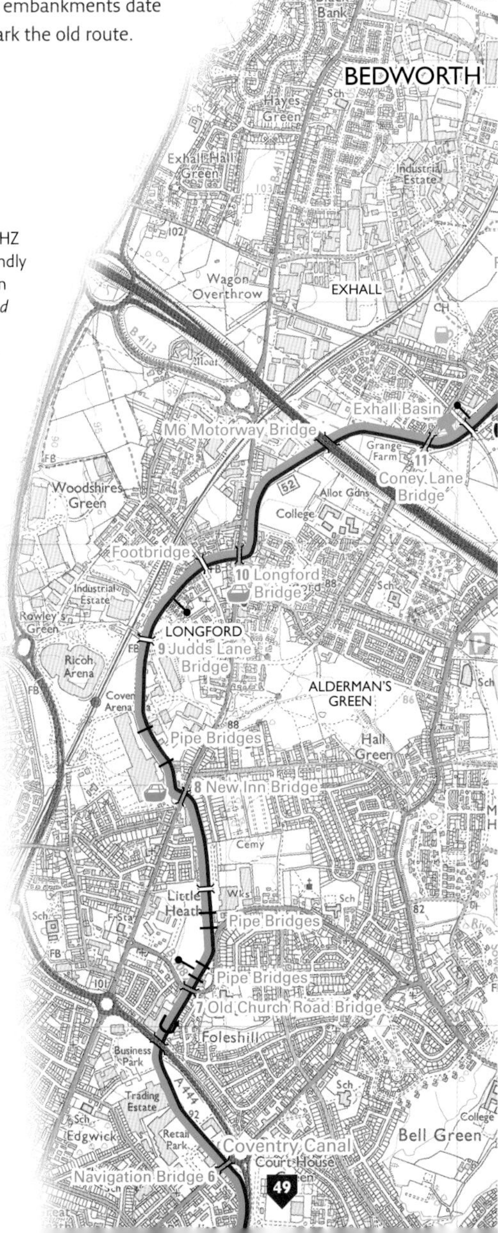

Pubs and Restaurants

1 The Rose and Castle Main Road, Ansty CV9 9HZ (024 7661 2822; www.theroseandcastle.co.uk). Friendly and welcoming canalside pub serving real ale and an extensive range of good food available *Mon-Sat L and E & Sun 12.00-21.30)*. Children welcome, play area and canalside garden. Moorings and [water tap symbol]. *Open Mon-Sat L and E & Sun 12.00-21.30.*

2 The Boat 31 Shilton Lane, Walsgrave, Coventry CV2 2AB (024 7661 2191). Sympathetically refurbished Victorian hostelry, dating from 1836, dispensing real ales and food *Mon-Sat L and E & Sun 12.00-17.00*. Garden, traditional pub games, sports TV and Wi-Fi. Children welcome when dining *until 21.00*. *Open 11.00 (Sun 12.00).*

3 The Old Crown 466 Aldermans Green Road CV2 1NP (024 7636 2438; www.facebook.com/oldcrowncov). East of Tusses Bridge (4). Welcoming and cosy pub with carved woodwork, beams, brasses and snug settees, serving real ale. Children welcome, garden with play area. Highly regarded food *L and E. Open 12.00.*

4 The Greyhound Longford CV6 6DF (024 7636 3046; www.greyhoundinn.org). A fascinating pub, dating from the early 1800s, situated beside Hawkesbury Junction, decorated with canal memorabilia and warmed by log fires in *winter*. An appetising selection of food is served *Mon-Thur 12.00-15.00* and *18.00-21.00; Fri* and *Sat 12.00-15.00* and *17.00-21.30* and *Sun 12.00-19.00*. The emphasis is on traditional pub food majoring on pies and salads. served in both the bar and restaurant. There is always a wide choice of real ales available. Children and dogs welcome. Canalside seating and moorings. Traditional pub games and real fires. *Open 11.00 (Sun 12.00).*

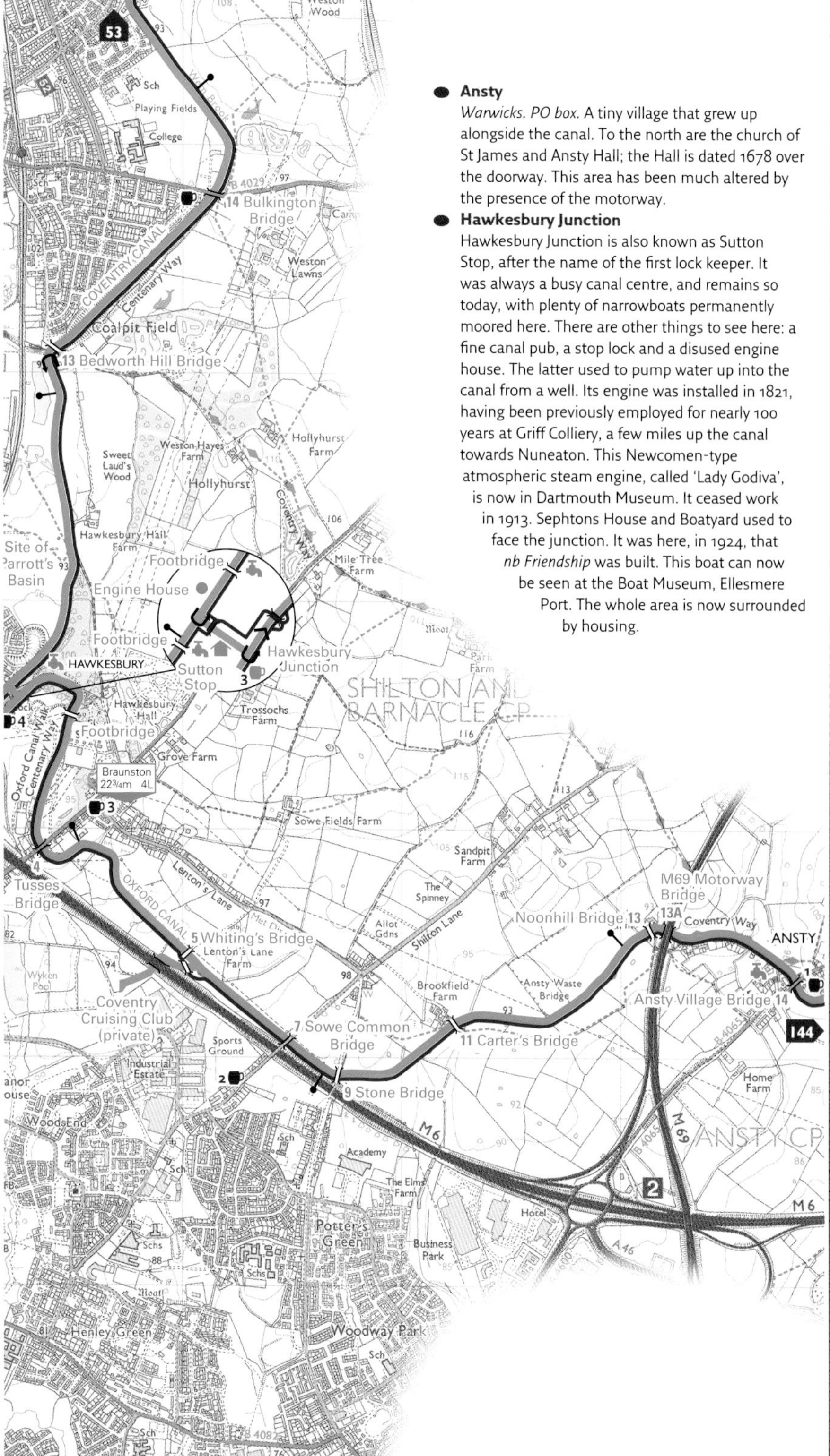

- **Ansty**

  Warwicks. PO box. A tiny village that grew up alongside the canal. To the north are the church of St James and Ansty Hall; the Hall is dated 1678 over the doorway. This area has been much altered by the presence of the motorway.

- **Hawkesbury Junction**

  Hawkesbury Junction is also known as Sutton Stop, after the name of the first lock keeper. It was always a busy canal centre, and remains so today, with plenty of narrowboats permanently moored here. There are other things to see here: a fine canal pub, a stop lock and a disused engine house. The latter used to pump water up into the canal from a well. Its engine was installed in 1821, having been previously employed for nearly 100 years at Griff Colliery, a few miles up the canal towards Nuneaton. This Newcomen-type atmospheric steam engine, called 'Lady Godiva', is now in Dartmouth Museum. It ceased work in 1913. Sephtons House and Boatyard used to face the junction. It was here, in 1924, that *nb Friendship* was built. This boat can now be seen at the Boat Museum, Ellesmere Port. The whole area is now surrounded by housing.

The Oxford Canal near Ansty

STAFFORDSHIRE & WORCESTERSHIRE CANAL: NORTH

MAXIMUM DIMENSIONS

Length: 72'
Beam: 7'
Headroom: 6' 0"

MANAGER

0303 040 4040
enquiries.westmidlands@canalrivertrust.org.uk

MILEAGE

AUTHERLEY JUNCTION to:
GREAT HAYWOOD JUNCTION: 20½ miles

Locks: 12

Construction of this navigation was begun immediately after that of the Trent & Mersey, to effect the joining of the rivers Trent, Mersey and Severn. Engineered by James Brindley, the Staffordshire & Worcestershire was opened throughout in 1772, at a cost of rather over £100,000. It stretched 46 miles from Great Haywood on the Trent & Mersey to the River Severn, which it joined at Stourport. The canal was an immediate success. It was well placed to bring goods from the Potteries down to Gloucester, Bristol and the West Country; while the Birmingham Canal, which joined it half-way along at Aldersley Junction, fed manufactured goods northwards from the Black Country to the Potteries via Great Haywood. In 1815 the Worcester & Birmingham Canal opened, offering a more direct but heavily locked canal link between Birmingham and the Severn. The Staffordshire & Worcestershire answered this threat by gradually extending the opening times of the locks until, by 1830, they were open 24 hours a day. When the Birmingham & Liverpool Junction Canal was opened from Autherley to Nantwich in 1835, traffic bound for Merseyside from Birmingham naturally began to use this more direct, modern canal. The Staffordshire & Worcestershire lost a great deal of traffic over its length as most of the boats now passed along only the ½-mile stretch of the Staffordshire & Worcestershire Canal between Autherley and Aldersley Junctions. The company levied absurdly high tolls for this tiny length. The B & LJ Company therefore co-operated with the Birmingham Canal Company in 1836 to promote in Parliament a Bill for the Tettenhall & Autherley Canal and Aqueduct. This project was to be a canal flyover, going from the Birmingham Canal right over the profiteering Staffordshire & Worcestershire and locking down into the Birmingham & Liverpool Junction Canal. The Staffordshire & Worcestershire company had to give way, and reduced its tolls to an acceptable level. In spite of this set back, the Staffordshire & Worcestershire maintained a good profit, and high dividends were paid throughout the rest of the 19th C. From the 1860s onwards, railway competition began to bite, and the company's profits began to slip. Several modernisation schemes came to nothing, and the canal's trade declined. Now the canal is used almost exclusively by pleasure craft. It is covered in full in *the Severn, Avon & Birmingham Guide* of this series.

Autherley Junction

Autherley Junction is marked by a big white bridge on the towpath side. The stop lock just beyond marks the entrance to the Shropshire Union: there is a useful boatyard just to the north of it. Leaving Autherley, the Staffordshire & Worcestershire passes new housing before running through a very narrow cutting in rock, once known as 'Pendeford Rockin', after a local farm: there is only room for boats to pass in the designated places, so **a good lookout should be kept for oncoming craft**. After passing the motorway the navigation leaves behind the suburbs of Wolverhampton and enters pleasant farmland. The bridges need care: although the bridgeholes are reasonably wide, the actual arches are rather low.

- **Autherley Junction**
A busy canal junction with a full range of boating facilities close by.

- **Coven**
Staffs. PO, tel, stores, chemist, baker, off-licence, takeaway, fish & chips. The only true village on this section, Coven lies beyond a dual carriageway north west of Cross Green Bridge. There are a large number of shops, including a *laundrette*.

Boatyards

Ⓑ**Napton Narrowboats** Autherley Junction, Oxley Moor Road, Wolverhampton WV9 5HW (01902 789942; www.napton-marina.co.uk). **D** Pump out, gas, narrowboat hire, overnight mooring, short term mooring, slipway, limited chandlery, provisions, books and maps, boat repairs, solid fuel, gifts. *Emergency call out.*

Ⓑ**Oxley Marina** The Wharf, Oxley Moor Road, Wolverhampton WV10 6TZ (01902 789522; www.oxleymarina.co.uk). **DE** Pump out, gas, day boat hire, over night and long-term mooring, slipway, solid fuel, winter storage, lifting facility, DIY facilities, boat sales and repairs, engine sales and repairs, welding and fabrication, toilets, car parking, *emergency call out*. Licensed bar *evenings and at weekends*. Snacks.

Pubs and Restaurants

1 The Pendulum 48 Blaydon Road, Wolverhampton WV9 5NP (01902 783779). North west of Blaydon Road Bridge. Rota of guest ales. *Food L and E (not Sun E)*. Children welcome. Outside seating, traditional pub games, regular quiz and music nights. Supermarket next door. *Open Mon-Thu 12.30 23.30, Fri-Sat 12.00-00.10 & Sun 12.00-00.00.*

2 Fox & Anchor Inn Brewood Road, Cross Green, Wolverhampton WV10 7PW (01902 798786; www.vintageinn.co.uk/restaurants/midlands/thefoxandanchorcrossgreen). Canalside by Cross Green Bridge. Large and friendly pub. Real ale, and meals available *all day*. Menu is traditional English, along with steaks and *Sun* roast. Children's menu, garden and good moorings. Wi-Fi. *Open daily 12.00-23.00 (Sun 22.30).*

WALKING AND CYCLING
The towpath is generally in good condition for both walkers and cyclists.

BIRD LIFE
The *Long-Tailed Tit* is a charming resident of woods, heaths and hedgerows. Feeding flocks of these birds resemble animated feather dusters. Their plumage can look black and white, but at close range there is a pinkish wash to the underparts and pinkish buff on the backs. The long-tailed tit has a tiny, stubby bill, a long tail, and an almost spherical body.

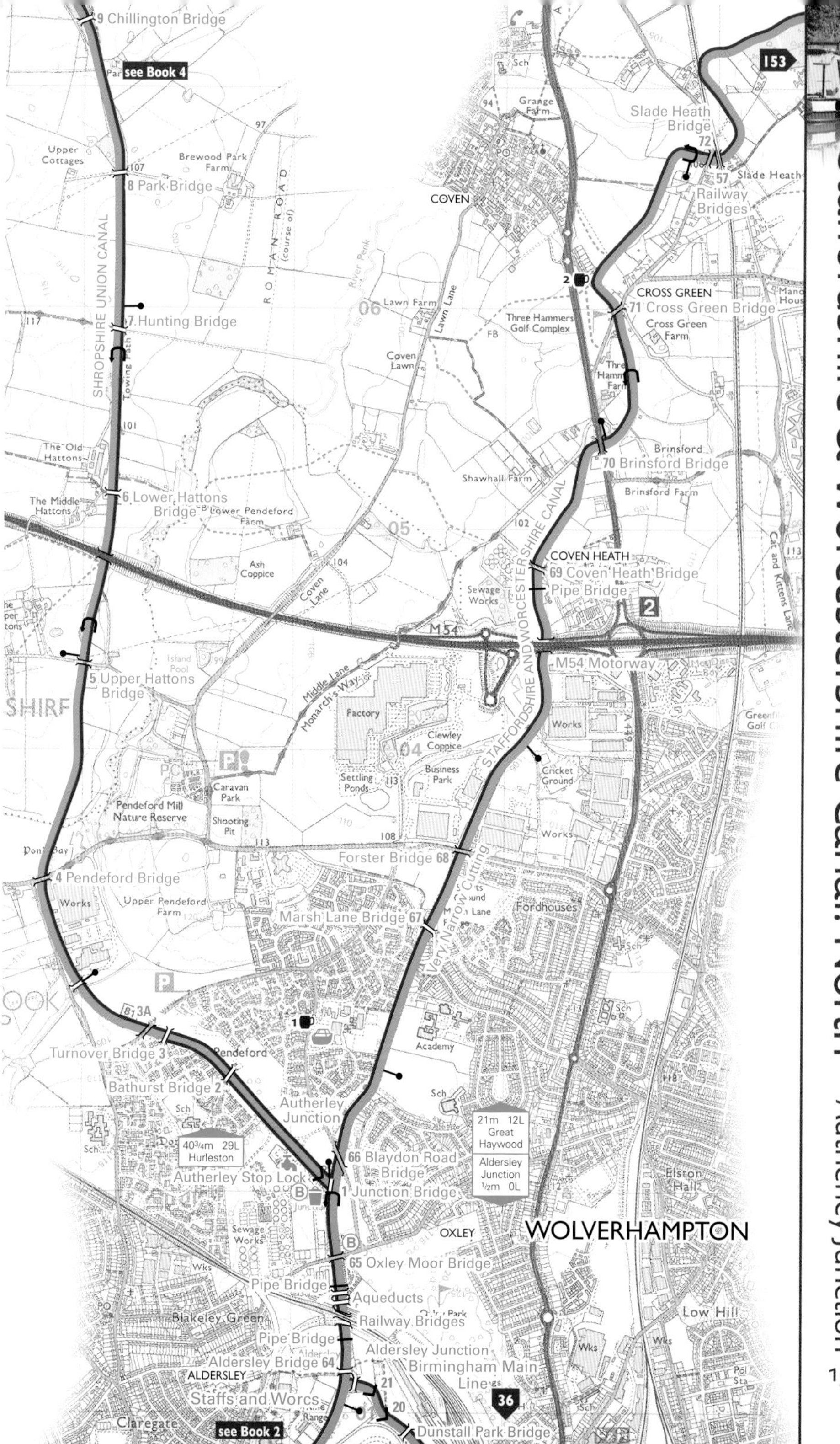
9 Chillington Bridge
see Book 4
153
Upper Cottages
Brewood Park Farm
97
107
8 Park Bridge
ROMAN ROAD (course of)
SHROPSHIRE UNION CANAL
Towing Path
7 Hunting Bridge
117
COVEN
Sch
Grange Farm
94
PO
Slade Heath Bridge
72
57
Slade Heath Railway Bridges
River Penk
Lawn Farm
Lawn Lane
06
2
CROSS GREEN
71 Cross Green Bridge
Cross Green Farm
Three Hammers Golf Complex
FB
Coven Lawn
101
The Old Hattons
The Middle Hattons
6 Lower Hattons Bridge
Lower Pendeford Farm
Brinsford
70 Brinsford Bridge
Brinsford Farm
Shawhall Farm
STAFFORDSHIRE AND WORCESTERSHIRE CANAL
05
102
104
Ash Coppice
Coven Lane
COVEN HEATH
69 Coven Heath Bridge
Pipe Bridge
Sewage Works
2
Cat and Kittens Lane
113
M54
M54 Motorway
Island Pool
99
5 Upper Hattons Bridge
SHIRF
Middle Lane
Monarch's Way
Factory
Clewley Coppice
04
Business Park
Settling Ponds
113
Works
Cricket Ground
A 449
Greenfield Golf C
PC
Caravan Park
Pendeford Mill Nature Reserve
Shooting Pit
110
108
113
Pond Bay
4 Pendeford Bridge
Works
Upper Pendeford Farm
Forster Bridge 68
Very Narrow Cutting
Works
Fordhouses
Marsh Lane Bridge 67
Sch
B
3A
Turnover Bridge 3
Pendeford
1
Academy
Bathurst Bridge 2
Sch
Autherley Junction
Sch
40¾m 29L Hurleston
21m 12L Great Haywood
Aldersley Junction ½m 0L
66 Blaydon Road Bridge
Autherley Stop Lock
B
1 Junction Bridge
Elston Hall
Sewage Works
OXLEY
WOLVERHAMPTON
Wks
65 Oxley Moor Bridge
Pipe Bridge
Aqueducts
PO
Blakeley Green
Railway Bridges
Low Hill
Pipe Bridge
Aldersley Junction
Wks
Wks
Aldersley Bridge 64
Birmingham Main Line
ALDERSLEY
21
36
Pol Sta
Staffs and Worcs
20
Claregate
see Book 2
Dunstall Park Bridge
Locks

Gailey Wharf

The considerable age of this canal is shown by its extremely twisting course, revealed after passing the railway bridge. There are few real centres of population along this stretch, which comprises largely former heathland. The canal widens just before bridge 74, where Brindley incorporated part of a medieval moat into the canal. Hatherton Junction marks the entrance of the former Hatherton Branch of the Staffordshire & Worcestershire Canal into the main line. This branch used to connect with the Birmingham Canal Navigations. It is closed above the derelict second lock, although the channel remains as a feeder for the Staffordshire & Worcestershire Canal. There is a campaign for its restoration. There is a *marina* at the junction. A little further along, a chemical works is encountered, astride the canal in what used to be woodlands. This was once called the 'Black Works', as lamp black was produced here. Gailey Wharf is about a mile further north: it is a small canal settlement that includes a *boatyard* and a large, round, toll keeper's watch-tower, containing a *canal shop* and there are *toilets* nearby. The picturesque Wharf Cottage opposite has been restored as a bijou residence. Half a mile west, along the busy A5, there is a useful *shop selling all manner of combustibles, from coal to kindling, and including gas.* The canal itself disappears under Watling Street and then rapidly through five locks towards Penkridge. These locks are very attractive, and some are accompanied by little brick bridges. The M6 motorway, and the traffic noise, comes alongside for 1/2 mile, screening the reservoirs which feed the canal.

Pillaton Old Hall Penkridge, ST19 5RZ (01785 712200). South east of bridge 85. Only the gate house and stone-built chapel remain of this late 15th-C brick mansion built by the Littleton family, although there are still traces of the hall and courtyard. The chapel contains a 13th-C wooden carving of a saint. Visiting is by appointment only: telephone 01785 712200. The modest charge is donated to charity.

Gailey and Calf Heath reservoirs 1/2 mile east of Gailey Wharf, either side of the M6. These are feeder reservoirs for the canal, though rarely drawn on. The public has access to them as nature reserves to study the wide variety of natural life, especially the long-established heronry which is thriving on an island in Gailey Lower Reservoir. In Gailey Upper, fishing is available to the public from the riparian owner. In Gailey Lower a limited number of angling tickets are available on a season ticket basis each year from BW. There is club sailing on two of the reservoirs.

Boatyards

Ⓑ**Hatherton Marina** Kings Road, Calf Heath WV10 7DU (07919 466368; hathertonmarina.co.uk). Short- and long-term moorings, dry dock, boat building and repairs, engine sales and repairs, boat painting and electrical work, boat fitting out, boat sales, bottom blacking, showers, toilets. BSC Examiner.

Ⓑ**Otherton Boat Haven** Ltd Otherton Lane, Otherton, Penkridge ST19 5NX (01785 712515; 07581 459309; www.othertonboathaven.co.uk). D Pump out, gas, overnight and long-term mooring, boat and engine sales and repairs, toilets, coal.

Ⓑ**J D Boat Services** The Wharf, Gailey, Stafford ST19 5PR (01902 791811; www.jdboats.sharepoint.com/Pages/default.aspx). D Pump out, gas, solid fuel, narrowboat hire, boat share, winter storage, DIY facilities, boat servicing and repairs, painting, wet dock, diesel heaters, boat and engine sales, boat building. Gifts, maps, guides, souvenirs, windlass's etc opposite in the Roundhouse (01902 791617). *Open daily 09.00-17.00.*

Ⓑ**ABC Boat Hire** At J D Boat Services (01905 610660; www.abcboathire.com). Narrowboat hire.

Pubs and Restaurants

1 Cross Keys Filance Lane, Penkridge ST19 5HJ (07810 080668). Canalside, at Filance Bridge (84). Once a lonely canal pub, now it is modernised and surrounded by housing estates. Family orientated, it serves real ale and food *daily 11.00-21.00.* Family-friendly, garden. Traditional pub games, real fires and sports TV. *Open daily 11.00-00.00).* There is a useful *shop and garage* ¼ mile west of Cross Keys Bridge 83A.

2 The Spread Eagle Watling Street, Gailey ST19 5PN (01902 790212; www.spreadeaglepubgailey.co.uk). Imposing road house, with a massive garden and children's play area, serving real ale and food *all day* (breakfast from *08.00). Daily* carvery, takeaway service and Wi-Fi. B&B. *Open 08.00-23.00 (Sun 22.00).*

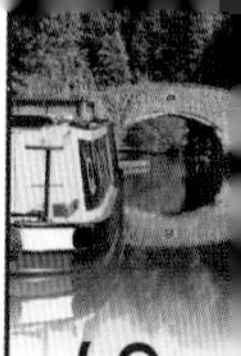

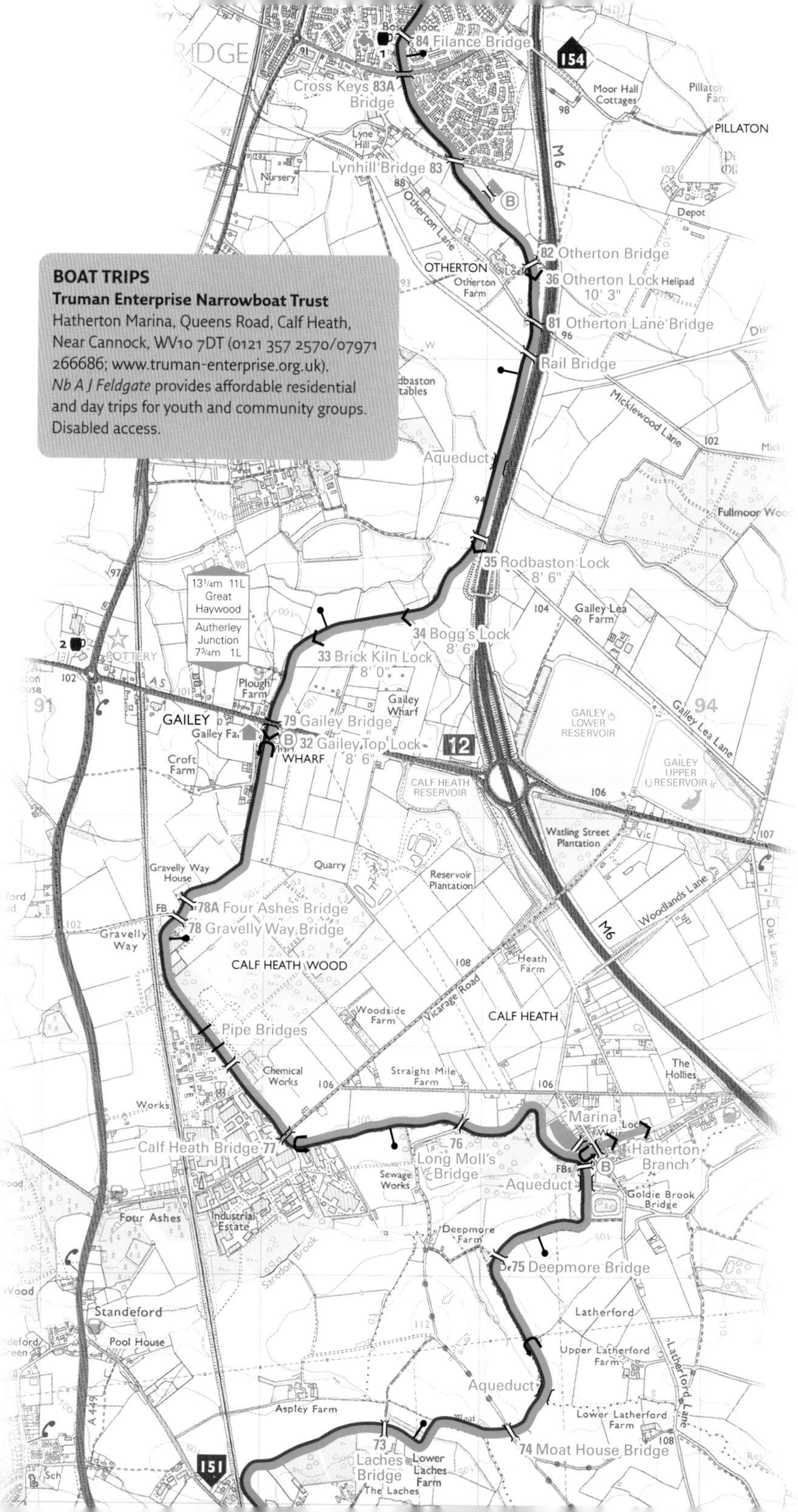
84 Filance Bridge
154
Cross Keys 83A Bridge
Moor Hall Cottages
Pillaton Farm
PILLATON
Lyne Hill
Nursery
Lynhill Bridge 83
Otherton Lane
M6
Depot
OTHERTON
Otherton Farm
82 Otherton Bridge
36 Otherton Lock 10' 3"
Helipad
81 Otherton Lane Bridge
Rail Bridge
Rodbaston Stables
Micklewood Lane
Aqueduct
Fullmoor Wood
35 Rodbaston Lock 8' 6"
13¼m 11L Great Haywood
Autherley Junction 7¾m 1L
Gailey Lea Farm
34 Bogg's Lock 8' 6"
33 Brick Kiln Lock 8' 0"
POTTERY
A5
Plough Farm
Gailey Wharf
GAILEY
79 Gailey Bridge
32 Gailey Top Lock 8' 6"
WHARF
12
GAILEY LOWER RESERVOIR
Gailey Lea Lane
GAILEY UPPER RESERVOIR
Croft Farm
CALF HEATH RESERVOIR
Watling Street Plantation
Quarry
Reservoir Plantation
Gravelly Way House
78A Four Ashes Bridge
78 Gravelly Way Bridge
Gravelly Way
Woodlands Lane
Oak Lane
CALF HEATH WOOD
Heath Farm
Woodside Farm
Vicarage Road
CALF HEATH
Pipe Bridges
Chemical Works
Straight Mile Farm
The Hollies
Works
Marina
Hatherton Branch
Calf Heath Bridge 77
76
Long Moll's Bridge
Sewage Works
Aqueduct
Goldie Brook Bridge
Four Ashes
Industrial Estate
Deepmore Farm
Saredon Brook
75 Deepmore Bridge
Standeford
Latherford
Pool House
Upper Latherford Farm
Latherford Lane
Aqueduct
A449
Aspley Farm
Lower Latherford Farm
73 Laches Bridge
Lower Laches Farm
74 Moat House Bridge
The Laches
151

BOAT TRIPS

Truman Enterprise Narrowboat Trust

Hatherton Marina, Queens Road, Calf Heath, Near Cannock, WV10 7DT (0121 357 2570/07971 266686; www.truman-enterprise.org.uk). *Nb A J Feldgate* provides affordable residential and day trips for youth and community groups. Disabled access.

Penkridge

The navigation now passes through Penkridge and is soon approached by the little River Penk: the two water courses share the valley for the next few miles. The Cross Keys at Filance Bridge (*see* page 152) was once an isolated canal pub – now it is surrounded by housing, which spreads along the canal in each direction. Apart from the noise of the motorway this is a pleasant valley: there are plenty of trees, a handful of locks and the large Teddesley Park alongside the canal. At Acton Trussell the M6 roars off to the north west and once again peace returns to the waterway. Teddesley Park Bridge was at one time quite ornamental, and became known as 'Fancy Bridge'. It is less so now. At Shutt Hill an iron post at the bottom of the lock is the only reminder of a small wharf which once existed here. The post was used to turn the boats into the dock.

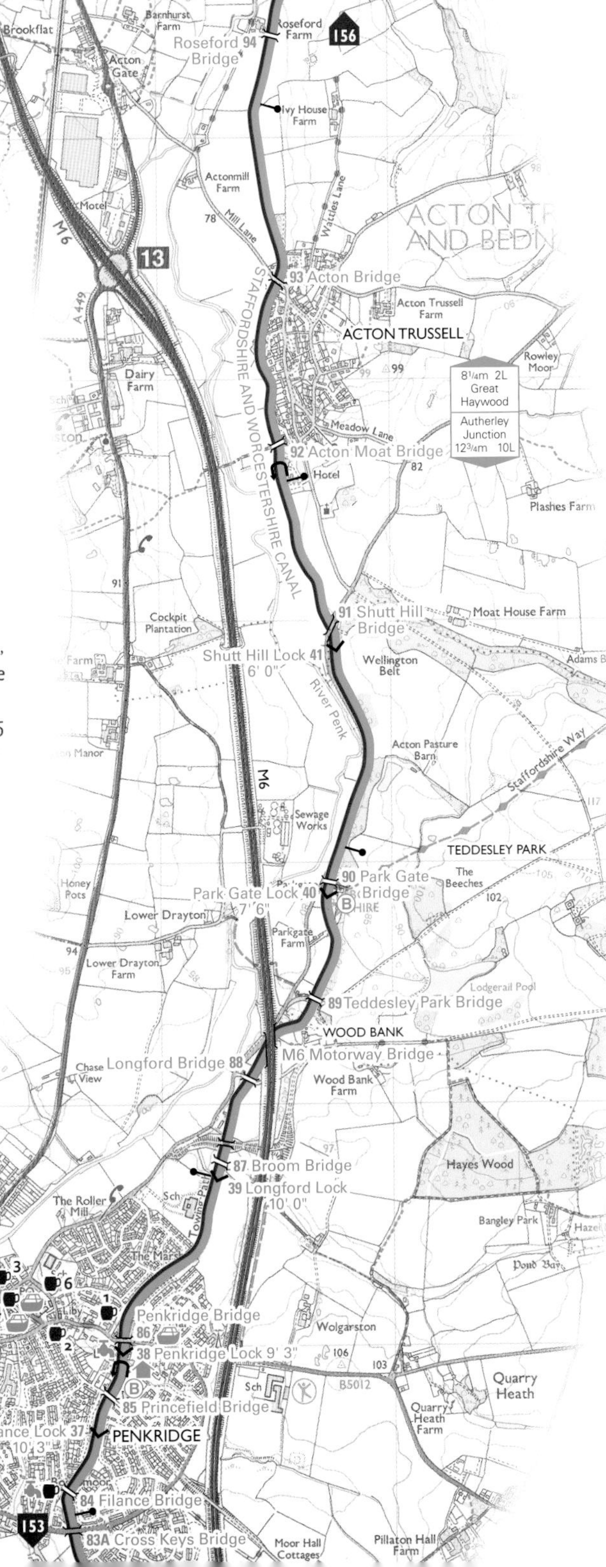

Penkridge

Staffs. PO, tel, stores, chemist, delicatessen, hardware, bank, butcher, baker, takeaways, fish & chips, off-licence, garage, station. Above Penkridge Lock is a good place to tie up in this relatively old village. It is bisected by a trunk road, but luckily most of the village lies to the east of it. The church of St Michael is tall and sombre, and is well-kept. A harmonious mixture of styles, the earliest part dates from the 11th C, but the whole was restored in 1881. There is a fine Dutch 18th-C wrought iron screen brought from Cape Town, and the tower is believed to date from c.1500. There are fine monuments of the Littletons of Pillaton Hall (*see* page 124), dating from 1558 and later.

Teddesley Park On the east bank of the canal. The Hall, once the family seat of the Littletons, was used during World War II as a prisoner-of-war camp, but has since been demolished. Its extensive wooded estate still remains.

Acton Trussell

Staffs. PO box, tel. A village overwhelmed by modern housing: much the best way to see it is from the canal. The church stands to the south, overlooking the navigation. The west tower dates from the 13th C, topped by a spire built in 1562.

Boatyards

Ⓑ**Teddesley Boat Company** Park Gate Lock, Teddesley Road, Penkridge ST19 5RH (01785 714692; www.narrowboats.co.uk). D Pump out, gas, narrowboat hire, overnight and long-term mooring, winter storage, crane (32 tonne), boat and engine sales and repairs, boat painting, books and maps. Midland Chandlers is next door, telephone 01785 712437.

Ⓑ**Tom's Moorings** Cannock Road, Penkridge ST19 5DX. Contact Streethay Wharf (01840 770128/07803 499111/07860 729522; www.bargemovers.com). Above Penkridge Lock. Overnight- and long-term mooring, electrical hook up, boat moving, cranage.

PLANT LIFE

The *Bluebell* is a familiar bulbous perennial, often carpeting whole woodland floors if the situation suits its requirements. The leaves are narrow and all basal. Bell-shaped flowers in one-sided spikes appear April–June.

Pubs and Restaurants

1 The Boat Inn Cannock Road, Penkridge ST19 5DT (01785 715170; theboatinn.org.uk). Canalside, by Penkridge Lock. Mellow and friendly red-brick pub dating from 1779. Real ale. Food is available *Mon-Fri L and E & Sat-Sun 12.00-20.00 (Sun 19.00)*. Child- and dog-friendly, garden. Sports TV. *Open Mon-Sun 12.00-23.00 (Fri-Sat 00.00).*

2 The Star Inn Market Place, Penkridge ST19 5DJ (01785 712513; thestarpenkridge.wixsite.com/home). Fine old pub serving real ale and bar meals *Mon-Thu L and E & Fri-Sun L*. Garden, traditional pub games and real fires. *Open Sun-Thu 12.00-23.00 (Thu 23.30) & Fri-Sat 12.00-00.00).*

3 White Hart Stone Cross, Penkridge ST19 5AS (01785 748598). This historic former coaching inn, visited by Mary, Queen of Scots, and Elizabeth I, has an impressive frontage, timber-framed with three gables. It serves real ale. Outside seating, dog-friendly. Traditional pub games, real fires, sports TV and Wi-Fi. *Open 12.00-00.00.*

4 The Horse & Jockey Market Street, Penkridge ST19 5DH (01785 716299). Opened in 1754 and still serving real ale! Family- and dog-friendly, beer garden. Traditional pub games, real fires, sports TV and Wi-Fi. *Open daily 12.00-23.00 (Mon 15.00).*

5 The Littleton Arms St Michael's Square, Penkridge ST19 5AL (01785 716300; www.thelittletonarms.com). Hotel, bar and restaurant. Real ale and excellent food available *Mon-Fri L and E & Sat-Sun 12.00-21.00*. Garden, dog- and child-friendly *(until 21.00). Open Mon-Sat 12.00-23.00 (Fri-Sat 00.00) & Sun 12.00-22.30.*

6 Flames Mill Street, Penkridge ST19 5AY (01785 712955). Contemporary eastern cuisine. Takeaway service. *Open daily 17.00-23.00.*

WALKING AND CYCLING

The Staffordshire Way crosses the canal between bridges 89 and 90. This 90-mile path stretches from Mow Cop in the north (near the Macclesfield Canal) to Kinver Edge in the south, using the Caldon Canal towpath on the way. It connects with the Gritstone Trail, the Hereford & Worcester Way and the Heart of England Way. A guide book is available from local Tourist Information Centres.

Tixall

Continuing north along the shallow Penk valley, the canal soon reaches Radford Bridge, the nearest point to Stafford. It is about $1\frac{1}{2}$ miles to the centre of town: there is a frequent bus service. A canal branch used to connect with the town via Baswich Lock and the River Sow. If you look carefully west of bridge 101 you can just about deduce where the connection was made – some remains of brickwork are the clue. A mile further north the canal bends around to the south east and follows the pretty valley of the River Sow, and at Milford crosses the river via an aqueduct – an early structure by James Brindley, carried heavily on low brick arches. Tixall Lock offers some interesting views in all directions: the castellated entrance to Shugborough Railway Tunnel at the foot of the thick woods of Cannock Chase and the distant outline of the remarkable Tixall Gatehouse. The canal now completes its journey to the Trent & Mersey Canal at Great Haywood. It is a length of waterway quite unlike any other. Proceeding along this very charming valley, the navigation enters Tixall Wide – an amazing and delightful stretch of water more resembling a lake than a canal, said to have been built in order not to compromise the view from Tixall House (alas, no more), and navigable to the edges. The Wide is noted for its kingfisher population. Woods across the valley conceal Shugborough Hall. The River Trent is met, on its way south from Stoke-on-Trent, and is crossed on an aqueduct. There is a wharf, and *fresh produce* (see page 189) can be purchased at the *farm shop* beside Bridge 75 on the Trent & Mersey, which is entered through an elegantly arched bridge. The bridge is the subject of a very famous photograph taken by the canal historian Eric de Maré. Immediately before this bridge there is a useful *boatyard* which, amongst other services, provides *Elsan disposal* (charge).

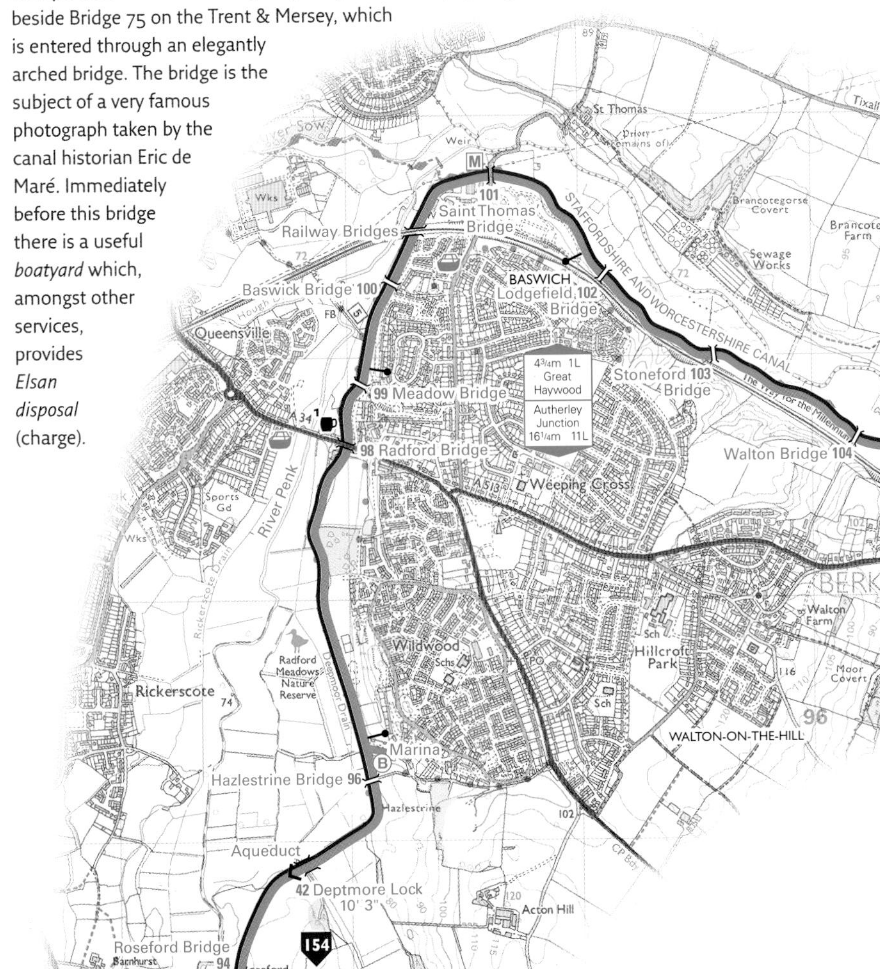

Boatyards

Ⓑ**Stafford Boat Club** Off Maple Wood, Wildwood, Stafford ST17 4SG (01785 660725/07716 960049; staffordboatclub.co.uk). At Bridge 96. D Pump out, gas, solid fuel, overnight and short-term moorings, limited winter moorings, slipway, wet dock, laundry, print shop, use of clubhouse (bar *open every evening and 12.00-15.00 Sun*).

Ⓑ**Anglo Welsh** The Canal Wharf, Mill Lane, Great Haywood ST18 0RJ (01889 881711; http://www.anglowelsh.co.uk/Locations/Bases/Great-Haywood). D Pump out (not *Sat*), gas, narrowboat hire, day-hire craft, overnight and long-term mooring, coal, engine repairs, chandlery, toilets, books, maps and gifts, ice cream and soft drinks. *Open daily 08.30-17.00 (Sun 09.00).*

Ⓑ**Great Haywood Marina** The Marina Building, Canalside Farm, Mill Lane, Great Haywood ST18 0RQ (01889 883713/07771 685731; www.greathaywoodmarina.co.uk). D Pump out, gas, short- and long-term mooring, boat sales and repairs, solid fuel, slipway, chandlery, laundrette, toilets, showers, Wi-Fi, CCTV. Farm shop adjacent.

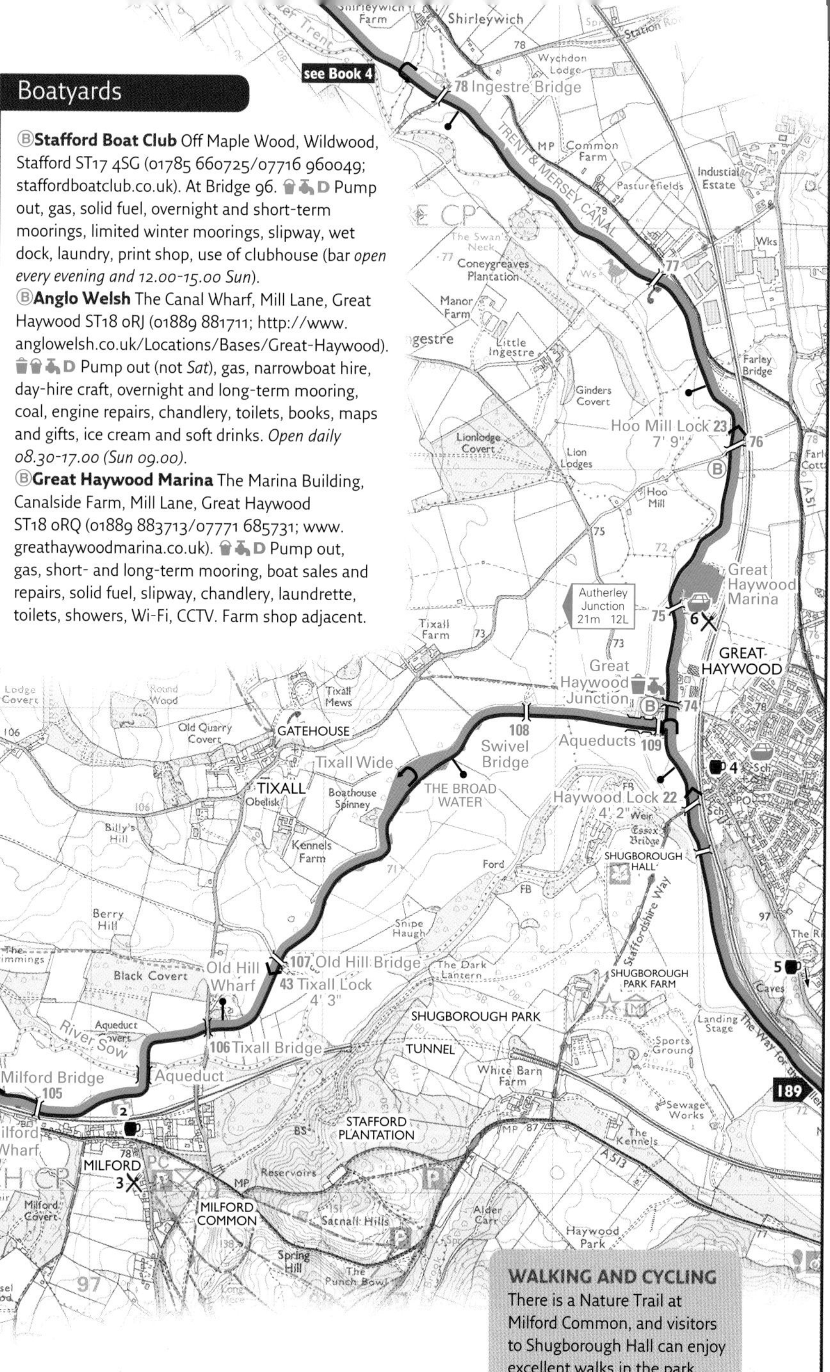

WALKING AND CYCLING

There is a Nature Trail at Milford Common, and visitors to Shugborough Hall can enjoy excellent walks in the park.

Stafford
Staffs. All services. This town is well worth visiting, since there is a remarkable wealth of fine old buildings. These include a handsome City Hall complex of ornamental Italianate buildings, c.1880. The robust-looking gaol is nearby; and the church of St Mary stands in very pleasing and spacious grounds. There are some pretty back alleys: Church Lane contains a splendid-looking eating house, and at the bottom of the lane a fruiterer's shop is in a thatched cottage built in 1610.
Tourist Information Centre Gatehouse Theatre, Eastgate Street, Stafford ST16 2LT (01785 619619; www.staffordbc.gov.uk/stafford-visitor-information-centre). *Open Mon-Sat 09.30-17.30.*

The Stafford Branch
Just west of bridge 101 there was once a lock taking a branch off the Staffordshire & Worcestershire to Stafford. One mile long, it was unusual in that it was not a canal but the canalised course of the River Sow.

Milford
Staffs. PO box, tel, takeaway Best reached from Tixall Bridge (106). Milford Hall is hidden by trees.

Tixall
Staffs. PO box, tel. Just to the east are the stables and the gatehouse of the long-vanished Tixall Hall. This massive square Elizabethan building dates from 1598 and is fully four storeys high. It stands alone in a field and is considered to be one of the most ambitious gatehouses in the country. The gatehouse is now available for holiday lets: telephone the Landmark Trust (01628 825925) for details.

Great Haywood
Staffs. PO, tel, stores, fishmonger. Centre of the Great Haywood and Shugborough Conservation Area, the village is attractive in parts, but it is closely connected in many ways to Shugborough Park, to which it is physically linked by the very old Essex Bridge, where the crystal clear waters of the River Sow join the Trent on its way down from Stoke.
Shugborough Hall Great Haywood, Milford ST17 0XB (01889 880160; www.nationaltrust.org.uk/shugborough-estate). Walk south along the road from bridge 106 to the A513 at Milford Common. The main entrance is on your left. The present house dates from 1693, but was substantially altered by James Stuart around 1760 and by Samuel Wyatt around the turn of the 18th C. The Trust has leased the whole to Staffordshire County Council who now manage it. The house has been restored at great expense. There are some magnificent rooms and treasures inside. *Opening times vary* so telephone or visit the website for further details. Charge.
Shugborough Park There are some remarkable sights in the large park that encircles the Hall. Thomas Anson, who inherited the estate in 1720, enlisted in 1744 the help of his famous brother, Admiral George Anson, to beautify and improve the house and the park. In 1762 he commissioned James Stuart, a neo-Grecian architect, to embellish the grounds. 'Athenian' Stuart set to with a will, and the spectacular results of his work can be seen scattered round the park.
Park Farm at Shugborough (01889 880160; www.nationaltrust.org.uk/shugborough-estate/features/park-farm-at-shugborough). Within Shugborough Park. Designed by Samuel Wyatt, it contains an agricultural museum, a working mill and a rare breeds centre. Traditional country skills such as bread-making, butter-churning and cheese-making are demonstrated. *Opening times vary* so telephone or visit the website for further details. Charge.

Pubs and Restaurants (pages 156-157)

1 Radford Bank Inn Radford Bank, Stafford ST17 4PG (01785 242825; www.stonehouserestaurants.co.uk/nationalsearch/eastandwestmidlands/theradfordbankinnstafford/foodanddrink). Canalside at bridge 98. Real ale. Food is served *daily 08.00-22.00* (including *weekday* breakfast *08.00-11.30).* Family-friendly, garden. Traditional pub games, sports TV and Wi-Fi. Quiz *Fri.* Takeaway service. *Open 08.00-23.00.*
2 The Barley Mow 28 Main Road, Milford ST17 0UW (01785 665230; www.eating-inn.co.uk/house/barley-mow-stafford). Predominantly aimed at the hungry, this pub also serves ales - food *09.00-22.00 daily* (including *weekday* breakfast *09.00-11.00*). Children's 'PlayZone' *open 11.00-20.00.* Garden and Wi-Fi. Quiz *Sun. Open daily 09.00-23.00.*

3 The Viceroy Indian Restaurant 8 Brocton Road, Milford ST17 0UH (01785 663239; www.viceroyrestaurant.co.uk). With its elegant, modern interior and warm welcome, this restaurant showcases its chef/proprietor's Indian and Bangladeshi culinary heritage. Food to savour is served *daily 17.30-23.00.* Takeaway service with online ordering.

Also try: **4 The Clifford Arm** Main Road, Great Haywood ST18 0SR (01889 881321; cliffordarms.co.uk) and **5 The Red Lion** Main Road, Little Haywood ST18 0TS (01889 881314).
6 Canalside Farm café Mill Lane, Great Haywood ST18 0RQ (01889 881747; www.canalsidefarm.co.uk). Café. *Open Apr-Oct, daily 09.00-18.00 & Nov-Mar, Tue-Sat 09.00-18.00 & Sun 10.00-17.00.*

STRATFORD-UPON-AVON CANAL: NORTH

MAXIMUM DIMENSIONS

King's Norton to Kingswood
Length: 70'
Beam: 7'
Headroom: 7' 3"

Kingswood to Stratford
Length: 70'
Beam: 6' 10"
Headroom: 6'

MILEAGE

KING'S NORTON JUNCTION to:
Hockley Heath: 9¾ miles
LAPWORTH, junction with Grand Union Canal: 12½ miles
Preston Bagot: 16¼ miles
Wootton Wawen Basin: 18½ miles
Wilmcote: 22 miles
STRATFORD-UPON-AVON, junction with River Avon: 25½ miles

Locks: 54

MANAGER

0303 040 4040
enquiries.westmidlands@canalrivertrust.org.uk

The opening of the Oxford Canal in 1790 and of the Coventry Canal throughout shortly afterwards opened up a continuous waterway from London to the rapidly developing industrial area based on Birmingham. It also gave access, via the Trent & Mersey Canal, to the expanding pottery industry based around Stoke-on-Trent, to the Mersey, and to the East Midlands coalfield. When the Warwick & Birmingham and Warwick & Napton Canals were projected to pass within 8 miles of Stratford-upon-Avon, the business interests of that town realised that the prosperity being generated by these new trade arteries would pass them by unless Stratford acquired direct access to the network. And so on 28 March 1793 an Act of Parliament was passed for the construction of the Stratford-upon-Avon Canal, to start at King's Norton on the Worcester & Birmingham Canal.

Progress was rapid at first, but almost the total estimated cost of the complete canal was spent on cutting the 9¾ lock-free miles to Hockley Heath within the first three years. It then took another four years, more negotiations, a revision of the route and another Act of Parliament to get things going again. By 1803 the canal was open from King's Norton Junction to its junction with the Warwick & Birmingham Canal (now part of the Grand Union main line) near Lapworth. Cutting recommenced in 1812, the route being revised yet again in 1815 to include the present junction with the River Avon at Stratford.

In its most prosperous period, the canal's annual traffic exceeded 180,000 tons. By 1835 the canal was suffering from railway competition. This grew so rapidly that in 1845 the Canal Company decided to sell out to the Great Western Railway. In 1890 the tonnage carried was still a quarter of what it had been 50 years before, but the fall in ton-miles was much greater. This pattern of decline continued in the 20th C, and by the 1950s only an occasional working boat used the northern section; the southern section (Lapworth to Stratford) was badly silted, some locks were unusable and some of the short pounds below Wilmcote were dry.

In 1955 a Board of Survey had recommended sweeping canal closures, including the southern section of the Stratford-upon-Avon Canal, but public protest was such that a Committee of Enquiry was set up in 1958, and this prompted the start of a massive campaign to save the canal. The campaign was successful: the decision not to abandon it was announced by the Ministry on 22 May 1959. On 16 October of the same year the National Trust announced that it had agreed a lease from the British Transport Commission under which the Trust would assume responsibility for restoring and maintaining the southern section.

The reopening ceremony was performed by Queen Elizabeth the Queen Mother on 11 July 1964, after more than four years of hard work by prison labourers, canal enthusiasts, Army units and a handful of National Trust staff. On 1 April 1988 control of the southern section of the Stratford-upon-Avon Canal was passed to the Waterways Board (now Canal and River Trust).

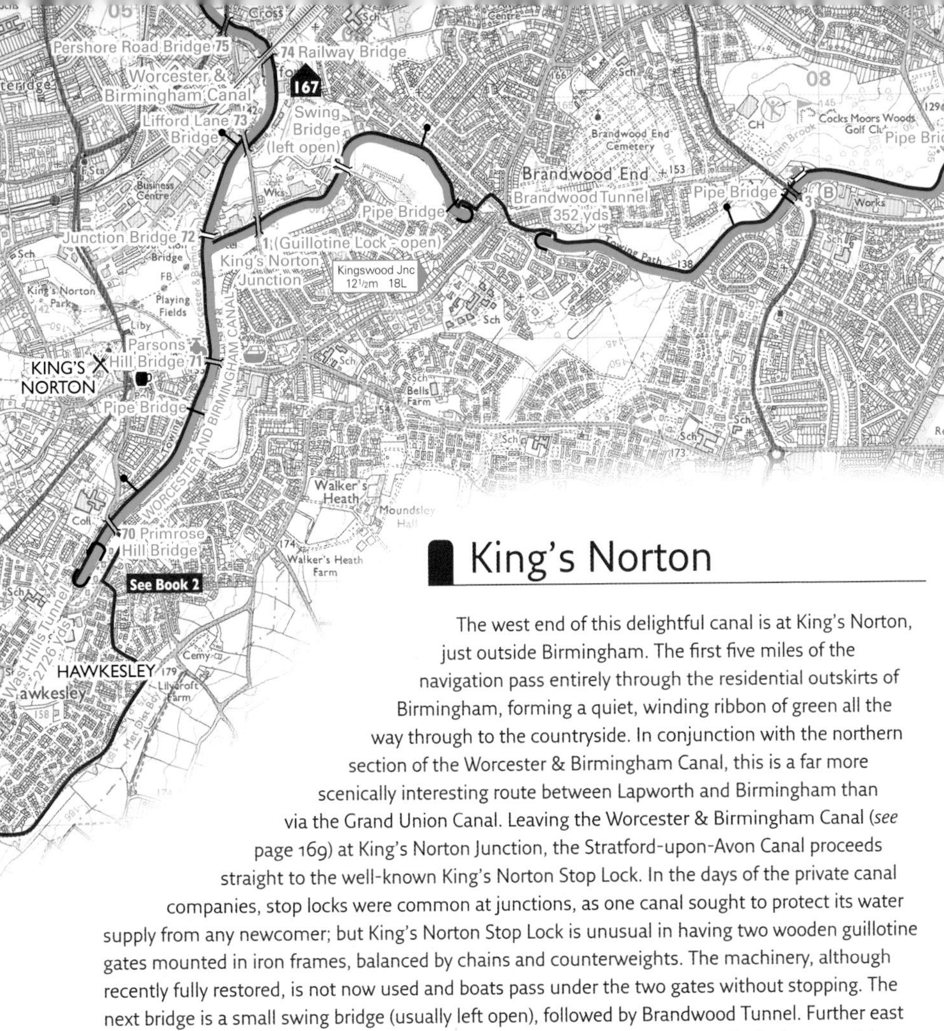

King's Norton

The west end of this delightful canal is at King's Norton, just outside Birmingham. The first five miles of the navigation pass entirely through the residential outskirts of Birmingham, forming a quiet, winding ribbon of green all the way through to the countryside. In conjunction with the northern section of the Worcester & Birmingham Canal, this is a far more scenically interesting route between Lapworth and Birmingham than via the Grand Union Canal. Leaving the Worcester & Birmingham Canal (*see* page 169) at King's Norton Junction, the Stratford-upon-Avon Canal proceeds straight to the well-known King's Norton Stop Lock. In the days of the private canal companies, stop locks were common at junctions, as one canal sought to protect its water supply from any newcomer; but King's Norton Stop Lock is unusual in having two wooden guillotine gates mounted in iron frames, balanced by chains and counterweights. The machinery, although recently fully restored, is not now used and boats pass under the two gates without stopping. The next bridge is a small swing bridge (usually left open), followed by Brandwood Tunnel. Further east is a beautiful tree-lined cutting, then a bridge with a *pub* beside it (*garage and telephone nearby*) and the remains of an old arm just beyond it. Passing over a small aqueduct, the canal reaches a steel lift bridge, which is raised and lowered electrically (see note below). Then beyond a railway bridge the canal begins to shed all traces of the suburbs, maintaining its twisting course in wooded cuttings through quiet countryside. The bridges over the navigation are mostly the generous brick-arched bridges typical of the canal between King's Norton and Lapworth Locks (in contrast to the much smaller bridges further south, and built when there were plans for a broad canal), but few roads of any significance come near the canal. At bridge 16 the canal emerges from a long cutting and is joined by a feeder from the nearby Earlswood Reservoir. Boats are moored along this, since it is the base of the Earlswood Motor Yacht Club. There are no villages along this rural stretch of canal.

NAVIGATIONAL NOTES

You will need a Watermate key to operate Shirley Drawbridge, 8. A single button completes the operation, and a line of piles guides you through.

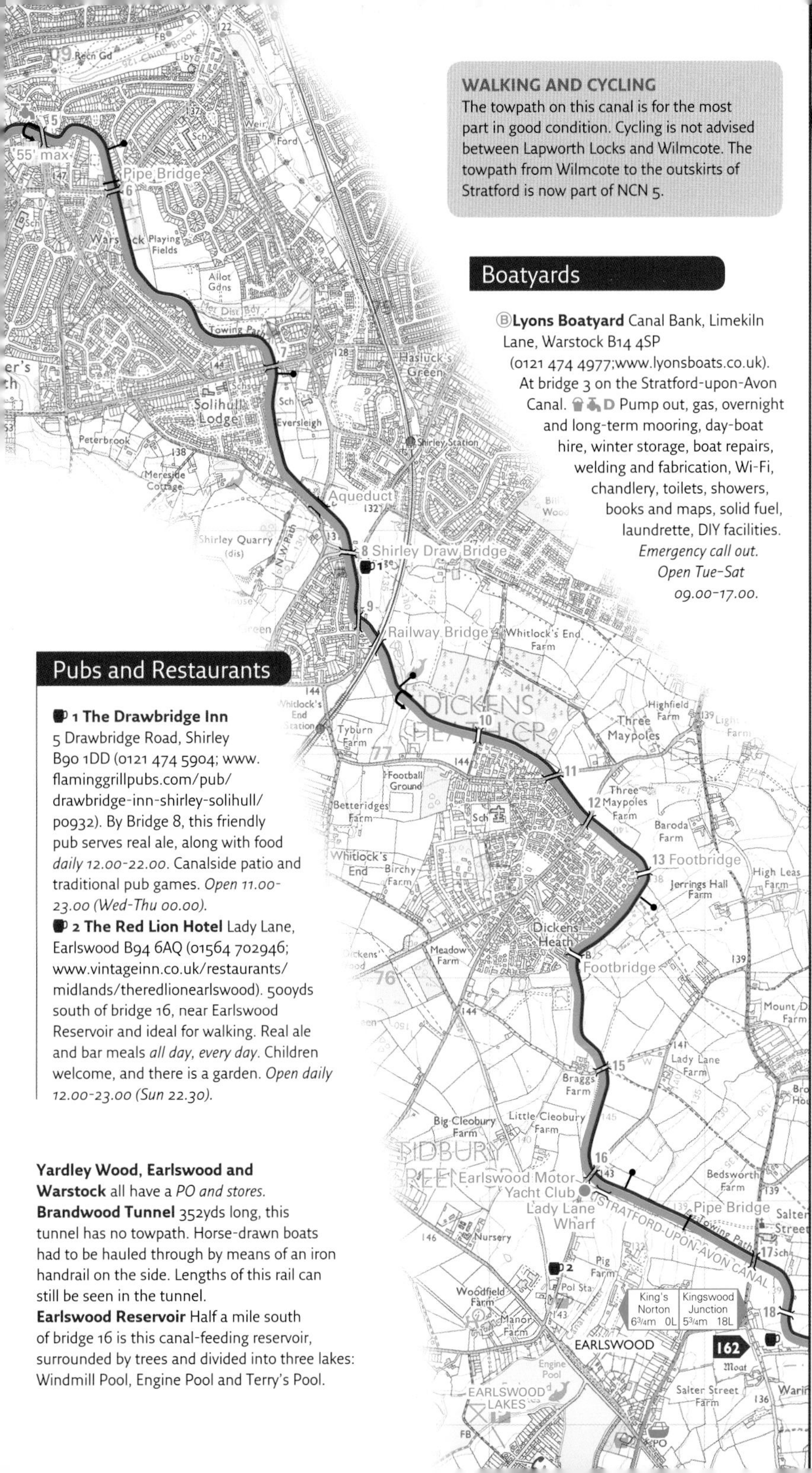

WALKING AND CYCLING

The towpath on this canal is for the most part in good condition. Cycling is not advised between Lapworth Locks and Wilmcote. The towpath from Wilmcote to the outskirts of Stratford is now part of NCN 5.

Boatyards

Ⓑ**Lyons Boatyard** Canal Bank, Limekiln Lane, Warstock B14 4SP (0121 474 4977;www.lyonsboats.co.uk). At bridge 3 on the Stratford-upon-Avon Canal. **D** Pump out, gas, overnight and long-term mooring, day-boat hire, winter storage, boat repairs, welding and fabrication, Wi-Fi, chandlery, toilets, showers, books and maps, solid fuel, laundrette, DIY facilities. *Emergency call out. Open Tue-Sat 09.00-17.00.*

Pubs and Restaurants

1 The Drawbridge Inn 5 Drawbridge Road, Shirley B90 1DD (0121 474 5904; www.flaminggrillpubs.com/pub/drawbridge-inn-shirley-solihull/p0932). By Bridge 8, this friendly pub serves real ale, along with food *daily 12.00-22.00*. Canalside patio and traditional pub games. *Open 11.00-23.00 (Wed-Thu 00.00).*

2 The Red Lion Hotel Lady Lane, Earlswood B94 6AQ (01564 702946; www.vintageinn.co.uk/restaurants/midlands/theredlionearlswood). 500yds south of bridge 16, near Earlswood Reservoir and ideal for walking. Real ale and bar meals *all day, every day*. Children welcome, and there is a garden. *Open daily 12.00-23.00 (Sun 22.30).*

Yardley Wood, Earlswood and Warstock all have a *PO and stores.*
Brandwood Tunnel 352yds long, this tunnel has no towpath. Horse-drawn boats had to be hauled through by means of an iron handrail on the side. Lengths of this rail can still be seen in the tunnel.
Earlswood Reservoir Half a mile south of bridge 16 is this canal-feeding reservoir, surrounded by trees and divided into three lakes: Windmill Pool, Engine Pool and Terry's Pool.

King's Norton 6¾m 0L | Kingswood Junction 5¾m 18L

162

Lapworth Locks

The canal continues on its south easterly course, passing through quiet countryside interrupted only by the incessant roar of the M42 motorway, crossing overhead. is an excellent, *combined bakery, delicatessen and café* just north of Bridge 20. There are no locks, and the bridges - especially those in the cuttings - are still the big brick arches built when a broad canal was planned. At Hockley Heath (bridge 25) there is a tiny arm that once served a coal wharf. Nearby the Wharf Inn overlooks the canal. East of here things change dramatically, for the first of the locks down to Kingswood Junction is reached. The top lock is numbered 2, as the old stop lock at King's Norton is number 1. The surroundings of the top lock are indeed pleasant: a white house enclosed by walls and hemmed in by trees stands beside the lock, while a cottage with a delightful garden faces the towpath just below. To the south west can be seen the spire of Lapworth church. After the first four locks, there is a ½-mile breathing space: then the Lapworth flight begins in earnest, with each of the next nine locks spaced only a few yards from its neighbour.

The short intervening pounds have been enlarged to provide a bigger working reservoir of water, so that one side of each lock is virtually an isthmus. The locks have double bottom gates so are not heavy going, and are interspersed with the old cast iron split bridges that are such a charming feature of the Stratford-upon-Avon Canal. These bridges are built in two halves, separated by a one inch gap

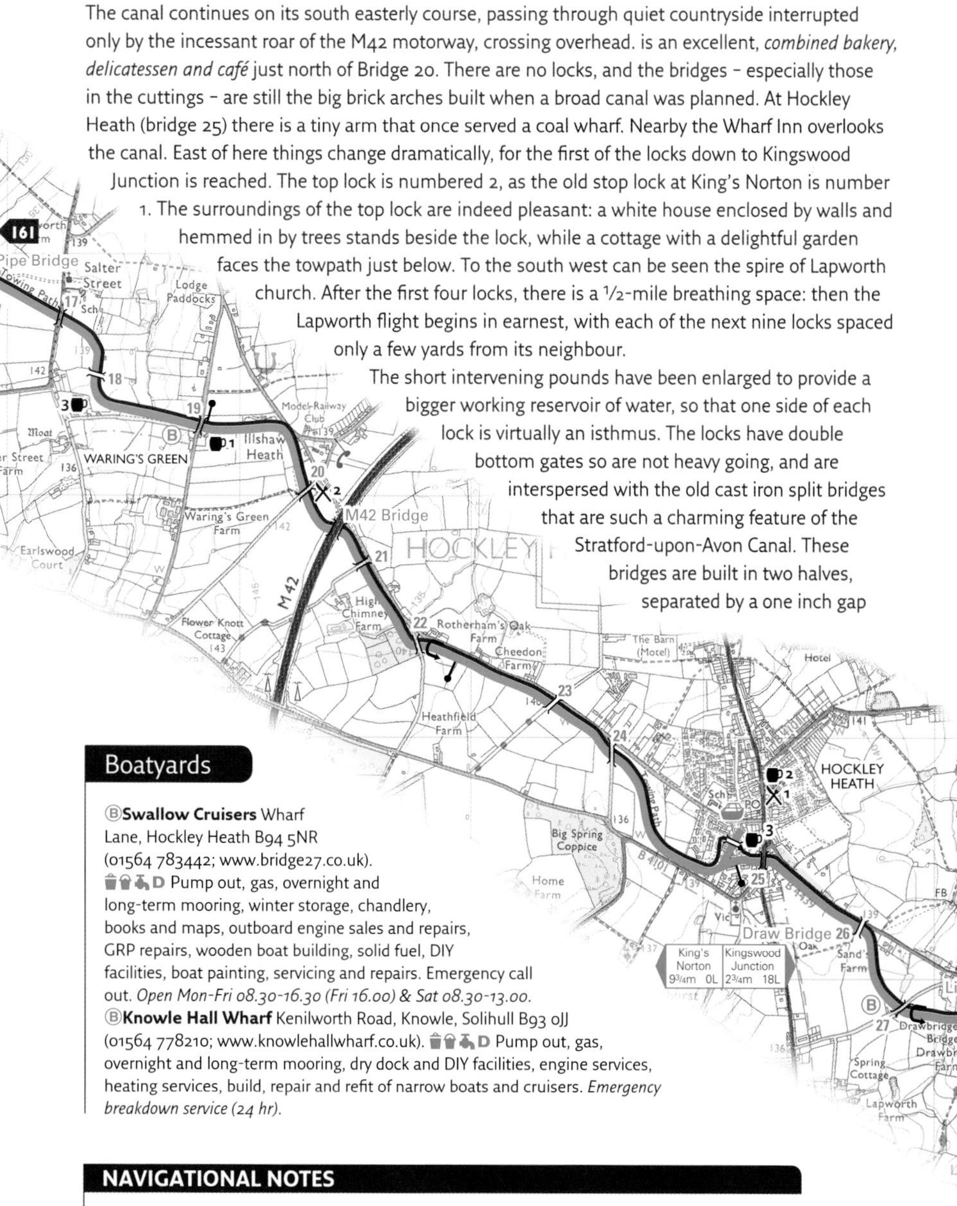

Boatyards

Ⓑ**Swallow Cruisers** Wharf Lane, Hockley Heath B94 5NR (01564 783442; www.bridge27.co.uk). D Pump out, gas, overnight and long-term mooring, winter storage, chandlery, books and maps, outboard engine sales and repairs, GRP repairs, wooden boat building, solid fuel, DIY facilities, boat painting, servicing and repairs. Emergency call out. *Open Mon-Fri 08.30-16.30 (Fri 16.00) & Sat 08.30-13.00.*

Ⓑ**Knowle Hall Wharf** Kenilworth Road, Knowle, Solihull B93 0JJ (01564 778210; www.knowlehallwharf.co.uk). D Pump out, gas, overnight and long-term mooring, dry dock and DIY facilities, engine services, heating services, build, repair and refit of narrow boats and cruisers. *Emergency breakdown service (24 hr).*

NAVIGATIONAL NOTES

1. *Please go slowly* to minimise your wash.
2. Bridges 26 and 28 operate hydraulically, using a lock windlass.
3. Due to rebuilding, the chamber of lock 15 on the Lapworth flight is now over 2ft shorter than the other locks. Those in full-length boats should take extra care when descending.

so that the towing line between a horse and a boat could be dropped through the gap without having to disconnect the horse. There are *shops* south of bridge 34. Below lock 19 is Kingswood Junction: boats heading for Stratford should keep right here. A short branch to the left leads under the railway line to the Grand Union Canal, or you can use the Lapworth Link after lock 22 if you are heading north to the GU, avoiding unnecessary lockage. There are *toilets* and a shaded *picnic area* Beside the car park adjoining the towpath at Lock 19.

Pubs and Restaurants

1 The Blue Bell Cider House Warings Green Road, Hockley Heath B94 6BP (01564 702328; www.thebluebellciderhouse.co.uk). A pretty, traditional cider house serving real draught cider and a range of real ales. Food available *Mon-Sat 12.00-20.30 & Sun 12.00-17.00*. Dog- and family-friendly, canalside garden. Traditional pub games, real fires, sports TV and Wi-Fi. Mooring. Quiz *Wed. Open Mon-Sat 11.30-23.00 (Fri-Sat 23.30) & Sun 12.00-22.30.*

2 Wedges Bakery and Delicatessen 495 School Road, Hockley Heath B94 6RP (01564 702542; www.wedgesbakery.co.uk). 100yds north east of Bridge 20. Set in the original bake house, dating from 1850, this café, delicatessen and bakery sells a tantalising selection of fresh food - both to eat in and take away - including breakfast, light lunches and afternoon teas. Courtyard seating. *Open Mon-Fri 08.00-17.30, Sat 07.00-17.00 & Sun 10.00-15.00.*

Also try: **3 The Bulls Head** 7 Limekiln Lane, Earlswood B94 6BU (01564 700368; www.thwaites.co.uk/hotels-and-inns/inns/bulls-head-at-earlswood/food-and-drink/menus/).

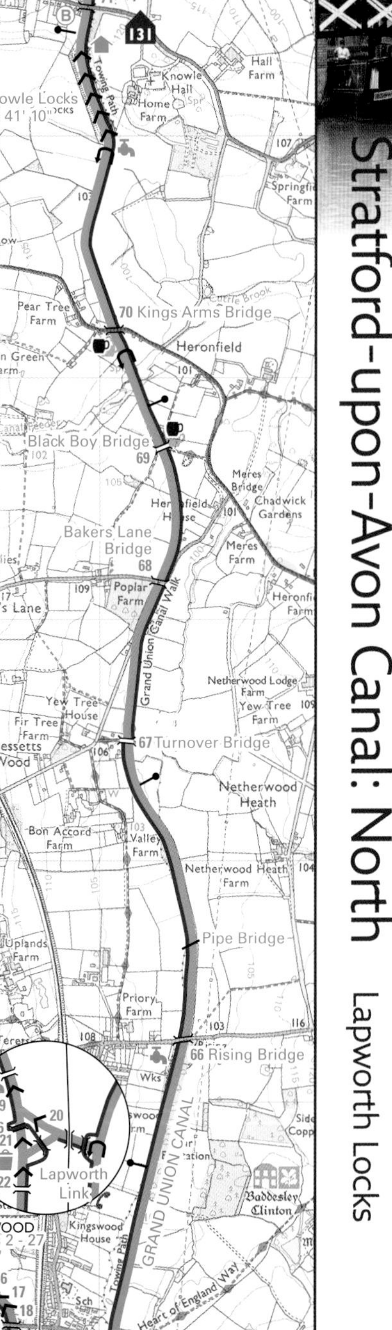

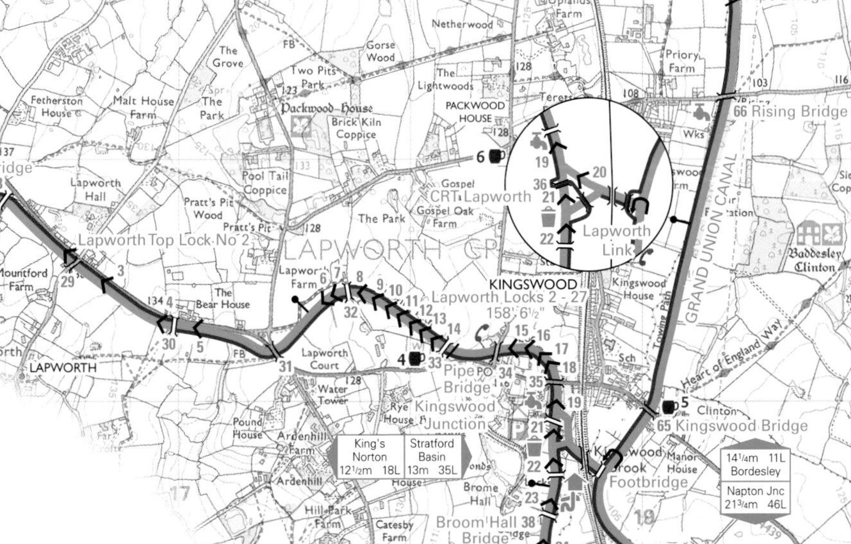

continued in Book 2

Hockley Heath

Warwicks. PO, tel, stores, butcher, delicatessen, fish & chips, garage (1 mile distant). A featureless place, but the several shops are conveniently close to the canal bridge, and the pub is pleasant. There is also a handy cycle shop: **Dynamic Rides** 2364 Stratford Road B94 6QT (01564 783332; www.dynamicrides.co.uk) which includes the Flying Squirrel Café. *Shop open 06.00-22.00.*

Lapworth

Warwicks. PO, tel, stores, off-licence, garage, station. Indivisible from Kingswood, this is more a residential area than a village. Two canals pass through Lapworth: the heavily locked Stratford-upon-Avon Canal and, to the east, the main line of the Grand Union Canal. These two waterways, and the short spur that connects them, are easily the most interesting aspect of Lapworth. The canalside buildings are attractive and there are two small reservoirs at the junction. The mostly 15th-C church is quite separate from the village and is 1½ miles west of the junction; it contains an interesting monument by Eric Gill, 1928.

Packwood House Packwood Lane, Lapworth B94 6AT (01564 782024; www.nationaltrust.org.uk/packwood-house). ¾ mile north of Bridge 31. Timber-framed Tudor house, dating from the late 16th C and enlarged in the 17th C, where Cromwell's general, Henry Ireton, slept before the Battle of Edgehill in 1642. Owned by the Featherstones until 1869, it was eventually purchased by Alfred Ash, who repaired the house and reinstated the gardens. Collection of tapestry, needlework and furniture. Park with formal grounds and 17th-C yew garden possibly laid out to represent the Sermon on the Mount, the trees taking the place of Jesus and his followers. Café. *Opening times vary* so telephone or visit website for details.

Pubs and Restaurants (pages 162–163)

1 Tagore Restaurant 2571a Stratford Road, Hockley Heath B94 6NL (01564 784800; tagorerestaurant.com). Well-regarded Indian Restaurant that will deliver a takeaway direct to your boat. *Open Mon-Sun 17.30-23.00 (Fri-Sat 23.30).*

2 Miller & Carter Steak House Stratford Road, Hockley Heath B94 6NL (01564 784137; www.miller andcarter.co.uk/millerandcarterhockleyheath). Traditional steak house serving much more besides, including real ale. Family-friendly, garden and Wi-Fi. *Open daily 12.00-23.00 (Fri-Sat 00.00).*

3 The Wharf Tavern 2390 Stratford Road, Hockley Heath B94 6QT (01564 782075; www.wharftavern.co.uk). A friendly, community pub overlooking the canal serving real ales and food *daily 12.00-22.00.* Child- and dog-friendly, canalside patio. Traditional pub games, sports TV and Wi-Fi. *Open 12.00-23.00 (Fri-Sat 00.00).*

4 The Boot Inn Old Warwick Road, Lapworth B94 6JU (01564 782464; www.lovelypubs.co.uk/the-boot-lapworth). Cosmopolitan country pub serving real ale. Fashionable bar meals *L and E.* Children and well-behaved dogs welcome; garden. Open fires. *Open Mon-Sat 11.00-23.00 (Fri-Sat 00.00) & Sun 12.00-22.30.*

5 The Navigation Old Warwick Road, Lapworth B94 6NA (01564 783337; www.navigationlapworth.co.uk). Real ales, real cider and food available *Mon-Thu L and E & Fri-Sun 12.00-21.30 (Sun 20.00).* Breakfast *Sat-Sun from 10.00.* Family-friendly, canalside garden. Traditional pub games, real fires and Wi-Fi. Camping & Moorings. *Open 11.30-00.00.*

Also try: **6 The Punchbowl** Mill Lane, Lapworth B94 6HR (01564 784564; www.thepunchbowllapworth.com).

Lapworth Locks

WORCESTER & BIRMINGHAM CANAL: NORTH

MAXIMUM DIMENSIONS

Length: 72' 0"
Beam: 7'
Headroom: 8'

MILEAGE

KING'S NORTON JUNCTION to:
BIRMINGHAM Gas Street Basin: 5½ miles

No locks

MANAGER

0303 040 4040

Diglis Basin to Wast Hills Tunnel south portal
enquiries.southwalessevern@canalrivertrust.org.uk

Wast Hills Tunnel south portal to Kings Norton Junction
enquiries.westmidlands@canalrivertrust.org.uk

The Bill for the Worcester & Birmingham Canal was passed in 1791 in spite of fierce opposition from the Staffordshire & Worcestershire Canal proprietors, who saw trade on their route to the Severn threatened. The supporters of the Bill claimed that the route from Birmingham and the Black Country towns would be much shorter, enabling traffic to avoid the then notorious shallows in the Severn below Stourport. The Birmingham Canal Company also opposed the Bill and succeeded in obtaining a clause preventing the new navigation from approaching within 7ft of their water. This resulted in the famous Worcester Bar separating the two canals in the centre of Birmingham, replaced by a stop lock in 1815.

Construction of the canal began at the Birmingham end following the line originally surveyed by John Snape and Josiah Clowes. Even at this early stage difficulties with water supply were encountered. The company was obliged by the Act authorising the canal to safeguard water supplies to the mills on the streams south of Birmingham. To do this, and to supply water for the summit level, ten reservoirs were planned or constructed. The high cost of these engineering works led to a change of policy: instead of building a broad canal, the company decided to build it with narrow locks, in order to save money in construction and water in operation.

The canal was completed in 1815. In the same year an agreement with the Birmingham Canal proprietors permitted the cutting of a stop lock through Worcester Bar. The canal had cost £610,000, exceeding its original estimate by many thousands of pounds. Industrial goods and coal were carried down to Worcester, often for onward shipping to Bristol, while grain, timber and agricultural produce were returned to the growing towns of the Midlands. However the opening of railways in the 1840s and 1850s reduced traffic considerably and had a profound effect on the fortunes of the canal.

By the early 1900s the commercial future of the canal was uncertain, although the works were in much better condition than on many other canals. Schemes to enlarge the navigation as part of a Bristol-Birmingham route came to nothing. Commercial carrying continued until about 1964, the traffic being mostly between the two Cadbury factories of Bournville and Blackpole, and to Frampton on the Gloucester & Sharpness Canal. After nationalisation, several proposals were made to abandon the canal, but the 1960s brought a dramatic increase in the number of pleasure boats using the waterway thus securing its future use. The whole of the canal is covered *in the Severn, Avon & Birmingham Guide*.

King's Norton

To the north of King's Norton Junction, where the Stratford-upon-Avon Canal (see page 160) joins the Worcester & Birmingham Canal, the canal passes through an industrial area, but thankfully seems to hold the factories at bay on one side, while a railway line, the main line from Worcester and the south west to Birmingham, draws alongside on its west flank. Canal and railway together drive through the middle of Cadbury's Bournville works, which is interesting rather than oppressive. Beyond it is Bournville station, followed by a cutting.

King's Norton
West Midlands. PO, tel, stores, chemist, takeaway, fish & chips, off-licence, bank, station. The village still survives as a recognisable entity, for the suburbs of Birmingham have now extended all around it, and the small village green, the old grammar school buildings (now converted into flats) and the soaring spire of the church ensure that it will remain so. The church is set back a little from the green in an attractive churchyard, and is mainly of the 14th C, although two Norman windows can still be seen. The grammar school is even older – it was probably founded by King Edward III in 1344. An interesting puzzle is that the upper storey is apparently older than the ground floor. The school declined during the last century and was closed in 1875. Now restored, it is an ancient monument. The shop is *open daily 08.00-21.00.*

Wast Hills Tunnel Once referred to as King's Norton Tunnel, this 2726yd bore is one of the longest in the country. It is usually difficult to see right through, and there are plenty of drips from the roof in even the driest weather. A steam-powered – and later a diesel-powered – tunnel tug service used to operate in the days of horse-drawn boats, as there is no towpath. The old iron brackets and insulators that still line the roof were installed to carry telegraph lines through the tunnel. Grandiose bridges (nos. 69 and 70) span the cuttings at either end.

Bournville Garden Factory Bournville, Birmingham B30 1UB. The creation of the Cadbury family, who moved their cocoa and chocolate manufacturing business south from the centre of Birmingham. The Bournville estate was begun in the late 1800s and is an interesting example of controlled suburban development. There were once old canal wharves here, which became disused when most of the ingredients travelled by rail – but the sidings closed in the late 1960s and now regrettably everything comes by road. There is a circular walking tour around Bournville village, visit www.bvt.org.uk for details.

Cadbury World Bournville, Birmingham (0844 880 7667; www.cadburyworld.co.uk). The ultimate chocoholic's dream come true – the chance to see it; feel it, smell it and taste it and then do it all over again. Restaurant, shops, snack bar, picnic and play areas. *Open all year, daily.* Opening times vary, so telephone for details. Charge.

Selly Manor and Minworth Greaves Maple Road, Bourneville B30 2AE (0121 472 0199; www.sellymanormuseum.org.uk/explore-visit-us/minworth-greaves). Two half-timbered Birmingham houses of the 13th- and early 14th-C re-erected in the 1920s and 1930s in Bournville. They contain a collection of old furniture and domestic equipment. *Open all year Tue-Fri 10.00-17.00, also Apr-Sep, Sat and Sun 14.00-17.00; closed Nov-Mar, Sat-Mon.* Charge. The nearest point of access from the canal is at Bournville station: walk west to the Cadbury's entrance. There is a public right of way (Birdcage Walk) through the works: bear right at the fork, then turn right at the village green. The two houses are close by, on the left. Selly Oak and Bournville both have a *PO*. For more information contact the Bournville Village Trust, Estate Office, Oak Tree Lane, Bourneville B30 1UB (0844 686 1164; www.bvt.org.uk).

Pubs and Restaurants

1 The Navigation Inn 1 Wharf Road, King's Norton B30 3LS (0121 458 1652; www.johnbarras.com/pub/navigation-inn-kings-norton-birmingham/p0754). About 100yds west of bridge 71. Guest real ales change regularly in this large rambling pub, which offers food *daily 12.00-22.00.* Family-friendly, garden and sports TV. *Open Mon-Sun 11.00-23.00 (Fri 22.30).*

2 The Red Lion 229 Vicarage Road, Kings Heath B14 7LY (0121 444 2803; www.emberpubanddining.co.uk/the-red-lion-kings-heath). ½ mile east of Bridge 75, along A4040 Pershore Road. An imposing piece of early 20th-C Grade II listed, Neo-Gothic architecture, this family pub serves real ales and classic pub fare, which is available *Mon-Sat11.30-22.00 & Sun 11.00-22.00.* Outside drinking area and a folk club *Wed.* Quiz *Thu & Sun.* Family-friendly, outside seating, newspapers, sports TV and Wi-Fi. *Open Mon-Fri 11.30-23.00 (Fri 00.00) & Sat-Sun 10.00-00.00 (Sun 23.00).*

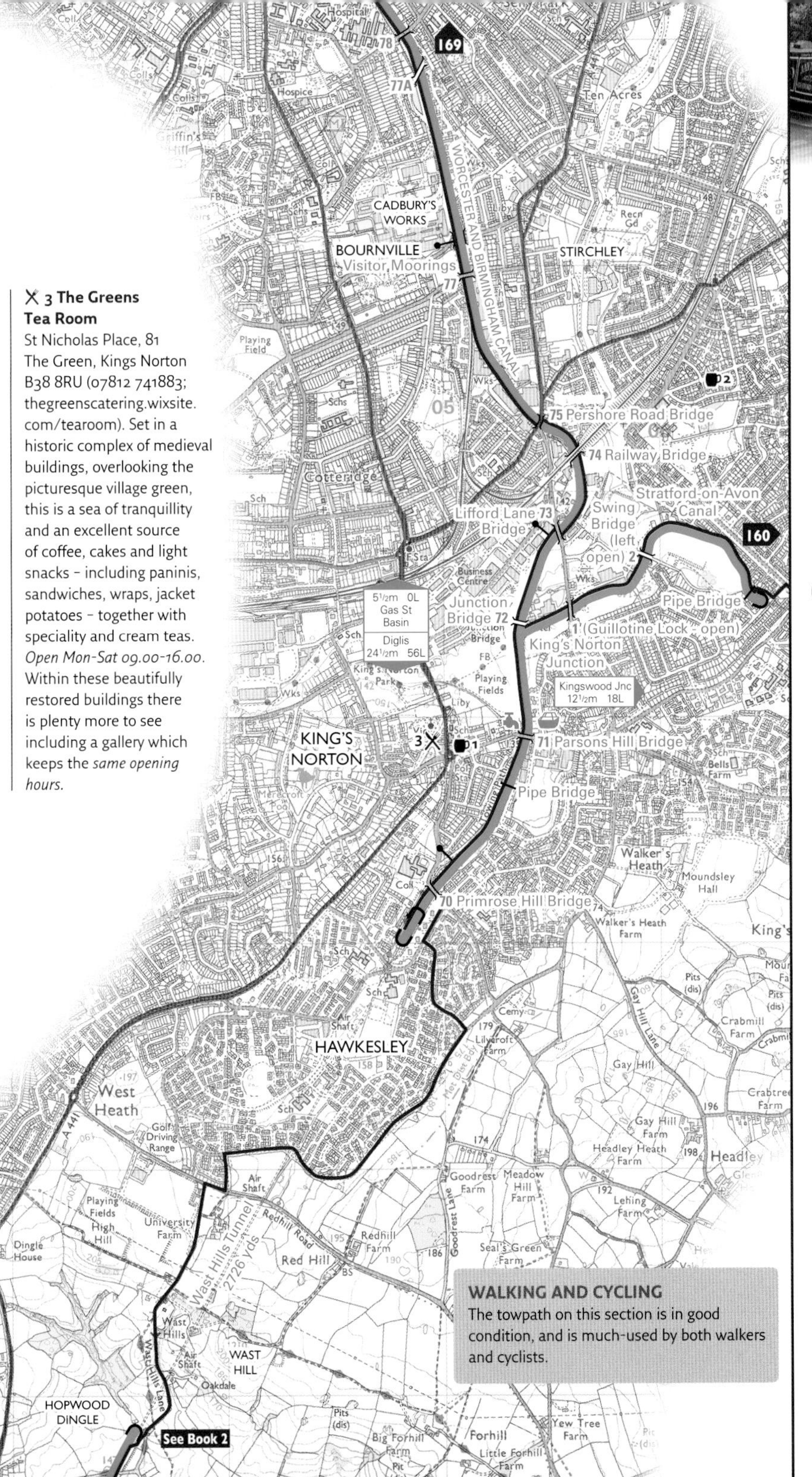

X 3 The Greens Tea Room
St Nicholas Place, 81 The Green, Kings Norton B38 8RU (07812 741883; thegreenscatering.wixsite.com/tearoom). Set in a historic complex of medieval buildings, overlooking the picturesque village green, this is a sea of tranquillity and an excellent source of coffee, cakes and light snacks – including paninis, sandwiches, wraps, jacket potatoes – together with speciality and cream teas. *Open Mon-Sat 09.00-16.00.* Within these beautifully restored buildings there is plenty more to see including a gallery which keeps the *same opening hours.*

WALKING AND CYCLING
The towpath on this section is in good condition, and is much-used by both walkers and cyclists.

Soon the railway vanishes briefly behind the buildings of Selly Oak. Between bridge 80 and the next, skewed, railway bridge is the site of the junction with the Dudley Canal, but currently little trace remains here now of either the junction or the canal itself. North of here the canal and railway together shrug off industry and town, and head north on an embankment towards Birmingham in splendid isolation and attractive surroundings. Below on either side is the green spaciousness of residential Edgbaston, its botanical gardens and woods. A hospital is on the west side. The University of Birmingham is on the east side; among its many large buildings the most conspicuous is the Chamberlain Campanile Tower, which was erected in 1900. At one of the bridges near the University, two Roman forts used to stand; but most of the evidence of them was obliterated by the building of the canal and railway. Only a reconstructed part of the larger fort now exists. There is a useful *supermarket* just south of bridge 80. Past the University's *moorings*, canal and railway enter a cutting, in which their enjoyable seclusion from the neighbourhood is complete; the charming old bridges are high, while the cutting is steep and always lined by overhanging foliage. It is a remarkable approach to Birmingham. The railway is the canal's almost constant companion, dipping away here and there to reappear a short distance further on; but trains are not too intrusive and in a way their appearance heightens the remoteness that attaches to this length of canal. At one stage the two routes pass through short tunnels side by side: the canal's tunnel, Edgbaston, is the northernmost of the five on this canal and the only one with a towpath through it. It is a mere 105yds long. The Worcester & Birmingham Canal now completes its delightful approach to Birmingham. The railway disappears underneath in a tunnel to New Street station, while the canal makes a sharp left turn to the basin. The terminus of the Worcester & Birmingham Canal is the former stop lock at Gas Street Basin; this is known as Worcester Bar: originally there was a physical barrier here between the Worcester & Birmingham Canal and the much older Birmingham Canal. The latter refused to allow a junction, and for several years goods had to be transhipped at this point from one canal to the other. This absurd situation was remedied by an Act of Parliament in 1815, by which a stop lock was allowed to be inserted to connect the two canals. Nowadays the stop gates are kept open and one can pass straight through, on to the Birmingham Canal (*see* page 39). Don't leave your boat unattended in this area, although Gas Street Basin should be OK.

The Dudley No 2 Canal This canal used to join the Worcester & Birmingham Canal at Selly Oak, thus providing a southern bypass round Birmingham. The eastern end of the canal is currently being restored under the auspices of the Lapal Canal Trust (www.lapal.org.uk) and will be partly re-opened in the not too distant future. The tremendously long (3795yds) Lapal Tunnel, now collapsed, emerged 2 miles from Selly Oak. This bore was more like a drainpipe than a navigable tunnel – it was only 7ft 9in wide, a few inches wider than the boats that used it, and headroom was limited to a scant 6ft. Boats were assisted through by a pumping engine flushing water along the tunnel, but it must still have been a night-marishly claustrophobic trip for the boatmen.

● **Edgbaston**
West Midlands. All services. A desirable residential suburb of Birmingham, Edgbaston is bisected by the canal.

Birmingham Botanical Gardens and Glasshouses Westbourne Road, Edgbaston, Birmingham B15 3TR (0121 454 1860; www.birminghambotanicalgardens.org.uk). Fifteen acres of beautiful gardens and four exotic glasshouses together with the National Bonsai Collection and a range of colourful birds and wildfowl. Gallery, sculptures and playground. Gift shop, plant sales and tearoom. *Open Apr-Sep Mon-Fri 10.00-18.00 & Sat-Sun 10.00-19.00 and Oct-Mar 10.00-17.00. Closed Xmas & Boxing Day*. Last admission *30 mins before closing*. Charge.

Perrott's Folly 44 Waterworks Road, Edgbaston B16 9AL (www.perrottsfolly.co.uk). About ¾ mile west of bridge 86, not far from the Plough & Harrow Hotel. This seven-storey tower was built in 1758 by John Perrott and claims to be Birmingham's most eccentric building. One theory as to its origin is that Mr Perrott could, from its height, gaze upon his late wife's grave 10 miles away. One of the Two Towers of Gondor, featured in J.R.R. Tolkien's *Lord of the Rings*, is thought to have been based upon this building. Tolkien's last address in Birmingham was at 4 Highfield Road, opposite the Plough & Harrow. From 1884–1984 the folly was used as a weather station and was subsequently renovated. For further insight into its more contemporary application visit www.theguardian.com/society/2013/jan/29/tower-inspired-tolkien-bought.

For more information on Birmingham, *see* page 41.

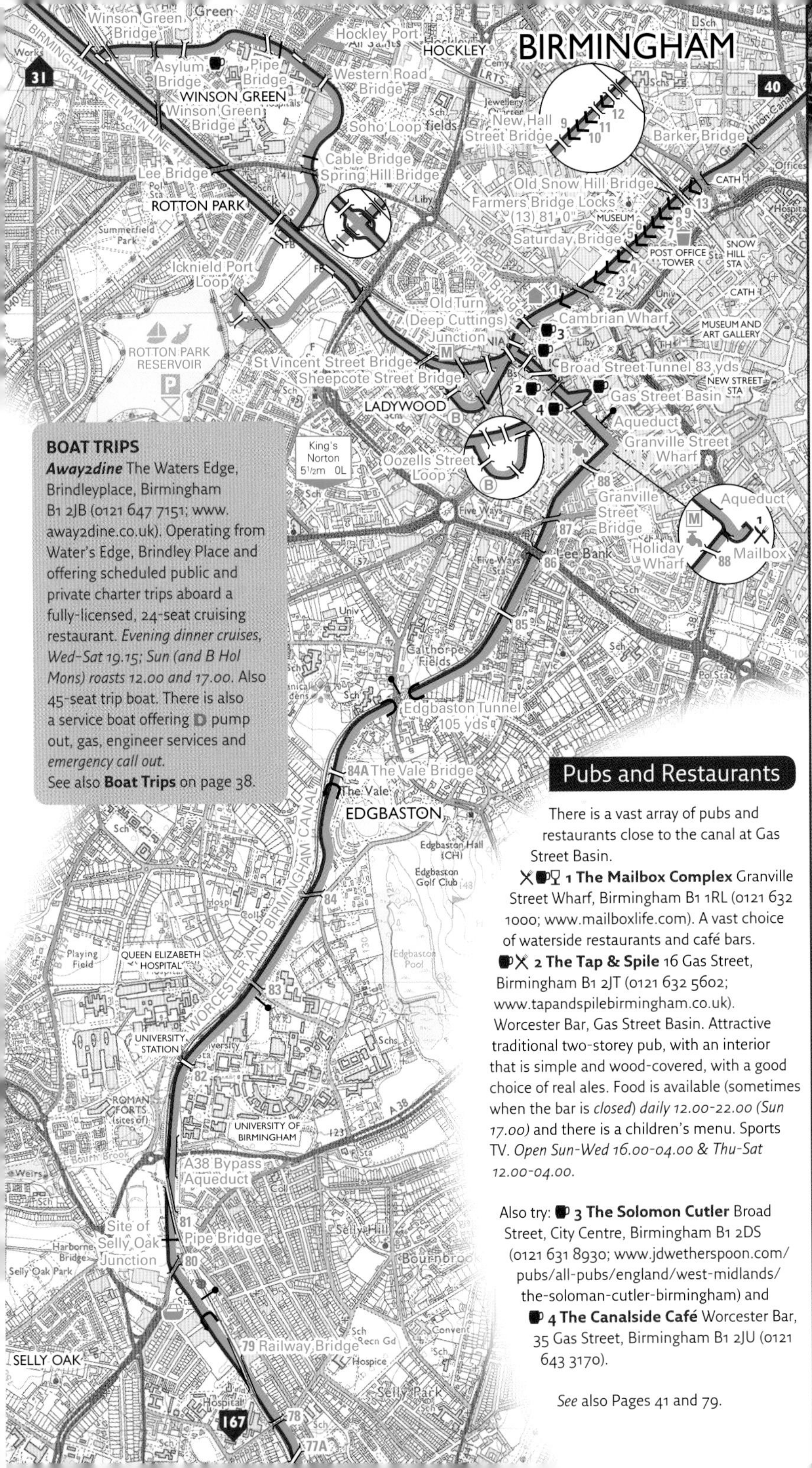

BOAT TRIPS

Away2dine The Waters Edge, Brindleyplace, Birmingham B1 2JB (0121 647 7151; www.away2dine.co.uk). Operating from Water's Edge, Brindley Place and offering scheduled public and private charter trips aboard a fully-licensed, 24-seat cruising restaurant. *Evening dinner cruises, Wed–Sat 19.15; Sun (and B Hol Mons) roasts 12.00 and 17.00.* Also 45-seat trip boat. There is also a service boat offering D pump out, gas, engineer services and *emergency call out.*

See also **Boat Trips** on page 38.

Pubs and Restaurants

There is a vast array of pubs and restaurants close to the canal at Gas Street Basin.

1 The Mailbox Complex Granville Street Wharf, Birmingham B1 1RL (0121 632 1000; www.mailboxlife.com). A vast choice of waterside restaurants and café bars.

2 The Tap & Spile 16 Gas Street, Birmingham B1 2JT (0121 632 5602; www.tapandspilebirmingham.co.uk). Worcester Bar, Gas Street Basin. Attractive traditional two-storey pub, with an interior that is simple and wood-covered, with a good choice of real ales. Food is available (sometimes when the bar is *closed*) *daily 12.00–22.00 (Sun 17.00)* and there is a children's menu. Sports TV. *Open Sun–Wed 16.00–04.00 & Thu–Sat 12.00–04.00.*

Also try: **3 The Solomon Cutler** Broad Street, City Centre, Birmingham B1 2DS (0121 631 8930; www.jdwetherspoon.com/pubs/all-pubs/england/west-midlands/the-soloman-cutler-birmingham) and **4 The Canalside Café** Worcester Bar, 35 Gas Street, Birmingham B1 2JU (0121 643 3170).

See also Pages 41 and 79.

WILDLIFE

The *Speckled Wood* is a double-brooded butterfly, flying April–June and July–September. It favours clearings and is fond of sunbathing. The upperwings are dark brown with pale markings; the underwings are rufous brown. The caterpillars feed on grasses.

The *Large Skipper* favours grassy places of all kinds and flies during June and July. The upperwings are dark brown and orange-brown with pale markings. The underwings are buffish orange with paler spots. In common with most other skipper butterflies, at rest the Large Skipper often holds its wings at an angle and can look rather moth-like. The caterpillars feed on grasses.

The *Holly Blue* actually appears silvery in flight. The violet-blue upperwings are seldom seen well as it rests showing white, black-dotted underwings. There are two broods, flying April–May, laying eggs on holly; flying August–September and laying eggs on ivy.

The *Orange-Tip* is an attractive spring butterfly, seen flying between April and June. The male has an orange patch on the dark-tipped forewing, which is absent in the female. The hind underwing of both sexes is marbled green and white. The larvae feed mainly on the cuckoo flower.

The *Banded Demoiselle* is an attractive damselfly, often found resting among waterside vegetation. Males are seen in small, fluttering groups hovering over water; the flight of the female is rather feeble. The body of the male is blue with a metallic sheen; the smoky wings show a conspicuous blue 'thumbprint' mark. The female has a green body, with metallic sheen, and greenish brown wings. Flies May–August.

The *Moorhen* is a widespread and familiar wetland bird: often wary, in urban areas they can become rather tame. The adult has brownish wings but otherwise mainly dark grey-black plumage. It has a distinctive yellow-tipped red bill and a frontal shield on its head, with white feathers on the sides of the undertail and a white line along the flanks. Juvenile birds have pale brown plumage. The moorhen's legs and long toes are yellowish. It swims with a jerky movement, with tail flicking. In flight the moorhen shows dangling legs.

The *Mute Swan* is a large and distinctive water bird, the commonest swan in Britain. The adult has pure white plumage, black legs and an orange-red bill. The black blob at the base of the bill is smaller in the female than the male. Young cygnets are often seen accompanying the mother. While swimming, the bird usually holds its neck in an elegant curve.

The *Great Crested Grebe* is a slender water bird with a long, thin neck. From a distance the bird looks strikingly black and white, although upperparts are mainly grey-brown and underparts white. In summer both sexes acquire a prominent orange-reddish-brown ruff and show a crest to their dark cap. In winter they lose the ruff but retain the dark cap and a suggestion of a crest. Pairs perform elaborate ritual displays in spring and build nests among the emerging vegetation.

The *Devil's-bit Scabious* is an erect perennial of damp grassland, woodland rides and marshes. The short, thick rhizome has an abruptly cut-off end – bitten off by the devil! The basal leaves are spoon shaped, in a rosette; the narrow stem leaves in opposite pairs, the upper ones narrow. Blue-purple flowers (rarely pink or white) are borne in rounded heads, 15–25mm across, and appear June–October. This plant is the food plant of the, declining Marsh Fritillary butterfly. The word scabious derives from the former herbal use of this and related plants to cure scabies and other unpleasant skin complaints. The lookalike Field and Small Scabious have lilac flowers, more than 25mm across.

The *Marsh Fritillary* has beautifully marked wings. It flies May–June but is only active when it is sunny. Favouring damp heaths and moors, but also dry chalk grassland, the larvae feed on devil's-bit scabious and plantains.

Boating through Shardlow

TRENT & MERSEY CANAL

MAXIMUM DIMENSIONS

Derwent Mouth to Horninglow Basin, Burton upon Trent
Length: 72'
Beam: 14'
Headroom: 7'
Stenson lock is very tight for 14ft beam craft and Weston Lock is tight for boats of 72ft length.

Burton upon Trent to south end of Harecastle Tunnel
Length: 72'
Beam: 7'
Headroom: 6' 3"

Harecastle Tunnel
Length: 72'
Beam: 7'
Headroom: 5' 9"

North end of Harecastle Tunnel to Croxton Aqueduct
Length: 72'
Beam: 7'
Headroom: 7'

Croxton Aqueduct to Preston Brook Tunnel
Length: 72'
Beam: 8' 2"
Headroom: 6' 3"

MANAGERS:

0303 040 4040

Derwent Mouth to south portal of Harecastle Tunnel:
enquiries.centralshires@canalrivertrust.org.uk
South portal of Harecastle Tunnel to Preston Brook:
enquiries.manchesterpennine@canalrivertrust.org.uk

MILEAGE

DERWENT MOUTH to:
Swarkestone Lock: 7 miles
Willington: 12¼ miles
Horninglow Wharf: 16½ miles
Barton Turn: 21¼ miles
Fradley, junction with Coventry Canal: 26¼ miles
Great Haywood, junction with Staffordshire & Worcestershire Canal: 39 miles
Stone: 48½ miles
Stoke Top Lock, junction with Caldon Canal: 58 miles
Harding's Wood, junction with Macclesfield Canal: 63¾ miles
King's Lock, Middlewich, junction with Middlewich Branch: 76¼ miles
Anderton Lift, for River Weaver: 86½ miles
PRESTON BROOK north end of tunnel and Bridgewater Canal: 93½ miles

Locks: 76

This early canal was originally conceived partly as a roundabout link between the ports of Liverpool and Hull, while passing through the busy area of the Potteries and mid-Cheshire, and terminating either in the River Weaver or in the Mersey. Its construction was promoted by Josiah Wedgwood (1730–95), the famous potter, aided by his friends Thomas Bentley and Erasmus Darwin. In 1766 the Trent & Mersey Canal Act was passed by Parliament, authorising the building of a navigation from the River Trent at Shardlow to Runcorn Gap, where it would join the proposed extension of the Bridgewater Canal from Manchester.

The ageing James Brindley was appointed engineer for the canal. Construction began at once and in 1777 the Trent & Mersey Canal was opened. In the total 93 miles between Derwent Mouth and Preston Brook, the Trent & Mersey gained connection with no fewer than nine other canals or significant branches.

By the 1820s the slowly-sinking tunnel at Harecastle had become a serious bottle-neck, so Thomas Telford recommended building a second tunnel beside the old one. His recommendation was eventually accepted by the company and the new tunnel was completed in under three years, in 1827. Although the Trent & Mersey was taken over in 1845 by the new North Staffordshire Railway Company, the canal flourished until World War I.

Look out for the handsome cast iron mileposts, which actually measure the mileage from Shardlow, not Derwent Mouth. There are 59 originals, from the Rougeley and Dixon foundry in Stone, and 34 replacements, bearing the mark of the Trent & Mersey Canal Society – T & MCS 1977.

Shardlow

The Trent & Mersey Canal begins at Derwent Mouth, some 2½ miles upstream of the point where the Soar Navigation enters the River Trent at a

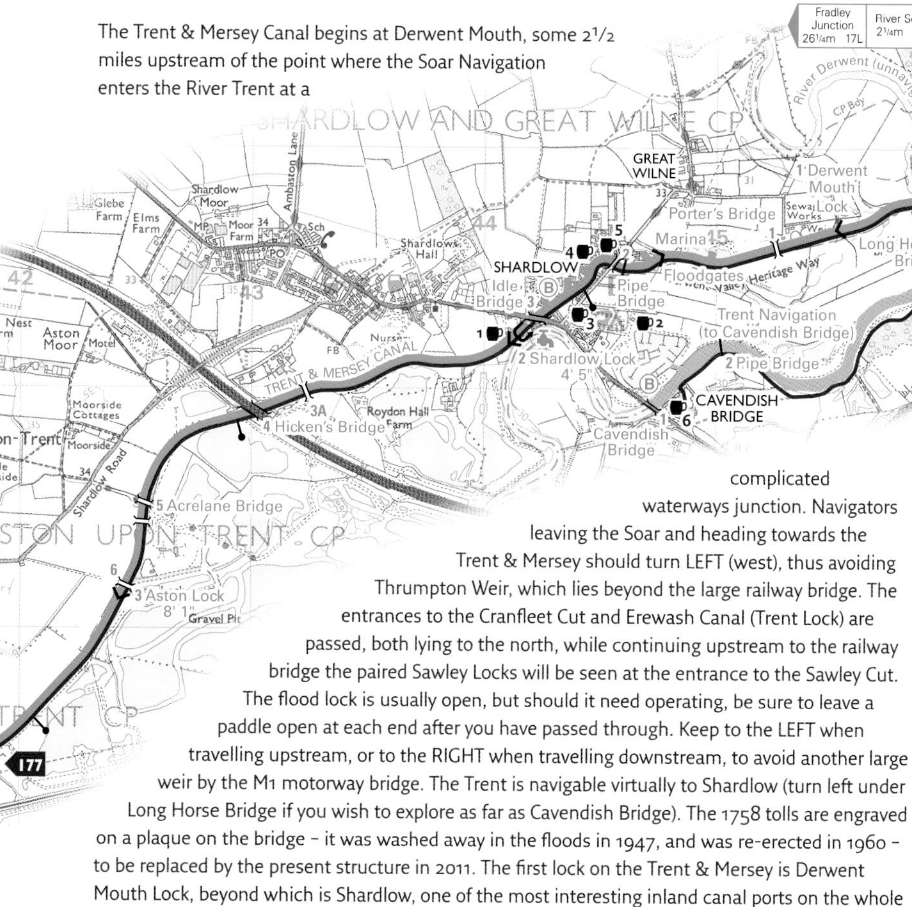

complicated waterways junction. Navigators leaving the Soar and heading towards the Trent & Mersey should turn LEFT (west), thus avoiding Thrumpton Weir, which lies beyond the large railway bridge. The entrances to the Cranfleet Cut and Erewash Canal (Trent Lock) are passed, both lying to the north, while continuing upstream to the railway bridge the paired Sawley Locks will be seen at the entrance to the Sawley Cut. The flood lock is usually open, but should it need operating, be sure to leave a paddle open at each end after you have passed through. Keep to the LEFT when travelling upstream, or to the RIGHT when travelling downstream, to avoid another large weir by the M1 motorway bridge. The Trent is navigable virtually to Shardlow (turn left under Long Horse Bridge if you wish to explore as far as Cavendish Bridge). The 1758 tolls are engraved on a plaque on the bridge – it was washed away in the floods in 1947, and was re-erected in 1960 – to be replaced by the present structure in 2011. The first lock on the Trent & Mersey is Derwent Mouth Lock, beyond which is Shardlow, one of the most interesting inland canal ports on the whole inland waterway network. Note, for example, the old salt warehouse by Shardlow Lock.

Boatyards

Ⓑ**J.D Narrowboats Limited** Dobson Wharf, The Wharf, Shardlow DE72 2GJ (01332 792271/07952 378679; www.jdnarrowboats.com). D Pump out, gas, bespoke boat and shell builders, long and short-term mooring, crane, boat and engine sales, slipway, engine repairs, diesel fuel cleaning, painting, solid fuel, toilets.

Ⓑ**Millar Marine** Warehouse C, 24 The Wharf, Shardlow DE72 2GH (01332 793358; www.chandleryuk.co.uk). Extensive chandlery (including on-line sales). *Open Mon–Sat 09.00–16.30 (Sat 15.00). Closed B Hol Mon.*

Ⓑ✕ **Sawley Marina** Sawley, Long Eaton, NG10 3AE (0115 907 7400; www.bwml.co.uk). P D Pump out, gas, overnight and long-term mooring, winter storage, slipway, boat and engine sales, engine repairs, telephone, chandlery, solid fuel, toilets, showers, restaurant (*closed Mon*), laundrette. groceries.

Ⓑ**Dobsons Boatyard** The Wharf, Shardlow DE72 2GJ (01332 792271; www.jdnarrowboats.com) D Pump out, gas, overnight and long-term mooring, slipway, boat building, boat and engine sales, engine repairs, wet dock, alterations, painting, blacking.

Ⓑ✕**Shardlow Marina** London Road, Shardlow DE72 2GL (01332 792832; www.shardlowmarina.co.uk). On the River Trent. Facilities for moorers only. D Pump out, gas, long-term mooring, slipway, boat sales, chandlery, laundrette, toilets and showers. Caravan and camping site. Bar and restaurant on site.

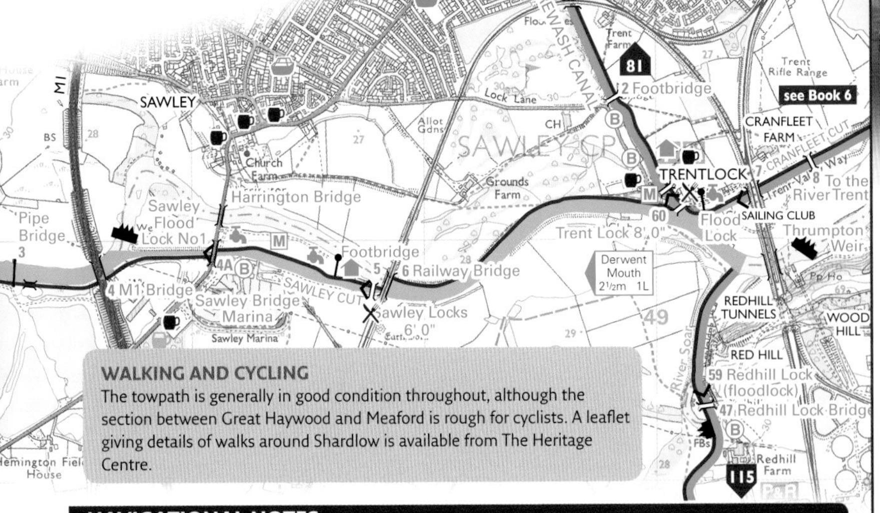

WALKING AND CYCLING

The towpath is generally in good condition throughout, although the section between Great Haywood and Meaford is rough for cyclists. A leaflet giving details of walks around Shardlow is available from The Heritage Centre.

NAVIGATIONAL NOTES

1. Those leaving the canal and heading towards the River Trent should not pass Shardlow floodgates if the warning light shows red.
2. The Derwent is not navigable north of Derwent Mouth and the Trent is not navigable beyond Shardlow Marina, Cavendish Bridge.
3. The entrance to Shardlow Marina can be difficult to spot and boaters should be aware of gravel banks in the area.

Sawley Cut
In addition to a large marina and a well patronised CRT mooring site, the Derby Motor Boat Club has a base on the Sawley Cut. There are windlasses for sale at Sawley Lock, as well as the more conventional facilities, and CRT showers. It is beautifully tended, with lots of flowers and some jokey sculptures. Have a look at the flood level markers – they are astonishing!

Shardlow
Derbs. PO, tel, stores. Few canal travellers will want to pass through Shardlow without stopping. Everywhere there are living examples of large-scale canal architecture, as well as long-established necessities such as canal pubs. By the lock is the biggest and best of these buildings – the 18th-C Trent Mill, now the Clock Warehouse. Restored in 1979, it has a large central arch where boats once entered to unload.
Shardlow Heritage Centre London Road, Shardlow DE72 2GA (adjacent to the Clock Warehouse (www.homepages.which.net/~shardlow.heritage/). Exhibitions of local canal history and replica of a narrowboat back cabin. Plus a calendar of canal-centred events. *Open Easter–Oct, Sat, Sun and B Hols 12.00–17.00.* Modest entry charge.

Pubs and Restaurants

1 The Clock Warehouse London Road, Shardlow DE72 2GL (01332 792844; www.clockwarehousepub.co.uk). Real ale, and food *L and E, all day.* Children welcome, and there is a garden. Moorings.
2 The Old Marina Bar & Restaurant Shardlow Marina, London Road, Shardlow DE72 2GL (01332 799797; www.theoldmarinabar.co.uk). Meals *L and E;* carvery *Sun 12.00–16.00;* specials during *week.* Outside seating. Children welcome. Live music *Fri and Sat.*
3 The Navigation Inn 143 London Road, Shardlow DE722HJ (01332 792918). By bridge 3. Haunted pub, serving real ale, and home-made food *L and E.* Garden with children's play area. Moorings. Live music *Fri.*
4 The Malt Shovel 49 The Wharf, Shardlow DE72 2HG (01332 792066; www.maltshovelshardlow.co.uk). By bridge 2. Friendly canalside pub, built in 1779 and serving real ale. Excellent food with home-made specials *L and Thu E.* Breakfasts. Children welcome. Outside seating. *Open all day from 11.00 Mon-Fri and 10.00 Sat & Sun.* Wi-Fi.
5 The New Inn 61 The Wharf, Shardlow DE72 2HG (01332 793330; www.thenewinnshardlow.co.uk). Next to the Malt Shovel. Real ale, and bar meals *L and E.* Children and dogs welcome. Garden and outside seating. Wi-Fi. *Open all day.*
6 The Old Crown Cavendish Bridge, Shardlow DE72 2HL (01332 792392; www.maltshovelshardlow.co.uk). Friendly riverside pub. Real ale. Bar meals served *Tue-Sun L & Tue-Thu and Sat E.* Children welcome. Garden with play area.

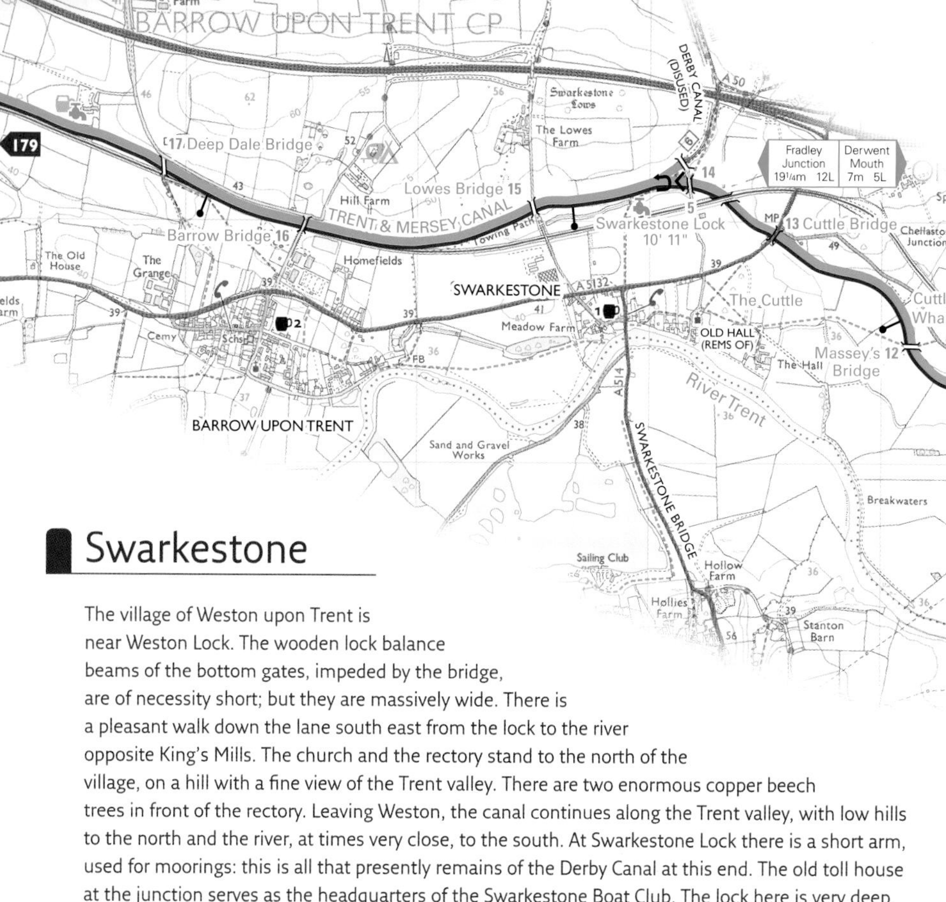

Swarkestone

The village of Weston upon Trent is near Weston Lock. The wooden lock balance beams of the bottom gates, impeded by the bridge, are of necessity short; but they are massively wide. There is a pleasant walk down the lane south east from the lock to the river opposite King's Mills. The church and the rectory stand to the north of the village, on a hill with a fine view of the Trent valley. There are two enormous copper beech trees in front of the rectory. Leaving Weston, the canal continues along the Trent valley, with low hills to the north and the river, at times very close, to the south. At Swarkestone Lock there is a short arm, used for moorings: this is all that presently remains of the Derby Canal at this end. The old toll house at the junction serves as the headquarters of the Swarkestone Boat Club. The lock here is very deep, with a fall of almost 11ft. As with the other deep locks, it has very low top gates which incorporate substantial paddles. The village of Barrow upon Trent lies between the canal and the river – the countryside is green and pleasant, with only the occasional train rumbling by to disturb the peace.

Weston upon Trent

Derbs. PO, tel, stores. A scattered village that is in fact not very close to the Trent. The isolated church is splendidly situated beside woods on top of a hill, its sturdy tower crowned by a short 14th-C spire. Inside are fine aisle windows of the same period. The lock gardens make the approach from the canal particularly attractive.

Swarkestone

Derbs. PO box, tel. The main feature of Swarkestone is the 18th-C five-arch stone bridge over the main channel of the River Trent. An elevated causeway then carries the road on stone arches all the way across the Trent's flood plain to the village of Stanton by Bridge. It was at Swarkestone that Bonnie Prince Charlie, in the rising of 1745, gave up his attempt for the throne of England and returned to his defeat at Culloden. In a field nearby are the few remains of Sir Richard Harpur's Tudor mansion, which was demolished before 1750. The Summer House, a handsome, lonely building, overlooks a square enclosure called the Cuttle. Jacobean in origin, it is thought that it may have been the scene of bull-baiting, although it seems more likely it was just a 'bowle alley'. Restored by the Landmark Trust, it is available for holiday lets – telephone (01628 825925) for details. The Harpurs moved to Calke following the demolition of their mansion after the Civil War. The pub in the village, and monuments in the church, which is tucked away in the back lanes, are a reminder of the family.

Barrow upon Trent

Derbs. PO box, tel. A small, quiet village set back from the canal. A lane from the church leads down to the River Trent. Opposite there is a 'pinfold', once an enclosure for stray animals. The surviving lodge house stands opposite a mellow terrace of old workmen's cottages.

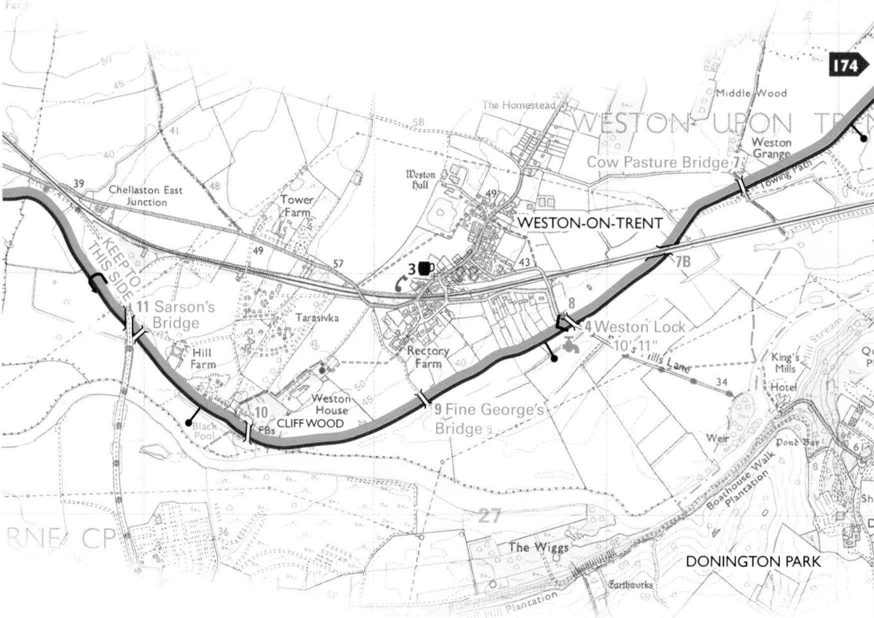

Pubs and Restaurants

1 The Crew & Harpur Arms Woodshop Lane, Swarkestone DE73 7JA (01332 700641; www.creweharpurpub.co.uk). By the river bridge. Real ale, and bar meals served *all day, every day* in this handsome pub. Riverside seating and garden. Children welcome. B&B.

2 The Brookfield Brookfield, Barrow upon Trent D73 7NA (01332 700128; www.barrowupontrentparish.co.uk/blog/?page_id=22). A friendly village pub, serving real ales and a variety of bar snacks, that welcomes walkers, cyclists and boaters. Children and pet friendly. Beer garden and large screen TV. Pool, darts and dominoes. *Open Mon-Fri E and all day Sat & Sun.*

3 The Coopers Arms Weston Hall, The Green, Weston upon Trent DE72 2BJ (01332 690002; www.thecoopers-arms.co.uk). So dark was the basement area of Weston Hall, that the Cooper family used it to force rhubarb and chicory. Today, re-invented as a country pub, this establishment serves appetising food *daily L and E*, together with a selection of real ales. Children welcome and garden. Regular *monthly* live entertainment. *Open all day from 11.30.*

A HOP, A SKIP, AND A JUMP TO DERBY

The Derby Canal, which left the Trent & Mersey at Swarkestone and joined the Erewash at Sandiacre, has long been disused. One condition of its building, and a constant drain on its profits, was the free carriage of 5000 tons of coal to Derby each year, for the use of the poor.

But one of the most unusual loads was transported on 19 April 1826, when 'a fine lama, a kangaroo, a ram with four horns, and a female goat with two young kids, remarkably handsome animals' arrived in Derby by canal 'as a present from Lord Byron to a Gentleman whose residence is in the neighbourhood, all of which had been picked up in the course of the voyage of the *Blonde* to the Sandwich Islands in the autumn of 1824'.

Willington

Just by bridge 18 is Arleston House, an attractive old building with ground-floor walls of stone and the upper tiers of brick. This is followed by Stenson Lock, the last of the wide locks until Middlewich – it has a massive fall of 12ft 4in, and is overlooked by a useful *coffee shop*. Stenson is a small farming centre and a popular mooring spot with a large marina. After passing through a railway bridge, the canal changes course and heads off in a south easterly direction towards Burton upon Trent.

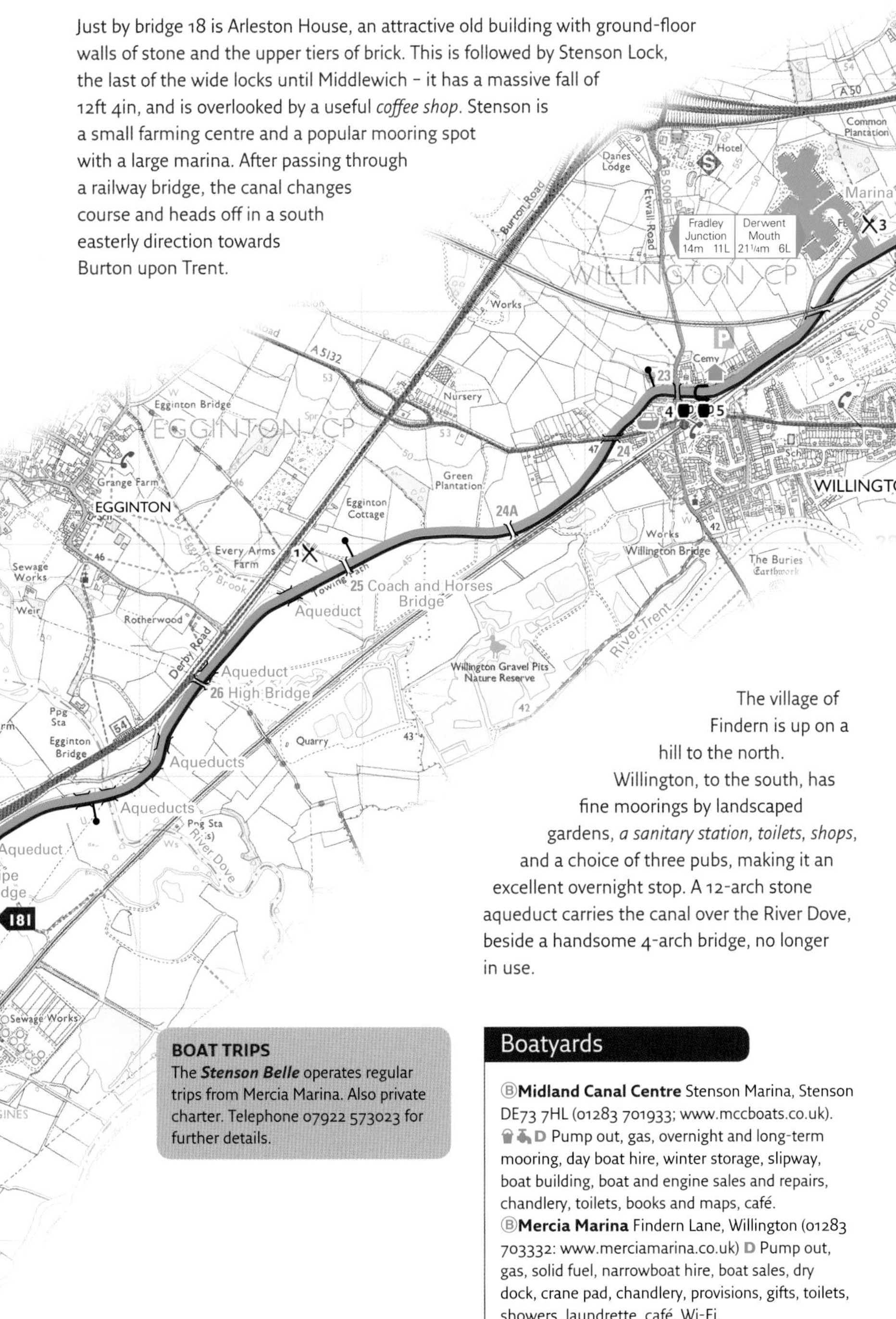

The village of Findern is up on a hill to the north. Willington, to the south, has fine moorings by landscaped gardens, *a sanitary station, toilets, shops*, and a choice of three pubs, making it an excellent overnight stop. A 12-arch stone aqueduct carries the canal over the River Dove, beside a handsome 4-arch bridge, no longer in use.

BOAT TRIPS

The ***Stenson Belle*** operates regular trips from Mercia Marina. Also private charter. Telephone 07922 573023 for further details.

Boatyards

Ⓑ**Midland Canal Centre** Stenson Marina, Stenson DE73 7HL (01283 701933; www.mccboats.co.uk). **D** Pump out, gas, overnight and long-term mooring, day boat hire, winter storage, slipway, boat building, boat and engine sales and repairs, chandlery, toilets, books and maps, café.

Ⓑ**Mercia Marina** Findern Lane, Willington (01283 703332: www.merciamarina.co.uk) **D** Pump out, gas, solid fuel, narrowboat hire, boat sales, dry dock, crane pad, chandlery, provisions, gifts, toilets, showers, laundrette, café, Wi-Fi.

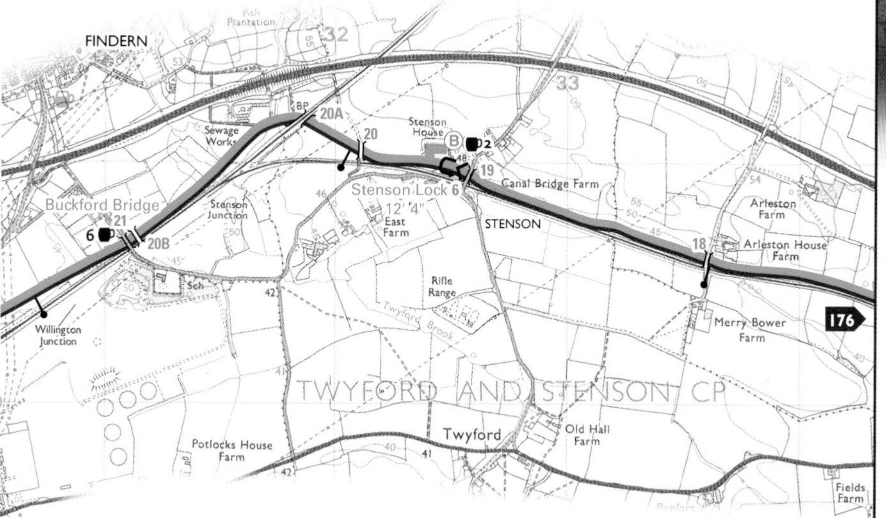

- **Repton**
  Derbs. PO. 1½ miles south east of Willington (over the River Trent) is Repton, one of the oldest towns in England, which was once the capital of Mercia. The crypt below St Wystan's Church was built in the 10th C. One of the finest examples of Saxon architecture in the country, this crypt was completely forgotten until the end of the 18th C when a man fell into it while digging a grave. Repton public school dates from 1557, and there is much of historical interest in the school and the town.
- **Willington**
  Derbs. PO, tel, stores, delicatessen, chemist, off-licence, takeaway, station. The railway bisects this busy little village on an embankment. There are three pubs, all close together.
- **Findern**
  Derbs. PO, tel, stores. A small, quiet village where Jedekiah Strutt, the inventor of the ribbed stocking frame, served a 7-year apprenticeship with the local wheelwright. At one time the village green was no more than a waste patch used by cars as a short cut, and a parking place. When suggestions were made to turn it into a formal cross roads, the indignant Women's Institute galvanised the villagers into actually uprooting all traces of tarmac from the green and turfing the whole area properly.
- **Egginton**
  Derbs. A quiet village lying off the A38. The church, set apart from the village, is pleasingly irregular from the outside, with a large chancel and a squat tower.

Pubs and Restaurants

1 Anoki Indian Restaurant Burton Road, Eggington (01283 704888; www.anoki.co.uk). Well regarded Indian restaurant and takeaway close to Bridge 25 serving meals *daily E.* Children welcome.

2 The Bubble Inn Stenson DE73 1HL (01283 703113; www.thebubbleinn.com). Alongside Stenson Lock and Marina, this modern pub in a converted barn serves real ale and bar meals *Mon-Fri L and E; Sat, Sun & B Hols all day.* Children welcome. Canalside garden. *Open all day.*

3 Willow Tree Tearoom Findern Lane, Willington DE65 6DW (01285 703700; www.merciamarina.co.uk/willow-tree-tea-room). *Open daily 08.30-17.00,* this tearoom serves a range of appetising food from breakfast through to lunches and afternoon tea, including toasties, salads, sandwiches, jacket potatoes cakes, coffee and teas.

4 The Rising Sun The Green, Willington DE65 6BP (01283 702116). Friendly village pub serving real ale. Reasonably priced bar food, including home-made pies, available *L and E.* Children welcome. Outside seating. Occasional live music.

5 The Dragon 11 The Green, Willington DE65 6BP (01283 704795; www.thedragonatwillington.co.uk). Popular and welcoming pub, with plenty of low beams. Real ale. Wide range of food available *Mon-Thu L and E; Fri-Sun & B Hol Mon all day.* Garden. Children welcome away from the bar. Moorings. *Regular* live music. *Open all day.*

6 Nadee 130 Heath Lane, Findern DE65 6AR (01283 701333; www.nadeerestaurant.co.uk). Adjacent to canal at bridge 21. Bar and Indian restaurant. Landscaped garden, including a 5-a-side football pitch. Children welcome. Marquee available for celebrations and parties. Mooring. *Open May-Sep Mon-Fri E & Sat, Sun and B Hol all day; Oct-Apr Mon-Sat E & Sun all day.*

Burton upon Trent

Ice cream, cold drinks and a *burger van* are available between Bridges 28 and 29. *Fish & chips* can be obtained 100yds north of Horninglow Basin, which has some services and a butterfly garden. The canal then passes along one side of Burton upon Trent, without entering the town. Many of the old canalside buildings have been demolished, but the waterside has been nicely tidied up, making the passage very pleasant. The lovely aroma of brewing - malt and hops - often pervades the town, usually strongest to the west. Dallow Lock is the first of the narrow locks, an altogether easier job of work than the wider ones to the east. Shobnall Basin is now used by a boatyard, and visitor moorings nearby are available from which to explore the town. The A38 then joins the canal, depriving the navigator of any peace. On the hills to the north west is the well-wooded Sinai Park - the moated 15th-C house here, now a farm, used to be the summer home of the monks from Burton Abbey. There is a fine canalside pub at Bridge 34. The village of Branston can be accessed from here via a pedestrian route passing under the busy A38 dual carriageway. The canal enters the new National Forest at bridge 30 - indeed an intricately carved seat reminds us of this - and will leave it just beyond Alrewas. The Bass Millennium Woodland, to the west of Branston Lock, is part of this major project.

Burton upon Trent
Staffs. All services. Known widely for its brewing industry, which originated here in the 13th C, when the monks at Burton Abbey discovered that an excellent beer could be brewed from the town's waters, because of their high gypsum content. At one time there were 31 breweries producing 3 million barrels of ale annually: alas, now only a few remain. The advent of the railways had an enormous effect on the street geography of Burton, for gradually a great network of railways took shape, connecting with each other and with the main line. These branches were mostly constructed at street level, and until recent years it was common for road traffic to be held up by endless goods trains chugging all over the town. Only the last vestiges of this system now remain. The east side of the town is bounded by the River Trent, on the other side of which are pleasant hills. The main shopping centre lies to the east of the railway station.
Marston's Brewery Visitor Centre Shobnall Road, Burton upon Trent DE14 2BG (01283 507391; www.marstonsbeercompany.co.uk). Tours of the brewery, including the unique and world-famous Burton Union system are available *Mon-Fri*. At the end of the tour you can enjoy a drink of real ale in the Visitor Centre. *Please telephone or visit website to check availability and to book.*
The Brewhouse Duke Street, Burton upon Trent DE14 1EB (01283 508100; www.eaststaffsbc.gov.uk/Brewhouse/Pages/default.aspx). Live entertainment in a 230-seat theatre, plus a gallery and bistro bar.
Tourist Information Centre Customer Service Centre, Market Place, High Street, Burton upon Trent DE14 1AH (01283 508000; www.enjoystaffordshire.com/Burton-Upon-Trent-Burton-upon-Trent-Tourist-Information/details/?dms=13&venue=2241503). *Open Mon-Fri 09.00-17.00 & Sat 11.00-16.00.*

Shobnall Basin
This is all that remains of the Bond End Canal, which gave the breweries the benefit of what was modern transport, before the coming of the railways.

Branston
Staffs. PO, tel, stores, chemist, takeaway, fish & chips. This is apparently the place where the famous pickle originated.

Boatyards

Ⓑ**Jannel Cruisers** Shobnall Marina, Shobnall Road, Burton upon Trent DE14 2AU (01283 542718; www.jannel.co.uk). In Shobnall Basin. D Pump out, gas, coal, overnight mooring, long-term mooring, winter storage, slipway, dry dock, chandlery, books and maps, boat-fitting, boat sales, engine repairs, surveyor, BSS inspections, toilets. ✕ **13 Café**.

WALKING AND CYCLING
Cycle Route 54 uses the towpath north of Burton upon Trent. It links Lichfield with Derby. Three walking trails around Burton upon Trent are available from the TIC. There are pleasant walks through Branston Water Park - telephone (01283) 508573 for more information.

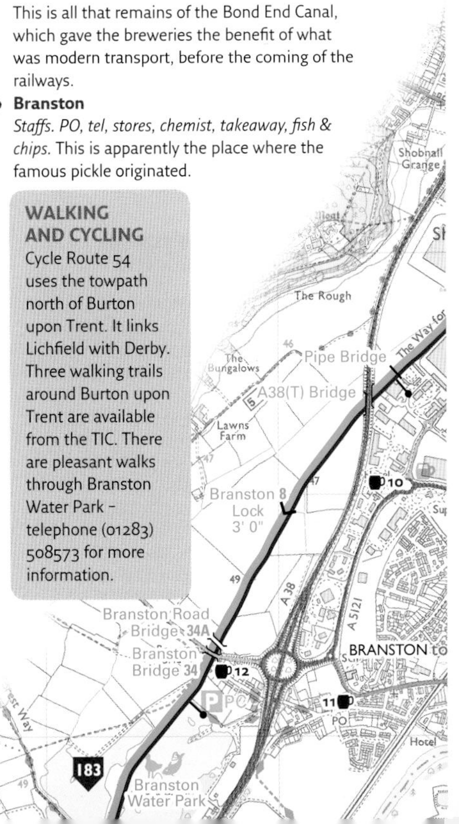

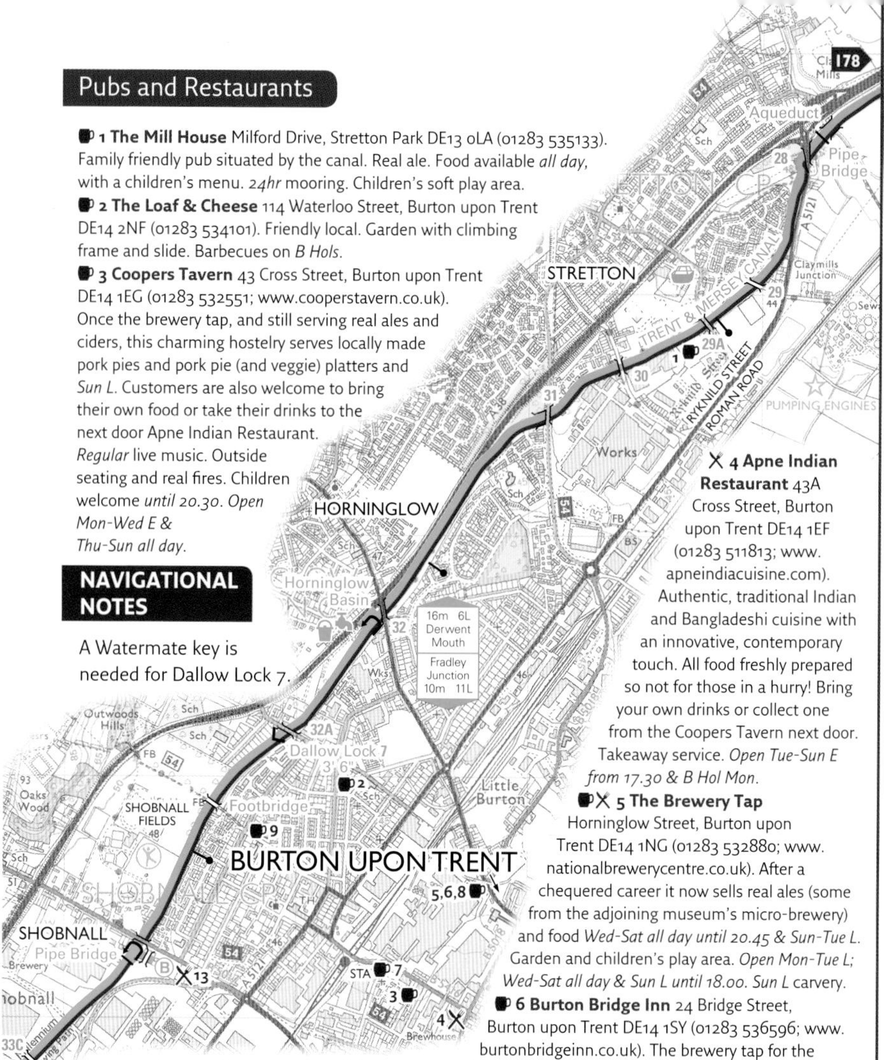

Pubs and Restaurants

1 The Mill House Milford Drive, Stretton Park DE13 0LA (01283 535133). Family friendly pub situated by the canal. Real ale. Food available *all day*, with a children's menu. *24hr* mooring. Children's soft play area.

2 The Loaf & Cheese 114 Waterloo Street, Burton upon Trent DE14 2NF (01283 534101). Friendly local. Garden with climbing frame and slide. Barbecues on *B Hols*.

3 Coopers Tavern 43 Cross Street, Burton upon Trent DE14 1EG (01283 532551; www.cooperstavern.co.uk). Once the brewery tap, and still serving real ales and ciders, this charming hostelry serves locally made pork pies and pork pie (and veggie) platters and *Sun L*. Customers are also welcome to bring their own food or take their drinks to the next door Apne Indian Restaurant. *Regular* live music. Outside seating and real fires. Children welcome *until 20.30. Open Mon-Wed E & Thu-Sun all day*.

4 Apne Indian Restaurant 43A Cross Street, Burton upon Trent DE14 1EF (01283 511813; www.apneindiacuisine.com). Authentic, traditional Indian and Bangladeshi cuisine with an innovative, contemporary touch. All food freshly prepared so not for those in a hurry! Bring your own drinks or collect one from the Coopers Tavern next door. Takeaway service. *Open Tue-Sun E from 17.30 & B Hol Mon*.

5 The Brewery Tap Horninglow Street, Burton upon Trent DE14 1NG (01283 532880; www.nationalbrewerycentre.co.uk). After a chequered career it now sells real ales (some from the adjoining museum's micro-brewery) and food *Wed-Sat all day until 20.45 & Sun-Tue L*. Garden and children's play area. *Open Mon-Tue L; Wed-Sat all day & Sun L until 18.00. Sun L* carvery.

6 Burton Bridge Inn 24 Bridge Street, Burton upon Trent DE14 1SY (01283 536596; www.burtonbridgeinn.co.uk). The brewery tap for the eponymously named brewers, this traditional 17th-C pub serves real ales (also a selection of malt whiskies and fruit wines) together with bar meals *Tue-Sat L*. Skittle alley and traditional pub games. Garden and real fires. *Open Sun-Thu L and E; Fri & Sat all day*. Takeaway ale service.

7 The Devonshire Arms 86 Station St, Burton upon Trent DE14 1BT (01283 562392; www.thedevonshire.co.uk). Another excellent Burton Bridge Brewery establishment, offering a warm, friendly welcome, and serving a wide range of real ales, together with freshly cooked bar meals and snacks *Tue-Sat L*. Patio seating and real fires in winter. Traditional pub games. *Open Mon E; Tue-Thu and Sun L and E & Fri-Sat all day*.

8 Lord Burton 154 High St, Town Centre, Burton upon Trent DE14 1JE (01283 517587; www.jdwetherspoon.co.uk/home/pubs/the-lord-burton). Once home to Woolworths, this busy pub now serves real ales, real cider and food *08.00-22.00*. Children welcome. Beer garden. Free Wi-Fi. *Open all day, every day*.

9 The Old Cottage Tavern 36 Byrkley St, Burton upon Trent DE14 2EG (01283 511615; www.oldcottagebeer.co.uk). Situated behind the town hall, this welcoming pub serves real ale and appetising food *Tue-Sun L & Fri-Sat E*. Garden and real fires in *winter*. Traditional pub games. *Open all day from 12.00*.

10 The Corner House Centrum 100, Wellington Road, Burton upon Trent DE14 2WF (01283 542321). North east of the A38 bridge. Friendly pub decorated with brewery memorabilia, serving food *all day*. Large beer garden with children's play area.

11 The Blacksmith's Arms Main Street, Branston DE14 3EY (01283 564332; www.blacksmiths.jthree.co.uk). Comfortable pub serving real ale and home-made food *Mon-Sat all day & Sun L*. Children welcome. Garden and patio. Large-screen TV, darts, pool and *regular* live entertainment.

12 The Bridge Tatenhill Lane, Branston DE14 3EZ (01283 564177; www.thebridgeinnbranston.co.uk). At Branston Bridge (34). Real ale, and good food *L and E*. Children welcome. Canalside garden. Mooring.

NAVIGATIONAL NOTES

A Watermate key is needed for Dallow Lock 7.

Barton Turn

Beside Tatenhill Lock there is an attractive cottage; at the tail of the lock is yet another of the tiny narrow brick bridges that are such an engaging feature of this navigation. Note the very fine National Forest seat just north of the lock – there is another at Bagnall Lock, along with a 'living willow' sculpture. After passing flooded gravel pits and negotiating another tiny brick arch at bridge 36, the canal and the A38, the old Roman road, come very close together – thankfully the settlement of Barton Turn has been bypassed, leaving the main street (the old Roman road of Ryknild Street) wide and empty. It is with great relief that Wychnor Lock, with its diminutive crane and warehouse, is reached – here the A38 finally parts company with the canal, and some peace returns. To the west is the little 14th-C Wychnor church. Before Alrewas Lock the canal actually joins the River Trent – there is a large well-marked weir which should be given a wide berth. The canal then winds through the pretty village of Alrewas, passing the old church, several thatched cottages and a charming brick bridge.

● **Barton-under-Needwood**
Staffs. PO, tel, stores, chemist, off-licence, library. Many years ago, when there were few roads and no canals in the Midlands, the only reasonable access to this village was by turning off the old Roman road, Ryknild Street: hence, probably, the name Barton Turn. The village is indeed worth turning off for, although unfortunately it is nearly a mile from the canal. A pleasant footpath from Barton Turn Lock leads quietly to the village, which is set on a slight hill. Its long main street has many attractive pubs. The church is battlemented and surrounded by a very tidy churchyard. Pleasantly uniform in style, it was built in the 16th C by John Taylor, Henry VIII's private secretary, on the site of his cottage birthplace. The former Royal Forest of Needwood is to the north of the village.

● **Wychnor**
Staffs. A tiny farming settlement around the church of St Leonards.

● **Alrewas**
Staffs. PO, tel, stores, garage, butcher, chemist, tearoom, fish & chips, takeaway, off-licence. Just far enough away from the A513, this is an attractive village whose rambling back lanes harbour some excellent timbered cottages. The canal's meandering passage through the village, passing well tended gardens and a bowling green, and the presence of the church and its pleasant churchyard creates a friendly and unruffled atmosphere. The River Trent touches the village, and once fed the old Cotton Mill (now converted into dwellings), and provides it with a fine background which is much appreciated by fishermen. The somewhat unusual name Alrewas, pronounced 'olrewus', is a corruption of the words Alder Wash – a reference to the many alder trees which once grew in the often-flooded Trent valley and gave rise to the basket weaving for which the village was once famous.

Alrewas Church Mill End Lane, Alrewas DE13 7BT. A spacious building of mainly 13th-C and 14th-C construction, notable for the old leper window, which is now filled by modern stained glass.

Boatyards

Ⓑ**Barton Turns Marina** Barton Turn, Barton-under-Needwood DE13 8DZ (01283 711666; www.bartonmarina.co.uk). D Pump out, gas, overnight and long-term mooring, winter storage, slipway, boat sales and repairs, engine repairs, chandlery, toilets, showers, books, maps and gifts, laundrette, Wi-Fi. Also pub, restaurant and shops, including a deli and bakery/butcher. Fly and course fishing.

Boat Doctor (01332 771622). Advice and information only

Ⓑ**Wychnor Moorings** Wychnor, Burton upon Trent DE13 8BY (07778 668388). Gas, private mooring, coal.

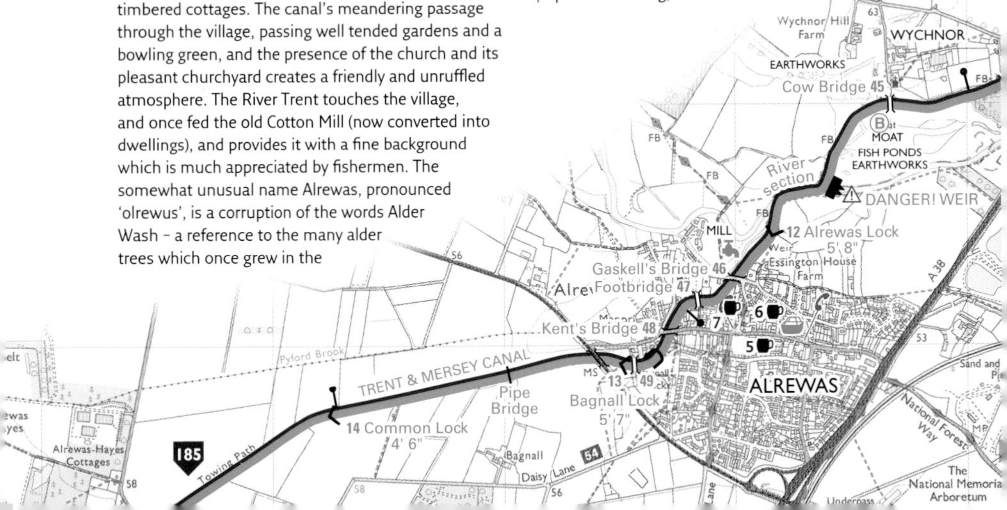

NAVIGATIONAL NOTES

In times of flood great caution should be exercised along the stretch immediately north of Alrewas Lock – keep well over to the towpath side at all times.

Pubs and Restaurants

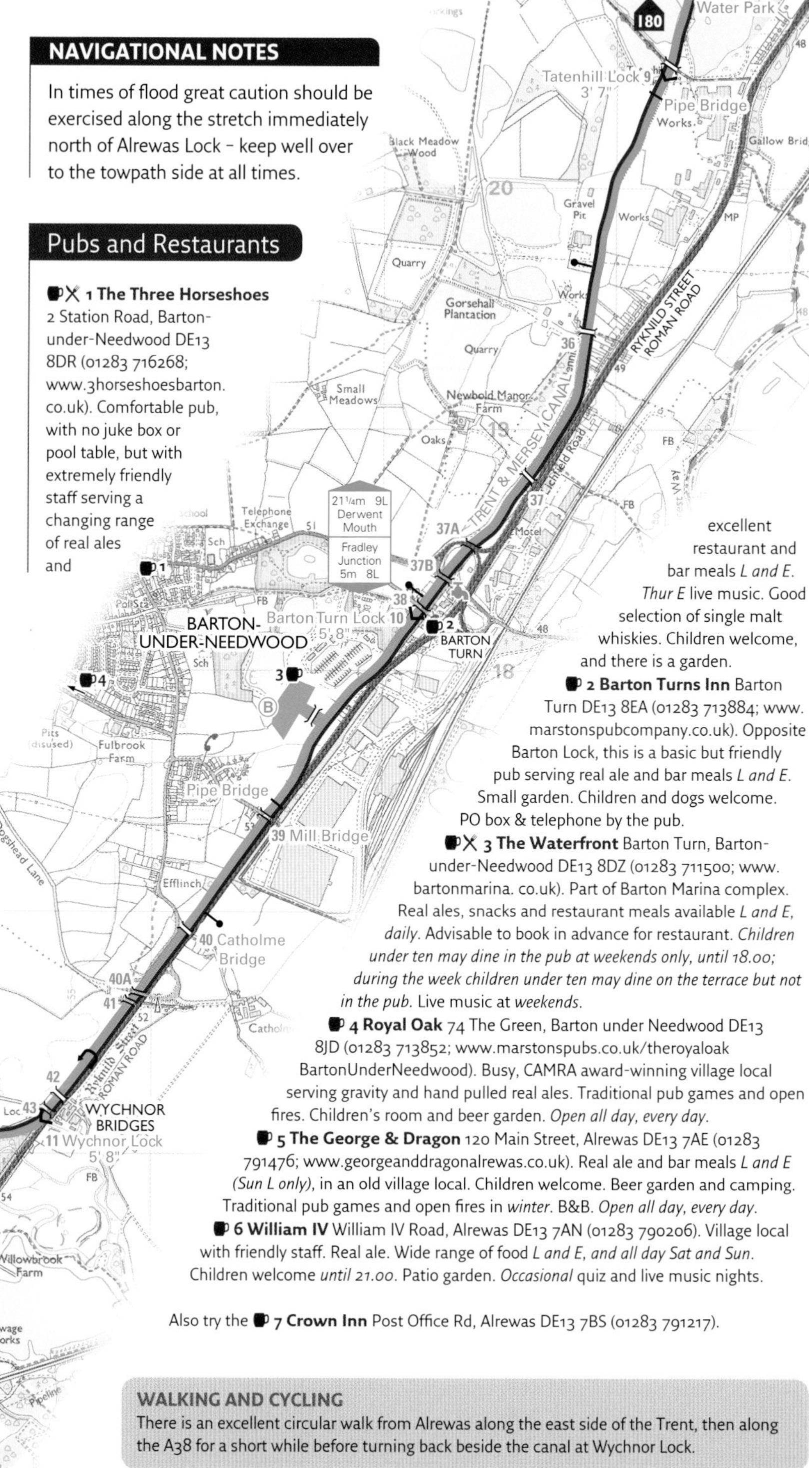

1 The Three Horseshoes 2 Station Road, Barton-under-Needwood DE13 8DR (01283 716268; www.3horseshoesbarton.co.uk). Comfortable pub, with no juke box or pool table, but with extremely friendly staff serving a changing range of real ales and excellent restaurant and bar meals *L and E*. *Thur E* live music. Good selection of single malt whiskies. Children welcome, and there is a garden.

2 Barton Turns Inn Barton Turn DE13 8EA (01283 713884; www.marstonspubcompany.co.uk). Opposite Barton Lock, this is a basic but friendly pub serving real ale and bar meals *L and E*. Small garden. Children and dogs welcome. PO box & telephone by the pub.

3 The Waterfront Barton Turn, Barton-under-Needwood DE13 8DZ (01283 711500; www.bartonmarina. co.uk). Part of Barton Marina complex. Real ales, snacks and restaurant meals available *L and E, daily*. Advisable to book in advance for restaurant. *Children under ten may dine in the pub at weekends only, until 18.00; during the week children under ten may dine on the terrace but not in the pub.* Live music at *weekends*.

4 Royal Oak 74 The Green, Barton under Needwood DE13 8JD (01283 713852; www.marstonspubs.co.uk/theroyaloak BartonUnderNeedwood). Busy, CAMRA award-winning village local serving gravity and hand pulled real ales. Traditional pub games and open fires. Children's room and beer garden. *Open all day, every day.*

5 The George & Dragon 120 Main Street, Alrewas DE13 7AE (01283 791476; www.georgeanddragonalrewas.co.uk). Real ale and bar meals *L and E (Sun L only)*, in an old village local. Children welcome. Beer garden and camping. Traditional pub games and open fires in *winter*. B&B. *Open all day, every day.*

6 William IV William IV Road, Alrewas DE13 7AN (01283 790206). Village local with friendly staff. Real ale. Wide range of food *L and E, and all day Sat and Sun.* Children welcome *until 21.00*. Patio garden. *Occasional* quiz and live music nights.

Also try the **7 Crown Inn** Post Office Rd, Alrewas DE13 7BS (01283 791217).

WALKING AND CYCLING
There is an excellent circular walk from Alrewas along the east side of the Trent, then along the A38 for a short while before turning back beside the canal at Wychnor Lock.

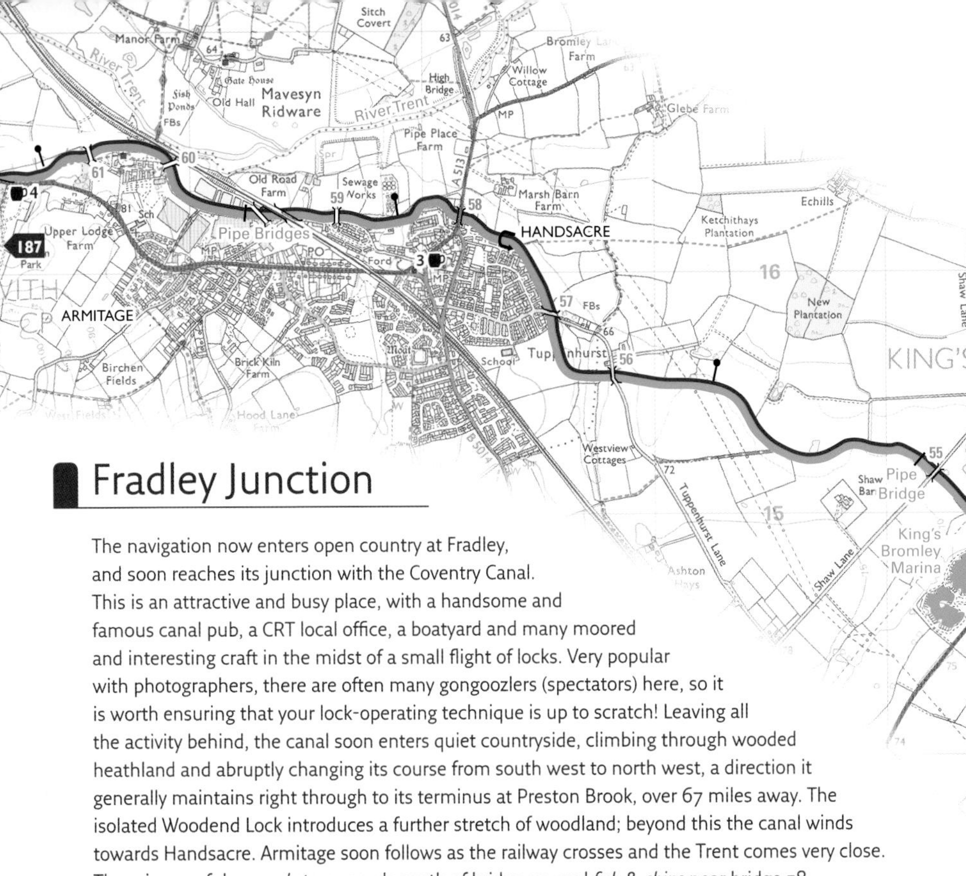

Fradley Junction

The navigation now enters open country at Fradley, and soon reaches its junction with the Coventry Canal. This is an attractive and busy place, with a handsome and famous canal pub, a CRT local office, a boatyard and many moored and interesting craft in the midst of a small flight of locks. Very popular with photographers, there are often many gongoozlers (spectators) here, so it is worth ensuring that your lock-operating technique is up to scratch! Leaving all the activity behind, the canal soon enters quiet countryside, climbing through wooded heathland and abruptly changing its course from south west to north west, a direction it generally maintains right through to its terminus at Preston Brook, over 67 miles away. The isolated Woodend Lock introduces a further stretch of woodland; beyond this the canal winds towards Handsacre. Armitage soon follows as the railway crosses and the Trent comes very close. There is a useful *general store* 500yds south of bridge 59, and *fish & chips* near bridge 58.

NAVIGATIONAL NOTES

West of bridge 61 the canal is very narrow, due to the removal of Armitage Tunnel, and wide enough for one boat only. Check that the canal is clear before proceeding.

Boatyards

Ⓑ**Fradley Marine Services** Fradley Junction, Alrewas, Burton-on-Trent DE13 7DN (01283 790332; www.fradleymarine.co.uk). **D** Pump out, gas, solid fuel, overnight and long-term mooring, DIY facilities, boat repairs, gift shop, chandlery, provisions, gallery of artists and crafters, tearoom. Can issue CRT boat licences.

Ⓑ**Bromley Wharf Ltd** Bromley Wharf, Riley Hill, Bromley Hayes, Nr Lichfield WS13 8HS (01543 419695/ 07815 577788; www.bromleywharf.co.uk). **D** Pump out, gas, solid fuel, covered dry dock, long- and short-term mooring, engineering services.

Ⓑ**King's Bromley Marina** Lichfield Road, Bromley Hayes WS13 8HT (01543 417209; www. kingsbromleymarina.co.uk). **D** Pump out, gas, solid fuel, overnight and long-term mooring, slipway, boat sales, chandlery, coal, toilets, showers, laundrette, Wi-Fi.

● **Fradley Junction**
Staffs. PO box, tel. A long-established canal centre where the Coventry Canal joins the Trent & Mersey. Like all the best focal points on the waterways, it is concerned solely with the life of the canals, and has no relationship with local roads or even with the village of Fradley. The junction bristles with boats for, apart from it being an inevitable meeting place for canal craft, there is a boatyard, a Canal & River Trust information centre and café (01283 790236, guided tours), CRT moorings, a boat club, a popular pub and another café at the holiday park – all in the middle of a 5-lock flight.

Fradley

Staffs. PO, tel, stores, fish & chips. A small village set to the east of the canal, and well away from the junction. It owed its prosperity to the airfield which is not used as such any more.

Armitage

Staffs. PO, tel, stores, chemist, butcher, baker. A main road village, whose church is interesting: it was rebuilt in the 19th C in a Saxon/Norman style, which makes it rather dark. The organ is 200 years old and it is enormous: it came from Lichfield Cathedral and practically deafens the organist at Armitage.

WALKING AND CYCLING

You can complete a circular walk if you head off along the Coventry Canal to Fradley Bridge (90), walk through the village and on to Alrewas, returning along the Trent & Mersey. Fradley Pool Nature Reserve can be accessed from the towpath, and makes for a pleasant walk.

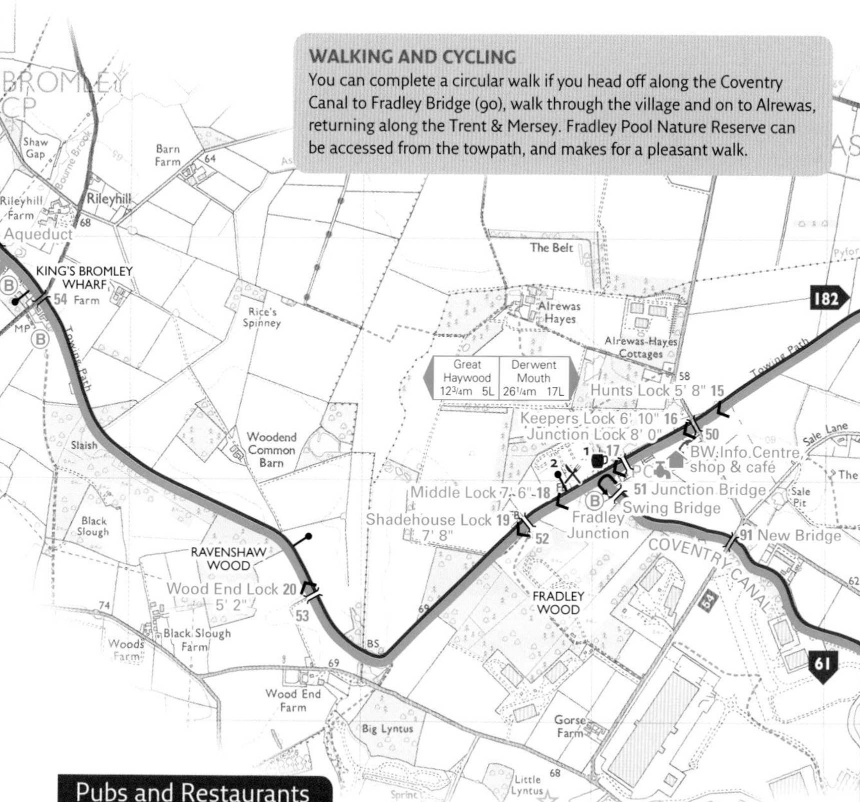

Pubs and Restaurants

1 The Swan Fradley Junction, Alrewas, Burton-on-Trent DE13 7DN (01283 790330). Known as 'The Mucky Duck'. Canalside, it is the focus of the junction and justly famous: this is reputedly one of the most photographed pubs in the country! It is in a 200-year-old listed building, with a fine public bar warmed by a coal fire, a comfortable lounge, and a vaulted cellar room. Real ale, and bar meals are served *L and E*, with a carvery *Sun L*. There is a flowered patio at the rear.

2 Kingfisher Canalside Café Fradley Junction, Alrewas DE13 7DN (01283 790407; www.kingfisherholidaypark.com). Beside the Swan Inn. Attached to the adjacent swimming pool and caravan park, this café serves a range of hot and cold snacks, drinks and light meals. *Open daily 09.00-17.00 (16.00* if quiet). Last orders *16.30*.

3 The Olde Peculiar The Green, Handsacre WS15 4DP (01543 491891; www.theoldepeculiar.co.uk). Traditional English pub. Real ale, and food available *L and E (not Mon or Tue L)*. Pretty garden. Children welcome. B&B. *Open Mon-Tue E & Wed-Sun L and E.*

4 The Plum Pudding Brasserie Rugeley Road, Armitage WS15 4AZ (01543 490330; www. plumpudding.co.uk). Modern, award-winning restaurant serving real ale and meals *L and E*. Children welcome for meals only. Outside seating, including large, covered, canalside area used for eating and drinking. *Open Mon-Fri L and E & Sat-Sun all day.*

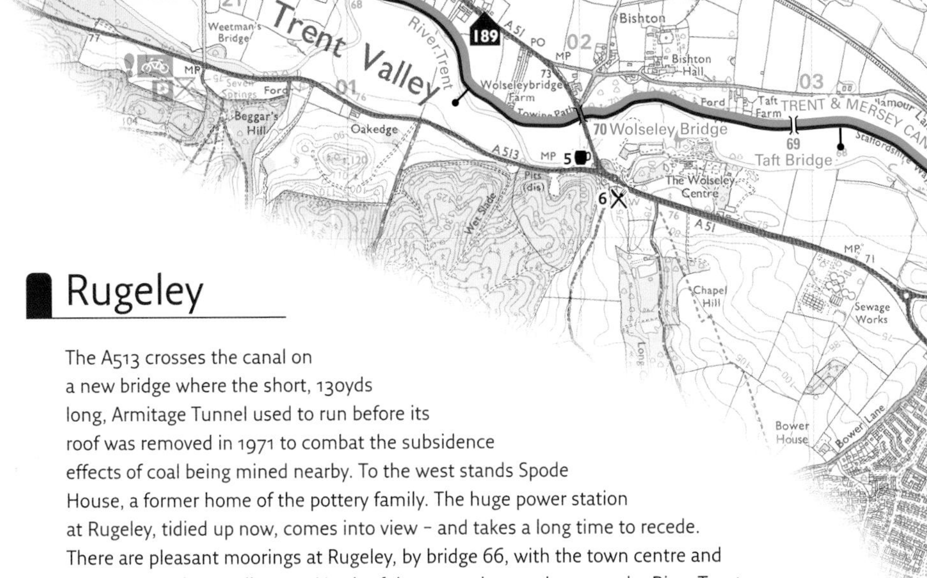

Rugeley

The A513 crosses the canal on a new bridge where the short, 130yds long, Armitage Tunnel used to run before its roof was removed in 1971 to combat the subsidence effects of coal being mined nearby. To the west stands Spode House, a former home of the pottery family. The huge power station at Rugeley, tidied up now, comes into view – and takes a long time to recede. There are pleasant moorings at Rugeley, by bridge 66, with the town centre and shops only a short walk away. North of the town, the canal crosses the River Trent via a substantial aqueduct. It then enters an immensely attractive area full of interest. Accompanied by the River Trent, the canal moves up a narrowing valley bordered by green slopes on either side, Cannock Chase being clearly visible to the south. Wolseley Hall has gone, but Bishton Hall (now a wedding venue) still stands: its very elegant front faces the canal near Wolseley Bridge. There is a *pub*, an *Indian restaurant* and an *antique, craft and garden centre* just a short way to the south.

- **Spode House** WS15 1PU Spode House and Hawkesyard Priory stand side by side. The priory was founded in 1897 by Josiah Spode's grandson and his niece Helen Gulson when they lived at Spode House. The Priory is now known as Hawkesyard Hall, and is a restaurant and spa.
- **Rugeley**
Staffs. All services. A bustling and much re-developed town, with many shops at the centre. There are two churches by bridge 67; one is a 14th-C ruin, the other is the parish church built in 1822 as a replacement.
- **Cannock Chase**
Covering an area of 26 square miles, and designated as an Area of Outstanding Natural Beauty in 1949, the Chase is all that remains of what was once a Norman hunting ground known as the King's Forest of Cannock. Large parts are recognised as Sites of Special Scientific Interest, and exceptional flora and fauna are abundant. This includes a herd of fallow deer whose ancestors have grazed in this region for centuries. An area of 4½ square miles forms a Country Park, one of the largest in Britain. Near the Sherlock Valley an area was chosen in 1964 as the site of the Deutscher Soldatenfriedhof, and was built by the German War Graves Commission. It contains the graves of 2143 German servicemen from World War I, and 2786 from World War II. It is an intentionally sombre place. A small area is devoted to the crews of German airships, shot down over the UK in 1916 and 1917. There were two huge army camps on the Chase during World War I, but today little remains, apart from some anonymous and overgrown concrete foundations.
Museum of Cannock Chase Valley Road, Hednesford WS12 1TD (01543 877666; www.cannockchasedc.gov.uk). This site was at one time the Valley Colliery. Local history and interactive galleries. *Open Jan-Mar & Oct-Dec 11.00-16.00 and Apr-Sep 11.00-17.00. Closed Xmas-New year.* Coffee and gift shops. Visitor information and walks. Free.

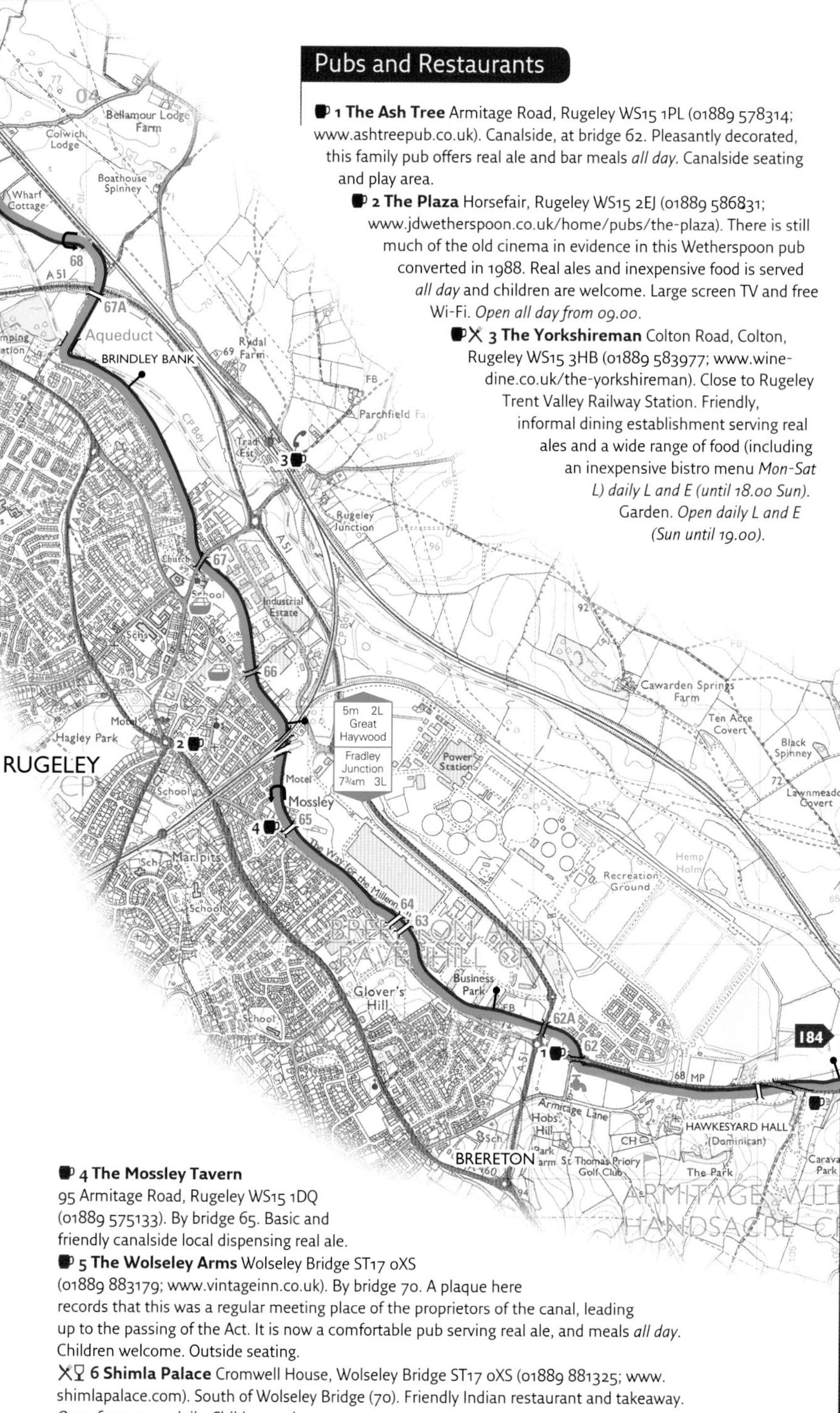

Pubs and Restaurants

1 The Ash Tree Armitage Road, Rugeley WS15 1PL (01889 578314; www.ashtreepub.co.uk). Canalside, at bridge 62. Pleasantly decorated, this family pub offers real ale and bar meals *all day*. Canalside seating and play area.

2 The Plaza Horsefair, Rugeley WS15 2EJ (01889 586831; www.jdwetherspoon.co.uk/home/pubs/the-plaza). There is still much of the old cinema in evidence in this Wetherspoon pub converted in 1988. Real ales and inexpensive food is served *all day* and children are welcome. Large screen TV and free Wi-Fi. *Open all day from 09.00.*

✕ **3 The Yorkshireman** Colton Road, Colton, Rugeley WS15 3HB (01889 583977; www.wine-dine.co.uk/the-yorkshireman). Close to Rugeley Trent Valley Railway Station. Friendly, informal dining establishment serving real ales and a wide range of food (including an inexpensive bistro menu *Mon-Sat L) daily L and E (until 18.00 Sun).* Garden. *Open daily L and E (Sun until 19.00).*

4 The Mossley Tavern 95 Armitage Road, Rugeley WS15 1DQ (01889 575133). By bridge 65. Basic and friendly canalside local dispensing real ale.

5 The Wolseley Arms Wolseley Bridge ST17 0XS (01889 883179; www.vintageinn.co.uk). By bridge 70. A plaque here records that this was a regular meeting place of the proprietors of the canal, leading up to the passing of the Act. It is now a comfortable pub serving real ale, and meals *all day*. Children welcome. Outside seating.

✕🍷 **6 Shimla Palace** Cromwell House, Wolseley Bridge ST17 0XS (01889 881325; www.shimlapalace.com). South of Wolseley Bridge (70). Friendly Indian restaurant and takeaway. *Open from 17.30 daily.* Children welcome.

Great Haywood

The pleasant surroundings continue as the canal passes Colwich. As the perimeter of Shugborough Park is reached the impressive façade of the Hall can be seen across the parkland. Haywood Lock and a line of moored craft announce the presence of Great Haywood and the junction with the Staffordshire & Worcestershire Canal (*see* page 157), which joins the Trent & Mersey under a graceful and much photographed towpath bridge: just the other side there is a useful boatyard which, amongst other services, provides *Elsan disposal* (charge). Beyond the junction the Trent valley becomes much broader and more open. There is another boatyard by Hoo Mill Lock.

● **Little Haywood**
Staffs. PO box, tel, stores, off-licence. An elegant residential village, with a shop and two pubs. There is an enterprising shop (01889 881579; www,generalstorebandb.co.uk) – *open daily 07.00 (Sun 08.00)-19.00* – which sells coal, firewood and kindling, as well as providing comfortable B&B.

● **Great Haywood**
Staffs. PO, tel, stores, fishmonger. The Centre of the Great Haywood and Shugborough Conservation Area, the village is not particularly beautiful, but it is closely connected in many ways to Shugborough Park, to which it is physically linked by the very old Essex Bridge, where the crystal clear waters of the River Sow join the Trent on its way down from Stoke. Haywood Lock is beautifully situated between this packhorse bridge (which is an ancient monument) and the unusually decorative railway bridge that leads into Trent Lane. The lane consists of completely symmetrical and very handsome terraced cottages: they were built by the Ansons to house the people evicted from the former Shugborough village, the site of which is now occupied by the Arch of Hadrian within the park, built to celebrate Anson's circumnavigation of the globe in 1740–44. About 100yds south of Haywood Lock is an iron bridge over the canal. This bridge, which now leads nowhere, used to carry a private road from Shugborough Hall which crossed both the river and the canal on its way to the church just east of the railway. This was important to the Ansons, since the packhorse bridge just upstream is not wide enough for a horse and carriage, and so until the iron bridge was built the family had to *walk* the 300yds to church on Sunday mornings! There is a fresh fish shop behind the Clifford Arms *open Tue-Fri 09.30-16.30*.

Shugborough Hall *NT*. Milford, near Stafford ST17 0XB (01889 881388; www.shugborough.org.uk). Walk west from Haywood Lock and through the park. The present house dates from 1693, but was substantially altered by James Stuart around 1760 and by Samuel Wyatt around the turn of the 18th C. It was at this time that the old village of Shugborough was bought up and demolished by the Anson family so that they should enjoy more privacy and space in their park. Family fortunes fluctuated greatly for the Ansons, the Earl of Lichfield's family; and crippling death duties in the 1960s brought about the transfer of the estate to the National Trust. The Trust has leased the property to Staffordshire County Council who now manage the whole estate. The house has been restored at great expense, and there are some magnificent rooms and many treasures inside.

Museum of Staffordshire Life This excellent establishment, Staffordshire's County Museum, is housed in the old stables adjacent to Shugborough Hall. Open since 1966, it is superbly laid out and contains all sorts of exhibits concerned with old country life in Staffordshire. Amongst many things it contains an old-fashioned laundry, the old gun-room and the old estate brew-house, all completely equipped. Part of the stables contains harness, carts, coaches and motor cars. There is an industrial annexe up the road, containing a collection of preserved steam locomotives and some industrial machinery.

Shugborough Park There are some remarkable sights in the large park which encircles the Hall. Thomas Anson, who inherited the estate in 1720, enlisted in 1744 the help of his famous brother, Admiral George Anson, to beautify and improve the house and the park. In 1762 he commissioned James Stuart, a neo-Grecian architect, to embellish the park. 'Athenian' Stuart set to with a will, and the spectacular results of his work can be seen scattered round the grounds. The stone monuments that he built have deservedly extravagant names such as the Tower of the Winds, the Lanthorn of Demosthenes and so on.

The Park Farm Designed by Samuel Wyatt, it contains an agricultural museum, a working mill and a rare breeds centre. Traditional country skills such as bread-making, butter-churning and cheese-making are demonstrated.
Open Apr–Oct daily 11.00–17.00. Charge. Parties must book. Tea rooms, shop.

Canalside Farm Mill Lane, Great Haywood ST18 0RQ (01889 881747; www.canalsidefarm.co.uk). Immediately east of Bridge 75, beside the marina. Selling an excellent selection of local (within 30 miles) seasonal, fresh produce. Butcher, baker and delicatessen. PYO strawberries and raspberries. Bedding plants and ice creams. Café. *Open Apr-Oct, daily 09.00-18.00 & Nov-Mar, Tue-Sat 09.00-18.00 & Sun 10.00-17.00.*

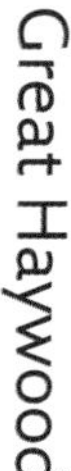

Pubs and Restaurants

1 The Clifford Arms Main Road, Great Haywood ST18 0SR (01889 881321; www.thecliffordarms.co.uk). There has apparently been a pub on this site for hundreds of years. At one time it was a coaching inn. Now it is a friendly village local with an open fire, serving real ale and bar and restaurant meals *L and E*. Small garden with Yews. Children in the bar welcome when dining. Traditional pub games and open fires in *winter*. Dogs welcome. *Open all day*.

2 The Red Lion Main Road, Little Haywood ST18 0TS (01889 881314). Village local with a comfortable lounge, serving real ale. Children welcome *until 20.30*. Garden.

3 Canalside Farm café Mill Lane, Great Haywood ST18 0RQ (01889 881747; www.canalsidefarm.co.uk). Café. *Open Apr-Oct, daily 09.00-18.00 & Nov-Mar, Tue-Sat 09.00-18.00 & Sun 10.00-17.00.*

Boatyards

Anglo Welsh The Canal Wharf, Mill Lane, Great Haywood ST18 0RJ (01889 881711; www.anglowelsh.co.uk). D Pump out *(not Sat)*, gas, narrowboat hire, day-hire craft, overnight and long-term mooring, coal, engine repairs, chandlery, toilets, books, maps and gifts, ice cream and soft drinks. *Open 7 days a week.*

Stafford Boat Club Off Maple Wood, Wildwood, Stafford ST17 4SG (01785 660725; www.staffordboatclub.co.uk). At bridge 96. D Pump out, overnight moorings, Calor gas, slip way, wet dock, use of clubhouse (*bar open every evening and 12.00-15.00 Sun*).

WALKING AND CYCLING

For a circular walk, head off along the Coventry Canal to Fradley Bridge (90), walk through the village and on to Alrewas, returning along the Trent & Mersey.

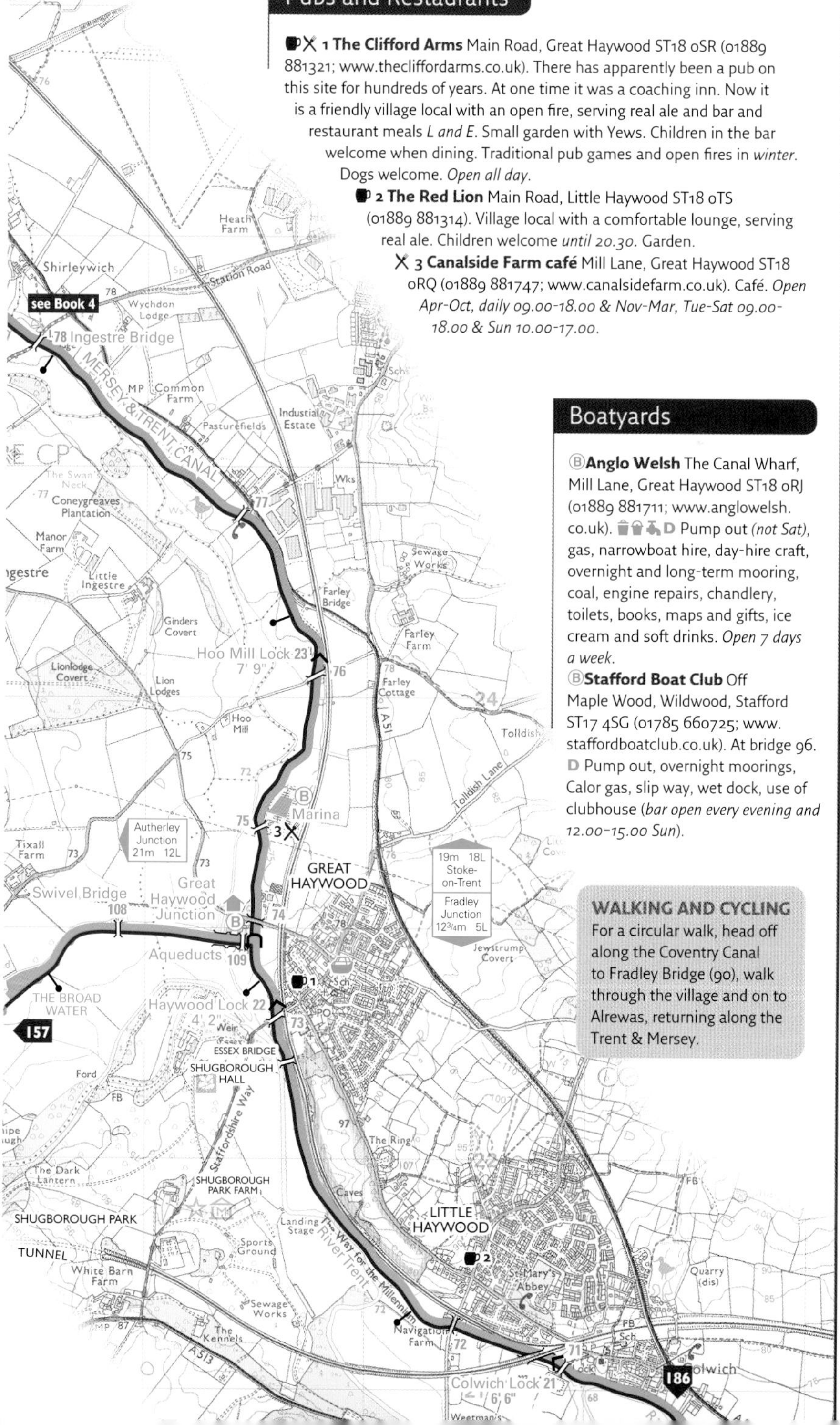

see Book 4

INDEX

Trent Falls

The mouth of the Trent curves gently to the east as it meets the Ouse: a layout that is largely of man's doing as much as by nature's design. Between the Wars an elaborate stone training wall was constructed on the western bank, easily visible at low water and marked by lights and wooden staffs at high water.

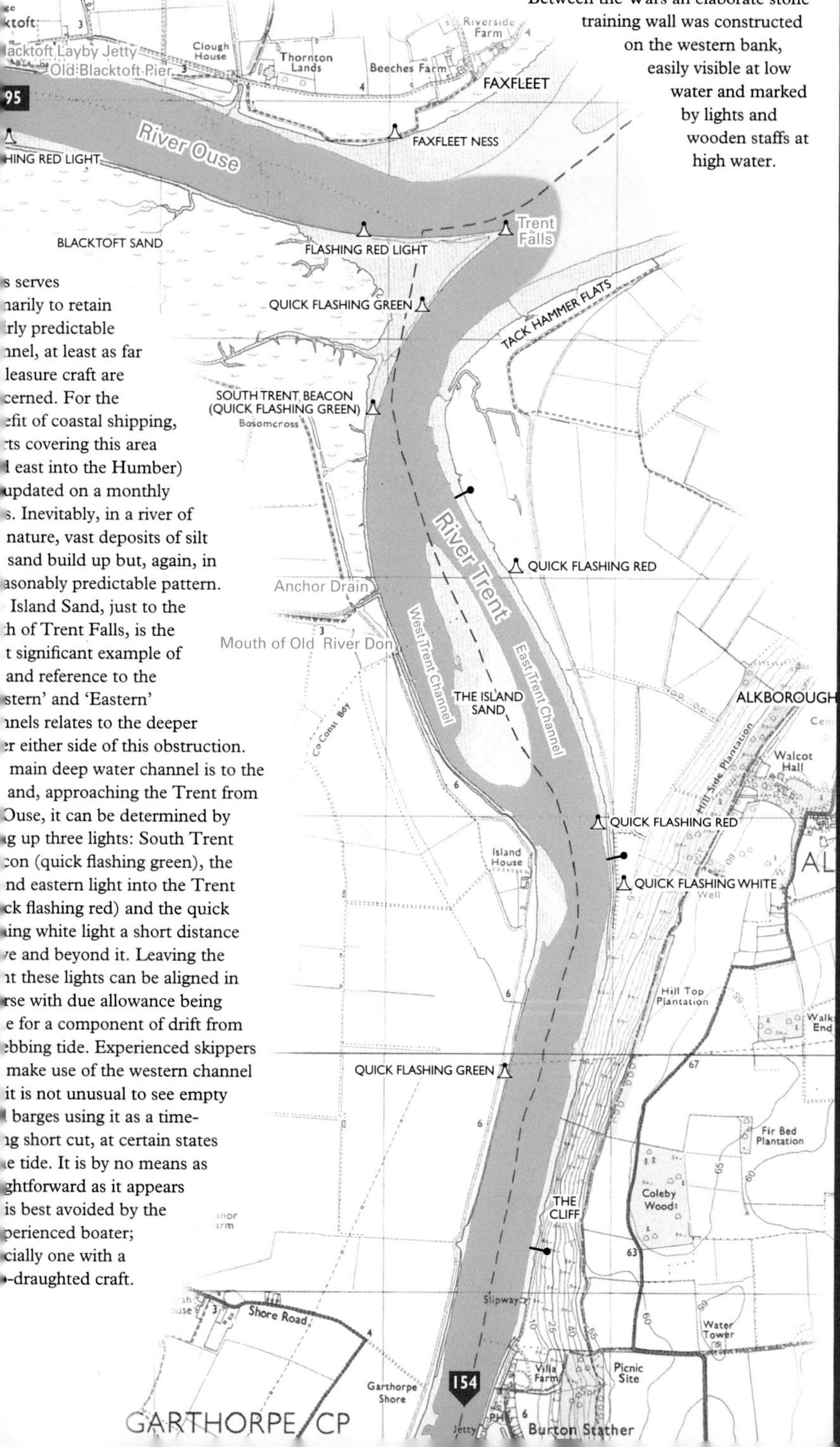

s serves
narily to retain
irly predictable
nnel, at least as far
leasure craft are
cerned. For the
efit of coastal shipping,
rts covering this area
l east into the Humber)
updated on a monthly
s. Inevitably, in a river of
nature, vast deposits of silt
sand build up but, again, in
asonably predictable pattern.
Island Sand, just to the
h of Trent Falls, is the
t significant example of
and reference to the
stern' and 'Eastern'
nnels relates to the deeper
er either side of this obstruction.
main deep water channel is to the
and, approaching the Trent from
Ouse, it can be determined by
g up three lights: South Trent
con (quick flashing green), the
nd eastern light into the Trent
ck flashing red) and the quick
ing white light a short distance
ve and beyond it. Leaving the
nt these lights can be aligned in
rse with due allowance being
e for a component of drift from
ebbing tide. Experienced skippers
make use of the western channel
it is not unusual to see empty
barges using it as a time-
ng short cut, at certain states
e tide. It is by no means as
ghtforward as it appears
is best avoided by the
perienced boater;
cially one with a
-draughted craft.

INDEX